**Same, Different, Equal**

# Same, Different, Equal

## Rethinking Single-Sex Schooling

ROSEMARY C. SALOMONE

Yale University Press    *New Haven & London*

Designed by James J. Johnson and set in Scala and
Meta types by The Composing Room of Michigan,
Inc. Printed in the United States of America by
Vail-Ballou Press.

Library of Congress Cataloging-in-Publication Data

Salomone, Rosemary C.
Same, different, equal : rethinking single-sex
schooling / Rosemary C. Salomone.
p.   cm.
Includes bibliographical references and index.

ISBN 978-0-300-10831-6
1. Single-sex schools—United States.   2.
Women—Education (Secondary)—United States.
3. Sex differences in education—United States.
4. Educational equalization—United States.
5. Feminism and education—United States.
I. Title
LB3067.4 .S35   2003
371.822—dc21
2002153145

A catalogue record for this book is available from
the British Library.

The paper in this book meets the guidelines for
permanence and durability of the Committee on
Production Guidelines for Book Longevity of the
Council on Library Resources.

*For*
Joe and Andrew

# Contents

# Preface

Books enter the world in different ways. Typically a book swells up as a concept in the author's mind and slowly takes shape before the first words begin to appear on the page. But there are also occasions when an unexpected event triggers the opportunity and even the necessity for a thoughtful response. That was the case here.

In the summer of 1996, while I was feverishly working against another book deadline, the Supreme Court struck down the all-male admissions policy of the Virginia Military Institute. Moved by the Court's sweeping decision on gender equality, I heatedly pulled together a commentary for the *National Law Journal* and figured my thoughts on the subject would rest there. But fortune took another turn. A few weeks later, I received a telephone call from someone I had never met. The caller introduced herself as Ann Rubenstein Tisch, a former news reporter and then sponsor of an all-girls public school that was scheduled to open in East Harlem that September. She told me that civil liberties groups were threatening to bring legal action and prevent the school from opening, as I was faintly aware from press reports. She urgently needed advice on the constitutional and Title IX implications. We spoke a bit about the school and I gave her my understanding of the VMI decision as well as the Title IX statute and regulations. Little did I realize that what seemed like a well-intentioned effort would mushroom over the coming months into a cause célèbre. Nor could I foresee how that initial conversation would redirect my attention and ultimately drive my intellectual energies for the next half-decade.

As I shifted back into my work, the East Harlem school continued to haunt me. How could anyone oppose a program that promised to heap benefits on disadvantaged girls? If nothing else, the school deserved a chance to prove its worth. I began to dig deeper into the question and spun out another commentary, this time for the *New York Law Journal*. Suddenly I became drawn into the public debate, called upon by the news media to comment on the merits of single-sex schooling. As the summer ended, the school did indeed open, and I was pleased to have played a small role in making it happen. But the issue continued to follow me. Later that year, Diane Ravitch invited me to prepare a paper on single-sex education for a conference she was planning with the Brookings Institution the following spring. At first reluctant to set aside my other work, I soon became engrossed in the project. Invitations to discuss and debate the legal and policy issues continued to come my way, and the interdisciplinary complexities gradually revealed themselves.

Meanwhile, I began for the first time in many years to consciously reflect on my own all-girls high school experience. I had long felt indebted to the school for having nurtured and validated my intellect at a time when society valued young women far more for how they looked than for what they knew or thought. But searching through the literature, I became keenly aware that it was not just the academic rigor of my alma mater that made such a profound and lasting impact on my life but also—and perhaps foremost—its all-female context and the experience of learning from and among smart women, who were passionate about their work and saw limitless possibilities. I recalled returning to the school as commencement speaker in the 1980s and telling the girls about the battles won and not yet won in the struggle for women's equality. I remembered being struck with the sense of continuity and ritual that had withstood the intervening years of vast social upheaval. Yet one thing had changed dramatically. The school's competitive sports program was riding the crest of Title IX, and the list of athletic scholarships now equaled the academic awards.

As I engaged in the public debate over the following year, and as the paper presented at the Brookings conference circulated around Washington and beyond, a number of individuals suggested that there was a book to be written here. That task initially seemed daunting; I realized that to effectively move the discussion beyond ideology, I would have to carefully examine every angle and to weave together a massive store of peripherally connected scholarship into a seamless policy argument. The Open Society Institute made this more possible with a generous fellowship that afforded me a concentrated stretch of time to make significant inroads on the work before me.

Carrying out this project has introduced me to dedicated educators in public and private schools serving the rich and the poor from New York to

California. From prestigious private schools on Manhattan's Upper East Side to public dual academies serving at-risk minority children in East Palo Alto, I have observed classes and talked to administrators, teachers, students, and parents who have graciously shared with me their thoughts and experiences. Seeing the education offered to the most privileged, I have come to recognize the realm of possibilities that schooling can and should offer the most disadvantaged. An invitation to work with lawyers and organizers in Chicago has afforded the added opportunity to help see the Young Women's Leadership Charter School of Chicago to fruition and to sharpen my understanding of the legal issues along the way. I have also entered the world of boys' schools, one totally alien to me, and have come to better understand their mission and their particular sensitivity to boys' needs. Most importantly, the project has laid before me the practical realities of gender and schooling and how they intersect with race, culture, and social class.

It has been an arduous but eye-opening journey, taking me over familiar and unfamiliar intellectual terrain to a destination that is still just barely on the horizon. What I have learned in the process is that the question of single-sex schooling is indeed complicated but not unanswerable if we simply look beyond preconceptions, consider the big picture, and embrace a more nuanced notion of gender equality than current discourse seems to admit. I hope this book provides insightful connections and cogent arguments that move both the law and educational policy in that direction.

# Acknowledgments

The arguments advanced and the thoughts presented here gradually developed over the course of several years and several prior publications, various portions of which I have incorporated into this work. Aside from early commentaries published in the *National Law Journal,* the *New York Law Journal,* and *Education Week,* my general thinking on this topic has evolved out of "Single-Sex Schooling: Law, Policy, and Research," which appeared in *Brookings Papers on Education Policy 1999* (Washington, D.C.: Brookings Institution Press, 1999). The discussion of the legal questions in Chapter 7 initially grew out of "Rich Kids, Poor Kids, and the Single-Sex Education Debate," *Akron Law Review* 34 (2000): 209–29, which was subsequently updated as "The Legality of Single-Sex Education in the United States: Sometimes 'Equal' Means 'Different,'" in *Gender in Policy and Practice: Perspectives on Single-Sex and Coeducational Schooling,* ed. Amanda Datnow and Lea Hubbard (New York: RoutledgeFalmer, 2002).

I deeply appreciate the time and interest of numerous school officials, teachers, parents, and students who shared with me their thoughts on single-sex schooling. I especially thank Ann Tisch and Maureen Grogan of the Young Women's Leadership Foundation; Landa McLaurin, principal of Western High School in Baltimore; and Geraldine Myles, principal of Philadelphia High School for Girls for welcoming me into their school communities, providing me with materials and data, and permitting me to play "fly on the wall." I also thank the many scholars across the country and across the globe who generously shared with me their published and unpublished research.

In the course of writing this book, I have benefited from a number of invitations to present my ideas in papers and lectures in scholarly and policy-making venues including the Brookings Institution, Sarah Lawrence College, Barnard College, Fordham Law School, Akron Law School, Wesleyan University, the Universidad Complutense de Madrid, the Association of American Law Schools 2002 Annual Meeting, the American Enterprise Institute for Public Policy Research, the U.S. Department of Education, and Capitol Hill. I thank the organizers and participants for the insights gained from those experiences. My sincere gratitude goes to the Open Society Institute for its generous support in granting me a fellowship that allowed a stretch of full-time work on this project. I especially thank Gara LaMarche, vice president and director of U.S. programs, and Gail Gordon, former program officer for individual project fellowships, for their willingness to think "outside the box" and envision the potential merits of my proposed research. I also wish to acknowledge St. John's University School of Law, whose Faculty Research Program provided me with several summer research stipends that significantly expedited the completion of this work, and my dean Joseph Bellacosa for his enthusiastic support.

As I gradually developed my ideas and arguments through a series of preliminary papers that have now converged in the chapters presented here, I have benefited immeasurably from the comments and suggestions of various scholars: Leonard Baynes, Michael Heise, Berta Hernandez-Truyol, Diane Ravitch, Cornelius Riordan, Kenneth Rowe, Catharine Stimpson, Michael Thompson, M. Elizabeth Tidball, Joseph Viteritti, and Stephen Yandle. I also owe much to my friend and neighbor Joan Gould, who never tired of sharing her keen insights on women and gender, or of offering words of encouragement as she diligently worked on her own grand opus. I attribute to each of these individuals the strengths of the book while ascribing any weaknesses to myself. In addition, I have also benefited from the research efforts of able and dedicated student assistants at St. John's: Margaret McConville Bateman (class of 1998), Cindy Schmitt (class of 1998), Stephanie Reday (class of 1999), Cara Morea (class of 2000), Laura Giles (class of 2002), Erin Cowen (class of 2003), and Kristina Wesch (class of 2003).

A word of thanks goes to the staff at the St. John's Law Library, particularly Aru Satkalmi, reference and documents research librarian, and Stanley Conrad, reference–interlibrary loan librarian, as well as Marilyn Narson, circulation supervisor at the main University Library. But my very special thanks go to Barbara Traub, head of reference services for St. John's Law Library. The rich body of interdisciplinary and international research threaded throughout this book is due in no small measure to her indomitable tenacity, unbeatable research skills, and unflinching good humor in the face of a continuous stream of near-impossible requests. My thanks also go to John Covell, my first editor at Yale University Press, who enthusiastically embraced this project from the very beginning; to Robert Flynn, whose support and good counsel saw it through critical stages; and to Erin Carter, who finally brought it to reality. And of course I thank Dan Heaton for smoothing out the rough edges with his skillful editing.

A major undertaking of this sort, however, can reach a successful conclusion only with the love and support of one's family and friends. And so I thank them for understanding my distraction and isolation and providing me, intermittently and just when needed most, with cheerful diversions. I especially thank my mother, Louise Salomone, for her unflagging faith in my ability over the course of a lifetime. Most important, I owe a world of gratitude to the two men who have lived with me through this seemingly endless venture: my husband, Joe Viteritti, for his invaluable emotional and intellectual sustenance as months of working weekends and summers have turned into years, and our son Andrew, who has never tired of my ramblings on sameness and difference and who has given me the joy of seeing at close view the very best that boys can be.

# 1
# Text and Subtext

It was the summer of 1996, not a particularly memorable summer by most accounts. Yet two oddly related events, one long-anticipated and the other a bolt from the blue, engrossed the media at least for the moment. In late June the United States Supreme Court struck down the all-male admissions policy of the Virginia Military Institute. That sweeping decision on the constitutional dimensions of gender equality set to rest not only the claims against VMI but also similar litigation against the Citadel in South Carolina.[1] Several weeks later, with the ink barely dry on the pages of that opinion, Community School District 4 in New York City announced the opening of the Young Women's Leadership School, an all-girls middle school serving inner-city minority students. Despite its almost unique set of facts, the VMI decision attracted national attention for its broader educational implications. Meanwhile, the New York school provided a challenging focal point for public discussion on single-sex schooling. The seeming incongruity of these two public acts immediately touched off a national debate that had been seething for at least a decade.

As Virginia reeled from the Court's decision, vacillating between resistance and mourning for its last stronghold of male privilege, parents in East Harlem eagerly readied their daughters for an academically empowering education that only the economically privileged had been able to buy. One could not possibly have imagined a more stark vision in contrasts. Yet it seemed that the destinies of these two institutions, miles apart in more than geography, might become inextricably intertwined. If so, the outcome could indelibly mark the educational landscape nationwide. The ensuing debate over this very possibility would plumb the depths of gender, race, and political ideology in the months and years to come.

For much of the public, the renewed interest in all-girls and all-boys schools seemed to have sprung upon the policy scene almost from no-where. For many, single-sex schooling was merely an intriguing educa-tional option, perhaps just a matter of personal preference. Others saw it as contextual, depending on who would benefit and who would be denied. For some it had an obsolescent, faintly Victorian, and even antifeminist quality about it. Still others believed that it was downright harmful and illegal un-der any circumstances. The East Harlem school hit an especially raw nerve for the American Civil Liberties Union and the National Organization for Women. Emboldened by an earlier court victory against Detroit's all-male schools, officials within the two organizations pounded the press with fiery accusations: single-sex schools smack of benevolent sexism, deny young women and men the interpersonal skills needed to function in the real world, reinforce persistent gender stereotypes, serve merely as a short-term political fix that ignores pervasive gender inequities in the schools. So they said, loudly and repeatedly.

As far as Anne Conners, president of NOW's New York City chapter, and Norman Siegel, executive director of the New York Civil Liberties Union, were concerned, school officials in New York had adopted "a Band-Aid ap-proach to educational equity for girls" that translated into "discrimination against boys." Holding firm in the belief that "public schools cannot segre-gate by gender or by race," Siegel accused the city of "trying to . . . turn the clock back [on integrating public schools]." Conners and her colleagues at NOW warned that we must not regress "to a time when sex stereotypes, up-held by private institutions, prevailed in society at large." They feared the re-turn to a pre–Title IX world—a world where gender-segregated public schools and vocational classes shortchanged girls of educational resources and tracked them into a fixed set of low-paying jobs and careers. As a mat-ter of law, both groups argued that separating students by gender violated the principle of *Brown v. Board of Education* that "separate" is "inherently un-equal." More directly, they questioned how any publicly supported single-sex school could possibly survive the Court's recent decision in the VMI case.[2]

The critics' apparent determination to keep the school from opening pro-voked an immediate and vigorous response from respected civil rights vet-eran and law professor Derrick Bell. In an aptly titled *New York Times* opin-ion piece, "Et Tu, A.C.L.U?" Bell chided the group for fighting a "misguided war against a girls' school in Harlem." For Bell as for others, the school held only a superficial resemblance to VMI. This was not a matter of exclusion from an elite institution but of inclusion and empowerment, offering girls "an environment free of the sexual pressures that are so prevalent in inner cities." He urged civil rights lawyers to recognize that their "views on what the Constitution permits are not always what poor, minority children need." With the hindsight of history, he warned that even successful legal actions sometimes "do no more than maintain a woeful status quo."[3]

To many liberals in particular, this all seemed a bit confusing. Hadn't the civil rights and women's movements put all these issues to rest? Hadn't American society concluded that coeducation was the more enlightened way to educate girls and boys so they could ultimately relate as women and men? Schools were supposed to provide girls with the same, not a different education from boys. Wasn't that the mark of true sexual equality? After all, that's what all the rumbling over VMI and the Citadel was about.[4] Besides, weren't public single-sex programs prohibited under Title IX? The answers to these questions became increasingly uncertain as the debate, replete with ironies, started taking shape in the local and national press. It was more than a faint reminder of the arguments raised several years earlier when cities like Detroit and Milwaukee had tried to open all-male academies for African-American boys. More immediately, it summoned up the heated discourse and high drama that had filled the pages of academic journals and national news reports as the Citadel and VMI lawsuits wormed their way through the federal courts.

It seemed as if the sands were shifting under the legacy of modern-day feminism and to some extent under the move toward racial integration. Women's rights advocates who had passionately denounced all-male admissions at state military academies were suddenly rallying to support public single-sex schools for inner-city girls in the name of affirmative action. Others, despite their avid support for that concept, were condemning such schools with equal resolve. The fragile women's rights consensus appeared to be unraveling at the seams. The issue clearly was a flashpoint for deeper social, political, and philosophical differences.

Apparently something critical had occurred since the 1960s and 1970s, when women's struggle for equal treatment and access had rocked the nation. That something was cautiously prodding single-sex schooling into the educational mainstream and creating this huge ideological rift. In the case of girls, it had all to do with widely publicized research on their loss of self-esteem as they approach adolescence, the popularly reported gender gap in math and science, the "chilly climate" for girls in public schools and college classrooms, and the arguable shortcomings within coeducation to meet their emotional and academic needs. In the case of minority girls and especially boys, there was mounting evidence that the current system of schooling was doing little to stop the downward spiral that increasingly has caught so many of them in its grip. Here the data on violence, dropout rates, and teenage parenthood, along with other indications of academic failure and social dysfunction, were staggering. Both lines of inquiry converged on the question of whether coeducation could effectively deliver on the promise of equal educational opportunity so integral to the larger civil rights agenda.

Beginning in the mid-1970s, with financial backing from private foundations and the federal government, researchers, educators, and gender equity advocates built an increasingly persuasive case on the "girl question." They argued for new strategies and initiatives, along with more resources to afford equal educational access to girls. Drawing on compensatory and pluralistic models borrowed from other disadvantaged and marginalized groups, they set in motion a sea change in policy and practice that profoundly affected the process and substance of schooling. They also brought renewed life to the age-old "nature versus nurture" debate and the question of whether females and males are essentially the same or different. In doing so, they traded the assimilationist goals of the women's movement for equitable outcomes based in controversial theories promoting gendered learning styles and women's unique "ways of knowing."

From the beginning, those theories drew harsh criticism from within feminist ranks. For some, "different" could dangerously be equated with "deficient." Eventually the policies and programs that this compensatory model spawned provoked into action a small but vocal backlash of other detractors who gradually grew louder in refuting the very premises of these arguments. In this case, the critics rejected what they perceived as an inaccurate and overstated case for girl "victimization" and joined with child psychologists in a dissonant chorus asking, "What about boys?" They pointed to data marking the dismal failure of schools to meet the academic and social needs of male students. Special education referrals were increasing and dropout and suspension rates were soaring. In fact, girls had begun to surpass boys on most indexes of academic performance, particularly in reading and literacy skills, while the gender gap favoring boys in math and science was progressively narrowing. These trends were not unique to the United States but rather reflected similar findings abroad in countries like England and Australia. In the meantime, brain research advanced by modern technology was telling us that differences in behavior and academic achievement between girls and boys might not be solely a matter of social conditioning, as many women's advocates have passionately argued, but perhaps partially a function of different maturational rates between the two sexes.

Amid all the academic mudslinging over the girl-boy/same-different controversy, urban school districts and parents from New York to California cautiously looked toward single-sex schooling both to address the much-publicized needs of adolescent girls across the economic spectrum and to resolve the compelling problems confronting inner-city boys. By the mid-1990s, public school systems more visibly explored comprehensive approaches that boldly defied the canon of coeducation in the name of gender equity for girls and equal opportunity for minority students of both sexes. School districts nationwide quietly experimented with single-sex math and science classes, extracurricular clubs for girls, and separate classes for minority boys.

At the same time, interest in single-sex education among private independent schools began to escalate. Between 1998 and 1999 alone, enrollment in all-girls schools increased by 4.4 percent. By the start of the new millennium, thirty-two new girls' schools had opened in the previous five years, while applications nationwide had increased by 37 percent and enrollments by 29 percent over the course of a decade. By 2002 enrollments rose by another 8 percent. In New York City, with its high concentration of private schools, applications jumped by a whopping 69 percent. Girls' schools were also outpacing boys' and coed schools in recruiting and retaining students of color. Obviously, something was convincing parents with adequate resources that single-sex education was a good investment in their daughters' futures.[5] And as the "boy question" slowly captured the public's imagination, a similar phenomenon started taking place among boys' schools, where enrollments have risen by 16.6 percent over the past decade.[6]

Energizing the debate in the public sector is the school choice movement in its varied forms, not the least of which is the burgeoning world of charter schools, which now number twenty-seven hundred nationwide. Families, and particularly inner-city minority parents, not unlike their more affluent urban and suburban neighbors, are more than ever looking to exercise a greater voice in the education of their children. No matter where one stands on the "school choice" issue, it is undeniable that the one-size-fits-all neighborhood school is slowly yielding to a new consumer-oriented model. And a small but increasing number of these consumers is choosing single-sex programs for their children.

Given this complex set of educational developments, political reactions, and legal events, it is not hard to understand why an approach that has gained renewed appeal within the private school network evokes such strong, inconsistent, and in some cases unanticipated responses from educators, policymakers, and scholars, especially when applied to public education. Even to the informed observer—and, I would speculate, to many of the participants themselves—the controversy over single-sex schooling simply revolves around two pressing concerns: whether it is legal within public schooling, and whether it produces educational benefits for girls or boys. These concerns form the text of the debate now swirling through education circles.

What is far less evident is that the interrelated developments of the past three decades, weighted down with historical and political baggage, form a veiled but intricately woven subtext inhabited with demons from the far and not so distant past. That subtext subtly roils public discourse on single-sex schooling and effectively immobilizes public policy. It is at this somewhat removed level that we find the deepest fears, hopes, and passions of advocates, skeptics, and opponents who continue to shout across a huge ideological divide, leaving parents and policymakers bewildered and frustrated as they search for definitive answers. And it is here at the subtext that I begin the discussion, clarifying the underlying philosophical disagreements over sex equality and sorting through the myths and realities of gender and schooling as they relate to ongoing arguments over whether schools are shortchanging girls or boys or both. By way of explanation, I use interchangeably the terms *sex* and *gender,* as is typically done in popular and scholarly literature, except where the distinction between biologically and socially determined characteristics is essential to the discussion, as in the case of sex discrimination or sex equality in the law.

But before wading through the details of this contentious debate, I first visit the real world of three inner-city all-girls' public schools, including two that have endured over a century and a half of sweeping social change. Looking through that prism, I move from the specific to the general, weaving through a vast and complex store of interdisciplinary scholarship and commentary. In the process, I uncover interesting connections and suggestive evidence that shift the debate from girls' victimization and the merits of sex-separation per se to the more constructive question of how best to provide an appropriate education for girls and boys, rich and poor, based not on group stereotypes but on informed understandings of individual needs as they at times coalesce around gender.

# 2
# A Tale of Three Cities

Single-sex education in the United States is and always has been predominantly a private school phenomenon. Even during the onslaught of mergers and closings in the 1960s and 1970s, a significant number of private same-sex schools survived, and they are still flourishing, along with new upstarts. The National Coalition of Girls' Schools now counts among its members 94 private day and boarding schools, while 114 schools in the United States, a fair number of them church-related, belong to the International Coalition of Boys' Schools.[1] Despite efforts to admit a racially and economically diverse group of students, most of these, particularly among the independent schools, are still elite institutions with a primarily white and privileged student body. Many still serve as springboards to prestigious colleges and universities.

This picture presents a striking contrast with what we find in the world of public schooling. Here the sweeping tide of coeducation dealt a fatal blow to single-sex schools nationwide. That inescapable movement dramatically transformed the landscape of large city school systems where single-sex schools had been the most numerous. New York City is a good case in point. In 1947 there were fourteen single-sex junior high schools and eleven vocational high schools in the borough of Manhattan alone. In 1970 these figures were reduced to two and eight, respectively. By the mid-1980s there were none except for one school in each of the five boroughs operating under the Pregnant and Parenting Teens Program. Even these schools technically were open to teen fathers, although in fact they were and still are schools of choice for pregnant girls.[2]

New York was just one among the many city school districts caught in the flow of educational and social reform. In subsequent years, those few urban school systems that have dared to establish some form of same-sex programs, no matter how well-intentioned, have found themselves marked as educational renegades. Most have capitulated under public scrutiny or gone undercover. Here taxpayer money and constitutional norms have increased the political and legal stakes. Efforts to establish programs for inner-city minority boys have met the strongest resistance, unable to shake the legacy of white male privilege historically associated with all-boys' schools, and even worse, the memories of racially segregated schools. The hard lessons of Detroit, Milwaukee, and other cities have rippled far and wide.

In the midst of this sea change, three urban school districts have stood out for their resolute stand that single-sex schools have something positive to offer adolescent girls. The current debate, in fact, owes much to New York City and the opening in 1996 of the Young Women's Leadership School in bold defiance of legal threats from civil rights groups. That single event pushed single-sex schooling into the vortex of educational reform and brought out of the legal shadows two long-established all-girls' public schools. Both the Philadelphia High School for Girls and Baltimore's Western High School have remained single-sex in fact, if not in law, since their founding in the 1840s, a time when girls were excluded from prestigious boys' schools that have since become coed. Both have weathered a century and a half of dramatic demographic and social changes and have undergone transformations in their student bodies from white merchant class to a racially and ethnically diverse and increasingly poor population. Both consciously affirm their rich history and tradition as all-girls' schools and enjoy loyal alumnae support. And both have steadfastly striven to stay alive and relevant in the face of shifting demographics, cultural norms, and professional knowledge.

In recent years, all three schools have drawn intermittent media attention while scholars and policymakers nationwide have debated their merits, largely as a matter of legal principle and abstract social ideals. Yet even the informed public still has only a vague sense of what makes these schools distinct and attractive to students, parents, and alumnae. And although a rigorous academic program plays a crucial role in their continuing appeal, that in itself is only part of it. There is something else happening in these schools that goes to the heart of their single-sex mission—a special something that their supporters maintain is impossible to replicate in a coeducational setting. Each school has an enlightening story to be told. In the case of Philadelphia and Baltimore, the sole remnants of "first-generation" all-girls' schools, it is a story of history, tradition, and gradual accommodation over a period spanning more than a century and a half. For New York, it is a tale of politics, planning, and process, initiated and driven by someone outside the system, to establish a "second-generation" model built not as a reactive counterweight to exclusion but as an affirmative vehicle for inclusion and an antidote to social disadvantage. It is a story of tradition in the making.

All three schools share common features that provide a wealth of untapped insights into the real world of single-sex schools both large and small. They also reveal how gender, race, and class intersect in the lives of inner-city adolescent girls. All three are designed to be academically rigorous, though none has the most academically selective admissions standards within its city. They all accept students with a range of abilities yet are viewed internally and externally as programmatically successful. They all have overcome legal threats and political opposition in a postfeminist world that remains highly skeptical of gender separation. Few schools, coeducational or otherwise, could withstand the intense scrutiny and continued demands for self-justification that all three have undergone.

Public pressure constantly weighs on these schools to prove that they are academically "better" than coeducational schools serving similar students. Yet anyone familiar with education research methods would agree that all the conditions for a valid, reliable, and useful comparative study simply do not exist here. The very virtue of these schools, that they are completely voluntary, turns out to be their methodological vice. Students attend as a matter of choice and not by random selection. So there is no definitive way to tell whether any differences in outcomes are the direct result of gender organization or merely the effect of background differences between student populations. Are the students who choose to attend these schools simply more motivated or academically inclined? Do their families hold higher aspirations for their daughters' success? Even if these factors could be controlled statistically, there is no way to account for a host of institutional features that inevitably affect learning. Schools differ from each other in subtle and not so subtle ways that are not quantifiable, from their curriculum to the instructional materials and approaches used, to their educational philosophy, academic expectations, teacher experience, and overall climate. Some readers undoubtedly will find this fact disappointing and even frustrating. Others will seize upon it as grist for the oppositionist mill.

Nonetheless, these limitations do not preclude other qualitative and useful ways of judging the merits of these schools. There is much hidden behind their doors by way of process and product that affirms their single-sex existence. Looking at them at close range and listening to the voices within helps us shed outdated misconceptions at the outset and more clearly understand that their single-sex nature is not an incidental and certainly not a harmful element as the opposing forces contend. To the contrary, it is a key ingredient that makes them "work" especially but not exclusively for a specific population of girls, many of whom come burdened with social problems that in other settings too often translate into academic deficits and failure.

I begin with the Young Women's Leadership School in New York, a relative newcomer that has subtly but decidedly revived and lent credibility to the discussion on single-sex schooling and broadened the debate over how we might best meet the needs of disadvantaged students.

## NEW YORK: WRITING ON A CLEAN SLATE

"Oprah's Words of Hope at Harlem Girls' H.S."

So read the headline in the *Daily News*. It was June 26, 2001, five years to the day since the Supreme Court had handed down its decision in the case against the Virginia Military Institute. Oprah Winfrey had come to New York's Metropolitan Museum of Art to address the first graduating class of the Young Women's Leadership School. The Grace Rainey Rogers Auditorium was packed with parents, educators, distinguished guests, and of course members of the media, who were there in full force. As expected, Oprah lent a stunning gloss of star power to the event. But even without her, this was a glorious day beyond the usual graduation pride and pomp. Everyone knew it. This was a special school that had defied the naysayers. And it was celebrating its success in grand style.[3]

It was a great day for the thirty-two graduates all dressed in white caps and gowns and all headed for college (except for one entering the air force). Most were the first in their families to go beyond high school. As the radiant face of each graduate flashed across a large screen, it conveyed a compelling sense of collective pride, individual hope, and institutional triumph. Typical of commencement exercises, several graduates spoke on behalf of their classmates. But rather than the usual droning speeches of personal goals and calls to civic duty, these brief remarks spoke volumes about the school, its mission, and the difference it had made in the lives of these young women. "In a world of followers," salutatorian Jeanette Dixon told the audience, "we dare to be leaders." Valedictorian Edriana Suarez could not hold back the tears as she told of overcoming the odds. "In the end, we are underdogs," she said with a gravitas that belied her youth and slight demeanor. "There are people who don't expect us to win and don't want us to win. The only thing we can do about these people is prove them wrong. And that's exactly what we're doing today." The audience broke into thunderous applause.

It was a great day for the families, many of them poor and working class, African Americans and Hispanics, most from East Harlem. They had taken a chance four years earlier and sent their daughters off to an educational experiment when the Young Women's Leadership School added a ninth-grade class in its second year. Their pride and excitement was palpable. It was a day of vindication for Ann Rubenstein Tisch, a former news reporter from the Midwest who had launched the school with her husband, Andrew Tisch, an executive in the family-owned Loews Corporation. Her vision and dogged determination had made this happen in the face of legal threats, unrelenting opposition, and personal assaults. Beaming with pride, she intently looked out at the front rows and said, "Girls, you have proven that this is what public education can be." And for Oprah, it was a chance to share struggles and triumphs that resonated deeply with the graduates. "I am here because of you," she told them. "I saw my life in your lives, I saw who I was and who I've been able to become." She entreated them to set their sights high but never to forget those who had come before them. "Excellence is the best deterrent to racism. It is the best deterrent to sexism. If you are excellent, the world notices." Five years earlier this was all a dream seemingly on the brink of unraveling.

The seeds for this school, however, were sown in the mid-1980s and that is where the story begins. As Ann Tisch tells it, her interest in the possibility of an all-girls' public school harkens back to her days as a national correspondent for *The NBC Nightly News*. She was especially struck by the impoverished lives of inner-city children. "You do the inner-city stories, you see the children who are dropping out, not coming back," she recalls. "I would be left scratching my head, saying, 'Gee, what could be done to solve some of those problems?' "[4] She was assigned to cover a story about a public school in Milwaukee that had opened a day care center for teenage mothers. In the course of her visit, she interviewed a group of girls. "Where do you see yourself in ten years?" she asked them. One of them started to weep quietly, shaking her head, Tisch recalls. It was clear that this girl "felt trapped." It was also clear that the answer was to "keep these girls off this path altogether." Tisch filed away the story, but it nevertheless proved a "turning point" in her thinking about the education of poor minority girls. Meanwhile, she moved to New York, got married, and left television reporting in 1991 after nineteen years in the business. She thought she would do political consulting, went to work for former New York congresswoman Geraldine Ferraro, and resumed news reporting part-time at ABC. But she never forgot the Milwaukee story.

By the mid-1990s, Tisch had become increasingly dismayed by the high dropout rate among Hispanic and African-American students. As she had learned from the Milwaukee experience, there was also a high pregnancy rate among these girls, and many of them left school to take care of their babies. At about the same time, reports started hitting the press of how coeducational schools and classrooms "shortchange" girls. Retrieving the image of the weeping girl from her "mental Rolodex," Tisch was convinced that minority girls would better focus on academics if set free from the distraction of boys. The more she thought about it, the more clearly she envisioned an all-girls' public school, one that would offer poor and working-class girls the educational opportunities available to the more privileged in the elite, private schools in New York—a school where they would be "valued for their intelligence and not their sex appeal."

Tisch started talking to people around the city—those in power as well as ordinary people on subway trains, those who had the clout to make things happen and those whose children desperately needed something positive to happen. She did her homework, visiting Baltimore's Western High School and Philadelphia's High School for Girls. She knew she had to find allies before she went to a school district. She explored partners—Girls Inc., Bronx Community College, the City University of New York, the Girl Scouts. At a book party for the historian Diane Ravitch, she talked it up with then–Chancellor of Schools Ray Cortines and several members of the central Board of Education, including Carol Gresser, the president of the board and a graduate of an all-girls' school. Cortines and Gresser both thought the idea was terrific.

She ran her idea by Seymour Fliegel and Coleman Genn, former school administrators who knew the system well. Together they had been instrumental in setting up small innovative schools in Community School District (CSD) 4 in East Harlem through the Center for Educational Innovation at the Manhattan Institute, a private think tank where they both were senior fellows. Ann Tisch was a member of the center's board. Here she found an enthusiastic response. Her idea dovetailed with a discovery made by Harvey Newman, the director of alternative schools in the district. As Newman later recalled, he had "found out that the city had been hiding data on an enormous gender gap in math and science scores. In black and Hispanic communities, the gap was starker still." A 1994 report from the Chancellor's Task Force on Sex Equity had revealed, for example, that African-American and Hispanic females had the lowest passing rate on the New York State Regents physics and chemistry tests—more than 20 percentage points below white females and more than 30 points below Asians.[5]

With Newman on board, Fliegel and Genn helped Tisch broker an agreement with the district superintendent, Evelyn Castro, who welcomed the idea. The setting was perfect. East Harlem was among the poorest neighborhoods in the nation. Data from 1993 showed that more than one in three residents was on some form of public assistance. In the early 1990s the number of violent crimes there was twice the city average.[6] Moreover, CSD 4 was no newcomer to school options. It already had twenty-three schools, some of them programs within schools, including three emphasizing math and science, two the performing arts, a writing school, a prep school, and a maritime school. The Young Women's Leadership School fit in well with this scheme.

Tisch and her small band of supporters fully realized that the school would generate controversy. A lot of people in the city told them, "You can't do that." They were resurrecting an approach that New York had buried a decade earlier and one that had provoked opposition and litigation elsewhere. So they continued to solicit advice and support from city and state officials, many of whom just happened to be graduates of single-sex schools from a bygone era. They sought counsel from former New York governor Mario Cuomo and congressman Charles Rangel. They engaged City Hall and the city's legal office, knowing that if a lawsuit ensued, the city's attorneys would have to defend them in court. As they set their legal and political ducks in order, they still had to find suitable space for the school, and so they talked to real estate brokers—a "time-consuming ordeal" as Tisch recollects. They finally found a home—the top three floors of an eleven-story gray brick commercial building that the Board of Education had already leased and renovated as a temporary site for a small alternative high school. Located on 106th Street off Lexington Avenue in East Harlem, or what New Yorkers call Spanish Harlem, the building also housed a film production company and an office of the city's Department of Housing Preservation and Development.

Months before the projected opening in fall 1996, the local community school board officially approved the school and hired a director and three teachers to begin planning the curriculum and recruiting students, mostly from the surrounding neighborhood. The school would emphasize math and science, two subjects in which girls have lagged behind boys in achievement and career interest. It would begin with fifty seventh-grade girls, add an equal number of ninth graders the following year, and gradually expand through grade twelve. It would incorporate both a middle school under community school district control and a high school which would report to officials at central headquarters. So they still had to move through the labyrinthine approval process of the central Board of Education. By the time the school was ready for a final sign-off in the summer of 1996, there was a new chancellor of schools, Rudy Crew, who did not share his predecessor's enthusiasm for the idea of an all-girls public school. According to the chancellor's press secretary, the "last thing" Crew wanted was "to put his imprimatur on a school that might be closed due to legal challenges."[7] There was also significant opposition to the school within the system itself. Many high-level officials considered single-sex schools socially backward at best and harmful at worst.

Just weeks before the vote was scheduled, it hit the newspapers that an all-girls public school was about to open in New York. The news immediately triggered a heated debate that swirled through the local and national press and the broadcast media. At the eleventh hour, the school's fate began to look tenuous. As prospective students pored over the books on their recommended reading list, got measured for school uniforms, and imagined what school would be like without boys, local organizers were locking horns with reluctant central Board of Education officials and fending off irate civil liberties groups. Norman Siegel, head of the New York Civil Liberties Union (NYCLU), immediately fired off a letter to the chancellor of schools. He warned that he would lend his support only if the district admitted boys and did not call it an "all girls school." Michael Myers, executive director of the New York Civil Rights Coalition, wrote to the president of the Board of Education to express concern that school officials had moved ahead on the school without giving the public the opportunity to comment. Like Siegel, he believed the school would violate federal law. Attorneys for both the chancellor and the board guardedly responded that the matter was still under consideration pending a thorough review of the law. The New York City chapter of the National Organization for Women (NOW) publicly joined the opposition, arguing that the school would not prepare girls for the real world.

Meanwhile, the New York Civil Liberties Union met with key figures, including CSD 4 officials, to gather more facts and present their case. There was a hint of déjà vu about this course of events. This was not the first occasion on which civil rights activists had found themselves in an incongruously adverse relationship with poor and working-class minority parents. Just a decade earlier, the NYCLU had threatened to sue the city if it did not convert the last all-girls school, Washington Irving High School, to coeducation. In that case Board of Education officials did in fact yield, despite vehement opposition from parents and students who unsuccessfully brought suit to stop the move.[8] In 1991 the NYCLU also had vigorously protested against the proposed Ujamaa Institute, an all-male school for at-risk African-American students. Again, officials capitulated and the school later opened as the coed Middle College High School at Medgar Evers College.

As city and school attorneys sifted through the ambiguities of the law, school officials hastened to fine-tune the program and ward off a federal investigation or, worse yet, litigation. As the scheduled opening day drew near, the central Board of Education finally met in closed session. John Ferrandino, the superintendent of high schools for the city, a career educator, and a graduate of an all-boys Catholic high school, argued it out with board members. As he later explained, "You have to be respectful of parents' choices. Parents know their kids better than we do. Students vary and if you maximize choice, you can better meet the students' needs."[9] With assurance from the city's attorneys that the school was legally defensible, the board unanimously approved a resolution extending the school to twelfth grade in subsequent years and endorsing it as an important educational option. Board officials announced that they would ensure the legality of the school by offering comparable programs in math and science enrichment and leadership to boys and girls in a coeducational school within the district. Although the school would arguably consider applications from boys, it actively recruited only girls for the entering class.

The following day, the New York City chapter of NOW, the New York Civil Liberties Union, and the New York Civil Rights Coalition filed a joint complaint with the Office for Civil Rights (OCR) of the United States Department of Education. The gist of the complaint was that the Young Women's Leadership School violated Title IX. More specifically, the complainants claimed that the school would "provide important educational opportunities to girls . . . not available to boys" and that it was "premised upon stereotypical views of the personality and behavior" of both girls and boys. A finding in their favor could have jeopardized nearly a billion dollars in education funds that New York City annually receives from the federal government. That same day, the chancellor of schools told the press that he "would not establish [a boys' school] as a 'quid pro quo' to keep the girls' school alive."[10]

As this drama slowly unfolded, the media had a field day and the Young Women's Leadership School became an international cause célèbre. From the *Rocky Mountain News,* to the *St. Petersburg Times,* the *Chicago Tribune,* the *Washington Post,* and even *Agence France-Presse,* the pros and cons of single-sex schools were laid open to public debate. Quickly the forces started lining up on either side and for different reasons. What some saw as educational innovation held hostage by civil rights politics, others considered a potential Pandora's box for legalizing two-tiered discrimination on a grand scale. Some recognized the merits of integrating students by race or sex, yet yielded to what seemed to be common sense and need. As one columnist put it, "There are already schools for gay and lesbian kids, for kids who can't take too much structure, for artsy kids and for kids who want to fly airplanes and run restaurants." This could just be a "remedial effort, a limited and carefully tailored way to correct past discrimination against girls."[11]

Others rejected "victim theory" with its "constant reminders of oppression, deprivation and second-class status to justify girls-only schools" but could accept the idea that some girls are freer to concentrate on schoolwork when removed from the distractions of boys. Yet for some girl advocates and feminists like Peggy Orenstein, author of the best-selling book *School-Girls,* the creation of a public girls' school not only was "risky" but ducked the real issue of how to make the "coeducational classroom, where most children will continue to be educated, work for both boys and girls." For Janet Gallagher, director of the ACLU Women's Rights Project, which was advising the NYCLU on the case, the idea that girls and boys inevitably distract each other was an "enormously dangerous presumption."[12]

For the parents of entering students, the school was a lifeline out of failing institutions. Most were attracted primarily to the academically challenging curriculum, although the absence of boys enhanced the school's appeal for many of them. In the opening weeks of school, the local press memorialized their motives, aspirations, and first impressions as well as those of their daughters. As one mother put it, "Just because you live in a poor area doesn't mean you can't reach for the stars. . . . Now we have to sit back and say we've done all this [integration], and we're still in the same spot." Another explained that she liked the "premise of the school—that it was a college preparatory school. My daughter wants to become a doctor, so for me, this school was perfect." For mothers like Marilyn Mercado, who was fifteen years old when her daughter was born, the school provided a way to keep their daughters "away from the boys."[13]

For the girls themselves, it was a refuge from the social pressures and apathy toward gender issues that they had experienced in coeducational schools. In talking to reporters, students noted that boys had dominated most of the classes in their previous schools. One student recalled how sometimes she "didn't even want to ever raise [her] hand and ask questions." They looked forward to the opportunity to excel and to just be themselves. "With boys around, you think of them and don't always concentrate on school," one girl remarked.[14] Another observed how "You can invent a whole new character. Girls get to be in charge of everything. You're not thinking all day, 'God, do I look okay?' " Still another recollected that at her former school, "Some girls worried so much about boys calling them fat that they wouldn't even eat."[15]

The school opened in September with a dark cloud of threatened litigation and a pending administrative complaint hanging over it. A lawsuit never did materialize. Civil rights groups simply could not find a boy willing to apply to the school and be denied admission. "We kept hoping," Norman Siegel of the ACLU later recalled. "No one ever surfaced. Once it becomes an all girls school, any boy who would go into that situation would probably be ridiculed."[16] So they had no live plaintiff whose legal rights had arguably been violated. Nonetheless, there was the real danger that the federal administrative axe could fall at anytime, forcing the school to admit boys or pushing the district to open a parallel boys' school. But federal officials were not about to jump to a hasty conclusion where the law was so unclear, nor were they eager to establish broad precedent on such a politically volatile issue. Besides, the Clinton administration was not averse to single-sex programs despite what Justice Department attorneys, still high from their victory against VMI, might have thought. After all, first lady Hillary Rodham Clinton was a proud alumna of Wellesley College.

Throughout the first year, the school hummed along. It led CSD 4 in reading, scoring 20 percentage points above the middle school average for East Harlem. One student took top prize in a citywide chess competition, and two more were winners in the district's science fair. The school's attendance was the highest in the district and among the highest in the city. Yet throughout that school year, the silence from Washington was deafening. It was not until the following September, as the school expanded into grades eight and nine, that some word was finally heard. The message was ambiguous at best. Office for Civil Rights officials conveyed a preliminary finding, not in writing but in a series of telephone calls to school board attorneys and opposing civil rights groups. The finding was that the school appeared to violate the law. The proposed remedy was either to admit boys or to open a comparable boys' school at a nearby location. Washington was obviously trying to mediate a compromise.

But neither side was willing to bend. As far as New York was concerned, admitting boys to the school would undermine the reason it had been created in the first place: "that teenage girls perform better, particularly in math and science, when boys are not in the room." Besides, CSD 4 already provided a myriad of opportunities for boys in coed schools, and those opportunities were equal to those that the girls at the Young Women's Leadership School were receiving. Civil rights groups, on the other hand, would settle for nothing short of the school's becoming coed. A letter sent that November to Secretary of Education Richard Riley by several New York congressmen supporting the school received a cordial but uncommitted response from the assistant secretary for civil rights, Norma Cantŭ. She basically stated that the Department of Education was still discussing alternatives with school officials. As Sy Fliegel later recalled, this was a "no-win situation" for the civil liberties groups. "If OCR forced the Board of Education to close the school, there would be TV cameras on site with 125 girls crying, parents protesting, and the NYCLU and NOW viewed as the villains. If OCR forced the Board to open a boys' school, there would then be not one but two single-sex schools and the NYCLU and NOW were even more concerned about boys' schools excluding girls."[17]

Neither scenario played out. Whether swayed by the display of support from New York Democrats or by the Clinton administration's apparent disinclination to pursue the issue any further, OCR officials did a complete turnaround in the following months. In a meeting with representatives from NOW-NYC, the NYCLU, and the New York Civil Rights Coalition that February, Cantú suggested that the city could justify the school as an affirmative action remedy and an exception to Title IX. "If this could provide an educational benefit for the girls, let them enjoy that benefit," Cantú was quoted as saying. The groups were outraged. For Norman Siegel of the NYCLU, the "exception" plan would turn the civil rights law "on its head." "Affirmative action is inclusionary. This is exclusionary." Michael Myers of the New York Civil Liberties Coalition called it "a sham and a ruse." Galen Sherwin, president of NOW-NYC, warned that it would "set up a double standard."[18]

According to press reports, New York could expect a final decision within the coming weeks. That was February 1998 and that was the last official word from Washington. In the meantime, single-sex schooling has gained bipartisan support within Congress, not to mention the ringing endorsement of now–New York Senator Hillary Rodham Clinton. This political turn is due in some measure to the continuing success of the East Harlem school and the public discussion it set in motion. At the same time, a new administration inclined toward school choice and local flexibility has taken hold of OCR's reins. And the Young Women's Leadership Foundation, the brainchild of Ann Tisch, the original force behind the school's engine, is stimulating interest and supporting local efforts to establish a national network of exemplary public girls' schools in other large cities. The first offshoot is the Chicago Young Women's Leadership School, a charter middle and high school designed by prominent women attorneys and corporate leaders, which opened in 2000.[19]

Back in East Harlem, first impressions are generally reliable, and so it goes with the Young Women's Leadership School, affectionately known as TYWLS by its students and staff. Set on a main thoroughfare with two-way traffic whizzing by and the rumbling of a commuter train line just beside it, the school is an oasis of excellence and hope in a desert of poverty, crime, and despair. On my first visit I was struck by the dissimilarity from other inner-city middle schools I had come to know over the years and by the striking contrast with the surrounding neighborhood. My immediate thought was that this was physically and emotionally a safe haven for these girls, a place where they could flourish emotionally and intellectually, free from the social distractions and sexual pressures that too often reach dangerous proportions in urban public schools.

The school now occupies the top five floors of a former warehouse subsequently converted and remodeled into an office building. You enter via an elevator dedicated solely to the school and run by an attendant who takes you to the ninth floor, where a female security guard politely asks you to sign in and show photo ID. As you slowly ascend, you leave behind the buzz, grime, and clamor outside for a place that is orderly and secure but with a palpable sense of energy and purpose. The high school's literature calls this "a public school with a private school mission" and it feels very much like a private school, one blending both traditional and progressive elements. Girls in plaid uniforms, navy in the middle school and gray in the high school, scurry about chatting as they move from class to class. Some wear skirts or slacks, white blouses, and a blazer or sweater. Others wear sweat pants and T-shirts for gym. All are neatly groomed. No funky hairdos or multipierced ears can be found. Jewelry is discouraged as "inconvenient and inappropriate." Sneakers must be worn at all times outside of dance and gymnastics classes. Teachers are dressed casually but professionally and neatly. Male teachers typically wear ties, a voluntary gesture.

The narrow hallways are painted a pale pink and the walls are lined with student art projects. The classrooms are green, pink, and turquoise, the remains from the previous tenant and not a sign of gender, as the staff apologetically explains. The space is carefully divided among classrooms, two science labs, two computer labs, a library, and a multipurpose room for performances and gym classes. Instead of a noisy cafeteria with the typical long, institutional tables, the girls eat lunch in a dining hall furnished with round tables more suited to conversation. The classrooms are small, with tables seating four neatly arranged to induce discussion and collaborative learning. Some, like the seventh-grade humanities classroom, have a sitting area with a comfortable couch and chairs for students to share creative thoughts and stretch their imagination. Some have rocking chairs and Oriental rugs, most of them furnished by the teachers themselves.

Everyone is on a first-name basis, from the principal on down. The staff has grown gradually to its present 27 teachers as the school has expanded from its first class of 50 seventh graders in 1996 to its current population of 365 students in grades seven through twelve. A hiring committee screens, interviews, and hires most faculty. The principal is a member of the committee, and the final decision is hers. The school has drawn upon local teacher-education programs, including the Bank Street College of Education, Teachers College, and New York University for recruits rather than seeking experienced teachers from within the city's public school system. The original professional staff of the school consisted of three women teachers and a female principal. Gradually men have joined the faculty, which remains predominantly female. Many of the teachers are young, and with their youth comes idealism, dedication, and willingness to take pedagogical risks. Some of them have taught in alternative schools and are inclined philosophically and temperamentally toward innovation.

The school is unequivocal in the values it aims to instill. Its clearly artic-ulated purpose is "to nurture the intellectual curiosity and creativity of young women." The mission statement talks of developing in students "a sense of community, responsibility and ethical principles." Leadership per-vades the program. Many of the extracurricular activities are geared to that end. Sixty hours of community service (twenty hours per year) are required for high school graduation. On the cover of the student handbook is a sketch of four young women in motion carrying flags. A speech bubble above says, "We Are the Leaders of Our Generation." The handbook lists twelve points of "Leadership Behavior," including "step[ping] aside to let adults enter or leave a room first," "be[ing] helpful to any visitors," and avoiding language that "may be hurtful and offensive to others." The school's discipline code calls for "discussion and demonstration of thought-ful habits of heart, mind, work and voice." It also lays down four "non-negotiable rules"—no violence, no drugs, no weapons, and no leaving cam-pus without a parent or guardian.[20]

The school makes a conscious effort to present students and parents with a positive sense of womanhood. The reception area of the main office dis-plays books with titles such as *Girls and the Physical Sciences* and *Raising Competent, Confident Daughters*. Women's achievements pervade the cur-riculum, providing proactive and thoughtful female role models. The li-brary boasts a sizable number of fiction and nonfiction books with strong women characters. The same can be said for the humanities program, where reading materials often present a female protagonist within a fiction-alized historical setting. In one classroom, a Barbie doll hanging by the neck from a ceiling light speaks volumes about the school's views on cul-tural representations of women. Just a decade after Mattel marketed Teen Talk Barbie whining, "Math class is tough," this school is determined to disabuse girls of that myth. The curriculum emphasizes math, science, and technology.

Classes, which last for fifty-five minutes, are relaxed and unfold more like a discussion than a lecture. Instruction is student-centered, project-based, collaborative, and interdisciplinary. The school expects all juniors and seniors to take courses on an advanced or honors level. Advanced Placement classes are offered in Spanish, English, science, and math. Se-niors can take college-level courses at Marymount Manhattan College. Some participate in summer programs for college or Advanced Placement credit. The school has tapped into the rich cultural and intellectual re-sources of its Manhattan location. The Science Fellows program at the New York Academy of Medicine and the astronomy program at the Rose Plane-tarium offer students invaluable opportunities to work on advanced science projects with professional researchers.

Students receive intense and personalized attention from the staff. The school makes every effort to maintain class size at about twenty to twenty-five students, larger than the typical private school but smaller than most city public schools. As in many private schools, every student is part of an "advisory group," and every teacher serves as an adviser. The groups meet every day, and once a week for an extended period, to discuss personal and social issues and to resolve any conflicts that may have arisen since the last weekly meeting. Each adviser is a combination of academic counselor, taskmaster, friend, and advocate. Advisers also serve a crucial role as liaisons to the home. It is almost impossible for any student to fall between the cracks. At the same time, the school openly values, recognizes, and rewards academic success. The school newsletter regularly publishes the names of students in various ranks within the honor roll and acknowledges students with perfect attendance. At a monthly "town hall" meeting for the entire student body, the honor roll is called and the girls cheer the success of their classmates.

The school actively recruits potential students from the surrounding community and gives them priority. A student is admitted on the basis of an interview (accompanied by a parent or guardian), a test (including writing and math components), attendance and discipline records from her prior school, and teacher recommendations. The school's literature makes it clear that academic achievement is only one factor considered in the admissions process. Equally important is an eagerness to learn and to excel in a college preparatory program. Given these parameters, the students are select in their attitudes and motivation but not necessarily in their academic preparation. A small number have learning disabilities or are not fluent in English. Approximately 40 percent of the student body is African American, 59 percent Hispanic, and the remaining 1 percent of various backgrounds. About 67 percent fall below the poverty line. Ninety percent are the first generation to attend college, and 25 percent are first-generation immigrants. A majority come from single-parent homes.[21] Since the school's opening in 1996, a small number of girls have left, mostly to attend a coed high school or because of difficulties in adjusting to the academic rigor and behavioral standards. Meanwhile, demand has grown exponentially. For the 2002–3 year there were more than 550 applications for the 60 openings in the seventh grade and a waiting list of 1,200 for 3 ninth-grade slots.[22]

The school's budget comes through the same channels as for other public schools in New York City, mostly local with some state and a smattering of federal funds, and at the same per-student level of allocation. In addition, the Young Women's Leadership Foundation provides approximately $1,000 per student, which pays for various support services, including a full-time college adviser, Chris Farmer, who makes college part of the girls' thinking from the day they enter in seventh grade. Farmer came to the school from St. Agnes Boys' High School in Manhattan, where he had served in a similar role. St. Agnes has now become the "brother" school for TYWLS. Farmer organizes group and individual college visits, helps students with their college essays, and navigates the application and financial aid process for them. He also works with families in helping them emotionally support their daughters in their college plans. The first graduating class in 2001 received offers from a wide range of public and private colleges. Most were within New York State, but also among them were Mount Holyoke, Regis, Trinity, and Howard. The second class began to move more solidly into the elite ranks, with offers from Amherst, Barnard, Columbia, Swarthmore, Wellesley, and Williams.

The foundation partially funds an SAT prep program, in which students receive back part of their payment if they have perfect attendance. It also supports various enrichment activities, including an intensive five-week summer science program at Smith College and field experiences in foreign countries, as well as professional development opportunities for the faculty and an annual "travelship award" for outstanding teaching. Ann Rubenstein Tisch, who heads the foundation, has helped the school forge alliances with the artistic, media, and corporate communities of New York City for a variety of collaborative efforts, including student internships. All students at TYWLS are eligible for full or partial scholarships for a variety of summer programs. A number of students have participated in the Urban Debate League in partnership with the University of Vermont. Others have attended the Smith Summer Program, a six-week intensive science and humanities course at Smith College. The foundation also supports a dance team and an art club at the school. College students serve as mentors throughout the school year, as do members of the Coalition of 100 Black Women.

The school shows all the vices and virtues that come with being small and innovative, along with all the growing pains of being new. Not unlike alternative schools of this sort, during the first several years there was considerable turnover in the teaching staff. Some could not adapt to the close coordination, the high expectations, and the intense rigor of the academic program. Others left for more lucrative positions. Similarly, in the first six years three successive principals brought very different leadership styles, and at least as many assistant principals came and went. The first principal, Celenia Chevere, came with a long history of creating unconventional yet academically successful schools, often in hostile environments. She was also an insider to the community, having grown up in East Harlem, the child of poor natives of Puerto Rico. Selected for exactly those reasons by the district superintendent, with the endorsement of Ann Rubenstein Tisch, Chevere laid out the original plans for TYWLS, handpicking the initial students, setting a traditional tone, designing the curriculum, and establishing high standards for students and staff. She saw the school through the first four years, but found herself increasingly at odds with uncompliant parents and with a Board of Education bureaucracy that wanted the school to serve a wider range of student needs than she had envisioned. She moved on to yet another innovative project, establishing a similarly challenging program, but this time coeducational and in a kindergarten-through-twelve school. She took with her eleven TYWLS students.[23] The second principal, Janet Scott, a Barnard graduate and passionate believer in all-girls education, served for one year in an interim-acting position. With an educational philosophy 180 degrees removed from that of her predecessor, she proved too dramatic a change for students, staff, and school district decision makers to embrace her tenure on a permanent basis.

The third and current principal, Kathleen Ponze, took over in fall 2001 and has brought a much-needed sense of stability. Raised as an "army brat," Ponze attended fourteen schools before graduating from Frankfurt American High School in Germany. Looking back, she states emphatically that her "most rewarding experience" was in a same-sex school. For her, leading TYWLS is a "career dream" fulfilled.[24] Her travels as a young person left her with an ability to adapt readily to new situations, which has served her well in her present post. As she sees it, the school is now at a crossroads in terms of its facility and its mission. Despite the addition of two floors in 2000, space is still a serious issue. There is no true gymnasium with a regulation court for team sports, nor is there an auditorium or practice space for the performing arts as you would find in a conventional high school. Without these, the sports and music programs are severely constrained. Despite these limitations, the school has generated increasing demand within and beyond East Harlem. As its reputation has grown, so has its appeal and so has the potential for becoming larger and more selective. Middle-class parents are taking their daughters out of private schools and sending them to TYWLS. The two burning questions now are whether to increase the school's population and thereby lose the intimacy of smallness, and whether to remain at the present site or move to a free-standing facility. The answers are potentially but not inevitably interrelated.

Ponze worries that to expand any further might disrupt the intense student-teacher relationships which are a significant part of the school's strength. She also fears that broadening the base of the student body would compromise the school's original mission to serve girls from the immediate neighborhood. As Ponze sees it, these girls "come with such issues—trying to find their voices and find themselves." The school, she says "draws from a community that has struggled in getting girls to college. Grooming a young woman to be a wife and mother" is the primary concern of many Hispanic households in East Harlem.

The school takes these girls and their parents from grade seven on forward and talks to them about college, a goal that is built into the life plan and consciousness of every girl. In that sense, the school provides a ticket out of the subculture, and only families who buy into this project enroll their children in the first instance. Heading many of these families are single mothers who decidedly want a better life for their daughters than they themselves have known. And as the word has traveled up and down the graffiti-lined streets of this beleaguered community, more and more of them are going to great lengths to seize that opportunity. Madeline Moore, former president of the New York Coalition of 100 Black Women, tells how mothers have pleaded with her to get their daughters into the school. Ponze suspects that the single-sex environment might be even more critical at the middle school level than the high school. She notes the importance of "harboring" them so that they can overcome the particular difficulties of these years.[25]

Critics of the school inevitably ask for the bottom line. Are students doing "better" at TYWLS than they would have at a coed school? That depends on what "better" means. Recent statistics demonstrate that the school is indeed working, and impressively so, when viewed both on its own and against the general backdrop of New York City. In 2000–2001 all students taking the Advanced Placement Spanish exam received scores of 3, 4, or 5. Meanwhile, 100 percent passed the New York State English, math, U.S. history, and biology Regents examinations. The school was one of 19 high schools, out of a total of 146 citywide, in which the entire graduating class passed both English and math exams. For the borough of Manhattan, TYWLS scores were second only to Stuyvesant High School, one of the city's most academically selective public schools, where admission is based on a rigorous entrance exam. At many schools the results were dreadful. Just blocks away at the well-regarded Park East High School, only 35 percent passed the math exam and 80 percent the English. Nearly a quarter of the class of 2001 citywide could not graduate because they had either failed or not taken either test.[26]

Within the first two graduating classes, every TYWLS student was accepted into college, compared with 50 percent citywide. Daily attendance remains consistently above 92 percent, as contrasted with 85 percent throughout New York City. With each successive year, students show stronger evidence of academic achievement. For 2001–2 the school boasted one finalist in the National Merit Scholarship Program and one in the New York Times Scholars Program. One student gained acceptance into the highly competitive New York University Film School Summer Program, and another won a summer scholarship awarded by the Asia Society for study in Korea.

Of course, the naysayers unrelentingly deny the critical role that the school's single-sex environment has played in achieving these remarkable results. To their mind, the school's apparent success rests solely on the quality of the educational experience. They point to small class size, a clearly articulated mission, a rigorous curriculum, a high level of parent involvement, an intense focus on college preparation, dedicated teachers, and the added resources of the Young Women's Leadership Foundation. It would be foolish to deny the importance of these factors. Critics assume, however, that you can reproduce these essential and tangible features of a good school in a coeducational setting and achieve exactly the same results. That assumption remains far from certain. In fact, if you talk to the young women attending the school, they make it clear that the all-girl setting incorporates certain intangible elements—a feeling of school pride, self-confidence, and security—that are conducive to academic achievement. As one teacher who had previously taught in a small coed school in the Bronx put it, "These girls are far more assertive and aware. They have a stronger sense of their future."[27] Assuming that to be true, then the school is succeeding in what it initially set out to achieve.

## PHILADELPHIA AND BALTIMORE: BLENDING THE OLD WITH THE NEW

Despite their many disagreements, supporters and opponents of the New York school agree on one point: its smallness is one of its virtues. Yet those who believe that size combined with outside resources are crucial to the school's success need only look two hundred or so miles west for compelling proof otherwise. The Philadelphia High School for Girls is a mélange of seeming contradictions, combining the largeness of scale emblematic of most American high schools and the ethos and mission of a small private girls' school, with some finishing school touches thrown into the mix. Its population numbers around 1,300, down from 2,000 in the 1980s. At that time, Central High, its all-male "brother" school, became coeducational under court order and began to offer for the first time an academically challenging option to girls. The teaching staff of Girls' High numbers about 65. Since 1958 the school has been located among row houses, health facilities, and other schools in the Olney section, a multiethnic low-income neighborhood just north of downtown Philadelphia.

Housed in a large building with a decidedly classical-style exterior, the long cavernous corridors of Girls' High evoke the factory model of public educational institutions born of the nineteenth century. Nonetheless, this is very much a twenty-first-century urban school where students enter the massive brick building each morning through city-mandated metal detectors, for which teachers and students are understandably apologetic and which are woefully incongruous with what lies immediately beyond. As in other public schools in this and other cities, the staff, including the principal, come via a citywide appointments process. Their employment is governed by union contract, and they work under the usual burdens of bureaucratic red tape. Many of the teachers have taught at the school for twenty-plus years. A number of them are alumnae and several of them hold doctorates.

But once you get past the size, the governance structure, and the security, you quickly realize that there is something uniquely special about this school. Reproductions of two statues of women, classical in pose and heroic in size, dominate an opulent entrance lined in pink marble. One is the Venus de Milo, originally acquired by the Alumnae Association in 1901 to grace the assembly room of a previous school site, along with other reproductions of ancient Greek and Roman art. The other is the Winged Nike from Samothrace, better known as Winged Victory. Funded by alumnae of the first thirty-six classes, the statue is dedicated to the memory of two members of the school's first faculty who died in a boating accident off the coast of Maine in 1905. Students have been known to place a penny on the statue's base for good luck on exams. The figures signify that this is a classical college preparatory school. Move further into the classrooms, science labs, art studios, and instrumental music rooms, and you experience a world with one eye toward the past yet both feet grounded in the present and future.

To best understand this paradox, one has to go back in time to the school's beginnings and move forward as it gradually fine-tuned its core mission to educate women. Girls' High traces its official origins to 1848, when the city established Girls' Normal School, with 6 teachers and 109 students. This was the first secondary public school for girls in the state of Pennsylvania and the first municipally funded normal school in the country. In 1860 the school was renamed the Girls' High and Normal School to more accurately identify its mission to train teachers and to offer specifically an academic program to girls. For the first thirty years of its existence, almost half of the school's graduates became teachers in the Philadelphia public schools.

In 1893 the school took its current name when the high school and normal school became distinct institutions. At that point, the school offered three parallel tracks—a three-year general course designed to prepare students for the normal school; a four-year classical course requiring four years of English, Latin, and French, with German added in the third and fourth years; and a three-year business or commercial course. Over the following decades, the school underwent further changes as the winds of educational and social reform blew over Philadelphia. In 1898 a Latin-scientific course was added to prepare students for prestigious institutions of higher education including Women's Medical College and the Seven Sister schools, as well as University of Pennsylvania courses open to women. Two years later, the business course merged into the newly established Commercial High School for Girls, which subsequently became reconfigured as William Penn High School.

As Girls' High entered a new century, it founded the *Iris,* a literary magazine providing a voice for student creative expression. Leadership and community service became embodied in the work of the Service Club, whose responsibility it was to develop "a code of conduct to foster finer womanhood" or what is now known as the Code of Honor and Courtesy of the Philadelphia High School for Girls. By 1911 one-third of the student body was enrolled in college preparatory courses. When alumnae, faculty, and friends of Girls' High successfully derailed an attempted remerger with William Penn in 1930, the school emerged with a more certain and lasting identity as an institution that educates academically talented young women. That identity was somewhat shaken in the 1970s and 1980s when two lawsuits brought by girls against Central High threatened to end single-sex education in Philadelphia. The second lawsuit spelled the demise of Central as an all-male institution but left Girls' High intact. The glaring resource disparities between the two schools that the litigation made public initially cast a cloud over Girls' High. But the surrounding media attention also mobilized staff, students, and alumnae to defend their beloved institution's reputation and demand more equitable treatment.

Throughout its more than 150 years, the student population of Girls' High has continuously changed with the demographics of the city. Originally serving the daughters of white Christian business owners and skilled workers, it gradually included Jews and other second-generation white ethnics and more recently African Americans, Hispanics, and Asians.[28] As the middle-class has left the inner city, the student population has become more socioeconomically diverse and increasingly poor. A glance through old school newspapers and yearbooks gives testimony to these changes, as do the names of student cultural groups, which now include the Asian and the Islamic Life Clubs. The school still attracts the daughters of foreign nationals from among the University of Pennsylvania faculty. In recent years, with increased migration from non-Western countries, both Asian and Muslim families have found the all-girls' environment particularly appealing. In most classes you find one or two girls wearing veils. The student body is now 59 percent African American, 21 percent white, 15 percent Asian, and 5 percent Hispanic. About half are eligible for free or reduced-price lunch. For the school's principal, Geraldine Myles, these changes have affected the school in direct and palpable ways. "Many of our students feel they must work after school, even though they maintain rigorous academic schedules. It interferes with extracurricular activities."[29] And unlike previous generations of students, they have far less innocence, having grown up with single working mothers, rap music, warnings of AIDS, and the threat of teen pregnancy.

Yet despite the marked differences between students of today and those of yesteryear, there is a continuous bond between the two that remarkably transcends time, race, religion, and social class. The school consciously and successfully cultivates what all reverently refer to as "The Intangible Spirit," which students and staff vaguely describe as a sense of school loyalty, shared vision, and common experiences that each girl "inherits" from previous generations. Along with the school motto, "Vincit qui se vincit" (she conquers who conquers herself), inscribed on a welcome mat in the main hallway, this spirit permeates every program and activity.

The Intangible Spirit assumes human form in a school mural created in 1989 and expanded in 1998 as part of the school's sesquicentennial celebration. The face of a 1905 graduate inspired the depiction. As described in the celebration's program, the figure "opens her arms in the symbolic gesture of embracing and receiving students." The program goes on to explain that this "represents her eternal presence, which offers the supportive and protective essence of the Philadelphia High School for Girls and its alumnae." Other aspects of the mural draw from the past and the present. Students appear dressed in the fashions of various time periods, including two representative gym uniforms. Female statuettes symbolize math and science, art and music. Two young women hold the Excellence in Education flag awarded to the school by the United States Department of Education. A dove in flight represents student dreams and aspirations. The images of young women of multicultural backgrounds reflect the diversity of the student body. And as a signal to the present and future, a student carries a laptop and an armful of books.[30]

As the mural reveals, in a school that prides itself on preparing young women to compete in a fast-changing world, tradition and ritual run high. Students clearly treasure and take great satisfaction in both. For an increasingly small number of students, a Girls' High education is something that is handed down from mothers, aunts, and cousins. Most graduates now move out of the city. Each freshman is assigned a "big sister" who not only offers academic and social advice but also passes on the traditions. Above the doorway in the main hall hangs an open book listing the name of each graduating senior. Each student is a member of a numbered graduating class. For example, the class of 2002 is "the 246," an identity that will remain with them forever as alumnae of the school. Each class participates in such time-honored activities as the Renaissance Fair, Women in Sports Day, the Soph Hop, the Junior Prom, the Senior Class Trip, and Move-Up Day. The last of these takes place at the end of the school year, when each grade except the seniors writes a theme song, designs a T-shirt emblem, and participates in an assembly in which students physically "move up" to fill the seats of the next grade. Each year the school hosts an eleventh-grade tea to instruct girls how to comport themselves in a receiving line—a traditional touch that makes some feminists wince. Perhaps it belies the school's academic and professional thrust and its modern fix on women's role in society. Yet it also signifies to the students a sense of social grace and civility now lost in many of their lives.

Each event is marked with conscious recognition of generations who preceded and celebrated in much the same way. At graduation, each girl wears a modestly designed white dress of her own choosing and carries a bouquet of red flowers, now carnations but in the past roses, like the girls of so many numbered classes in years past. As part of the school's sesquicentennial celebration in 1998, fifteen similarly dressed alumnae representing decades from the "roaring twenties" to the "electronic eighties" marched with graduates in the commencement exercises.

An active Alumnae Association, organized in 1889, is highly instrumental in keeping the spirit and traditions alive. The current site includes an alumnae board room, an unusual feature in a public school building. The room was funded by the son of a graduate who attended the school in the late 1800s. The association's board of directors, elected by a membership of more than 4,500 graduates, hosts an annual alumnae luncheon, organizes class reunions, and publishes the *Alumnae News,* which includes an impressive list of alumnae notes. It maintains an e-mail and address list on the school's website so that graduates can keep in touch with each other and, implicitly, with the school. Each year the association grants awards for merit, service, and honor to its members. It also administers to graduating seniors numerous named scholarships, prizes, and awards funded largely through unsolicited donations. The association maintains an archives room where one finds a treasure trove of memorabilia—from mannequins draped in white graduation dresses of years gone by to athletic trophies, a photomontage of past principals (all male until 1930), a visitors' book with signatures dating back to 1933, and a store of old photos, newspaper clippings, yearbooks, and school newspapers, all evoking a history of continuity in the midst of change.

The school proudly touts its famous graduates and repeatedly affirms their accomplishments. Among them are counted numerous "firsts"—the first African-American woman bishop in the Episcopal Church, the first woman partner in a major Philadelphia law firm, the first African-American woman to graduate from the University of Pennsylvania Medical School, the first woman and African American to serve as superintendent of the Philadelphia public school system, the first African-American woman to hold a faculty position in Temple University's School of Law, one of the first women to argue a case before the U.S. Supreme Court, the first woman president of the American Medical Association, and the first woman president of the University of Pennsylvania. In addition, the school boasts a string of doctors, lawyers, entrepreneurs, scientists, and novelists, as well as world-renowned artists and instrumentalists who trained in the school's first-rate arts and music program. Many of these women now hold a place in the Court of Honor of Distinguished Daughters of the Philadelphia High School for Girls. From these names, which are engraved on a plaque in the archives room, students gain inspiration and motivation. The message is that Girls' High produces leaders.

Tradition is not all the school has to offer, nor does the school rest on its laurels. Girls' High continues to define itself as a "highly competitive college-preparatory school for gifted women of multi-cultural backgrounds" whose mission it is to "equip students with the academic, social, emotional, and cultural foundations for success in an ever changing society." When *Teacher* magazine profiled the school in 2000, it found the same factors attracting students as it had observed in 1991—an emphasis on promoting self-esteem, high academic standards, and leadership opportunities, combined with school safety, a rare commodity in many urban areas.[31] The curriculum follows a traditional college preparatory model, with four years of English, three years of math, three years of science, at least two years of a foreign language, and five major academic electives.

As a magnet school, it draws its student population from across the city and actively recruits prospective students to the idea of an all-girls education. For admission, applicants must demonstrate a ranking in at least the 85th percentile on citywide math and reading tests, no more than one grade of C, and excellent attendance and behavior records. The school expects every student to continue to higher education, most to colleges and universities but others to music schools or technical institutes. All classes are considered college preparatory, and a certain number also are taught at the honors level. Special courses accommodate a small number of students identified as "mentally gifted." Students can choose among six modern languages as well as Latin, and among fifteen Advanced Placement electives, including calculus, physics, and statistics.

Students with special talents and interests can pursue an intensive major in the school's art and music programs, which have gained a reputation for producing notable professionals. The school library houses a gallery displaying the works of graduates spanning fifty years. The music program is a particular draw for talented girls who bypass performing arts schools for a unique offering of strong academics combined with music performance. The well-equipped music program centers around a music suite that includes six practice rooms and a listening room. The All-City Orchestra, which the school's music director conducts, practices at the school, and students have use of the full range of the orchestra's instruments. The program engages more than two hundred students a year in two vocal ensembles, a choir of more than one hundred students, a seventy-five-piece orchestra, a jazz band, and several chamber music ensembles. Girls here have the opportunity to play large instruments without feeling intimidated. As the music director, a veteran of thirty years, proudly notes, "At coed schools rarely would a girl play the saxophone or trombone. Here it is a common event. And for theatrical productions, girls build the entire sets."[32] There are no boys to do the heavy lifting.

The school still occasionally boasts a National Merit Scholarship semifinalist, though the numbers are down from 1967, when there were twelve. That decline is not unusual for urban schools, where a growing number of students now struggle to overcome social and economic disadvantages. Yet among Philadelphia's public high schools, Girls' High continues to prove its academic worth. Aside from one school specifically designated for gifted students, Girls' High ranks second behind Central High School, out of a total of forty-one secondary schools, on statewide reading, math, and writing tests. The percentage of students taking Advanced Placement exams is higher than the state average except in math and computer science, and the percentage scoring 3 or higher also exceeds the state average on all exams except those covering math, computer science, and science. One hundred percent of those taking Advanced Placement exams in art and music, where the school has distinct strengths, scored 3 or higher in the 1999–2000 school year. For English the figure was 89.5 percent, and in foreign languages 85.7 percent, all well above the state average.

In recent years, Girls' High has been one of just three city high schools with a dropout rate of zero across the grades, compared with 55 percent among ninth graders citywide. Each year more than 98 percent of Girls' High graduates go on to college.[33] Most attend public and small private colleges, many within the state. But there is always a small number of top achievers who gain admission to such prestigious institutions as Columbia, Cornell, Yale, Swarthmore, Wellesley, and the University of Pennsylvania.

How has the school managed to avoid a legal challenge to its single-sex status? It simply has no official written policy excluding boys. When an occasional boy inquires about applying, the school helps him find an acceptable and suitable alternative among the city's other magnet schools. In fact, he need go no further than down the street to Central High, which offers a college preparatory program with similar course offerings. Yet this quiet deflection does not come without a price. Title IX prohibits the school from offering any program that cannot be found in another school within the city system. These constraints apparently caused the demise in the early 1990s of the highly regarded International Baccalaureate (I.B.) Program started at the school in 1984 with funding from the Gulf Oil Company. The I.B. is a two-year diploma program that enables advanced students to enter colleges and universities around the world with sophomore standing. As the only public school in Philadelphia offering this option, it would have had to admit any qualified boy seeking admission.

Girls' High is a rare blend of tradition and resilience among urban secondary schools. But it is not unique. Baltimore's Western High School has followed a strikingly similar trajectory through the twentieth century and into the twenty-first. Its history, rituals, and values echo those of Girls' High. Western prides itself on being one of the first two publicly supported high schools for girls in the country. The other, Eastern High School on the other side of the city, has since merged with another school and become coed. The school opened in 1844 as Western Female High School "to provide females who have manifested superior abilities the best and most appropriate education possible." The first class included thirty-six female students taught by one male teacher, who also served as headmaster. These young pioneers studied elocution, moral philosophy, astronomy, rhetoric, grammar, ancient history, and botany. And like the early graduates of Girls' High, they subsequently moved on to teaching careers, though many soon married and became mothers, fulfilling culturally defined expectations.

It was nearly a century before the school hired a female principal and even longer before an African-American student or teacher crossed its threshold.[34] Baltimore schools were racially segregated until forced to integrate by law in 1954 following the Supreme Court's decision in *Brown v. Board of Education*. The school is now 85 percent African American. Approximately 40 percent of the students are eligible for free or reduced-price lunch. Many families choose the school not only for its academic reputation but also for its physically safe environment. About seven girls a year from outside the city limits pay tuition of $2,000 to attend the school. About the same number of girls each year transfer from private schools.

Like Girls' High, Western thrives on traditions and rituals, many of which it too has memorialized in an archives room, with the aid of the

Archives Club, a student organization. Here we find the usual awards, photos, news clippings, and other memorabilia marking the evolution of the school and the accomplishments of its graduates. We also find a series of creative writing anthologies with titles like *The Inkling* (1949) and *The Scriptorian* (1950). Members of the Alumnae Association, founded in 1897 "to support the standards set by the women who have graduated from Western," give generously of their time, serving as mentors to students and funding scholarships to graduates. Counted among them are the actress Anna Deavere Smith and Nancy Grasmick, the Maryland state superintendent of schools, as well as numerous judges, lawyers, artists, educators, and businesswomen. As Grasmick recalls her student days, "We were used to being everything, the president of the student council, president of the class. That expectation was there to be a leader." The current principal, Landa McLaurin, is also an alumna with a firm commitment to all-girls schooling and a passionate belief that her students can excel in spite of social disadvantages.[35]

With a racially and socioeconomically diverse population of approximately nine hundred students, Western also has come a long way from its days as a training ground for educating the daughters of white merchants either to teach in Baltimore's public elementary schools or to work as secretaries. In the 1970s the school eliminated most of its secretarial science courses and became primarily a college preparatory school. The school proudly exalts and affirms that mission in a large and highly visible listing of graduating students and the colleges they will attend that sprawls across the Western Wall of Fame facing the main office. Another list highlights the names of students of "distinction," "honor," and "merit" on the Principal's Honor Roll.

For admission, eighth graders must demonstrate an 80 overall average, 90 percent attendance, and performance at or above grade level on national standardized tests. From the moment they are admitted, applicants and their parents are drawn into the school's academic community. Parents sign a "Parent Pledge" agreeing to send their daughter to school on time, to check her homework, to participate in school activities, and to reinforce a set of core values. Before entering ninth grade, students attend a three-week summer program that includes classes in algebra and English, a freshman seminar, and preparation for the statewide functional tests. Students then choose among three academic tracks: the accelerated college preparatory, the honors college preparatory, and the honors business college preparatory. Students in the accelerated program pursue Advanced Placement or college-level work in the eleventh and twelfth grades.

Students can also participate in a comprehensive advanced science and technology course, which introduces them to various aspects of engineering. The course is offered under the Maryland Mathematics Engineering Science Achievement (MESA) program based at Johns Hopkins University's Applied Physics Laboratory. Nineteen Western students won trophies in regional and statewide competitions sponsored by MESA in 2001. The school aims to educate the whole student, offering more than forty clubs, organizations, and sports activities. A showcase of gleaming athletic trophies in the main hallway gives testament to the school's winning sports teams. Its basketball team rarely places lower than first in the state.

Like Girls' High, Western lives in the shadow of its formerly all-boys counterpart, Polytechnic Institute. Poly, as it is familiarly known, began accepting girls in the mid-1970s not under court order but under pressure from girls who were pushing to attend what many considered to be a superior academic school. Since 1968, when Poly was still all-male, the schools have been situated in adjoining buildings within the Poly-Western Complex. They share an auditorium, an Olympic-sized swimming pool, tennis courts, and a common courtyard where students of both schools congregate before and after school and during lunch. Founded in 1883, Poly quickly developed a reputation as one of the country's outstanding engineering high schools. Its curriculum still has that focus, so the school draws the top math and science students in the city. It also offers the Ingenuity Project, which is an accelerated and advanced mathematics, science, and research program that prepares students for competitions including the prestigious Intel Science Talent Search. Poly's admissions requirements are somewhat more rigorous than Western's, and its student population remains predominantly male.

Nevertheless, on all indexes of academic success, including SAT, Advanced Placement, statewide test scores in reading, math, and writing, college admissions, attendance, and dropout rates, Western fares favorably when compared with Poly and other public high schools in the city. The school has an annual dropout rate of only 1.88 percent and an attendance rate of 94.4 percent, compared with Poly at 1.78 percent and 94.6 percent. The school ranks third among Baltimore high schools in SAT scores, trailing Poly and Baltimore City College. In 2000–2001 the average combined SAT score was 912, versus 789 districtwide. Among Western's eleventh graders, 98.5 percent passed all three state tests, compared with 100 percent at Poly and 82.3 percent across the city. More than 82 percent of the graduating class goes on to college full-time, compared with 83 percent at Poly. Many remain within the Maryland public system, but a generous sprinkling of them move on to such prestigious southern institutions as Duke, the University of Virginia, and nearby Johns Hopkins.[36] Like Girls' High in Philadelphia, Western does not officially exclude male students as a matter of policy. Whenever a male has sought admission, however, officials have referred him to Poly or another college preparatory school within the Baltimore system. Here too, the strategy has proven successful.

This is a school with well-defined values that are clearly articulated and constantly reinforced. The school's motto is *Lucem accepimus; lucem demus*— we have received light; let us give light. Terms like *responsibility* and *respect* pervade the school's literature. The student handbook tells students that it is their "responsibility to carry and pass the torch of academic excellence, Quiet Dignity, civility, grace, and sisterhood." Flyers bearing the phrase "Quiet Dignity" and the school's symbol of a dove hang from classroom walls. As the handbook makes clear, Western's philosophy and goals are all about empowerment, offering its students the skills and attitudes to "assume leadership roles" and to "take charge of their own lives."

## VOICES FROM WITHIN

A school's history and present-day offerings tell only part of its story. To fully appreciate what a school is all about, one has to listen to the staff and students who give it life. What brought them to the school to begin with? What special qualities keep them returning on a daily basis, year after year? What evokes such passionate loyalty and continued commitment in its graduates?

As I visited these three schools and spent time listening and observing, I was struck by the orderly learning environment, the challenging academic program, the high expectations set for the students, the consistently articulated and pervasive values and strict code of behavior, and the commitment and enthusiasm of the teachers. Obviously all of these elements of an effective school can be replicated in a coeducational setting. But there is something else in all three schools that is almost intangible yet nonetheless powerful and definitive. There is a spontaneity, a synergy, an emotional security, and a sense of community that seem to flow out of shared experiences and common purposes as young women. What I saw and what I heard from students, parents, staff, and alumnae was that these schools are safe harbors where girls can securely weather the storms of adolescence while nurturing their spirit and intellect.

At all three schools girl after girl noted how the absence of boys relieves students of social pressures while at the same time creating a feeling of camaraderie. As a tenth grader at TYWLS told me, "I don't know if I'd be as focused [in a coed school]. Girls here don't gossip like they do in other schools. No one has a problem with sharing personal issues." Coming from an Egyptian background, she credited the school with having so helped her shed her initial shyness when she entered in seventh grade that three years later she was president of the student government. The same themes echoed throughout discussions at Girls' High and Western. Girls recalled that they had found boys distracting and disruptive in their previous schools, and observed that they now felt more confident speaking out in class. As one Western senior put it, "Here, being smart is cool. You're not afraid to talk up and know all the answers. People don't think you're a nerd or just trying to act smart. They look to you for help. Girls in coed schools are always conscious that some guy is looking at them. Here you can run in and your hair is frizzy, but you have to finish your bio project."

Students noted that the schools have pushed them to "ask questions," to "take initiative," to become more "outgoing and aggressive." They talked about admiring the academic stars in the class, trying to be more like them. They often used the language of family in describing their relationships with each other—"We're all like sisters." There seem to be fewer cliques. There is no one "most" or "least" popular girl. And because the student body is so racially and ethnically diverse, particularly at Girls' and Western, there are different notions of beauty. Students also noted how they have become "distanced" from their old neighborhood friends. They realize that their schools are moving them into another sphere and believe that they have been well prepared for a coed college. But they also understand that these schools are not for every girl.

Students appear to be self-aware without the self-consciousness of most adolescents. As one Western student said, "You learn so much about life here. You know you have a common bond. It's okay to talk about experiences in an open environment with teachers." Girls noted that topics like weight and body image are freely addressed in health and psychology classes, for example. A Western mother, herself a Radcliffe graduate, described the institutional opportunity for female bonding. "The way women regard women throughout their life is affected by going to an all-girls' school. The other girls don't judge you by your physical characteristics but [by whether] you are civilized, courteous, and responsible." Teachers observed that the students are less likely to be intimidated in larger settings outside the school. "In citywide meetings," one teacher noted, "you can pick out the Western students. They're more assertive." A Girls' High teacher, comparing his experiences there and at a coed school, observed that the Girls' High students have "more focus." They "come to class on time" and "don't delay in the halls talking to their boyfriends."

At all three schools, students treasure the traditions and rituals that are a significant part of the academic year. They seem to savor the many rites of passage along the way to the diploma and consciously appreciate the value of the diploma itself. They particularly cherish the various rituals surrounding the graduation ceremony. At TYWLS there is a palpable excitement in making history, being pioneers, setting the path for others to follow. At

Girls' High and Western, students mention that their grandmothers, mothers, aunts, and cousins who attended the school made lasting friendships there. They are also aware of the networking opportunities afforded through alumnae. For them, being a student at the school gives them a certain status that they will carry into the future.

As far as these girls are concerned, the benefits gained far outweigh any minor burdens on their social life. In fact, when the subject of boys comes up, they do not seem to give it much weight. Girls' High and Western students in particular enjoy the benefits of boys from coed schools in close proximity. Yet they have neatly compartmentalized their intellectual and social lives for the time being and feel confident that the skills and attitudes they develop in an all-girls setting will serve them well when they move on to a coed college. Obviously, there are those students who feel less positively about the absence of boys, but they appear to be a distinct minority. One reasonably can assume that students who find such schools socially stifling are likely to transfer to coeducational schools.

For students and their families, these schools undeniably represent a conscious academic choice in which the single-sex environment plays an integral role both in their minds and in its practical effect. Yet there are those who consider single-sex schools anachronistic at best and harmful at worst. Within the wide gulf between the personal reality and this distantly fixed perception lies a complex maze of conflicting arguments—grounded in history, philosophy, and law and informed by developmental psychology—that weave in and out in search of a definitive answer. That is where the discussion now turns.

# 3
# Equality Engendered

For most observers, the controversy over single-sex schooling comes down to a matter of law and policy, and undoubtedly that is how it will come to rest, at least for the time being. But listen carefully to the arguments in court and the sound bytes culled from the media, and you quickly grasp a philosophical dimension, set against the history of women's exclusion and subordination, that quietly but forcefully drives the debate. Here is where we find the most fundamental disagreements. And it is here that we find the wellspring from which the opposition has grown.

At the heart of the debate lies the concept of equality, and particularly sexual equality, with its overlapping and conflicting meanings. Over the past half-century, the abstract ideal of equality has gained widespread support as a worthy objective for social action. Nevertheless, sharp divisions have arisen over how best to realize that ideal. Does it mean formal equality in the sense of equal treatment, or does it demand different or special treatment in order to achieve substantive results? Does different treatment impose other harms?

Certainly these are not novel questions in the world of public policy. What is remarkable is the alignment of the parties and the animosity the single-sex issue has bred among traditional allies in the civil rights movement. In the past, such issues as school desegregation, bilingual education, and preferential treatment in admissions have generated predictable responses from conservatives and liberals. Conservatives, for whom equality means identical treatment, oppose government intervention to accommodate group differences. Liberals take the opposite approach and recognize that sometimes equality in the end can best be achieved with different treatment based on group characteristics. Single-sex schooling, however, defies such political labels, attracting support from the political right while pitting liberals against each other in some typical and other atypical alliances. Scratch the surface of this controversy and you find unresolved questions concerning the nature of sex differences, whether biologically determined (and therefore inevitable) or culturally constituted (and thus avoidable). Dig deeper and you find basic disagreements over women's role in society. At the core lies a tension among competing views on women's rights that need to be examined in historical perspective if we are to fully comprehend the seeming intractability of the problem and the rift it has created especially among those who champion the cause of sex equality.

Supporters, though not monolithic in their views, conceptually embrace single-sex education for various reasons, some in the name of liberty, others in the name of equality, and still others in an amalgam of both. Those who consider themselves libertarians—in the classical liberal tradition of Adam Smith—base their support in free-market theory. Individuals should be free to make their own choices about schooling, and the availability of single-sex or coed schools should reflect those individual decisions, free of government intervention.[1] Social and religious conservatives, on the other hand, view single-sex schooling as a means to accommodate what they consider the inherently different capabilities, tendencies, and preferences of women and men.[2] Both, to some degree, tie single-sex schooling to the broader issue of educational diversity, and particularly to school choice initiatives that now dominate much of the discussion over school reform. Here conservatives find themselves locked in a paradox, constructively supporting a notion of equality that takes into account group differences cloaked in the language of individual liberty, free choice, and family autonomy. Yet in marked contrast to other controversial issues, conservatives have remained on the periphery of the legal dispute while demonstrating sporadic interest at the national policy level. For whatever the reason, until quite recently they have left it to the liberals to fight this one out in the judicial and administrative arenas, and more visibly in the court of popular opinion.

What has ensued is a bitter debate within the civil rights community and particularly among women's rights advocates. Here the equality ideal, a core element of the American liberal project, has taken center stage. Although some within liberal ranks stand more resolute in their position than others, most remain uneasy in the resulting schism. In some cases, bewilderment has turned to anger. Individuals who have passionately fought side by side for sex equity are now facing off against each other in court, in the broadcast media, and in the pages of local and national newspapers and professional journals. Few issues have caused such a deep divide in the dwindling and aging ranks of scholars, advocates, and public intellectuals who still proudly carry the "feminist" banner or who, at the least, believe that women have not totally won the battle for equal citizenship.

For more than a decade, the National Organization for Women and the American Civil Liberties Union have swiftly moved to stop school districts dead in their tracks at the mere suggestion of single-sex schooling, although some of their members do not share these sentiments. Distinct differences of opinion also have surfaced within the National Association for the Advancement of Colored People, while the organization itself has officially denounced the concept. Yet the Coalition of 100 Black Women has rallied to the support of the New York school at which its members actively serve as mentors. Supporters of the concept call the opposition misguided and ideological, while opponents rail against the other side's perceived naïveté. The resulting confusion and ambiguities reveal profound disagreements concerning the purposes and values underlying gender equality as a legal standard, a moral principle, and a policy objective.

Each side claims the high road on gender and justice. Proponents argue that single-sex education is necessary, at least under certain circumstances, to promote substantive equality, or equality of opportunity. For them, sometimes "equal" means "different." Many women within this group, although certainly not all, attended academically rigorous single-sex schools or colleges, which proved for them a positive and even a defining experience. No doubt their personal familiarity with the notion eases some of the serious concerns that classifications based on sex typically evoke.

Opponents, on the other hand, look to formal equality, or equal treatment, and argue that single-sex programs undermine equality. Their argument typically takes one of three approaches. The most absolutist among them maintain that, following *Brown v. Board of Education,* "separate educational facilities are inherently unequal," whether the qualifying factor is race or gender. *Separation* is a euphemism for *worse,* and represents subordination and inferiority, perpetuating harmful stereotypes and, in the case of single-sex schools, stigmatizing girls. Others take a more moderate position, arguing that it is not separateness per se but unequal treatment that violates the equality principle. For them, what is offered to members of one sex must be offered to members of the other sex. To others the two programs need not be identical but must be substantially equal. Still others look to both social history and social consequences and draw the line either on sex or economics. Here such programs are acceptable where they serve girls but not boys or where they address the needs of disadvantaged students but not the more privileged.

Implicit in these arguments are two related concepts, each of which has become a political hot button in recent years. The first is *compensation*, or *remediation*, which obviously evokes images of affirmative action or preferential treatment. The second is the related dichotomy of *sameness* and *difference*, which has engaged feminist scholars in heated debate for the past two decades. The participants have followed one of several strategies: to deny the extent or essential nature of differences between women and men, to recognize and even celebrate them, or, more recently, to discard them by redefining the terms for debating gender relations.[3]

These competing perspectives elicit a host of controversial questions, all revealing the many contentious points implicit in gender equality. Should public policy initiatives support same treatment because women and men are the same? Alternatively, should women be treated differently because they are biologically different from men or because their social conditioning is different, thereby creating different "ways of knowing"? Or do women need to be compensated because traditional cultural norms have created in them different attitudes, aspirations, and expectations that limit their life opportunities and options? Should the sameness-difference dichotomy be discarded for an antisubordination principle, whereby law and policy address the subordinate role historically forced upon women in the face of male dominance? Does the sameness-difference argument wrongly assume an "essential" women's (and for that matter, men's) experience, independent of other realities like race, class, ethnicity, religion, handicapping conditions, or sexual orientation? If so, should equality in law and public policy recognize these differences? How do these questions bear on single-sex schooling? What hopes drive supporters of the approach? What fears drive the opposition?

The arguments raised on both sides are not mere political saber rattling; rather, they draw their substance from a heightened consciousness intensified in the modern-day women's movement and the synergistic advocacy and scholarship that movement has spawned. Here a post-sixties generation, through theory and practice, has struggled to apply the equality principle to the real-life experiences of women. That attempt has evolved through roughly four schools of thought grounded in feminist jurisprudence and heavily informed by theoretical developments in psychology, sociology, history, and literary studies.[4] Within this discussion, the concepts of *sameness, difference, dominance,* and *(in)essentialism* provide a theoretical framework and language for examining the question of whether single-sex programs advance or undermine educational equality for females as well as males. When applied to the various permutations of the facts, these concepts lend clarity, if not closure, to the more subtle questions regarding particular student populations and educational contexts. An understanding of this contemporary exploration into the "woman question" and its historical backdrop is essential to unraveling the paradoxes and dilemmas inherent in the seemingly irresolvable debate over single-sex education.

## SEPARATE SPHERES IDEOLOGY

The modern-day struggle to achieve equality for women has its roots in mid-nineteenth-century activism. Over the previous century, as political liberalism had gained favor, it challenged traditional hierarchies, including the conventional notion of women as subservient to men. In place of that belief emerged a cult of domesticity. Society still considered women physically and intellectually unequal to men and expected them to act submissively, while encouraging them to develop literacy skills. At the same time, society valued women for their moral rectitude and piety, through which they might help to preserve the republic by rearing children of similar virtue. This bifurcated view of reality, dating back at least to classical Greece, immersed the social order in a *separate spheres* ideology, consigning women to the private sphere of home and family while men held dominance over the *polis* or public sphere of work, politics, and intellectual life. Even the renowned chronicler of American mores Alexis de Tocqueville, touring the United States in 1831, was struck by the constraints endured by the American married woman as compared with her European counterpart. Tocqueville observed how the American woman "irrevocably lost" her independence "in the bonds of matrimony," living in her husband's home "as if it were a cloister," forbidden to "step beyond" the "narrow circle of domestic interests."[5]

For females of that day, biology was truly destiny. Until the states began adopting the Married Women's Property Acts in 1839, a woman could not even maintain her right to the property that she brought to marriage, much less the wages she earned. The reasoning was that if she could hold property in her own name, then her husband's creditors could not take it if he went bankrupt. It would take another half-century before states such as New York would grant women a right to their own earnings. This pervasively constricted notion of women's place in society was notoriously captured in *Bradwell v. Illinois*. In that decision the United States Supreme Court denied Myra Bradwell the constitutional right to practice law in the state of Illinois. In language forever etched in the annals of women's history, Justice Bradley in his concurring opinion unabashedly acknowledged that "the civil law, as well as nature herself, has always recognized a wide difference in the respective spheres and destinies of man and woman. The natural and proper timidity and delicacy which belongs to the female sex evidently unfits it for many of the occupations of civil life. The constitution of the family organization ... indicates the domestic sphere as that which properly belongs to the domain and functions of womanhood."[6]

But the Victorian "cult of true womanhood" carried within it the seeds of discontent and ultimately of its own destruction. Confined within this deeply entrenched collective psyche, the first wave of organized women's advocacy in America had to devise an effective yet realistic strategy. This era produced such leading figures as Lucy Stone and Elizabeth Cady Stanton, veteran abolitionists. Others like Susan B. Anthony came to press for women's equality via the temperance movement. The causes they pursued represented the few endeavors, aside from work in settlement houses and schools, in which women could extend their assigned domestic role into the public sphere. Although considered radical among their contemporaries, these women did not advocate sweeping reform but rather focused on specific issues.

As they attended to the vital social issues of their day with political and intellectual passion, they soon learned firsthand the unjust limitations placed on women in the public sphere. Denied voting rights and forced to sit in the gallery because of their sex, Stanton and other women delegates to the 1840 World Anti-Slavery Convention in London were faced with the stark reality of their inferior status. Outraged and emboldened by the experience, Stanton became the moving force behind the first women's rights convention, held in Seneca Falls, New York, in 1848. There the participants adapted the language of the Declaration of Independence to explicitly include women. Their Declaration of Sentiments proclaimed as follows: "We hold these truths to be self-evident: that all men and women are created equal."

In language that was shockingly extreme for its time, the document talked about the "absolute tyranny" that man had established over woman, having "created a false public sentiment by giving to the world a different code of morals [for each sex]," having "monopolized nearly all the profitable employments," and having denied "the facilities for obtaining a thorough education" and endeavored in every way "to destroy her confidence in her powers, to lessen her self-respect, and to make her willing to lead a dependent and abject life." Women's exclusion from public and political life lay at the heart of their continued subordination. The Declaration, including a resolution claiming suffrage for women, demanded rights and privileges equal to men's. It passed by a slim majority.[7]

As the historian Nancy Cott has recounted, this first wave of activism deeded to its successors a "Janus face." Spurred on by nineteenth-century liberalism infused with Enlightenment rationalism, proponents passionately advocated the dignity of women as humans. Because women were like men, they argued, they deserved the same rights to education, employment, property and political representation. Heartened by the success of Oberlin College, the first American institution to grant the A.B. degree to women in 1841, they championed the right to coeducation as a crucial precondition for liberating woman from her "separate sphere." They used the growing women's press to drive that message home. As editor in chief of the *Women's Journal,* Lucy Stone, herself an Oberlin alumna, declared: "Women's educational institutions of whatever pretensions, wherever they exist, whether legal, medical, or collegiate, hold inferior rank to those of men, and always will. . . . We do not believe in colleges for women alone, anymore than for men alone."[8]

At the same time, however, the early feminists viewed women as being different from men. In particular, they maintained that women could bring special talents and capabilities to public life. They focused specifically on the right to vote and based their argument in women's higher moral sense and their common experience as mothers. Women merited the vote because they were "virtuous, sober, devout, respectable, and maternal." Men, on the other hand, were "competitive, aggrandizing, belligerent, and self-interested." Women would cleanse government of corruption and vice and make the nation safe for children.[9]

This basic duality was in part a matter of political strategy in the face of suspicion and open opposition to their cause. By stressing the benefits that women's unique contributions could bring to society, they would prove less threatening to the male establishment and perhaps gain access, however limited and incremental, to that world. But on a deeper level, their position also reflected their true belief in women's moral superiority and manifested what they believed was women's social mandate based in mainstream Protestantism. For nineteenth-century feminists, "women's sphere" was not merely a "point of oppression"; it was their "point of departure." Womanhood was their defining feature and they insisted that it be considered a "human norm." Jane Frohock, writing in the reform journal *Lily,* captured these sentiments. "It is woman's womanhood, her instinctive femininity, her highest morality," she noted, "that society now needs to counter-act the excess of masculinity that is everywhere to be found in our unjust and unequal laws."[10]

As the women's movement marched into the twentieth century, it embraced these seemingly conflicting visions, both reinforcing and challenging the social order. At the same time, as it became apparent that the vote was an effective mechanism for mobilizing group interests, women's activists continued to define their group by conventional standards—as mothers, housekeepers, and caregivers. In doing so, they used the stereotypes of difference to portray the vote as necessary on such issues as education, health care, and prisons, where society most needed women's nurturing skills.[11]

With rapid industrialization, fueled by massive waves of immigration, pushing lower-class women out of the private sphere of the home and into the public sphere of the workforce, collective action on behalf of women's rights cast an even wider net that included the working class. In this effort the interests of labor became merged with the interests of universal suffrage. Reformers combined the fight for economic justice through decent wages and working conditions with a call for legislation providing maximum working hours and minimum wages for women. By 1907, twenty states had passed legislation limiting women's hours of work. The following year, the Supreme Court upheld protective legislation for women workers although it had previously struck down such laws for all workers on constitutional grounds. As the justices saw it, "woman's physical structure" placed her "at a disadvantage in the struggle for subsistence." The "inherent difference between the two sexes" justified "a difference in legislation."[12]

As late as 1968, thirty-eight states still had maximum hour and overtime prohibitions, ten states had weightlifting exclusions ranging from fifteen to fifty pounds, eighteen states prohibited or regulated night work, and twenty-six states excluded women from certain types of work such as bartending and mining.[13] But protectionist laws carried a price that effectively denied women equal rights with men and, in the end, protected men's interests. Maximum hour and weightlifting legislation, for example, also precluded women from opportunities for job advancement. Targeted restrictions on night work and overtime often preserved the most desirable jobs for men and deprived women of the flexibility they needed to care for family members during the day or to enhance their salaries.

Generally these restrictions did not apply to domestics, cleaning women, and others who performed "women's work" with low pay and low status. Until revised in 1969, New York labor laws required that women (but not men) obtain a permit to work after midnight in a factory or in a dining room or kitchen. No permit was required for hat check girls, cigarette girls, or ladies' room attendants. Obviously, the motives underlying such "reforms" were less than noble. Yet as the law considered women naturally good and pure, it also considered bad women to be far worse than bad men. As late as the mid-1970s, a female minor in New York State could be imprisoned for a nonviolent crime as a "person in need of supervision" until the age of twenty, compared with a maximum age of eighteen for males.

Although women gained the right to vote in 1920, they would lose their citizenship if they married a foreign national, as my paternal grandmother painfully learned. And while the states could allow women to refuse jury service on the basis of sex alone until the mid-1970s, they could also refuse to pay the salaries of women (but not men) who, in fact, volunteered to serve on juries.[14] The mindset of difference thereby justified and validated the institutionalization of discrimination, exclusion, and second-class citizenship. Difference served as "inequality's post-hoc excuse, its exclusionary artifact."[15]

Some of these distinctions were remnants of the common-law doctrine of *coverture*. Based partially on biblical notions of the "unity of flesh" of husband and wife, as described by Blackstone the doctrine considered woman's legal existence "suspended during the marriage . . . or at least incorporated and consolidated into that of her husband." The basic idea was that a woman performed every act under her husband's "wing, protection, and cover." Other distinctions were manifestations of sex stereotyping with no ostensible rationale other than to maintain the social and political inferiority of women. Whatever the justification, by the 1960s and nearly half a century after the "suffragettes" had taken their grand prize and withdrawn from the public scene, the civil rights movement sufficiently sensitized a generation of women to pierce through these distinctions and challenge them before the law.[16]

Meanwhile, Betty Friedan's *Feminine Mystique,* a devastating exposé of widespread dissatisfaction among American women, touched a raw nerve in both sexes and paved the way for a new discourse on women's rights and women's place in society. That discourse, in fact, had been quietly working its way through Western culture for the previous decade, since the publication of Simone de Beauvoir's *Second Sex.* Although Friedan wrote primarily about upper-middle-class college-educated women, her message soon brought to light stark inequities in job opportunities and earnings across social and economic strata.[17]

## LIBERAL EQUALITY

The modern-day women's movement formulated its early strategies against this confused legacy of protection, exclusion, and subordination. Throughout the 1970s, women's rights advocates, many of them trained in social activism within the civil rights and antiwar movements, used the law to dismantle barriers that historically had impeded the advancement of women. Strategically they focused on equal rights, attempting to capitalize for the women's movement on the gains made for racial minorities under the Fourteenth Amendment equal protection clause. They drew from legal precedent and defined equality as the similar treatment of individuals who are similarly situated. Troubled by the harmful stereotypes and inequalities that inevitably flowed from separate spheres ideology, women's rights advocates unequivocally rejected difference theory and focused on the similarities between men and women. Finding a significant overlap between the sexes on most characteristics related to social roles, they challenged the prevailing biological determinism as fundamentally misguided. Whatever sex differences existed were legally irrelevant. As the law was color-blind, so it should be sex-blind. They demanded formal equality in the sense of same treatment, echoing the call of the abolitionist and feminist Sarah Grimke back in 1837: that men should grant no special favors to women, but merely "take their feet off [women's] necks and permit [them] to stand up straight."[18]

A 1969 report prepared by the Presidential Task Force on Women's Rights and Responsibilities laid bare this "restive" state of women over "denial of equal opportunity, equal responsibility, and even equal protection of the law." Task force members made clear their agenda: "Women do not seek special privileges. They do seek equal rights. They do wish to assume their full responsibilities. . . . Inequities within our society serve to restrict the contribution of both sexes. We have witnessed a decade of rebellion during which black Americans fought for true equality. . . . Nothing could demonstrate more dramatically the explosive potential of denying fulfillment as human beings to any segment of society."[19]

Feminists of that era defined their goals by what was valued and possessed by white, middle-class men: respect and recognition in the public sphere, gratifying careers with the attendant monetary rewards and status, and freedom from the social expectation of bearing and raising children. By proving that women were the same as men on whatever the relevant criterion happened to be, they hoped to break down sex-based distinctions that denied women the same benefits or rights. And by focusing on equal rights, they could avoid the complicated and controversial question of whether the differences between the two sexes were biologically or socially constructed. The immediate aim was not to radically transform society but to gain for each woman equal access, independence, and autonomy based in an individualistic liberal ethos. Integration was their ultimate goal, and social androgyny was their underlying principle.[20]

This perspective on the equality ideal, sometimes referred to as liberal feminism, draws philosophically from the writings of the English writer and activist Mary Wollstonecraft and the philosopher John Stuart Mill, along with his wife, Harriet Taylor. They approached women's issues via eighteenth- and nineteenth-century liberal theory on individual rights. Wollstonecraft's *Vindication of the Rights of Woman* (1792) was the first full-scale book supporting women's equality with men. It deeply inspired the nineteenth-century women's movement as well as the more radical feminism of the 1920s. Arguing that men possessed no innate superiority over women, Wollstonecraft railed against the social constraints and deficient education that made women subordinate, oppressed, and dehumanized.[21]

In a similar way, the Mills advocated equal political rights in their essay *The Enfranchisement of Women.* Although the essay was originally published in 1851 under John Stuart Mill's name, there are those, including the sociologist Alice Rossi, who argue forcefully that its primary author was Harriet Taylor, one of the first women in England to press for women's rights. The Mills questioned whether it was "right and expedient that one-half of the human race should pass through life in a state of forced subordination to the other half." Years later, in *The Subjection of Women,* a short but eloquent work widely read and hotly debated when it appeared in 1869, John Stuart Mill rejected outright the alleged inferiority of women. "What is now called the nature of women," he wrote, "is an eminently artificial thing—the result of forced repression in some directions, unnatural stimulation in others." As a remedy, Mill proposed that women be afforded educational and vocational opportunities equal to men's through a principle of "perfect equality." The philosopher Bertrand Russell later credited this work with having transformed him into a "passionate advocate of equality for women." But even Mill succumbed to the nineteenth-century distinction between married and unmarried women. For him it was simply more economical and efficient for married women to stay at home regardless of their talents and inclinations.[22]

The prevailing legal strategy and political spirit of the 1970s was best captured in the movement to adopt the Equal Rights Amendment (ERA). Debated in consecutive Congresses since 1923 and proposed by both houses in 1971–72, the amendment stated that "equality of rights under the law shall not be denied or abridged by the United States or by any State on account of sex." It would have authorized Congress to enact implementing legislation. The ERA exemplified the key premise underlying the 1970s feminist agenda—that is, the belief that men and women are equal and therefore should be treated equally before the law. It embodied a moral judgment that society could no longer relegate women to an inferior social and economic position. Proponents rejected any suggestion of a dual system of rights, even one that attempted to upgrade women's status. Women would no longer be given automatic preference for child custody in divorce suits, they would have to assume equal responsibility for alimony and child support within their means, and they would be subject to the military draft.[23] As far as ERA advocates were concerned, any classification by sex would inevitably lead to overclassification, including within its ambit even those who did not possess the relevant characteristic.

Two exceptions, however, would have held: cases in which pertinent characteristics were unique to one's sex, such as women's ability to bear children, and situations in which special treatment would be necessary to remedy past denial of equal rights. Supporters disavowed any hint of a separate-but-equal doctrine, then discredited as to race. They viewed this as an invidious device for subordinating disfavored groups in society—a principle still invoked in court by civil liberties organizations and threaded through the opposition to publicly supported single-sex schools.[24] As that controversy has demonstrated, such an absolutist position inexorably proves constitutionally fatal.

Engrafting this notion of formal equality into the American social contract, although a seemingly modest effort, proved in the end too abrupt and radical in its potential social and political consequences. Although the amendment expressly applied only to governmental action, it came to symbolize a society in which sex would be totally irrelevant. Equality would come with a cost, and many women preferred the protections of the old regime to the responsibilities that the ERA would impose on them. The amendment fell to defeat in 1982, falling three states short of the required thirty-eight when the extended period for ratification expired.

In the meantime, activists were not sitting idly as the amendment was winding through the states on what they knew from the outset was a perilous and uncertain path. Rather, they advanced a collateral but more incremental attack in the federal courts, prodding the judiciary to recognize that governmental distinctions drawn on sex, like those drawn on race, were impermissible and that women were due the same rights as men under the law. In fact, most of the laws that ERA proponents identified as evils when the amendment was debated in 1972 ultimately became presumptively unconstitutional over the following decade. Moreover, many of the changes that the ERA promised, including the widespread dismantling of single-sex schools, have since become reality through either legislative fiat or political pressure.[25]

Equal access to education and to employment were two of the primary goals for 1970s activists. The application of their theory to judicial action was particularly successful in the realm of education, where women aspired to share in the male-defined world on its own terms. In the case of employment, however, equal treatment proved to be an inadequate remedy in view of the differing experiences, social roles, and values of women as a group as compared with men. Neither the courts nor legislatures were ready to address the implications that inevitably flowed from those fundamental differences. Women's advocates themselves were sharply divided, as they still are, on the political wisdom of bringing these differences to the fore of the debate.

Most elite women's colleges sprang into being specifically in response to women's exclusion, until modern decades, from the most prestigious colleges and universities. By the early 1970s many all-male institutions, whether under political pressure or by legal mandate, had begun to open their doors to women, but only technically. Coeducation in itself was not the cure-all for deeply institutionalized attitudes toward women. Discrimination in counseling, hostile classroom environments, and a curriculum devoid of women's experiences and accomplishments soon surfaced as serious impediments to their full participation.

A lesser-known fact is that these institutions, as well as academically selective public secondary schools, often held female applicants to higher admissions standards than males. Most often they drew this distinction in order to maintain an even gender balance in the student body. Such was the case of Lowell High School in San Francisco, for example, where women applicants tended to present higher admissions credentials. But some school systems, like Boston's, adopted even more invidious differential policies. There the number of seats allocated at the prestigious all-boys Boston Latin was twice that allocated at Girls Latin, where girls had to meet higher standards to compete for half the seats. In the past women quietly resigned themselves to such blatant inequities, but by the early 1970s they were poised for legal action. In both San Francisco and Boston, federal district courts found that the use of different admissions criteria based on the sex of the applicants violated the equal protection clause of the Fourteenth Amendment.[26] As a matter of legal right, girls and boys who demonstrated equal academic performance were constitutionally entitled to the same consideration. In the case of Boston Latin, that meant admitting girls.

A key player in this early stage of the movement was Ruth Bader Ginsburg, who understood firsthand the perils of separate spheres ideology. Years later, as a Supreme Court justice, she recounted that Justice Felix Frankfurter had rejected her nomination for a Court clerkship despite her extraordinarily impressive academic credentials, including editorial positions on the law review boards of both Harvard and Columbia. "The Justice was told of my family situation," she recalled. "I was married and had a five-year-old daughter. For whatever reason, he said no." That initial rebuff made her keenly aware that educational opportunity alone was not the sole answer. Social and economic barriers had to be broken down before women could claim their rightful place in society.[27]

As founding director of the American Civil Liberties Union Women's Rights Project (WRP), Ginsburg, while teaching on the Columbia University law faculty, led ACLU attorneys in a carefully planned litigation program that challenged sex stereotypes in a variety of contexts. Some of these technically benefited men and not women.[28] To her mind, gender distinctions, even when benign, not only reflected a traditional way of thinking about women but also reinforced outmoded stereotypes and misconceived notions that belied individual ability, often resulting in unequal opportunities. Over a five-year period from 1971 to 1976, she and her WRP colleagues gradually whittled away at separate spheres doctrine, using legal liberalism and "equal treatment" to win a series of Supreme Court victories for women.[29] They strategically structured their briefs and oral arguments and successfully moved the Court to more carefully scrutinize gender-related distinctions.

The WRP also met some defeats, particularly on the issue of pregnancy and its relation to other disabilities for purposes of employee benefits. Nevertheless, the group remained steadfast in its pursuit of equal treatment, a strategy it has continued to pursue, for example, in its persistent opposition to single-sex schooling. The Supreme Court's equality decisions have followed a similar course. With the exception of reproductive rights, the justices have rejected distinctions based on sex because they tend to reinforce archaic and overbroad stereotypes. In the Court's words, such distinctions merely perpetuate the "romantic paternalism" that historically placed women "not on a pedestal, but in a cage."[30]

The most striking example of the ACLU's fixed position came in the mid-1980s, when along with the NOW Legal Defense and Education Fund the group vigorously yet unsuccessfully argued that it was sex discrimination for the state to mandate that employers grant paid pregnancy leaves to women but not disability leaves to other workers who were incapacitated for comparable periods. The plaintiffs claimed that the state disability benefits should be extended to all workers regardless of sex. Such protective legislation based on biological differences, they maintained, only served to harm women in the long run. As Justice Ginsburg counseled in a 1999 lecture, "Patriarchal rules long sequestered women at home in the name of 'motherhood.' . . . It is not always easy to separate rules that genuinely assist mothers and children from those that confine women to their traditional subordinate status."[31]

Liberal feminists maintained that to the extent that women are the same as men, they are entitled to all the benefits that are granted to men. Of course, the underlying assumption that men define the norm accepts without question the clear inferences of male privilege. But the corollary to that proposition is equally true. To the extent that women and men differ, as in the case of pregnancy, then formal equality may offer women no protection, and that is where the principle fell short. Here women could not merely look for assimilation into a world of work as constituted by men. That world itself would have to be reconstituted in order to address certain preconditions to equality and to accommodate fundamental biological, social, and economic differences between the sexes.

Women's rights advocates had learned this hard lesson a decade earlier when they unsuccessfully challenged California's exclusion of women from the disability benefits program offered to state employees. The plan covered a long list of other disabilities including such sex-specific procedures as circumcisions and prostatectomies. In an infamous sleight-of-hand, the Supreme Court rejected the argument that the exclusion of pregnancy constituted sex discrimination. As far as the justices were concerned, the exclusion merely demonstrated that the state had decided to remove one physical condition—pregnancy—from the list of compensable disabilities. The fact that only women could experience pregnancy was of no consequence. The Court, using male employees as the norm, refused to consider real biological differences between the sexes.[32] The decision implicitly recognized that equality entitled women only to those benefits that the state had granted to men based solely upon male experiences and needs. The Court seemed blind to the fact that the exclusion of pregnancy was based on stereotypical notions of women and their commitment to the workforce.

Some equal rights feminists have subsequently claimed that the decision reflected not weaknesses in their theory but rather the constraints of relying on the judiciary to bring about fundamental social change. Others, however, have suggested a modified vision of equality, with assimilation as a general rule but subject to exceptions grounded in sex-specific physical differences. They recognize that most alleged differences between women and men, such as height, weight, lifespan, mathematical ability, and capacity for nurturing, are merely statistical generalizations—more true in the aggregate than in individual cases. Yet they also suggest that there are clear biological reproductive sex differences that demand different or special treatment for women, but only where they are being utilized, as in the case of pregnancy and childbirth, for reproductive purposes. They consider these differences as a functional attribute of sexual identity rather than as an inherent characteristic. In doing so, they leave open the possibility that child care benefits can be assigned to either sex based on who carries out the function of caregiver. Modifying the assimilationist model in this way, they attempt to reconcile the ideal of equality with the reality of biological differences.[33]

Still others, nevertheless, have concluded from the pregnancy conundrum that formal equality rings substantively hollow for women. For them, the issue is emblematic of the cultural limitations inherent in the liberal vision. First, it is impossible to determine, using objective and value-free criteria, exactly which individuals are similarly situated or which groups are comparable. More important, the formal equality approach fails to disrupt the inherently unequal paradigm of male normativity. The use of the male norm as the definitional standard relegates women to the position of what

Simone de Beauvoir called "the incidental ... the inessential ... the Other."[34] These perceived shortcomings have since become the target of heated criticism.

## DIFFERENCE EQUALITY

As the 1970s drew to a close, the notion of formal equality as a legal precept for achieving sex equity came under increasing attack within the feminist community. At this time, a body of theoretical and empirical research presented legal scholars with an alternative paradigm for examining the "woman question." Rather than avoid gender differences for fear of reviving the different-nature ideology that legitimized age-old exclusions, a new generation of feminist scholars across the disciplines began to celebrate women's distinct characteristics. This scholarship emphasized women's affiliational or relational values, which, some argued, emanate from mothering and the mother-child relationship. A seminal and popularized work within this particular genre was Nancy Chodorow's *Reproduction of Mothering*. Chodorow presented the much-analyzed and highly controversial images of the relational woman and the autonomous man.[35]

A growing cadre of women in the legal academy began to draw on this body of scholarship as they became increasingly troubled with the limitations of formal equality in effectively realizing justice for women. Calling "sameness" into serious question, they selectively resurrected and redefined nineteenth-century "difference" in the hope of developing a more robust theory of gender equality that would have more immediate impact on the lives of women, one that would recognize the concrete ways in which women's lives differed from those of men. Thus was born an intellectual battle, which has still not abated, between a jurisprudence of formal equality and a jurisprudence of difference.

Based in what is ordinarily referred to as relational or difference feminism, this perspective on equality soon took root in the research of the education psychologist Carol Gilligan. Her provocative book *In a Different Voice* has won both praise as the beginning of a new moral theory and condemnation as methodologically flawed and even antifeminist.[36] The only point upon which both sides agree is that her work has left an indelible mark on theory and practice. Not only did it broaden the discourse on gender and difference, but it unexpectedly revived interest in single-sex education. Its implications are still being debated and explored two decades later.

Gilligan staked her argument on two main points: that women differ from men in their fundamental orientation to life, and that existing psychological theories devalued women's orientation. Drawing on the work of Chodorow and other ego psychologists, Gilligan questioned the conventional wisdom on the disparity between women's experience and the representation of human (male) development. Leading psychological theorists had previously either cited the difference as evidence of women's deficient moral development (Sigmund Freud), ignored perceived sex differences by articulating a theory based solely on men (Jean Piaget), or merely noted that women's development was different from men's without defining the difference (Erik Erikson and Bruno Bettelheim). In all cases, men were considered the norm and women judged by how closely they fit that norm.

Gilligan specifically disputed the theory of cognitive moral development put forth by her Harvard mentor and colleague Lawrence Kohlberg. She maintained that Kohlberg had misrepresented female moral development as a result of his biased samples and faulty theoretical assumptions. In fact, females simply did not appear in Kohlberg's research, even though he claimed universality for his conclusions. He based his empirical findings on a study of eighty-four boys whose development he had followed over the course of twenty years. According to Kohlberg, individuals pass through six distinct stages of moral development from childhood to adulthood. At the two highest levels, they critically evaluate accepted social norms and form moral judgments based on abstract concepts of moral right. At stage four they subordinate relationships to rules, and at stages five and six they subordinate rules to universal principles of justice. Women, however, seemed to cluster at the third stage, where "morality is conceived in interpersonal terms and goodness is equated with helping and pleasing others."

Gilligan was struck by the paradox in Kohlberg's theory. The very traits by which society traditionally defined and valued women—their care and sensitivity to others—marked them as deficient in moral development on Kohlberg's scale. She set about to derive developmental constructs specifically from the lives of women, using a mode of thinking that was contextual and narrative as opposed to formal and abstract. She drew her findings from the results of three studies based on interviews that included the same sets of questions. She examined conceptions of self and morality, together with experiences of conflict and choice. The first study included twenty-five randomly chosen college sophomores enrolled in an elective course on moral and political choice. They were interviewed as seniors and again five years following graduation. The second study drew from interviews of twenty-nine women in the first trimester of pregnancy as they were contemplating abortion. The third study involved 144 males and females matched for age, intelligence, education, occupation, and social class at nine points across the life cycle.

As she listened to women resolve serious moral dilemmas, Gilligan discovered among them a "morality of responsibility" centered on relationship and connection. Individuals operating within this mode, she argued, determine their moral choices inductively within the particular context and from the experiences that each brings to the situation. What she defined as an "ethic of care" stood in sharp contrast to Kohlberg's "morality of rights" with its emphasis on separation, autonomy, and the application of abstract rules and principles. She called this approach an "ethic of justice." Kohlberg himself subsequently questioned this dichotomy in orientations, as well as their link to gender, arguing that many moral situations evoke a response that integrates both orientations in women and in men. In fact, since 1978 he had revised his scoring system to incorporate levels of relationship and caring into both lower and higher levels on his scale of moral development.[37]

Without placing priority on one over the other, Gilligan claimed both care and justice as universal elements of the human condition. Both, she asserted, should be equally valued. She maintained that the different voice she described was "characterized not by gender but by theme." Although she traced it empirically through women's voices, she claimed that it was neither "absolute" nor a generalization about either sex but merely represented "two modes of thought." She estimated that one-third of men and women combined an ethic of care and an ethic of justice in their moral perspectives, while two-thirds focused on one set of concerns or the other. The women in this latter group were equally divided in each approach, while the exclusive focus on care, with only one exception, was absent among men. In other words, while the care focus was not characteristic of all women, it was almost exclusively a "female phenomenon, at least in her sample of educationally advantaged North Americans."[38]

Gilligan made no claims about the origins of the differences. Yet she noted that they "arise in a social context where factors of social status and power combine with reproductive biology" to shape the experiences of men and women and their relationships with each other. She also stated explicitly that the aim of her research was to provide "a clearer representation of women's moral development" and for women to recognize the "integrity and validity" in their thought. These gender-specific assertions apparently conflict, at least to some degree, with her denials of gender specification in her findings. Even the title of her book suggests that her ethic of care is a universal feminine trait. Her subsequent research on adolescent girls continued the relational theme as applied to gender differences. Her later work theorized both justice and care in these terms, the one speaking to the "unjust use of unequal power" and the other speaking to the "dissociations that lead people to abandon themselves and others." She proposed that a relational voice would "set the key" for psychology, political theory, ethics, and philosophy and would free "the voices of the disciplines from patriarchal structures."[39]

Gilligan's claim that women and men differ in their moral sense was not a novel one. Throughout history, a variety of groups have shared similar beliefs—from nineteenth-century suffragists who used woman's moral superiority to support voting rights, to twentieth-century radical feminists who argued that it would save the world from self-destruction, to contemporary social conservatives who reject government intervention into the private realm in order to preserve the unique sensibilities that women bring to family life. Gilligan's work quickly gained a global popularity of almost epic proportions. Her book was translated into nine foreign languages. *Ms.* magazine named her Woman of the Year, 1984. The *New York Times* endowed her with a front-page story. Newspaper columnists, political pollsters, and management experts all seized on her research to explain the gender gap.[40] Gilligan had struck a chord that resonated for many women and for some but not all feminist scholars.

Gilligan's research soon found its way into the legal academy. Her apparent thesis was that there exists a predominantly female and a predominantly male approach to moral reasoning. Her assertion that certain feminine characteristics such as deference, self-doubt, and dependency represent strengths and not weakness inspired a strand of feminist jurisprudence based in gender difference. Between 1989 and 1995, her work received 365 citations in law review articles, a clear indication of her influence on legal scholarship.[41] For the first time, there was a critical mass of legal scholars who recognized a downside in the longtime exclusion of women not only from the substance of the law but also from the process of shaping its structure. Here the discussion shifted from denial of equal opportunity as the root cause of gender inequality to a focus on the historical devaluation of women's experiences and perspectives. Rather than women accommodating to the male norm, social institutions would have to change to accommodate women's lives.

Using Gilligan's studies as a touchstone for their research, feminist scholars embracing the difference principle have suggested that woman's unique perspective could help correct the distortions of the male-constructed individualist liberal paradigm.[42] Some have speculated that her ethic of care could change the practice of law, moving it away from its win-lose confrontational style.[43] Others have seen the potential of women's different voice for changing substantive law in areas as diverse as torts, bankruptcy, family law, and constitutional law.[44] They draw from other contemporary psychologists who argue that women's different life experiences, combined with academic learning, produce different forms of knowledge or "ways of knowing" as compared with men.[45] Reinforced by Gilligan's ethic of care and its sense of connection, subjectivity, and responsibility, women's different perception of reality could result, they believe, in legal rules that focus less on individual rights as an abstract concept and reflect more of a concern for the injured and the isolated.[46]

Advancing these varied but related claims celebrating women's unique characteristics and circumstances, this core of feminist scholars has coalesced around the difference principle and redefined gender equality. Setting aside the formal equality or equal treatment of the 1970s, they have embraced a notion of substantive equality grounded in different treatment and equal results. For them, equality has to be assessed in the context of individual lives and experiences, which for women as a group differ sharply from those of men. They recognize that care, connection, and relationship are not necessarily intrinsic characteristics but perhaps historically necessary traits that women have had to develop to survive in a male-dominated world. At the same time, they view these as positive characteristics regardless of their source. Their position evokes Beauvoir's counsel from a half-century ago that "patience is one of those feminine qualities which have their origin in our oppression but should be preserved after our liberation."[47]

Yet other scholars across the disciplines have criticized Gilligan for sending inconsistent messages. Is she talking about women or "the feminine"? Although she claims that the different voices are not always tied to gender, her argument is rife with gender-based assumptions. Beyond the ambiguities, some see danger lurking behind her "different voice." Some have drawn an analogy to the "scientific racism" that flourished throughout the IQ-testing movement in the early twentieth century. Others fault relational feminists in general for having reclaimed the "compliments of Victorian gender ideology" while "rejecting its insults," effectively reifying separate spheres ideology. In celebrating women's mothering instincts, critics argue, difference feminism in some of its forms actually resembles some of the assertions made by antifeminists. Even worse, by ascribing certain commonalities among women, the difference strategy could have the unintended effect of not only perpetuating traditional gender stereotypes but also embedding those traits within women. Moreover, by failing to account for cultural, political, and social forces that shape gender, including race and class, difference feminism implies that gender differences are natural, immutable, and traceable to a feminine essence or "innate womanhood." As one commentator has put it, "Gilligan describes how women make lemonade out of the lemons they have inherited. She does not tell how to transform the lemons into chocolate."[48]

For the sociologist Cynthia Fuchs Epstein, such bipolar conceptions of women and men assume difference as a given, rather than as a "process" with significant roots in the law. She sees gender distinctions emanating from two sources: from the decisions of powerful gatekeepers and from the self-monitoring of those who rationalize the attributes ascribed to them as "natural and proper." Justice Sandra Day O'Connor has also brought this point home, warning that difference feminism threatens to confine women to new categories of "women's work" while excluding men. Yet herein lies the "dilemma of difference." Whether we recognize differences or ignore them, either way they carry a stigma.[49]

These pernicious tendencies, in fact, surfaced most recently in the Virginia Military Institute's defense of its all-male admissions policy. VMI officials relied specifically on Gilligan's research to assert that women's "tendencies" and "capacities" made them unfit as a group to withstand the institution's rigorous military training program. Gilligan challenged these assertions in a forceful brief submitted to the appeals court. She emphatically warned that there is "too much variation within each sex to argue that psychological differences result from 'real' differences between the sexes." This was not the first time that the perils inherent in Gilligan's findings had surfaced in high-profile litigation. In the late 1980s, in the case of *EEOC v. Sears Roebuck,* the company's expert witness, the renowned feminist historian Rosalind Rosenberg, had cited Gilligan to support the proposition that women subordinate work to family, are "more relationship centered" than men, and are "less competitive." The unfortunate upshot of Rosenberg's testimony was that a particular woman was denied a job simply on the basis of ascribed group traits and preferences despite the fact that she was fully qualified.[50]

These and similar stories lend credence to the argument that difference feminism can at least in some contexts prove demeaning and harmful to women. Although it arguably celebrates the positive qualities, whether innate or socially conditioned, that women as a group bring to the political and social table, its most extreme categorical form insidiously allows those same qualities to be turned into negatives and suggests that women must make a special claim to virtue to gain entrance into public life and public discourse. It leaves them, as Katha Pollitt tells us, "marooned on Gilligan's Island."[51]

## EQUALITY AND POWER

Throughout the 1980s, as difference feminists became buried in the many perils implicit in the difference principle, a third and equally controversial strain of feminism emerged from the legal academy, shifting the focus from the moral to the political—from difference to power. Among this diverse group of scholars, the struggle to reconcile equality and difference merely obscures the one difference that really counts: that women are politically, socially, and economically subordinate to men. They see gender as primarily a question of inequality, the problem being to eliminate the unequal consequences that flow from sex differences—to achieve equality despite them. The critical issue is not difference itself, but "the difference difference makes." The debate over whether differences are "natural" is inconsequential, they claim. For feminists within this camp, the key question is whether recognizing such differences (whatever their origin) as a matter of law in a particular case would more likely reduce or reinforce sex-based political, social, and economic disparities. Nonetheless, they believe that any attempt to promote equality between the sexes must also consider alternative social arrangements.[52] Unlike difference feminism, in which the project is to shape normative rules to fit existing reality, the ultimate goal of this strain of feminism is to change reality itself. At the same time, proponents realize that treating individuals in unequal positions identically, as embodied in the liberal project, can produce injustice. Motives do not matter. Results do.

Within this discourse the concept of power, whether subtly suggested by some or stridently invoked by others, plays a pivotal role. The chief architect and most radical proponent of this view is Catharine MacKinnon, one of the most provocative and controversial feminist scholars of our time. Best known for having defined the concept of sexual harassment in the law and for her advocacy against pornography as a form of female subjugation, MacKinnon has challenged the very premises of both liberal feminism and difference feminism. In doing so, she has dramatically shifted the grounds of the gender debate. Setting aside the language of equality, which inevitably turns on a comparison of women to the male norm, she posits in its place a theory based on dominance.[53]

MacKinnon rejects liberal feminism's pursuit of sameness. In her view, arguments couched in terms of equal treatment merely validate entrenched patriarchal values and fail to acknowledge the connection between sex and power. She also argues against celebrating women's difference from men, a notion infused, she warns, with hierarchical implications. For her, discrimination against women emerges not from distinction but from dominance. Relational feminism, she tells us, merely celebrates the terms of women's oppression. "Difference," she says, is "inequality's post hoc excuse . . . its outcome presented as origin," the "velvet glove on the iron fist of domination." MacKinnon asks: "Why do women become these people, more than men, who represent these values?" The answer for her is clear; it rests in women's subordination.

Although MacKinnon accepts Gilligan's observations on the "different voice" as accurate, she views it as merely the "voice of the victim." Woman's voice, she argues, is not her own but only what male supremacy has made it out to be. "His foot is on her throat," she graphically explains, echoing the nineteenth-century feminist Sarah Grimke. The difference between the sexes is all about power. Men have it and women as a group do not. For MacKinnon, the critical equality concern is "whether the policy or practice in question integrally contributes to the maintenance of an underclass or a deprived position because of gender status."[54]

## (IN)ESSENTIAL EQUALITY

As the advocates of feminism's divergent and overlapping strands have tugged and pulled at the "woman question," voices within and without the legal academy have questioned the notion of a unitary "woman's experience." Feminist scholarship, these critics have argued, has mistakenly claimed to speak for all women. By using the abstract woman as a referent, the movement has disregarded such factors as race, ethnicity, age, religion, class, handicapping conditions, and sexual orientation, all of which play a crucial role in shaping women's lives and experiences. Each of us sits at the "intersection" of various categories, some of them more salient than others.[55]

Liberal, difference, and radical feminism have all come under siege for assuming an "essential" woman, defined by a fixed bundle of traits, beneath the realities of difference within the female sex. According to critics, even when these competing theories have taken into account various forms of identity and oppression differences, such analysis has been additive, as if the forces were distinct rather than interrelated. Critics argue that feminist scholarship merely reflects the values and concerns of white, middle- and upper-middle-class, heterosexual, college-educated women, constructing its own form of privilege. In that sense, the movement to define feminism has replicated the privilege and demographics of the status quo it criticizes.[56] It simply has failed to recognize that different social groups "live" gender differently.

Women scholars of color, in particular, have criticized this pervasive inattention to the diversity in women's experience. For them, dominance theory and relational feminism present white womanhood as universal truth while at most relegating to footnotes issues of race. Dominance theory in particular, they argue, overlooks the fact that all men do not share a privileged social status or benefit equally from sexism. They draw a distinction between the exploitation and discrimination suffered by women collectively and the oppression, with its incident lack of choices, endured by women of color. The latter, sitting on the bottom of social power hierarchy, are the one group not allowed an institutionalized "other" to exploit or oppress. Dominance for African-American women, they argue, ineluctably flows from the intersection of racism, sexism, and often classism, with their antecedent myths, stereotypes, and images. Not only do males oppress them, but so do other females—as, for example, employers in the context of domestic work. And not only does oppression victimize women, it also victimizes some groups of men in our society, particularly African-American men.

In that sense, as the feminist author bell hooks points out, liberal feminism is off the mark in setting women's social equality with men as its goal. At the same time, dominance theory fails to recognize that men, too, have been oppressed. The very fact that African-American men and women have been tied in their struggle for liberation has made African-American women averse to viewing men as the enemy. In spite of the pervasiveness of sexism, African-American communities have long valued the indispensable role that women historically have played in maintaining their social institutions. The same cannot be said for white society, which has marginalized women's contributions. A similar contrast can be drawn for family, which for African-American women is not a source of oppression but rather a site of resistance against racism.[57]

The ideology of motherhood that some relational feminists have presented further defies the historical experience of African-American women for whom mothering and wage labor have not been opposing choices.[58] Both exist as integral parts of their lives. As a result, they typically and understandably project an image of independence, autonomy, resourcefulness, and self-reliance. As teenagers, they fare better on tests of self-confidence and self-esteem than white or Hispanic females. Yet their self-assurance is often not enough to overcome countervailing social and economic forces that derail their life plans. This disconnect between personal traits and actual performance is too often overlooked in the conventional educational setting.

The debate within feminist legal scholarship over gender essentialism underscores the paradox at the core of feminism. As Elizabeth Spelman has noted, "Any attempt to talk about all women in terms of something we have in common undermines attempts to talk about differences among us, and vice versa." Yet some scholars, Catharine MacKinnon among them, have argued that antiessentialism is harmful to women. From a politically pragmatic viewpoint, the success and even the possibility of a coherent argument supporting women's equality require a singleness of voice and purpose.[59]

## EQUALITY AND SINGLE-SEX SCHOOLING

Over the past three decades, feminist scholars have struggled mightily to articulate a workable theory that most effectively produces equal participation for women in the public sphere. Each approach presents contrasting views on the time-worn dispute over whether women and men are the same or different, whether differences are biological or cultural, and whether the law or public policy should accommodate these differences. Despite inherent limitations, each of the various perspectives that have evolved presents features that have contributed in a unique way to advancing public discourse on the equality ideal as it applies to gender.

At the onset of this era, liberal feminism scored an amazing record of success in raising women's expectations and placing their concerns into the stream of discussion. Women won most of their judicial and legislative victories under the banner of liberal feminism—the right to vote, access to employment and educational opportunities, and the right to serve on juries, among others. By articulating their concerns in the language of equal rights and equal treatment, advocates provided policymakers and particularly the courts with a familiar standard that appealed to fundamental notions of fairness and justice. Difference feminism presented a theory for valuing attributes, whether inherent or socialized, that may appear more common among women as a group, and for recognizing caring, relation, and affiliation as important to a just society.

Dominance theory, although at times overstated, realistically has reminded us that we cannot discuss equality honestly without considering the question of economic, social, and political power. Rather than sentimentalize difference, it sets our focus on the consequences that flow from it. It suggests a constitutional bottom line that proves particularly useful in the case of single-sex schooling—that is, whether the policy contributes to or in fact remedies the harm that comes from a deprived position related to gender. In that sense, it permits us to move away from absolutes and to look at programs in the context of the population served. Meanwhile, the nuances that "inessentialism" has brought to the fore have significant bearing on efforts to achieve sex equity across a diverse population of women and also of men. The insights gained from examining intersectionality and multiple identities have particular importance in the current dispute over single-sex education, where racial and economic differences among student groups seem to get lost in competing political views on gender.

There remains, however, an interesting and perhaps revealing paradox in this rich body of scholarship. Feminist scholars, with few exceptions, supported the Supreme Court's decision striking down the all-male admissions policy at the Virginia Military Institute. Yet, again with rare exception, they have remained on the sidelines of the public debate surrounding the implications of the decision for elementary and secondary education.[60] Few among them have attempted to apply theory to practice or propose a workable solution.[61] That silence, I suggest, reflects the complexity of the underlying issues and the difficulties many experience in arriving at a fixed and easy position that accords with their larger views on women's place in society. Some of this hesitance stems from the opaqueness of the VMI decision itself and the question of how one reconciles the Court's renunciation of VMI's admissions policy and its proposed parallel program for women with support for other models of publicly supported single-sex education. It also stems from the dark history of separate spheres ideology and educational exclusion. Both those memories produce understandable discomfort among women's rights advocates whenever policy decisions are based on sex differences, albeit for arguably benign reasons. Even some feminists who recognize the leadership opportunities and self-affirmation that sex-segregated education offers women have difficulty accepting any justifications for all-male institutions.

Yet the various strands of feminist theory have much to offer not only the legal but also the policy discussion on publicly supported single-sex schooling. As I shall demonstrate in the following chapters, the tension among the competing theories inevitably reveals itself in both policy initiatives and court decisions and particularly in the efforts of school districts to meet the educational needs of inner-city students, both male and female. While opponents remain transfixed in equality as sameness, advocates continue to weave through the maze of sex differences, women's historical subordination, and inequalities based on race and social class while struggling to avoid the deep and dangerous pitfalls of deficiency, essentialism, and categorical stereotypes.

# 4
# Myths and Realities
# in the Gender Wars

For three decades, researchers and advocates have drawn on the equality principle, and above all on the emotive force of difference and subordination, to level the educational playing field for girls. This remarkably successful yet still unfinished project forms the backdrop against which the current debate over single-sex schooling has evolved. The arguments and counterarguments that have emerged are undoubtedly crucial to understanding how the approach has recaptured the public imagination and why it evokes almost visceral responses among educators, policymakers, scholars, and civil rights groups. Unfortunately, much of the research and findings have become mired in myths, misunderstandings, and half-truths peppered with ideology that collectively obscure the realities of gender and schooling for girls and boys. Yet without a shared understanding of competing concerns there is no common ground for educators and policymakers to reach a reasoned consensus. It is to that task that I now turn, sifting through the research and scholarly discourse on gender and education as it has developed and continues to take shape.

## THE (CO)EDUCATION OF GIRLS

Throughout history, the education of women has been subject to intermittent waves of resistance, ambivalence, and qualified support, each reflecting enduring disagreements over women's place in society. Until recent times, the fiercest and most rancorous battles were fought on the fields of higher education. Nothing captures the opposition more clearly than the now legendary views expressed by Dr. Edward Clarke, a member of Harvard's Board of Overseers and a former member of Harvard's medical faculty. Clarke warned with great certainty that secondary and higher education would harm women's reproductive abilities. He was particularly averse to educating women in the masculine and academically demanding atmosphere of the coeducational school. To counter Clarke's arguments, a Special Committee of the Association of Collegiate Alumnae, which later became the American Association of University Women, conducted a survey of women college graduates. Not surprisingly, they found that among the 705 replies received, college alumnae were in fact in better health than the working girls of Boston with whom Clark had compared them. Undoubtedly the differences were at least in part a function of social class, which points up the irrelevance of the comparison itself.[1]

That finding, nevertheless, did not seem to weaken Clark's argument within the academy. His book, *Sex in Education,* was widely read for decades and weighted down early efforts to extend education to women beyond the primary grades. Obviously his thesis sounds irrational and absurd by today's standards. Yet it still jogs the conscience, and understandably so, given that the struggle for women's access to prestigious institutions, traditional gateways to privilege and professional success, is barely a generation behind us. The austere portraits of presidents embellishing the administrative halls of countless colleges and universities still denote a lineage cast exclusively in a male mold until very recent years. More significantly, the stereotypical attitudes that historically forced women's categorical exclusion still linger in remote and perhaps not so remote corners of academe, even three decades after most institutions removed admissions barriers. That grim and shameful history and present-day truth, replicated in same and different ways in secondary schools, has made some women's advocates fear what they believe are the inevitably harmful consequences of single-sex education at any level and for any reason, however benign.

Higher education forms an important piece of the collective memory of sex discrimination. Within elementary and secondary education, on the other hand, that sense of awareness is somewhat less clear, though nonetheless real. Coeducation, the dominant form of schooling for most Americans, has provided a veneer of equality. The pervasive preference for educating girls and boys together is long-standing, predating the common school movement of the mid-1800s. The early American colonists, for example, believed that educating young girls and boys together would replicate relations within the family and the church. But equality had its limits. For the Puritans, at least, basic literacy was important for girls to read the

Bible and fulfill their religious duties, but that is where their education ended. Boys, in contrast, would move on to the town school or private academy, and in many cases to Harvard.

It was not until the post–Revolutionary War years, infused with the spirit of equality for all, that the public cry began to be heard for more systematic schooling for women. The underlying rationale was consistent with mainstream Protestant thinking. It was also cast in a way that was decidedly non-threatening to male patriarchy and the reigning social order. Women's education would serve the needs of the family and the republic. As Thomas Jefferson believed when proposing his Virginia Bill for the More General Diffusion of Knowledge, three years of schooling for girls would prepare them for marriage and motherhood. It would give them the intellectual and moral training needed to raise their children, and particularly their sons, in the principles of free government. It would also make them more interesting companions to their husbands. To these questionable ends, elementary schools in the North began to open their doors to girls, though often on a limited and segregated basis—either after the boys' schoolday ended or during the summer months.

In the early nineteenth century, pioneers like Emma Willard and Mary Lyon used similar reasoning to extend female education beyond the primary grades. They maintained that education would train unmarried women to teach young children. As a temporary career, teaching was ideal preparation for motherhood. In 1821 Willard obtained support from the New York State legislature and from private citizens to open the Troy Female Seminary, now known as the Emma Willard School, a forerunner of similar institutions that sprang up throughout the country in the following decade. In 1837 Lyon founded what became Mount Holyoke College, the first women's college in the United States. Just as these female seminaries prepared teachers for the early common schools, their cautiously conservative rationale supported the efforts of reformers like Horace Mann to include women within the orbit of common schooling for the masses.[2]

Despite this early tinge of egalitarianism, as common schools grew exponentially, the decision to choose one organizational form over the other had as much to do with custom and pragmatic considerations as any grand theory of child development, pedagogy, or even social arrangements. An 1883 government report intended to respond to inquiries from abroad noted how "the 'common school' in the United States is and has been a 'mixed school,' . . . and is the only school that three-fourths of the people ever attend." The report unapologetically concluded with a reminder that if coeducation were discontinued, school systems would more likely deny "educational privileges" to girls than bear the cost of additional buildings and teachers.[3]

In sparsely populated rural areas in particular, the gender organization of schools was purely a matter of economics and convenience. With few students at any given grade level, coeducation simply was cost-effective, as demonstrated in the much-sentimentalized "one-room schoolhouse." In contrast, such eastern cities as Boston and New York initially resisted coeducation. Here again the dominant consideration was financial, but in this case it was shaded with social sensitivity or elitism, depending on how you view it. School officials feared losing their more privileged clientele to the private academies. The upper classes were averse to having their children, and particularly their daughters, intermingle with lower-class boys, especially those from immigrant families. Particularly through the primary grades, even where one school appeared to serve both sexes, boys and girls often entered through different doors and remained separate throughout the schoolday. The model was "coinstitutional" rather than "coeducational."

Only in the late 1840s and the 1850s did such large seaport cities as Baltimore, Boston, New York, and Philadelphia afford any secondary education to girls even in separate schools. For example, Boston Latin offered boys a classical education dating from the 1630s and later became a feeder school for Harvard. It took more than two centuries for city officials to establish a secondary school for girls or for Girls Latin to offer anything approaching the academic quality of its male counterpart. Again, school boards often justified girls' schools only grudgingly, as teacher-training grounds for the primary grades. Typically the education in these schools was narrower and less well subsidized than the education offered to boys. These striking disparities continued to exist well into the twentieth century, as the litigation against Philadelphia's all-male Central High School ultimately demonstrated.

Coeducation, which had always been the norm in the primary grades, gradually took hold in the high schools of densely populated cities. By the turn of the century, except for extreme cases like Philadelphia, which had no coeducational high schools, and Baltimore, where they existed only for African Americans, 98 percent of the public high schools nationwide were mixed-sex. Girls and boys generally studied the same subjects, but with strikingly different profiles and outcomes. Girls far outnumbered boys, generally outperformed them, and graduated in higher numbers. Only 12 cities out of 628 reported that they operated any single-sex schools, and those that remained were generally in older and more central areas.[4]

As girls gained basic access to education, their apparent success relative to boys gave rise to a disquieting response that dramatically limited the horizons of generations of women to come. Educators began to consider what became known as the "boy problem," whose roots they ascribed to the "woman peril." Their concerns focused on the rising dropout rates and academic disinterest among working-class boys. Searching for a cause, they feared that boys were becoming "feminized" from close daily contact with girls, and especially from the influence of women teachers who had come to dominate the profession. A vocal and persistent proponent of this view was G. Stanley Hall, the president of Clark University. Along with Dr. Clarke of Harvard, Hall decried the evils of coeducation, warning that it was biologically and socially harmful to girls and threatened the virility of boys. Although this extreme view never gained widespread credibility within the education community, it stoked the fires of a debate over coeducation that spanned several decades. In the early 1900s, a small number of school districts heeded these ominous warnings and briefly experimented with single-sex classes and schools specifically geared toward preventing boys from dropping out. Their reasoning was that separation would spare boys the social distraction and academic competition of girls, an interesting reverse from present-day arguments supporting girls' schools, yet one that is regaining resonance in the current discourse on boys.[5]

Massive migration and rapid industrialization carried the problem to new heights. The more widespread and lasting response was to make coeducational schools more practical. In the end, that meant more blatantly gendered and sex-segregated programs. In 1918 the National Education Association's Commission on the Reorganization of Secondary Education published its Cardinal Principles. The group proposed a reform of the high school curriculum, tying schooling more closely to the world of work through a system of vocational education that was highly differentiated by sex. In doing so, the educational establishment coupled the "boy problem" with "domestic feminism" and reimposed a clear gender ideology with particular consequences for the high school. Progressive reformers believed that some children were simply beyond academic redemption. Counted among these were the most disadvantaged—children of immigrants from southern and eastern Europe and the nonwhite, including African Americans, Native Americans, and Mexican Americans. These beliefs in practical education became tied into the IQ-testing movement, which perpetuated negative assumptions about the innate abilities of certain groups.

Throughout this process, schooling came to reflect and validate clearly demarcated traditional roles in society, despite the continued rhetoric of coeducation. "Equal opportunity" for the masses meant vocational training, and going to school simply became a way of getting a job.[6] That meant that schools prepared boys as breadwinners and girls as homemakers regardless of individual interests and true abilities. The fact that girls as a group had been flourishing in the academic curriculum was of little consequence. They too had to conform to the new educational agenda, especially if they became identified for the vocational track.

In the upper elementary grades, schools separated students into home economics classes for girls and wood shop classes for boys, each taught by a teacher of the students' sex. In the high schools, vocational programs were more comprehensive and at the same time more targeted. School officials tracked certain male students into drafting, woodworking, and auto mechanics and females into classes geared toward low-paying careers in domestic service, dressmaking, and secretarial skills. Some of these classes were sex segregated as a matter of school policy, others as a matter of "choice" severely constrained by social convention. The only vocational program that cut across gender lines was commercial education, which gradually lost its status as it became predominantly female. By 1930 girls outnumbered boys by three to one in stenography.

Gender demarcations also spilled over into certain academic courses that were judged more appropriate for girls or boys. Boys maintained a slight edge in mathematics and outnumbered girls by about three to two in physics despite the fact that the female school population was significantly larger. After all, how useful was physics in the home? A few districts offered a differentiated curriculum in physics as well as in chemistry to suit different purposes—the boys' coursework being more scientific and technical for higher education and the working world, the girls' geared toward domestic matters.

Meanwhile, large urban school districts like New York's went even further in promoting a specifically gendered program. In 1909, when the board of education authorized the establishment of vocational schools, it expressly stated that "boys and girls shall not be permitted to attend school in the same building" except for "special cases" in which officials had authorized separate classes. Vocational education became institutionalized in separate schools with self-defining names such as Girls' Commercial High School and Aviation High School for Boys. Many of these remained until the 1970s, when they were closed or reorganized under mandate of federal law. Originally intended primarily as a form of "compensatory education" for boys, this highly differentiated curriculum again reinforced not only gender but also racial, ethnic, and class biases that existed in society. It also restricted girls' access to certain areas of knowledge, most notably and notoriously, science and mathematics.[7]

Again, vocational tracking was not the only aspect of education with built-in inequities. It was simply the most visible one and the one that educators could most readily eliminate when the time came. But as the women's movement of the 1960s gained force, activists also fought to tear down admissions barriers in the limited number of academically selective all-male public secondary schools, like Boston Latin and Philadelphia's Central High School, and in the more numerous elite private schools, colleges, and universities. Throughout the 1970s, leaders within the movement for women's equality shared a set of firm beliefs—that single-sex schooling reinforced stereotypical notions of women's abilities and interests, that women could and should develop the same aspirations and career goals as men, that they should be mainstreamed into the social and economic life of the country, and that coeducation was the most effective approach for achieving these goals. Embracing the ideas of liberal feminism, they built their equality agenda on an assimilationist model. They believed that girls and boys entered school with the same cognitive abilities and that, given equal opportunities, the outcomes could and should be the same.

This mindset clearly affected the public's attitudes and interest. Single-sex schooling seemed to be dying a slow but certain death. As in most western societies, coeducation was perceived as more socially appropriate, liberating, and enlightened. The impact was initially most dramatic among private independent schools, where, between the mid-1960s and mid-1970s, the balance shifted from 62 percent single-sex to 66 percent coeducational. But it was ultimately devastating for public education. By 1981, among 6,000 public school districts surveyed by the federal Office for Civil Rights, there were only 86 all-male and 106 all-female schools. The majority of the boys' schools were vocational and technical, while many of the girls' schools were for pregnant students. Five years later, New York City converted to coeducation its last remaining single-sex school, Washington Irving High School, which primarily had served low-income girls. Although the school was a remarkable success (between 85 and 90 percent of its graduates going on to postsecondary education), and despite strong opposition from parents who unsuccessfully challenged the conversion in court, city officials remained resolute in providing an educational environment that "mirror[ed] the diversity of modern society." In the end, the tide of coeducation was unstoppable.[8]

It soon became apparent, however, that perhaps at least equally troubling and pervasive problems lay directly in coeducation itself with its superficial and deceptive air of gender neutrality. It was at this point that the distinction between single-sex schooling and coeducation began to take shape as a matter of critical and conscious concern. And just as the "boy problem" had driven educational reform in the early part of the twentieth century, the "girl problem" set that movement in reverse. As females gained increased access to elite institutions and as vocational programs lost their gender identification, women's advocates began to look more broadly at both the overt and hidden curricula and the widespread institutional sexism of coeducational schools.

It was not long before researchers turned their attention to the problem, gathering data to support that view. Studies successively showed that women were underrepresented in textbooks and in the literature studied in schools and that subjects were highly polarized by gender—math and science viewed as more masculine and English and foreign languages more feminine. They found that beginning in the middle school years, boys were more confident in learning math and science and perceived these subjects to be more useful, while teachers tended to interact more frequently and provide more instructional feedback to them. The conclusion was drawn that these external and internal factors, taken together, initially influenced girls' attitudes, subsequently their achievement and course enrollment, and ultimately their choice of careers.[9]

American feminists pushed for greater equality within the coeducational model, unlike many radical feminists in Great Britain, for example, who rejected coeducation outright as a vehicle for reproducing male patriarchy and dominance.[10] It was not until the 1990s, when a confluence of intellectual and social forces drew national attention to the education of girls in coeducational schools, that single-sex education appeared on the American radar screen of gender equity and became a matter of heated controversy. But the inflammatory language of oppression and subordination gave way to a distinctly American cry for equality of opportunity touched with the spirit of pluralism.

## GIRLS, ADOLESCENCE, AND SCHOOLING

If asked to name one defining work that energized the modern-day debate over education and gender, most educators and scholars probably would point to Carol Gilligan's *In a Different Voice*. Although this was essentially a study on moral development, it set the stage for subsequent scholarship on gender differences that had a profound effect on educational policy. As I have noted, it also energized a focal shift begun in the 1970s, when feminist scholars started looking at gender differences through the lens of cognitive styles rather than cognitive abilities. They consciously considered the possibility that women and men differ in how they conceptually organize their environment and in the strategies they use to address unfamiliar problems.

Gilligan maintained that women, or those culturally defined as "female," are oriented toward attachment, connectedness, and caring, which inclines them toward human relationships. Men, or those culturally defined as "male," are oriented toward "separateness" and abstract thinking, which predisposes them toward individual achievement and the subordination of relationships. Some academic feminists railed against the gender stereotypes implicit in Gilligan's theory, while others welcomed the high moral ground it suggested for women. Gradually it spawned a loosely defined school of thought, with various disciplinary branches making Gilligan's name an icon in the scholarship of "difference."[11]

The book created a theoretical base for Gilligan's later work with adolescent girls. And though its title came to represent her research in a broad sense, it was her later studies, conducted mainly in collaboration with graduate students, that made a pronounced mark on educational thinking. Gilligan's collective findings and conclusions added up to a general theory of female adolescent development. Again, the basic assumption of her research was that the way people "talk about their lives," the "language they use," and the "connections they make" constitute a window onto their world and how they perceive it. She and her colleagues defied orthodox quantitative research and gathered data by engaging in conversations with young women as they moved from preadolescence to adolescence.

Gilligan's initial work with students at the Emma Willard School in Troy, New York, in the years 1981 to 1984 led her to describe the age range she studied as a critical period in the lives of women, calling it a "watershed in female development, a time when girls are in danger of drowning or disappearing." She found that girls' knowledge seems to become buried between the ages of twelve and fifteen (the time, she noted, when dropping out of school becomes more common in the inner city). She saw young women caught in a struggle to balance their own sense of caring and relationship against the male-dominated culture's values of autonomy and self-sufficiency. She observed that girls are more likely than boys to manifest such psychological problems as depression and eating disorders, that they respond more negatively to stressful challenges in early adolescence, and that they reveal more disturbances in self-image.[12]

Gilligan subsequently confirmed these observations among a broader group of girls between the ages of seven and eighteen attending the Laurel School in Ohio. Based on a series of conversations between 1986 and 1990, she compared early adolescence in women's development to early childhood in men's. For her, each is a time of "compromise between voice and relationships." As she saw it, for girls that compromise is tied to the subordinate role of women in society. Girls deem it necessary, she tells us, because it removes or relieves the tension between their own voices and the "regeneration of patriarchal and male-voiced cultures." But exactly which cultures was Gilligan talking about? One of the criticisms leveled against her was that she seemed to consider all girls as generic, without taking into account the effects of race, ethnicity, and class on female development. She later addressed that concern and found that girls from public schools and diverse cultural backgrounds expressed similar feelings of isolation and loss, although often with more candor and without the same psychological and economic supports of her earlier and more privileged subjects.[13]

Gilligan's findings supported the general proposition that men and women are not necessarily the same, whether innately or through social conditioning, and that their distinct ways of perceiving reality should be equally recognized. Gilligan was not the first to call for a model of human development that included females as well as males. Feminist psychologists from the 1970s like Nancy Chodorow in her book *The Reproduction of Mothering* made similar claims that women as contrasted with men experience a sense of self in connection with others.[14] But Gilligan's focus on adolescent girls and how they hide or silence parts of themselves to maintain relationships held a distinct resonance for many women of her generation. Her conclusions lent theoretical credence to the empirical findings of educational researchers and women's advocates examining gender equity over the following decade. At the same time, her research on the unique issues faced by young adolescent women struggling to develop a sense of self gave academic currency to the escalating debate over the education of girls, particularly in the middle school years.

Gilligan's well-known proposition that girls are "confident at 11, confused at 16" became the mantra of gender equity advocates. Her emphasis on the importance of connection and relationship among female students translated into a move toward collaborative or group learning in classrooms nationwide. It also suggested gendered learning styles that, in an unintended way, supported the concept of single-sex classes and schools. In the end, her evolving research, generously underwritten by major foundations, laid the groundwork for a discussion that continues to provoke comment and critique to the present day.

Gilligan was primarily concerned with female adolescent development and used the school as the venue for conducting her research, although her later writing has ventured into policy recommendations. Throughout the 1980s and 1990s, other researchers concerned with the achievement gap favoring boys and the relationship between experience and self-esteem directly focused on schools as the cause. Operating in the gender equity mode, some examined the classroom itself as a sociopolitical setting and the differential messages conveyed to and received by girls and boys. Most prominent among these were David and Myra Sadker, professors at American University, who spent more than a decade observing classroom interaction and talking to teachers and administrators across the country. Their widely read book *Failing at Fairness* sparked an intense look at the impact of coeducational schools on female students. In observations of more than one hundred fourth-, sixth-, and eighth-grade classrooms, they found "two worlds: one of boys in action, the other of girls' inaction." Boys dominated discussion and called out more frequently than girls, while teachers were more likely to praise, correct, help, and criticize them. Teachers tended to initiate more communication with boys, ask them more complex, abstract, and open questions, and give them more detailed instructions—all techniques, the Sadkers argued, that foster self-esteem and achievement.[15]

While the Sadkers were initially reporting their findings in academic journals and at professional meetings, the American Association of University Women (AAUW) published several pamphlets followed by a series of reports that used the Sadkers' research, along with Gilligan's, as a touchstone for confirming serious and widespread gender bias in the schools. The ominous tone of these reports and the broad media coverage they attracted inadvertently sparked renewed interest in single-sex education. The first report, released in 1991, presented the results of a nationwide survey of almost three thousand students (2,374 girls and 600 boys) in grades four through ten and from varied racial and ethnic backgrounds. Based on responses to a series of statements, the AAUW concluded that girls experienced a disproportionate loss of self-esteem as they approached adolescence. Given the statement "I am happy the way I am," 67 percent of the boys responded affirmatively in elementary school, but only 46 percent agreed with the statement in high school. For girls, the decline between elementary and middle school was more dramatic, dropping from 60 to 37 percent, then to 29 percent in high school. The loss was most pronounced among Hispanic girls, whose affirmative responses decreased by 38 points between elementary and high school. Yet the drop among black girls was only 7 points.

The report drew a causal connection between self-esteem and how girls perceive their abilities in math and science. "As girls 'learn' they are not good at these subjects, their sense of self-worth and aspirations for themselves deteriorates," the AAUW concluded. According to the data presented, the percentage of girls reporting that they "like math" dropped from 81 to 61 during those years, compared with a drop from 84 to 72 percent among boys. Interest in science showed a similar decline, from 75 to 63 percent among girls and from 82 to 75 percent among boys within the same age range. The report noted that the competitive learning environment of most classrooms puts girls at a disadvantage, as most girls learn better in "cooperative settings." Citing the Sadkers' findings, the AAUW concluded unequivocally that "schools set girls up to fail."[16]

The following year, a second report prepared for the AAUW by the Center for Research on Women at Wellesley College drew data from more than 1,300 previous studies and confirmed earlier findings: that women were underrepresented in school textbooks and curriculum, that teacher behavior and standardized tests tended to favor boys, and that girls lagged seriously behind boys in math and science. The report listed the Sadkers as contributors to the section on curriculum. A third and perhaps the most controversial report, published in 1993, presented the results of a survey on sexual harassment. Among a group of 1,630 eighth- through eleventh-grade students, the study found that 85 percent of girls and 76 percent of boys reported that they had experienced in school "unwanted and unwelcome sexual behavior" that interfered with their lives. Although the gender gap here was surprisingly insignificant, it widened further when frequency was considered. Girls were more likely to report having been targeted "often" as compared with "occasionally" or "rarely." Educators found this report to be the most troubling of all and were understandably reluctant to embrace its findings. As subsequent litigation has proven, the data on sexual harassment in the schools carried serious legal implications.[17]

The AAUW then set its sights directly on the social and institutional challenges that young adolescent girls face as they form identities and negotiate the middle school environment. Here researchers presented the results of classroom observations and interviews with staff, students, and parents in six schools representing rural, suburban, and urban communities. They found the process to vary depending upon each school's political and cultural interpretation of gender. They also found that in schools with large minority populations, gender equity was difficult to disengage from issues of race, culture, and economic class.[18]

Gilligan, the Sadkers, and the AAUW together painted a painful portrait of growing up female in America. Their critical findings and controversial conclusions touched off a national debate among educators, psychologists, policymakers, feminists, and antifeminists concerning gender equity and gender differences. Their influence on public policy and on the nation's consciousness became increasingly palpable, establishing "gender bias" as a high priority in school reform. As one critic wryly noted, "In some school districts, the AAUW forced more changes in education policy in the space of a few short years than had advocates for black children in forty." Private foundations as well as federal and state agencies responded to the call, infusing millions of dollars into new educational programs for girls. In introducing the Gender Equity in Education Act in Congress in 1993, Congresswoman Patricia Schroeder cited both the AAUW's self-esteem study and the Wellesley report to support the purposes of the legislation. That year, the Ms. Foundation launched Take Our Daughters to Work Day to counter the loss in self-esteem and broaden the career horizons of young women. A *San Francisco Chronicle* editorial decried the "Dreadful Waste of Female Talent," while the *New York Times* warned that "Bias Against Girls is Found Rife in Schools, with Lasting Damage."[19]

In 1994 alone, three widely read books drew media attention and popularized the notion of a national crisis among adolescent girls: journalist Peggy Orenstein's *School Girls*, written in association with the AAUW; psychologist Mary Pipher's *Reviving Ophelia,* which reached number one on the *New York Times* best-seller list; and the *Washington Post* columnist Judy Mann's *The Difference.* Each of these confirmed that, as Pipher put it, the "selves" of young adolescent girls "crash and burn in a social and developmental Bermuda Triangle." Like Shakespeare's Ophelia, they lose their voice and the silencing goes hand in hand with falling self-esteem. Pipher's book in particular became the bible for scores of mothers trying to help their daughters navigate the turbulent waters of the preteen and adolescent years. It is still widely read and cited almost a decade later.[20]

As the 1990s wore on, listening to the individual and collective voices of girls became a major strategy in girl advocacy. Driving that project was a proliferation of books that permitted us to listen in on the inner life of girls. We saw girls spontaneously talking about identity, sexuality, school, body image, and the sometimes "over the top" claims of popular culture. Apparently there was a sizable population of self-selected young women who were eager to share their thoughts and feelings, and our confessional culture was just as eager to hear and absorb them. The most popular among this new genre of social history, *Ophelia Speaks,* written by a high school student, also made its way to the *New York Times* best-seller list. Meanwhile, despite all the criticism of her work, Carol Gilligan was still racking up notable commendations. In 1996 *Time* magazine cited her as one of "America's 25 most influential people," while the following year she received the Heinz award for upending "the paradigm for what it means to be human."[21]

The impact of this nationally publicized common wisdom soon began to reach the admissions offices of private all-girls schools. Enrollments swelled for the first time in a decade—by almost two thousand—between the 1995 and 1996 school years. That figure increased by another thirty-five hundred between 1997 and 1998.[22] It also generated a flurry of activity in public school districts around the country, with after-school programs, mentoring projects, and single-sex math and science classes all focusing on the pressing needs of girls. But the response was not all favorable. Gradually there appeared an increasingly visible and vocal backlash bent on setting the record straight and refocusing the gender equity agenda.

## THE BACKLASH

In 1995 the AAUW Educational Foundation president explicitly stated that "girls [were] not receiving the same quality, or even quantity, of education as their brothers."[23] Yet in fact the data seemed to be moving in the opposite direction. As the media hype continued to escalate and the educational establishment became increasingly driven by the "girl crisis," a slow but steady backlash began to take shape. Initially targeted at the prevailing research on gender equity and female adolescence, a small core of scholars and activists challenged the findings and underlying methodology, explicitly posing the question, "What about boys?"

On the organizational level, the Independent Women's Forum (IWF) in Washington, a counterweight to groups such as the AAUW and the National Organization for Women, has led the way in gathering data to debunk what they consider the myth of girls' victimization. By far the most outspoken, unequivocal, and unremitting voice in the backlash chorus is that of Christina Hoff Sommers, a philosophy professor at Clark University, currently a resident fellow at the American Enterprise Institute for Public Policy Research, and chairwoman of the IWF advisory board. Her books *Who Stole Feminism?* and *The War Against Boys* have made her both a popular and a controversial figure on the lecture and talk-show circuit. In the first book in particular, Sommers exposes what she considers the excesses of the feminist agenda and the dangers it has posed in trying to resocialize boys. In Sommers's view, the feminist establishment has shifted course from "Enlightenment principles of individual justice" to a view of women joined in a "common struggle against patriarchy," and in doing so it has overstated the "girl crisis" by a long stretch. In both books Sommers squarely takes on Gilligan, the Sadkers, and the AAUW reports.[24]

Sommers takes Gilligan to task for not providing empirical data to support her theory of moral development, calling it "nothing more than a seductive hypothesis, without evidential basis" and contesting her conclusion that girls lose their "voice" as they approach adolescence. Sommers likewise questions the scientific validity of the Sadkers' classroom observations, pointing out that teacher responses to student "call outs" are subject to observer bias and that student-teacher interaction may vary widely depending on the grade level and the particular teacher. She heaps equal criticism on the AAUW report on self-esteem. Not only is self-esteem an unstable and therefore difficult construct to define and measure, she says, but what you ultimately find depends on how you frame the question and group the responses.[25]

Yet Sommers's critics hold that she herself at times has played fast and loose with the facts. They point out that she inflated the price tag of the Gender Equity in Education Act from an actual figure of $5 million to $360 million in new money. She mistakenly implied that the AAUW had intentionally downplayed the results of a study it had commissioned with the educational researcher Valerie Lee, who has subsequently explained that she and her coauthors had in fact retained the copyright so that they could publish their findings in a scholarly journal. In a frontal attack on Carol Gilligan and the Sadkers, Sommers suggested that none of their research had undergone the peer review that is conventional practice in scientific circles. Gilligan and David Sadker have publicly refuted that claim. Both have sparred in the press with Sommers over the truth of her accusations and the accuracy of their retorts. Many of their disagreements hinge on semantics: what constitutes "peer review," what characterizes "scientific" rather than "interpretive" research, what "calling out significantly" means as a quantitative measure.[26]

Without excusing any arguable failings, it is difficult to deny that Sommers does in fact reveal significant gains made by girls and women in recent decades. "It is boys, not girls, who are languishing academically," she tells us. Citing federal Department of Education data, she notes that girls get better grades, spend more time on homework, participate more in Advanced Placement programs, and enroll in high-level math and science courses in slightly greater numbers than boys. Girls outnumber boys in student government, in honor societies, on student newspapers, and in debating clubs. They also outperform boys on tests of artistic and musical ability. On the other hand, she points out, more boys are suspended from school, are held back, and ultimately drop out. Boys are more frequently enrolled in special education programs and diagnosed with attention deficit hyperactivity disorder. More boys than girls are involved in crime, alcohol, and drug abuse. And although suicide attempts are more common among girls, she says, more boys actually kill themselves. Statistics bear out all her assertions.[27]

These sobering truths could set the struggle for gender equity on a more balanced plane. Yet like the early AAUW reports, Sommers too speaks in absolutes and oversimplifies what we now know are complex issues. Furthermore, she goes beyond the quantitative evidence, positioning herself in the far more contentious debate over sexually identified characteristics. She argues that the "equity enthusiasts" are dead wrong in believing that girls and boys are the same, and that Gilligan and the "difference feminists" are mistaken in believing that differences are "socially constructed" and capable of being "reconstructed" differently. As far as Sommers is concerned, the search for statistical parity between the sexes is an exercise in futility. Boys and girls are simply hardwired differently. Girls, she says, have better verbal skills, which she suggests may account for their greater emotional expressiveness. Boys, on the other hand, have better spatial reasoning skills, which gives them an edge in math, engineering, and architecture. Boys are also more physically active and take greater risks, which, she argues, makes them "proto-criminals" in the eyes of the "equity specialists." And what schools now consider "sexually harassing" behavior she claims has little to do with "misogyny, patriarchy, or sex discrimination" but all to do with the propensity of children, regardless of sex, to "bully and be cruel."[28]

Although few approach the depth or breadth of Sommers's invective, she is not alone in beating the drums of girls' achievement and challenging their continuing image as victims. Other scholars have argued that many of the deficits noted in the AAUW reports from the early 1990s had already been remedied by that time. The historian Diane Ravitch, who served as an assistant secretary of education in the first Bush administration, also has been a vocal critic of what she calls the AAUW's "phony crisis." For Ravitch, the group's 1991 report on math and science "might have been the right story 20 years earlier, but coming out when it did was like calling a wedding a funeral." The report merely diverted attention from the serious gap between racial groups, Ravitch argues. On every measure of school achievement, she points out, African Americans are far behind their white peers: "The average black 17-year-old scores the same as the average white 13-year-old." Ravitch is more temperate in her views than Sommers. She recognizes that social and economic inequities continue to burden women. Yet she also suggests that schools no longer bear the blame. Concerns about equal pay, she advises, should be taken to employers, while complaints about stereotypical representations of women should be laid at the doorsteps of movie and television commercial producers, not teachers and principals.[29]

The sociologist Cornelius Riordan, best known for his work on single-sex schooling, presents a like-minded view of the AAUW studies. By 1992, he maintains, females possessed "a clear and significant advantage on most central educational-outcome indicators, on average." In fact, at that point, women accounted for 54 percent of students receiving B.A. and M.A. degrees. Riordan further challenges the connection between low self-esteem and academic achievement, a basic premise underlying the AAUW's argument. In 1972 and 1980, he reports, girls had higher self-esteem than boys, even though their educational expectations and opportunities were lower than that of boys. Riordan suggests that self-esteem actually may decrease with education, perhaps the result of "greater expectations and demands."[30]

Judith Kleinfeld, a psychology professor at the University of Alaska, Fairbanks, also presents a more measured view in a 1998 report prepared for the Women's Freedom Network in Washington. Like Sommers, she takes issue with the Sadkers' research. In addition to the difficulties in conducting and interpreting classroom observations, she points out, "getting attention from the teacher" can mean many things. In elementary school in particular "attention" can be associated not with positive reinforcement but with discipline. In fact, Kleinfeld maintains that unpublished research findings from the AAUW itself, which both she and Sommers found difficult and costly to obtain, contradict the Sadkers' argument. According to those findings, at least as students perceive it, boys and girls receive substantially equal amounts of attention; in fact, teachers tend to show some favoritism toward girls and not boys. Kleinfeld also looks at achievement test scores, and presents a reasoned analysis of more current data that clarifies some of the confusion over the apparent gender gap. She drives home a now well-publicized fact, that the female advantage in reading and writing "substantially outstrips" the male advantage in math and science achievement.

The researcher Valerie Lee drew similar conclusions from her 1995 AAUW study, using a national database of middle school students. Although she found gender differences that favored boys in social studies and science, the differences favoring girls in reading achievement and engagement with school were of equal or greater magnitude. She observed no significant differences in math achievement. But why is it that males continue to score higher than females on the Scholastic Aptitude Test I (SAT) and most Advanced Placement (AP) tests? The reason Kleinfeld offers is that males tend to display greater variability, so more end up at the upper tail on the bell curve. But as she points out, more also end up at the lower end. That phenomenon at least partially explains the higher number of boys with extraordinarily high test scores.[31]

## THE BOY QUESTION

Threaded through at least some of this commentary is a sense of "feminism run amok." Clearly the objective is not only to debunk the widespread perception that schools and society continue to victimize girls but also to shift attention to the "boy question." Psychologists have entered the fray with best-selling books whose subtitles advise us to "protect" and "rescue" boys. They too agree that there is a "boy crisis"—that boys not only are failing academically but are "depressed, suicidal, emotionally shut down." They differ, though, on the reasons for the crisis.[32]

Probably the most controversial among these commentators is the family therapist Michael Gurian, whose books *The Wonder of Boys* and *A Fine Young Man* helped launch the "boys' movement" in the 1990s. While purportedly supportive of "gender equality" and aware of cultural influences, Gurian also sings the antifeminist refrain, blaming misguided feminist efforts to make boys more like girls: by denying basic biological differences between the sexes, "radical" feminists have robbed boys of their boyhood. Boys are hardwired for "action and risk-taking," and girls are destined to be "nurturers." Among his other works, *Boys and Girls Learn Differently!* tells us exactly what its provocative title suggests. Drawing on brain studies,

Gurian presents a drumroll of sex differences that affect cognitive development, academic performance, and even emotional responses. Nature seems in large measure to eclipse nurture. In his latest book, *The Wonder of Girls*, Gurian goes even further, replacing feminism with what he calls "womanism." He posits a new way of thinking about males and females—one whose rationale he says is devoid of arguments based on male privilege, female victimization, empowerment, and androgyny. Needless to say, women's groups consider the book an inaccurately monolithic and static portrayal of feminism at best, and at worst a dangerous "throwback," despite the author's denials.[33]

Other clinical psychologists present a less oppositionist examination of the "boy problem." Popular books like Dan Kindlon and Michael Thompson's *Raising Cain* and William Pollack's *Real Boys* have received wide acclaim from parents and educators and propelled their authors into the media limelight. Rather than merely embrace some variant of the classic "boys will be boys" position, they persuasively reveal the difficulties that young boys experience in adjusting to a school climate that is geared toward the faster developmental pace of girls. Without casting aspersions on feminists or others, both books suggest that the structure and behavioral expectations of most coeducational schools, particularly elementary schools, tend to favor female students and that teachers have become "well sensitized to girls' voices." The authors note that boys mature more slowly than girls, have a higher activity level, and are slower to develop impulse control. That helps explain their typically poorer school performance, especially in the early grades, the greater likelihood of their being diagnosed with attention deficit hyperactivity disorder, and consequently their low self-esteem.

These authors admit that girls and boys each have distinct neurological advantages as a group, whether it is girls' ease with language and reading or boys' ability to throw a ball. Nonetheless, they recognize that nurture plays a significant role in enhancing and reinforcing these skills. They also affirm the importance of connection in the lives of boys, as Carol Gilligan did in the lives of girls. Society must permit boys to gain more "emotional literacy," they argue. For them the key to understanding boyhood is to understand masculinity. Kindlon and Thompson tell us how male peers present the young boy with a "culture of cruelty," which forces him to deny emotional neediness, "routinely disguising his feelings." Pollack refers to this as the "boy code" and the "mask of masculinity"—a false bravado that boys adopt to hide their fears and vulnerability. If girls "lose their voice" as they approach adolescence, something equally insidious happens a lot earlier to boys, profoundly affecting their sense of self and their relationships with others.[34]

The urgent attention given this issue is neither unique nor original to the

United States. This country, in fact, is still behind the curve on this score as compared with other developed nations. Scholars and researchers in Australia and England, for example, have afforded this question intense study and discussion. The Australian government launched a parliamentary inquiry into boys' education in 1994. At about the same time, the British government commissioned a five-part report on gender differences, performance, and achievement. Meanwhile, Germany was establishing educational programs for boys outside the schools while Japan was debating the prospects of a new "men's studies." Those who attended a 1995 conference in Sweden on "Gender and Education—into the 21st Century" heard repeated commentary from across the globe on the increased concern about boys' education in policy discourse.[35] One significant factor, however, distinguishes the United States in a critical and immediate way. Although other Western countries are faced with a growing population of poor and unskilled immigrants, the United States has still not resolved the lingering effects of legally sanctioned racial segregation. That historical fact continues to manifest itself in a downward cycle of poverty, violence, and academic failure into succeeding generations.

The AAUW more recently has softened its rhetoric and embraced a more inclusive concern for boys while showing greater sensitivity to the growing racial and ethnic diversity of the nation's student population. In its 1999 report, *Gender Gaps,* the organization called for institutional changes to be set in place in order to achieve equitable outcomes for both sexes. Here the group recognized the gains made by girls since its 1992 report and acknowledged that boys have also been left behind in certain subject areas and skills, including reading and writing. Unfortunately, the AAUW based some of its arguments on data that were at least five years old at the time of publication. Whatever was new and noteworthy in the report was lost in the "old news."[36]

Carol Gilligan herself in recent years has acknowledged that "unsettled issues" remain in the study of both girls' and boys' development. With almost two decades of media buildup, controversy, and educational reform behind her, she now points out that her research results "do not lend themselves to simple statements such as 'Girls are thriving' or 'Girls are at risk.' " Gilligan acknowledges: "Girls and boys are strong and vulnerable, although in somewhat different ways." In hindsight, she questions whether the attention that her work attracted might have unintentionally restricted society's perception of boys. Along with several doctoral students at Harvard, Gilligan has taken up studying young boys to see whether something is missing from the psychological literature on their development.[37]

But for Christina Hoff Sommers, this is still bad medicine. Gilligan and her associates, she says, "are embarked on a large-scale program to save the boys of the future by changing the way society socializes them in what Gilligan calls the 'patriarchal social order.'" They have "set about the task," Sommers tells us, "of liberating boys from their maleness." Sommers does not rest her case with Gilligan. Rather she inveighs against the "crisis writers" in general, including Pipher and Pollack and "their many colleagues," who speak of "saving, rescuing, reviving" and in doing so "irresponsibly portray . . . healthy American girls and boys as pathological victims of an inimical culture."[38]

## REACHING A TRUCE

As the media and researchers now shift the gender gap discussion to the "boy question," there is still a tendency to mistakenly present the problem in a bipolar frame—schools are failing to meet the needs of girls or boys, rather than failing in different and equally damaging ways to meet the needs of both. The new wave of popular literature on boys, in fact, has an aura of déjà vu. Similar to the research on girls, it can seem alarming and overstated if taken to the extreme. It should not be forgotten that here we have the perspective of psychologists who tend to view human behavior, and in this case boyhood, through the lens of their clinical practice. Generalizing from their middle-class, suburban, white clients, they too run the risk of falling into the trap of "gender essentialism"—a criticism that women of color have leveled against feminists—rather than sorting through the various shades of "maleness" and the various populations of boys with distinct needs. Social context matters, and it matters significantly. Boys raised in the streets of Harlem obviously demonstrate attitudes, self-expectations, and emotional needs largely related to social and economic pressures that are sharply different from those experienced by boys raised in the mansions of Beverly Hills or the mountains of Tennessee, to present the point in starkest contrast. Equally troubling is the fact that in the popular enthusiasm to "rescue the boys," the unique and persistent problems facing disadvantaged adolescent girls are in danger of being lumped together with those of the larger female population, whose gender-related issues have become increasingly less weighty or pressing over time.

Meanwhile, we should not discount the profound influence that three decades of increased attention to girls' education has had on narrowing the achievement gap favoring boys. The enormous gains that young women have made are due in no small measure to a massive body of empirical research responding to the "wake-up call" sounded by Gilligan, the Sadkers, and others, regardless of their methodological weaknesses. I do not deny that their conclusions were somewhat overblown and one-sided. I also realize that this smacks of an "end justifies the means" argument. But in those conclusions lay more than a kernel of truth: schools were failing girls. Moreover, the widely publicized findings of these authors, along with legal mandates, made gender equity a top educational priority nationwide. The numerous programs and policies put in place since the 1970s, when there was in fact a severe crisis in women's education, no doubt contributed to the higher math and science scores and increased enrollment in advanced courses that we now find among female students. And while that effort perhaps diverted attention and arguably resources from the unique problems confronting boys, those problems have mounted over the years for social and economic reasons unrelated to the women's movement or gender equity.

That being said, a measured reading of the "boy" literature carries a wealth of insights into boys' distinct developmental and emotional needs. It also challenges some of the lingering myths and outdated assumptions surrounding the boy-girl debate, making the public recognize that gender inequities cut both ways. It is not simply a question of female virtue and male vice. As Valerie Lee rightly points out, gender equity "should not be restricted to only those outcomes on which girls are disadvantaged. . . . Gender differences that disadvantage boys in reading are just as problematic as those disadvantaging girls in science. Why shouldn't we pay attention to all of these?" Painting girls as "victims in an unjust world," Lee warns, merely serves to politicize the gender question.[39] Taking that broader view opens up the single-sex debate to new and potentially more appropriate rationales based on what we currently know and continue to learn about boys and girls, their similarities, and their differences.

# 5
# Who's Winning, Who's Losing, and Why?

Sifting through the opposing arguments on gender and schooling proves somewhat exasperating. Are schools meeting the academic and emotional needs of girls and boys at different age levels and among distinct racial and social groups? If not, then why not? Is it just institutional failure or does it have something to do with the sexes themselves? Or is it a combination of both? In searching for an answer to these questions, it is often difficult to distinguish between fact and opinion, and the opinions are indeed forcefully expressed. Personal feelings and professional reputations are not spared. Objectivity at times gives way to passion. Advocacy gets passed off as science. As the protagonists in this drama have staked their claims, leaving behind a wealth of conflicting interpretations, others have established some useful and thought-provoking guideposts. After more than two decades of intense and inconclusive debate, it is now time to travel back over this vast and winding landscape in search of present-day meaning and direction, all the while mindful of the profound implications for same- versus mixed-sex schooling.

## ACADEMIC ACHIEVEMENT

As the 1990s drew to a close, even the most committed girl advocates realized that the gender gap was cutting both ways. The American Association of University Women (AAUW), whose studies had fueled much of the debate over gender and schooling, acknowledged in a 1999 follow-up report that boys also face inequities in school and that social conditioning may skew their educational experience just as it does for girls. At the same time, the group recognized that girls have made significant strides in recent years and that they now predominate in advanced English courses and in foreign language and arts classes. The report nevertheless pointed out that course-taking patterns and scores on standardized achievement tests still reinforced traditional beliefs about the relative strengths of girls and boys.[1] The AAUW was definitely on the right course. Nonetheless, the problem is not quite as simple as it appears. In fact, a more thorough analysis of comparative data reveals that the educational experience and outcomes for girls and boys are far more complex than advocates or the popular press has led the public to believe.

An appropriate place to begin is with initial cognitive and behavioral differences. Boys make up 61 percent of infants and toddlers receiving early intervention services under federal law and 65 percent of those with developmental delays. Girls enter kindergarten with a small but noticeable advantage in reading skills, as well as in fine and gross motor skills. Teachers and parents also rate girls higher than boys on various measures of preparedness and social behavior. About 5 to 7 percent more girls than boys are able to identify colors, count to twenty or more, and read or pretend to read when they begin formalized schooling. Girls are more likely to recognize letters and write their own names. The gaps favoring girls, in fact, are equal to or larger than the racial gaps favoring white students. Boys, on the other hand, tend to be more restless and to have shorter attention spans.[2]

All of these deficits together indicate that boys as a group are at a serious disadvantage from the beginning. For some boys, these indications have meant the delay of kindergarten entry—what has come to be known as "academic redshirting"—an increasingly common practice whose long-term benefits researchers are beginning to question. For others, and particularly for economically disadvantaged boys, these perceived developmental lags have translated into retention in kindergarten for an additional year. As boys progress through school, many continue to lag at the lower ends of various academic success measures. Data on learning disabilities, lack of basic skills, and consequent dropout rates and disciplinary dismissals all make this point clear. Boys are twice as likely as girls to be enrolled in special education programs and four times as likely to demonstrate school-related disabilities, including dyslexia, autism, and stuttering.[3]

Yet despite this conventional wisdom on boys, an emerging stream of research findings suggests that these gender differentials may not be due solely to the prevalence of male students with learning disabilities but may reflect the fact that referrals to special education are based more on challenging behaviors than on poor academic performance. There is some indication that schools tend to underidentify girls with attention deficit hyperactivity disorder (ADHD), for example, because girls are less likely to engage in disruptive or oppositional behavior in the classroom. Signs of developmentally inappropriate behavior typically alert teachers to attention deficit disorders in general. One could reasonably speculate that if schools evaluated girls by reference to other girls rather than to a mixed-gender norm, they might in fact identify more girls with cognitive deficit and related problems. Similar gender bias may occur for learning disabilities across the spectrum, such that girls must demonstrate more significant deficits before schools refer them for special services.

With girls better able to "play school" or "look busy," they run the risk of being rewarded for learning to underachieve and for being inconspicuous. But the short- and the long-term consequences can prove devastating. Studies have shown that nearly 65 percent of homeless and runaway youth exhibited learning disabilities, while only 35 percent of them had previously been diagnosed. Similarly low rates of diagnosis have been found among welfare recipients, 98 percent of whom were women. At the opposite end, girls are less often referred for assessment on giftedness. Between 1989 and 2002, 61 percent of the students referred were male and only 39 percent female.[4]

Gender disparities at the extremes of cognitive abilities obviously demand further consideration. But the partially related and broader question of academic achievement and gender differences is the one that has attracted the most attention and generated the most heat. A 1997 report from the Educational Testing Service begins to give new clarity to the many fine points that have heretofore gone unnoticed. The report drew information from more than four hundred tests and other measures and more than fifteen hundred datasets, including nationally representative samples of students. Researchers found that girls' advantage over boys in test performance for writing and language use significantly increases from the fourth to the eighth grade, at which point the difference in most areas levels off or declines. In contrast, boys significantly increase their performance advantage over girls in math concepts, geopolitical subjects, and natural science from the eighth to the twelfth grades. The differences, however, begin even earlier. Among the five million fourth- through eighth-grade students participating in the National Geography Bee in 2001, a stunning 76 percent of the 15,252 school winners were boys, while only two of the state winners were girls. All of the top ten finalists were boys, as seems to be an annual pattern. There is some evidence that this striking disparity is a function of small but real differences between boys and girls in their knowledge of geography rather than any innate cognitive factors affecting their performance. The unanswered question is, "Why?"[5]

The girl-verbal/boy-math dichotomy becomes less definitive when we break the disciplines into component parts. For example, although there are noticeable differences favoring girls in writing and language use, the differences in reading and, to an even greater extent, vocabulary reasoning are considerably smaller. Likewise, although males outperform females on math concepts and spatial skills, females outperform males on computation and abstract reasoning. By twelfth grade, the gender differences are generally small, except for girls' advantage in verbal-writing, language use, and perceptual speed, which remain in the medium range, while boys' advantage on mechanical/electronic tests is substantially larger. The ETS study also found a greater spread among males across numerous datasets, with four females for every five males below the 10th and above the 90th percentiles. As Judith Kleinfeld has similarly noted, the low-end result manifests itself in the greater number of boys assigned to special education programs, while the high end is seen in the greater number of boys in certain high-performing categories.[6]

There is no doubt that the overall gender gap for girls has narrowed. Nevertheless, data gathered by the federal government reveal continuing differences in math and science achievement and attitudes. Fourth-grade girls are as likely as boys to agree with the statement "I like mathematics," while eighth- and twelfth-grade girls show less agreement than boys. At all three grade levels, females are still less likely than males to agree with the statement "I am good at mathematics." Although equal percentages of males and females report that science is a hard subject in both fourth and eighth grades, by twelfth grade the percentage of boys reporting this perception increases by 7 points, whereas the percentage of girls increases by 18 points.

It could be the case that information based on self-reporting has little or no connection to ability nor any influence on achievement. Student self-perceptions can easily distort responses. Perhaps girls are more self-critical or more comfortable in admitting their academic weaknesses. Test-score differences at higher grade levels, however, reflect similar tendencies. Although there are no significant gender differences in math scores on the National Assessment of Educational Progress (NAEP) at grade four, these differences do in fact become significant in favor of boys by grades eight and twelve. In fact, girls' math scores in twelfth grade have actually declined significantly since 1996. Females also continue to lag behind males in science. Between 1996 and 2000 the score gaps favoring males widened by three points at grade four and by five points at grade eight. Where girls seem to lose out most in math and science is at the highest levels of achievement. At grade twelve boys outperform girls at the "proficient" level in science (21 vs. 16 percent) and in math at both the "advanced" (3 vs. 1 percent) and "proficient" (20 vs. 14 percent) levels.[7]

That being said, the overall differences favoring boys in math and science pale in comparison with the ones favoring girls in reading and writing. The gender gap among students who score at or above the "proficient" level in reading progressively widens as students move from grade four (6 percentage points) to grade eight (13 points), and on to grade twelve (15 points). International data reveal a similar picture across developed countries, including the United States, where the average score difference favoring females in reading literacy is a statistically significant 29 points. Ability is, not surprisingly, tied to interest. In every country, females agree more frequently than males that reading is a favorite hobby. In writing skills, among those scoring at or above the "proficient" level, differences favoring girls peak at 19 percentage points in grade eight, before declining to 15 points by grade twelve. A recent report from the U.S. Department of Education concluded that the average eleventh-grade boy writes with the proficiency of the average eighth-grade girl.[8]

Yet NAEP and other broad-scale testing data tell only part of the story on gender differences. Results from "high stakes" tests provide equally interesting and important details. As the pool of test takers becomes progressively more select, girls lose their verbal advantage. For example, on the Preliminary Scholastic Aptitude Test (PSAT), the initial screening tool for millions of dollars in college scholarships awarded by the National Merit Scholarship Corporation, far more boys qualify as semifinalists, even though significantly more girls take the test. For years, women's and civil rights groups had argued that the PSAT underpredicted girls' college performance. The National Center for Fair and Open Testing (FairTest), an organization that advocates against the use of standardized tests for high-stakes decisions, filed a Title IX gender-bias complaint against the test with the Department of Education in 1994. In response, the College Board added a multiple-choice writing component to the PSAT in 1997. That addition alone narrowed the gender gap by 40 percent in the first year. Each of the three components of the test is based on a scale of 20 to 80. In 2000 girls scored an average of 1.1 points higher than boys on the writing section but 0.5 points lower on the verbal and 3.3 points lower on the math. Again, the disparities were most striking at the highest performance levels. Only 15 percent of females scored at 60 or higher, compared with 27 percent of males.[9]

This pattern replicates itself on the Scholastic Aptitude Test (SAT) I. Looking back over the past decade and a half, the SAT math gender gap appears largely intractable even while overall math scores have increased. In 1984 the gap in average scores was 40 points. A decade later, it was 36 points. When the SAT was renormed in 1996, the gap was 35 points, and there it remains. The gap has been consistently greatest at the upper percentile levels. For example, in 2000 20 percent of females but 30 percent of males scored at or above 600. Meanwhile, contrary to popular belief, boys have not only closed the gender gap favoring girls on the verbal section of the SAT I, but they now hold a slight edge.[10]

The same pattern emerges from Advanced Placement exams. Whereas an equal percentage of female and male test takers now achieves an overall score of three or higher on a scale of one to five, boys continue to outperform girls in all areas with the exception of art and foreign languages. That is the case even in biology and in English language and composition, where girls typically excel in classwork. And although the differences in math and science have progressively decreased over the years, they are still noteworthy. Girls comprise 47 percent of students taking the Advanced Placement AB calculus exam, with a mean score of 2.84, compared with 3.13 for boys. For the more advanced BC calculus exam, 38.6 percent of the test takers are girls and their mean score is 3.41 compared with 3.75 for boys. Among students taking the physics B exam, 35 percent are girls, with an average score of 2.44, compared with 2.91 for boys. Of those students planning to take advanced standing in college calculus, only 25 percent are female. This pattern repeats itself in the admissions tests to medical and law school despite the higher number of female test takers. Males continue to achieve higher average scores on all subtests of the Medical College Admission Test (MCAT), including verbal reasoning and the biological sciences. The same holds true for the Law School Admission Test (LSAT).[11]

These differences belie the fact that female college-bound students are more likely than males to enroll in advanced and honors classes in all subject areas except for computer-related ones. Females are also more likely to graduate in the top 10 percent of their high school class.[12] Apparently females do far better in their schoolwork than on high-stakes tests. Some of these group differences and skewing at the higher percentile ranks can be explained by the fact that many more lower-performing girls than boys plan to attend college and consequently take the PSAT, SAT, and Advanced Placement tests. But that still does not account for the decline in girls' math scores as they approach adolescence and the lingering gender differences on more inclusive standardized tests, such as those used in the National Assessment of Educational Progress. Looking at it another way, one can speculate that if all students below the 10th percentile, with its greater representation of male students, were eliminated from the NAEP calculations (as they arguably are absent from more selective testing data), then males might demonstrate even more consistently higher average achievement levels across the grades. If that were the case, then perhaps the female advantage in verbal ability would also diminish or even disappear.

Researchers have tried to comprehend the "disconnect" between girls' school grades and their test performance, particularly in math. One plausi-

ble explanation is that achievement tests typically use a multiple-choice format and place a high premium on speed and strategic guessing, skills more
commonly observed among boys. Mathematics courses, on the other hand,
present more complex and personally relevant problems and place a premium on sustained reasoning, skills more common among girls. In such
countries as the Netherlands, England, and Australia, which use a different
test format and require students to solve several long math problems, girls
fare considerably better.[13]

As the AAUW has more recently documented, the main area in which
the gender gap continues to disfavor girls is technology, specifically the use
of computers. Similar to advanced mathematics, a working familiarity with
information technology is fast becoming a filter for screening subsequent
career options. Such knowledge is now a strong asset in an increasingly
competitive job market. Yet females are underrepresented in computer-
learning environments, from computer camps to enrollments in secondary
school classes and continuing into college and graduate school. The data
confirm this reluctance and ambivalence. On the Advanced Placement
computer science A exam, which covers the first college semester of calculus, girls account for only 17 percent of test takers (down from a high of 22
percent in 1995), and their average scores are 0.44 points lower than boys'
(up from a 0.40-point difference in 1997). The proportionate decline in
girls taking the exam and the widening gap in average scores reverses years
of a narrowing trend. Similar to the AP calculus exams, boys proportionately outnumber girls among those receiving the highest grade of five.

The choice of college majors and subsequently of careers reflect these
disparities. According to the College Board, only 18 percent of those planning to major in engineering in 2000 were women. Among those planning
a major in computer or information sciences, only 22 percent were women,
a sharp decline from a peak of 37 percent in 1984. Although women earn
42.5 percent of awarded doctorates overall, including 64 percent in education and 54 percent in the social sciences, they receive only 14.8 percent in
engineering.[14]

In some respects, this is a startling reversal of history. Many of the computer pioneers were women. During World War II, the military assigned
women, known as the "ENIAC girls," to program the first operational computer. In the 1960s Grace Hopper was largely responsible for developing
COBOL, the first widely used programming language. In the 1970s, when
computer science surfaced as a discipline on college campuses, women
were counted among the early students. In the nascent days of the industry,
65 percent of computer operators were women. Fast-forward to the present
and the contrast is striking. Female students who enroll in computer
classes in high school or in community colleges are significantly more

likely than boys to be found in clerical and data-entry classes. Yet at the same time, high school coursework is a critical factor for girls in their career choice at the more advanced levels. A multiyear study of computer science students at Carnegie Mellon University, the site of one of the premier programs in the country, found that for almost one-third of the women interviewed, a high school programming course had been the key element in their decision to major in computer science. The same was true for only 9 percent of the male students, for whom the appeal of computing had begun much earlier, at home or with their friends. According to a 1999 survey, there is a 4:1 male-to-female ratio in the information technology profession, where women's earnings are 85 percent that of men. The gaps consistently appear across a range of job categories and are unrelated to job experience.[15]

These figures taken as a whole present a troubling image of gendered exclusion arguably driven less by overt discrimination than by culture, including the culture of university programs themselves. Perhaps it is not merely a question of math and science or of being outnumbered by males. Women have overcome those drawbacks in such traditionally male dominated fields as law and medicine, where the attraction for some and perhaps many women has been the potential for helping people and making a difference in society. Engineering programs are finally beginning to recognize that potential and are developing more real-world orientated teaching strategies under more flexible accreditation guidelines. Whether these changes will increase the number of female students remains to be seen.[16]

More progress undoubtedly needs to be made before females demonstrate test performance and participation equal to males' in certain math and science-based areas that serve as gateways to high-prestige and high-salaried careers. At the same time, more attention needs to be placed on developing literacy skills among male students, particularly those who are sorted out early in their school years and never make it into the pool of high-stakes test takers. It goes without saying that verbal reasoning and writing skills are critical to effective participation in an information-based society.

## VOICE, SELF-ESTEEM, AND INNER CONFIDENCE

Researchers have shown and the numbers prove that girls as a group have made significant academic strides since Carol Gilligan, the Sadkers, and the American Association of University Women made their findings. Yet the first-generation researchers all tried to assess personal traits that might arguably bear on academic success. Obviously the constructs they used, such as voice and self-esteem, lend themselves to varying definitions and methods of measurement. For that reason alone, the link between these concepts and academic achievement remains unproven with any degree of certainty. Gilligan herself in recent years has admitted, "It feels palpably different. . . . Girls are [now] visible and audible in this culture."[17]

Subsequent research presents a textured and hazy picture. For example, Gilligan's "loss of voice"—that is, decline in the ability to speak one's experience and the negative consequences of that loss on self-esteem—may in fact be less specific to girls and perhaps more sensitive to context than Gilligan perceived. The widely cited research of the psychologist Carol Harter suggests that both girls and boys are more or less comfortable expressing their opinion depending on whether they are speaking to friends or classmates of the same sex, or to their parents, teachers, or to members of the opposite sex. Meanwhile, it could be the case that "gender orientation" rather than sex itself is the significant factor. Girls who hold a stereotypical female orientation may be particularly uncomfortable articulating their views in school and in social situations with boys. Of course, the definition of female orientation remains open to question. Nevertheless, one can reasonably speculate that girls who value a broader role than traditionally allowed for women in society or who embrace less clearly defined gender bounds may do so with greater ease regardless of context. Harter warns against a "singular focus on enhancing girls' voices." As she notes, there are also boys in the "silent ghetto" of the classroom.[18]

There is likewise evidence that self-esteem or the individual's evaluation of him- or herself may vary across race, culture, and class not just for girls but also for boys. Although self-esteem admittedly is not the sole construct associated with emotional well-being, it seems to be the one most closely associated with such traits as goal directedness, high achievement, motivation, competitiveness, and assertiveness. Most cultures, including our own, still tend to identify these traits with men. It is also widely believed that these traits relate to academic success. The AAUW's study in 1991, measuring self-esteem, found that white girls were the least likely to report that the assertion "I am happy the way I am" was "always true." Hispanic girls were the most likely to respond positively to that assertion in the elementary grades and African-American girls in middle and high school. More boys than girls agreed with the statement at all grade levels. The AAUW concluded that self-esteem is low among white girls and diminishes among Hispanic girls as they enter adolescence.[19] Yet white girls, as a group, demonstrate higher academic performance than minority girls, while boys, as a group, appear to be failing at least on some measures relative to girls. If self-esteem is positively related to academic success, then there is something patently peculiar about these irreconcilable findings.

The inconsistency here may stem in part from the measurement technique itself. Perhaps self-reporting is particularly sensitive to differences in the way girls and boys express emotion rather than actual emotional differences. For boys the responses may reflect a false bravado, while girls may feel more comfortable revealing their insecurities, similar to their reporting on math and science. If so, the argument can be made that boys suffer more in the end by hiding their insecurities behind a mask of self-assurance. As the rash of school violence among adolescent boys in recent years has painfully demonstrated, repressed emotions can ultimately blow up with horrific results. Another possibility is that the way the researchers phrased the statement may have skewed the responses. They may have elicited evidence of a personal type of self-esteem related to family and community affirmation but unrelated to such traits as self-confidence and efficacy typically associated with success in school.[20]

A more recent meta-analysis of more than two hundred studies specifically examining "global self-esteem"—the self as a whole rather than specific domains such as family or social situations—suggests that gender differences are perhaps not as large as the AAUW study indicated, nor is the outlook on female self-esteem as bleak as the AAUW and others have maintained. Here the researchers found no evidence of a "drastic decline" among teenage girls but only small gender differences that grow somewhat larger during adolescence and reverse themselves as adulthood approaches. The researchers point out the potential costs of the cultural belief that boys have markedly higher self-esteem, while the trait plummets in adolescent girls. On the one hand, the stereotype can create a self-fulfilling prophecy in girls. On the other, the mistaken implication that boys do not suffer any self-esteem problems works to the detriment of boys who do. For example, one most significant source of both self-esteem and social status among adolescent boys is athletics. Those who are not athletically inclined or interested in sports therefore may be viewed as not measuring up to this image of masculinity, and that public perception might lead to low self-esteem.[21]

Subsequent research on various measures of inner confidence, which arguably correlates to some extent with self-esteem, has yielded even less definitive results. On a 1997 national survey of students in grades seven through twelve, half of the teachers reported that girls appeared to have "more inner confidence" in achieving their goals than boys, while a third believed that boys were more confident. The gender disparities varied by family income, growing larger as community income decreased while nearly equalizing where the estimated household income was $50,000 or higher. Perhaps disadvantaged boys receive less affirmation from the school setting than other students. A parallel survey of students found that minority boys from urban schools showed the lowest confidence in achieving their future goals as did Hispanics as a group. Among white students, the responses were consistent regardless of sex. The study looked at class participation as a measure of confidence. Boys and girls almost equally enjoyed participating in class (62 percent vs. 65 percent). Minority girls enjoyed it the most (69 percent) and minority boys the least (56 percent). Minority girls also appeared to be the most cautious, raising their hands only when they were certain that they knew the right answer. White boys were the least cautious.[22]

These findings taken together underscore the limitations inherent in Gilligan's, the Sadkers', and the AAUW's research. The questions they posed apparently were more complex and the conclusions they drew less certain than initially believed.

## CLASSROOM INTERACTION

The level at which students participate in classroom discussion is governed in part by factors operating in the classroom itself. Proponents of single-sex education for girls maintain that coeducational schools and classrooms do not provide girls with an overall climate that is conducive to learning. Drawing on the Sadkers' research, one piece of this argument focuses on classroom verbal interaction, including communications between teachers and students and among students themselves. In coeducational classrooms, we are told, boys monopolize the linguistic space and the attention of the teacher. It follows that a classroom without boys affords girls greater confidence in their abilities and permits them to develop communication and abstract thinking skills.

Early studies, particularly from Britain, support the Sadkers' observations and conclusions.[23] Others, though, reveal that teacher-student interaction is not merely a matter of gender differences. Teacher attention in itself is not necessarily a positive sign of acceptance or affirmation. As any teacher will attest, at least some of the attention given to boys is in fact directed toward maintaining discipline, communicating appropriate procedures and behavior, or—especially in the early primary grades—just containing their high energy levels.[24] "Boy advocates" and particularly proponents of boys' schools validly argue that schools should "channel" that energy rather than contain it, as coeducational settings tend to do.

There is no doubt that the classroom climate is now more open to girls and respectful of their views than it was two and three decades ago, when the Sadkers collected their data. Again, their findings and the widespread recognition they received stimulated a wealth of research, along with innumerable programs that have increased public and professional awareness, sensitized teachers to gender equity issues, and raised students' expectations for equitable treatment. But these changes also demand a reassessment of earlier findings. Moreover, any conclusions drawn even from more recent classroom observations are confounded by a number of factors beyond gender. Significant among these are student characteristics (race, ethnicity, socioeconomic background, ability, achievement levels), subject matter, grade level, class size, teacher attitudes and behavior, the structure of the activity (small or large group, science lab, problem solving, theoretical discussion), and the gender dominance of the group (male or female). And of course, it is not just the quantity of interactions that counts; at least as important is the substance of the interactions.[25]

It is tempting to dismiss the issue of "linguistic space" as a remnant of a bygone era or as simply a construct incapable of being measured in any meaningful way. Nonetheless, the issue appears to remain salient at least in those intellectual domains traditionally considered "masculine" where women's participation or achievement has lagged. At the middle and secondary school levels, researchers have focused on math and science in an effort to understand why women are underrepresented in high school physics and calculus classes, college technology majors, and careers in the physical sciences and engineering. A number of these studies were conducted in the 1970s and 1980s, yet more recent findings continue to support earlier conclusions.

In a study from the early 1990s among seventh- to twelfth-grade students enrolled in various science courses, researchers found that female students were more likely to respond on task and raise their hand rather than call out or respond in a way that was not germane to the task. Yet teachers were four times less likely to ask high-level questions of girls than of boys. By asking girls low-level questions, the researchers concluded, teachers were sending them negative cues about their ability level while conveying the opposite to boys. The researchers suggest that over the course of time, as female students move from one science class to another, they may attribute their success to luck and their failure to low ability, leading them ultimately to exercise less effort and to avoid enrolling in science classes at higher levels. A more recent study produced similar evidence from sixth- through eighth-grade students participating in a performance-based science program. Boys were found to volunteer more than girls, so teachers called on them more frequently. In a related study of the same students, boys handled the equipment more, "hogging the resources," as the researchers put it, leaving girls involved in such passive behavior as making suggestions and taking notes.[26]

This phenomenon seems to extend to other male-typed areas of the curriculum. For example, boys have been found to dominate computer-based cooperative learning activities. In a study of fifth- and sixth-grade students randomly assigned to same- and mixed-gender classes, students had significantly different experiences depending on the gender composition of the group. Boys tended to become more verbally active and girls less so in mixed-gender groups and particularly where there was an equal ratio of girls and boys. The researchers explained these differences on the basis of "status characteristics." In mixed-gender groups, males are presumed to have higher social status. Consequently, they are more active and exert more influence in the overall interaction process than female students. On the other hand, girls in the study more actively sought and more successfully obtained help from their peers in groups that were either all-female, predominantly female, or equally male and female. Similar findings emerge from other studies of girls and boys working together with computers.[27]

These findings obviously hold implications for such areas of the curriculum as math, science, and technology that are more generally regarded as "masculine" and in which the gender gap remains to some degree. They also present a paradox regarding small-group collaborative activities. Educators have come to recognize the educational, motivational, and social value of collaborative talk, in which pupils listen to each other and build on each other's ideas. Schools increasingly encourage these activities in part to accommodate the arguably preferred learning style of many female students. There is some evidence that girls in fact perform better in cooperative rather than competitive groups and express more positive attitudes toward subjects like geography and computers when working in this mode.[28] But at the same time, collaborative learning in mixed-gender groups may produce the unanticipated effect of "freezing girls out" from the learning process in some of the very areas in which they need the most encouragement to develop their potential.

There is yet another aspect to this occurrence that seems to get lost in the literature on classroom interaction. Boys are socially programmed into a conventional masculine mold that identifies success with achievement through competition and independent work. They are therefore less inclined to seek help or to work collaboratively with other students unless asked to do so. Yet research indicates that boys in fact show the greatest gains in performance from collaborative learning activities, particularly when grouped only with boys. Male students working in this manner have shown better success in problem solving and greater persistence in reaching their learning goals than students working in competitive groups or individually. This suggests that students who arguably dominate discussion may set themselves at a disadvantage, particularly in small groups. By denying others the opportunity to contribute to the task at hand, they deny themselves the benefit of those views and consequently inhibit their own learning.[29] Relating these findings to the single-sex schooling question, both girls and boys may derive educational benefits when they work coopera-tively with members of their own sex.

Reports that male students dominate classroom discussion in certain contexts resonate deeply among those of us who teach young women and men at the far end of their formal education. Lani Guinier's study at the University of Pennsylvania School of Law in the 1990s lent credence to this belief. Female students expressed feelings of alienation and silencing that negatively affected their sense of self-worth and for some their academic performance. More systematic observations across eight law schools like-wise found a gender-skewed classroom dynamic. Of course, the specific na-ture of legal education, especially the intense questioning of the Socratic method, produces a unique type of interaction in the law school classroom. Yet researcher Catherine Krupnick's classroom observations from elemen-tary through law school over more than two decades support these findings. In particular, her study at Harvard College in the mid-1980s and her later observations of freshman classes at a former women's college that had re-cently admitted men produced similar evidence of male dominance. This was so even though females outnumbered males and it was particularly ev-ident in classes in which students, rather than the teacher, controlled the conversation. On the other hand, female students in the Harvard group spoke almost three times as much when taught by women as they did when taught by men. Similar research in high school classrooms found that while males controlled discussion in math and science and often in social science classes, females took the lead in English, a subject conventionally marked as "female" and one in which boys traditionally have lagged behind girls in interest and achievement.[30]

So although girls may be outstripping boys on most indexes of academic performance and enrolling in college in record numbers, as a group they remain in certain contexts at what Krupnick calls the "bottom of the con-versational heap—some passive, others competing for the scarce resource of conversational space." This appears to be especially true in settings in which men dominate either numerically or historically. Researchers have suggested a number of reasons for this occurrence—that men tend to have a more competitive style of talking, are more willing to take risks, and are more prone to respond spontaneously; or that women are more vul-nerable to interruptions, are more comfortable speaking in small groups, tend to cluster their talk in short "runs" between longer stretches of male talk, or need time to prepare a reasoned response. These rationalizations suggest that "rewards" for classroom participation may simply be a matter of "quick" rather than "deep" thinking. They also suggest that the dis-course rules more common among girls are destined to fail in a competi-tive arena because girls tend to surrender individual power in the interest of group success, a strategy that boys typically interpret as a sign of weakness.[31]

The linguist Deborah Tannen's popularized work on the differential use of language by males and females, although questioned in some feminist circles for its air of "linguistic determinism," pushes the discussion into broader view. According to Tannen, males tend to engage in ritual opposition, with a blatant statement followed by challenge and argument. Women, she tells us, find this communicative style antithetical to the way that they prefer to learn. In observing college students, Tannen has found that females and males as a group have different "ethics of participation." Students who speak frequently in class, many of them men, assume that those who "remain silent have nothing to say," while others who "rein themselves in" assume that the talkers are "selfish and hoggish."[32] That may be so, but in the end the nonparticipants—whether women, other minorities, or less verbally assertive men— are denied an equal opportunity to engage in the give and take of discussion. Yet that kind of exchange is critical to developing more abstract thinking skills and mastering the vocabulary and thought processes of the discipline.

Certainly one can argue that Krupnick's data are somewhat outdated, and both she and Tannen drew their conclusions largely from college classes. One might expect that the post–Title IX generation of female students would prove more comfortable and competitive in mixed-sex classrooms. Nevertheless the observations reported by the Sadkers, Guinier, Krupnick, and Tannen have a qualified ring of truth when I consider my own experiences teaching in two contrasting academic situations. The first is the law school setting, where males historically have dominated the academy and the profession. The second is a graduate program in education, where gender dominance in the profession itself varies somewhat by level and discipline.

Over the past decade and a half, I have observed a gradual increase in class participation among my female law students as the incoming classes have become more gender balanced. Women as a group now appear more comfortable in volunteering to join in the discussion. They also demonstrate greater ease and confidence when I call upon them. Nevertheless, there is something decidedly different about their interaction style when compared with that of men. Proportionately more males formulate their own questions and comments, and challenge me as well as other students. Female students, on the other hand, are far less likely to raise their hand to ask a question, offer a comment, or challenge anyone. They tend to save their questions and comments for an after-class one-on-one informal chat with me, although even this is a rare occurrence. Nor can I recall a female student who has ever tried to control classroom discussion or totally absorb my attention as male students occasionally do. I have observed a pattern similar to females among minority students of both sexes. Perhaps these differences have something to do with status and power, which are often but not always related to sex. Many of my colleagues have confirmed these observations.

One wonders whether this phenomenon is merely a continuation of what occurs from early childhood through secondary school, or whether it is unique to the competitive atmosphere of certain traditionally male-dominated fields of study such as law. Or perhaps it is a bit of both. There is still some evidence in the research that boys tend to ask more questions and shout out more answers than do girls. Yet girls' questions, while less frequent, are typically more constructive. The psychologists Eleanor Maccoby and Carol Nagy Jacklin have noted the prevalence of male dominance in mixed-sex interactions even among preschool children. Among boys, social interactions tend to create a pecking order, whereas girls engage in more turn taking, with all group members participating in decisions. Talking serves a noticeably different function for each group. Girls use speech to "maintain relationships of closeness and equality," to "criticize others in acceptable ways," and to "interpret accurately the speech of others," the researchers tell us. Boys, on the other hand, use speech to "attract and maintain an audience," to "assert one's position of dominance," and to "assert one's self when others have the floor." Maccoby and Jacklin suggest that while mixed-sex encounters may offer boys "confidence-building leadership experiences," this may not be the case for girls. They question whether leadership experience in all-female groups might better prepare girls to "hold their own" in mixed-sex occupational settings as adults.[33]

But something else is operating at the adult level beyond the residue of childhood interactions. As Tannen points out, "No one's conversational style is absolute; everyone's style changes in response to the context and others' styles."[34] For example, the same students, both male and female, who are "ghosts" in large lecture classes are often far more visible and verbal in small seminars, where the pace is slower, the discussion is more reflective, the opportunities for student talk are more frequent, and there is "nowhere to hide." It could also be the case that only students who have a certain degree of comfort with engaging in class discussion enroll in seminar classes in the first instance. Yet I have observed the same behavior patterns in nonseminar classes with lower enrollment.

I cannot help but compare my law school observations with a more mixed experience in the early 1980s, when I taught education law in two separate programs within a graduate school of education. In the regular degree program, the students were mainly midcareer professionals studying full-time toward a master's degree in education. A smaller number were enrolled in the doctoral program, and an even smaller number were law students participating as cross-registrants. Women dominated the student body, as they did the profession, and participated at least as actively as men even in large lecture classes. Male students rarely tried to take over the discussion, but then again neither did the females.

At the same time, I also taught the law segment in a summer certificate program for high-level college and university administrators. In that case, men numerically dominated the student body (by about four to one) as well as the professional ranks they represented. They also dominated classroom discussion in much the same way as the law students I have since encountered. They participated actively and they challenged me as well as each other. The women typically took a back seat but were more apt to come up after class to share a thought or ask a question, as did the men. I was teaching similar subject matter in the same classrooms at the same institution, but with a different gender ratio, professional mix, and gender-based status characteristics that evoked different verbal interactions and different classroom dynamics.

Again, the question of classroom interaction and linguistic space is not simply a matter of gendered language styles or tendencies. It is also at least in part a matter of contextual factors. How the two intersect in today's coeducational elementary and secondary classrooms within different instructional settings and among diverse groups of students obviously merits further exploration. The short-term effects on girls' attitudes and achievement, especially in math and science, and perhaps boys' attitudes and achievement in English and foreign languages, as well as the long-term effects on advanced course taking and career choices, present interesting questions for future research. At the same time we cannot deny that there remains an overall gender polarity that tends to position "attitude" (questioning, challenging) as masculine in opposition to "academic application" (diligence, pleasure in learning) as feminine. Yet this dichotomy is both false and damaging. Attitude is useless without application and at the same time essential to deep learning.[35] That being said, educators are challenged to create learning environments that encourage all students, regardless of gender, to develop a comfort and affinity for both behaviors across the curriculum.

## SAMENESS AND DIFFERENCE

Perhaps the most contentious question inevitably raised in discussions over single-sex schooling is whether girls and boys are in fact different in cognitive abilities and learning preferences. If so, then do they require distinct educational approaches? The popular literature has drawn these arguable differences out in detail. But there is also the baffling observation that although girls now surpass boys in school performance, they still lag behind them in testing programs where the academic and professional stakes are high. However we look at it, it seems that girls and boys interact with the educational environment in different ways.

The obvious question is "Why?" Is it simply a matter of biology? Are commentators like Michael Gurian right after all when they assert that girls and boys are simply hardwired differently, accounting for their different interests and academic performances? Do infants enter the world programmed either for "caretaking" or "warmaking"? If so, how do these innate differences affect their learning, and where should schools intervene? Can specific teaching strategies overcome innate cognitive "deficiencies," as Gurian suggests?[36] What role, if any, does socialization play in creating or enhancing the development of certain abilities and learning styles in girls and boys? How does prior experience affect performance? And even given observable differences, are these small compared with the differences within each sex, as many social scientists have suggested?

The answers to these questions go well beyond the scope of this book. The etiology of gender differences spans a massive literature. At most I can offer a sense of research trends while focusing on those traits related to the most commonly observed performance and achievement differences between girls and boys. Meanwhile, it should be kept in mind that the evidence on the sources of differences remains somewhat circumstantial, merely suggestive, and nondefinitive.

Until recently, feminists and others strongly resisted research on sex differences. They believed that the issue itself was unscientific, politically motivated, and inevitably harmful to women's social equality. Even those who ascribed to distinct female "ways of knowing" avoided the question of innate differences. For them, it was largely a matter of social conditioning, discrimination, and denied opportunities. That position is beginning to shift as new statistical techniques and technology have made research findings more reliable. With the exception of a few "die-hards" at either extreme, the current consensus appears to be that individuals are shaped both by nature and by nurture. There exists reasonable evidence that social, experiential, and biological factors interact in many of the differences found between males and females. Nevertheless, the relative strength of each of these factors, the magnitude of differences themselves, and the degree to which individuals can enhance their innate abilities through practice and training remain subjects of intense controversy.[37]

Over the past several years, this discussion has filtered through the pages of the news media, where the question of hormonal influence on learning and behavior has become a topic of considerable public interest. Brain research has given scientific legitimacy to the belief that the structure of the brain differs slightly from birth, depending on the amount of testosterone present at that point. It is believed that this variation may influence such conventionally identified male traits as aggression and competitiveness. Other studies have suggested that hormonal changes in puberty may influence phonological processing skills, which in turn, may account for the higher percentage of male dyslexics particularly identified past childhood. Since the late 1980s functional magnetic resonance imaging (MRI) scans, along with electroencephalograms (EEGs), have enabled scientists to view how men and women process information and how their brains develop from childhood through adolescence and into adulthood. Studies now document the more rapid maturation of the female brain, as well as sex differences in the regions of the brain activated for phonological processing (related to language and reading skills) and spatial performance (related to mathematical skills).[38]

Conclusions drawn from these studies are tentative although increasingly compelling. Yet despite the differences that seem to be emerging, there is widespread agreement that innate abilities respond to outside influences which either reinforce their strength or counteract their weaknesses. Maccoby and Jacklin made this point clear almost three decades ago in *The Psychology of Sex Differences*. They too found that girls have greater verbal ability and boys excel in the visual-spatial and quantitative realms. Yet they also suggested that where one sex is more biologically disposed to perform certain tasks, this difference in ability influences popular beliefs and expectations about the sexes. As a result, innate tendencies help to create a "cultural lore" that children pick up from their environment. Hence they adapt themselves further to a normative view grounded in biological reality. At the same time, both home and school reinforce the initial differences by providing children from an early age with activities and experiences suitable to their perceived talents.[39]

Maccoby more recently has reaffirmed that girls and boys have different growth timetables, not only in language development but in the "inhibitory capacities" underlying the regulation of emotions. From infancy boys also have a higher basal metabolism rate and, far more than girls, "are excited by threats, challenges, and competition." Yet she again makes clear that humans have an extraordinary ability to learn and adapt to their sociocultural context.[40]

Girls and boys engage in different pastimes and hobbies that provide them with different language opportunities and place them on progressively divergent learning trajectories. The 1997 Educational Testing Service report demonstrates that girls engage in such leisure activities as taking classes in music, art, language, and dance, as well as talking and doing things with their parents. Boys more frequently report that they participate in sports and use computers. As a result of these different socialization patterns, children develop different ways of responding and making sense of their environment. That, in turn, affects how and what they learn as well as what behaviors are appropriate for them. Meanwhile, the higher energy levels and less advanced verbal ability commonly found in boys at the beginning of schooling create in many but not all school communities a cultural expectation of antiacademic behavior among males and studentlike behavior among females. As the psychologist William Pollack, author of *Real Boys*, has remarked, "By the time boys come out of K, 1, 2 they already have a belief they are not as good at reading and that reading is for girls—and they start to give up." In this way, the school and the home unintentionally collaborate in facilitating a certain normative behavior. Nature and nurture thus reinforce each other in a continuous cycle.[41]

The use of computers is a clear example of this phenomenon. Technology is generally considered a male endeavor related to math and science. The computer "geek" is now a well-positioned male stereotype. Boys have far more opportunities to develop a familiarity and comfort with computers just through play activity at an early age. Across the globe, there is a rich market in computer games that are designed to appeal to boys. Part of that appeal may have some connection with boys' shorter attention span and the rapid-fire sequences that many popular games present. But American society also socializes girls and boys in very different ways. Boys' attraction to these games undoubtedly has much to do with the common war scenarios, physical adventures, sports, and images of male power that reflect cultural stereotypes of manliness. The market has not responded in a similar way to activities and subjects that might appeal to girls, including women's sports.

Girls, whether consciously or subconsciously, tend to recognize computer games as sexist and excessively violent. It is therefore not surprising that by the time girls enter school, they demonstrate less interest in computer technology than boys. With computers as with observed patterns in math and science, girls as a group tend to develop less of what social learning theorists call "self-efficacy"—that is, a belief that they can carry out the task successfully. This problem is not unique to the United States but has been documented in other countries, including England and Australia.[42]

Nonetheless, if we look beyond the violence and misogyny that pervade many of the computer as well as video games targeted toward boys, these games may have a positive side to them. In an odd and undoubtedly unintentional way, they provide boys with a sense of "movement," along with the ability to explore "unfriendly spaces" and take risks that may in fact enhance their self-confidence, competitiveness, and sense of control over their environment. These are all traits that will serve them well in the adult world. But they would serve girls equally well and yet game producers, and society as a whole, have failed to address the potential of action games for girls. As one commentator has put it, perhaps girls need to play games where "Barbie gets to kick butt."[43] The same gender dichotomy manifests itself in toys targeted toward girls or boys, from Barbie again at one extreme to GI Joe and the Power Ranger action figures at the other. Then again, perhaps girls would feel no attraction to or connection with a Barbie who in fact "kicks butt."

In the meantime, there is some suggestion that computer games can potentially foster higher-level cognitive skills that may transfer to more demanding learning environments. Many of the games popular among boys require planning and troubleshooting abilities. They engage the player in learning a formal system and manipulating its features to solve problems. These skills are similar to those used in math problem solving and in physics, for example. If that is the case, then the gender differences in recreational computer use may have some effect on the continued differences in math achievement and advanced course enrollment in math and science despite the concerted efforts of educators to counter that historical trend.[44]

Boys are believed to have more developed spatial visualization skills than girls, although the differences appear to be small. They can better visualize two- and three-dimensional objects in space and rotate them in their minds. This ability is thought to facilitate performance especially in math but also in science. The gender differences seem most pronounced beginning in early adolescence at the same time that certain sex-related differences in mathematics achievement also appear. Researchers have further found strong and consistent gender differences, as early as grades one through three, in the strategies used to solve math problems. Girls tend to use more "concrete" strategies, like counting and modeling, while boys are more apt to use more "abstract" strategies that reflect deeper conceptual understanding of important ideas on which further mathematical learning is based. These early differences may relate to those found in performance on complex mathematical tasks, such as problem solving, in early adolescence. But this is also the time when girls appear to question their own competencies.[45] The question remains whether girls are unsure of their ability because of their lower performance or whether they perform poorly because they are unsure of their ability.

Studies conducted in the 1970s found that boys were significantly more confident than girls with mathematics and believed that it was more useful.[46] Perhaps boys' innate ability has created a popular belief that math is a "boy" subject. Boys in turn respond by living up to the stereotype, while girls conform to the contrary view. Yet as these preconceptions have weakened in the intervening years, girls' performance has indeed improved. The fact that increased intervention strategies on the part of schools, along with changing attitudes in society, have narrowed the gap favoring boys in math and science indicates that ability in these areas is changeable and not carved in biological stone.

There is also evidence that at least part of the achievement gap in math is due to boys' higher ability at math-fact retrieval. This split-second calculation difference may free up mental capacity for other kinds of math problems, especially on timed tests. It could further be associated with boys' more impulsive behavior in testing situations, as well as their inclination to take risks. In any event, it may bear on boys' general performance advantage on multiple-choice questions. It may also at least partially explain girls' lower performance on achievement tests as compared with class work. Nonetheless, research findings indicate that whatever the source of this ability, it is not genetic and improves significantly with practice. At the same time, girls tend to perform better on verbal-processing tasks where the gender differences are greatest at the low ends of the score distribution. That explains in part the larger differences favoring girls in school grades and in general testing programs such as the National Assessment of Educational Progress, in which everyone participates, compared with more highly selective tests such as the SAT I or Advanced Placement exams.[47]

But why does the gender gap favoring girls in reading become progressively wider as students move through the grades even though boys presumably catch up in brain maturational levels by the end of secondary school? One plausible reason is that female students as a group have longer attention spans, and attentiveness has been found to be a salient predictor of literacy achievement, although literacy achievement may even more strongly reduce inattentive behavior. The interrelation between the two may, in fact, create a vicious cycle for some boys. In recent years, both the curriculum and assessment measures, not only in the United States but also in other English-speaking countries, have increasingly focused on activities that require higher levels of sustained attention than in the past. The emphasis has shifted away from the acquisition of knowledge toward the process of learning and the application of facts in different contexts. In lieu of short-answer and "check-the-box" activities, schools now present students with tasks that require more advanced verbal reasoning skills, such as writing extended prose and completing independent research projects, activities in which girls have a decided maturational advantage. So what appears as a widening gender gap in achievement may be partially a function of changes in schooling itself.[48]

In addition, a critical socialization factor that contributes to boys' underachievement in reading and language skills is their relative reluctance to read. Researchers have found that, from an early age, boys tend to perceive

English as a "feminine" subject. Perhaps this view comes from their weaker verbal skills at school entry, or from the fact that women usually teach young children how to read, or from the emphasis in the curriculum on reading and writing fictional stories presenting personalized themes that do not necessarily interest many boys.[49] And although the noted propensity of boys to engage in prolonged computer and video activities arguably enhances their skills in other areas, it may seriously detract from developing their reading ability.

## RACE, CULTURE, AND SOCIAL CLASS

It is a rather odd circumstance that much of the debate about gender and schooling proceeds as if girls and boys were each members of distinct and cohesive groups. One gets the sense that except for those studies using large national databases, most look at students who are primarily white and economically secure. What seems to get lost in the push toward gender equity and the frequent one-upmanship is the powerful influence of race, culture, and social class on the present and future lives of vast numbers of American students. No constructive discussion of single-sex education, or any educational reform, for that matter, can take place without factoring in and sorting through these important differences.

Concerns over whether boys or girls excel in math and science or foreign languages lose much of their immediacy in comparison with the academic and social desolation experienced by poor and minority students. Only by looking at the surrounding demographic data can we clearly comprehend the depths of these problems and the intricacies of gender equity as it interconnects with a complex constellation of mutually enforcing factors, particularly in urban schools. And only then can we fully appreciate the growing interest in single-sex education among urban educators and parents who desperately search for a remedy.

African Americans and Hispanics now account for nearly one-third of schoolchildren nationwide. Demographers predict that this figure will grow to two-thirds over the next fifteen years, particularly with the rapid growth in the Hispanic population. At the same time, in cities across America the number of these children living in impoverished neighborhoods has risen to staggering levels, reaching 97 percent for African Americans in Washington, D.C., and Atlanta, 93 percent in Baltimore, and 86 percent in Detroit. Throughout the 1990s, the number of children in working-poor families increased from 4.3 million to 5.8 million despite the economic boom in the latter part of the decade. Many of these children are minority group members. As those reaching the middle class have fled major cities, they have left behind blighted neighborhoods where churches and community organizations no longer possess a leadership base for defining and monitoring norms and values.[50]

Although public attention has focused on minority and especially African-American males, I will put that question aside for the moment and examine the case of inner-city girls, who often demonstrate extraordinary resilience and self-confidence in the face of adverse circumstances. Yet like their male counterparts, they too succumb frequently to negative social forces that impair their ability to succeed academically. Empirical studies have shown that race and social class mediate the schooling experience and influence how students perceive its importance to their future lives. Among disadvantaged minority girls, the gender gap in math, science, and technology is merely one of the compelling challenges that they face.

For many of them, the developmentally harmful influences of early disadvantage manifest themselves in teenage motherhood. Although it is true that teen pregnancy has declined over the past decade, almost one million adolescents still become pregnant each year, resulting in nearly half a million teen births, 83 percent from low-income families. And although birth rates have dropped by 23 percent for African Americans and 5 percent for Hispanics between the ages of fifteen and seventeen, the overall numbers are still dramatically higher than for whites. Minority adolescent girls, particularly those with poor basic skills, feel more vulnerable to male pressure. Viewing life through the lens of few available options, they perceive their economic and social situations as hopeless and resort to early and repeat motherhood as a source of competence and significance. Unfortunately, they soon learn the realities of raising children on their own without the emotional and financial support of a husband.[51]

Of course, it is easy to overgeneralize about cultural values and practices within racial and ethnic groups. Yet between- and within-group differences at times have a significant impact on how individuals live their lives. Hispanics, for example, vary not only in their country of origin but also in their socioeconomic background, migration status, generational status (first, second, or third), and levels of acculturation and assimilation. Teen pregnancy rates reflect these differences. There are twice as many teenage mothers among U.S.-born Hispanics as among foreign-born Hispanics. There are also considerable differences in pregnancy rates among subgroups of Mexicans, Puerto Ricans, and other Central and South American populations.[52] African Americans likewise differ depending upon whether their families lived in the United States or draw their more recent origins under British rule in the Caribbean. For decades following the end of slavery in the states, American society marginalized and displaced African-American males and left women to bear the burden of keeping the family on course. Caribbean families, having lived through a different emancipation experience, tend to embrace more traditional family structures and values, especially for their daughters.

Nonetheless, members of these groups still share some salient cultural values. For many Hispanic girls, the adolescent quest is not to develop individuality but to remain interdependent with their families. Traditional values of *marianismo*—honoring self-sacrifice and nurturance—further push them into early marriage and pregnancies. The impact on their future lives often proves devastating. Only seven out of ten teen mothers complete high school, and they are less likely to go on to college than other young women. Set on a predictable path of low-wage jobs at best and unemployment at worst, they continue a cycle that perpetuates itself into the next generation.[53]

Research shows that children born to teenage mothers are more prone to have low birth weight, which places them at risk for physical disabilities including mental retardation and chronic respiratory problems, as well as later diagnosis for dyslexia, hyperactivity disorder, and other learning disabilities. Throughout their young years, they are also more often the victims of abuse and neglect. They are twice as likely to drop out of school and almost twice as likely to have a child before they are eighteen, compared with children of mothers who delay childbearing until their early twenties. The teen sons of adolescent mothers are two and one-half times as likely to end up in prison. These circumstances become magnified within the African-American community, where racism and poverty historically have required women to enter the labor market as they struggle with single parenthood. Young African-American girls share the experience of their mothers, whose tenuous relationships with men force them to work outside the home, leaving scarce time or energy for their children's educational and developmental needs.[54]

Girls also represent the fastest-growing segment of the juvenile justice population, of which two-thirds of the females are minorities. And although girls are still far less likely than boys to become involved in the system, between 1981 and 1997 the arrest rate for females age seventeen and under increased by a staggering 103 percent, compared with a 27 percent increase among males. For many girls, physical, sexual, and emotional victimization is the first step along the path leading to the juvenile justice system. A high proportion of them enter as runaways seeking to escape abusive homes.[55]

The confluence of race and social class affects minority boys in ways that are even more alarming. Nearly seven out of ten young people in secure confinement facilities and more that 75 percent of those newly admitted into state prisons are members of minority groups. Men in general have a 9 percent chance of going to prison during their lifetime, compared with 1 percent for women. For African-Americans, that chance is 16.2 percent and for Hispanics 9.4 percent, compared with 2.5 percent for whites. Sixty-three percent of jail inmates in 1996 were from racial or ethnic minorities, and 90 percent of them were male. In 1999–2000 there were more African-American men in prison than in higher education. Homicide is the leading cause of death among African-American males ages fifteen to twenty-four. In fact, their rate of death from firearms is nearly five times that of white males within the same age range. Suicide rates among African-American males also have skyrocketed, up 100 percent since 1980, with more than 95 percent of them involving the use of guns. The soaring rate of drug and alcohol abuse within this population is highly correlated with academic failure, delinquency, and accidental deaths.[56]

The debilitating effects associated with race and ethnicity, which are often linked to poverty, reveal themselves most clearly in learning deficits even before formalized schooling begins. Among three-to-five-year-olds, only 19 percent of poor children, compared with 45 percent of nonpoor, show three or more signs of emerging literacy. Among preschoolers, only 14 percent of Hispanic children, 25 percent of African Americans, and 30 percent of others can recognize all the letters of the alphabet. Hispanic children are far less likely to count to twenty or higher, while African-American children are less likely to read or pretend to read. Not surprisingly, what is widely known as the "achievement gap" appears as early as kindergarten in reading and math skills. But educational deficits typically reach a critical point during the middle school years. As poor children progressively fall farther behind in the classroom, they become far more likely to drop out of school, which in turn increases the odds of unemployment and marginal employment in the years to come.[57]

In 1999, 12.6 percent of African Americans and 28.6 percent of Hispanics between the ages of sixteen and twenty-four had dropped out of school, compared with 7.3 percent of whites. And despite the decline in dropout rates for all groups since 1972, the rate has not changed significantly for Hispanic males, due partially at least to the growing immigrant population. The problem is most acute in urban areas, where 6 percent of those between the ages of fifteen and twenty-four who were enrolled in school in 1998 dropped out, compared with a national rate of 4 percent. According to a national study of ten large school districts, African-American students were three to five times more likely than white students to be suspended or expelled from school. In San Francisco, for example, African Americans constituted 16 percent of the public school enrollment but accounted for 52 percent of students removed from school for disciplinary reasons.[58]

Thirty years of statistics from the National Assessment of Educational Progress (NAEP) confirm this troubling picture of academic downslide.

Despite overall achievement gains, the test-score gap between white and African-American students has been widening since the mid-1980s in nearly every age group and in every subject, reversing the gains made in the previous decade and a half. Results among Hispanics have been mixed. In reading and math, the differences for both groups as compared with whites across grade levels are at least 25 points. Nearly two-thirds of African-American and Hispanic fourth graders are functionally illiterate. The gaps are especially striking at the top of the achievement spectrum. Only one-tenth of those who score at the advanced level on the NAEP reading, math, and science tests are African American, Hispanic, or Native American.[59]

The disparities in test scores continue into higher education. African Americans on average score 94 points less than whites on the SAT I verbal test and 104 points less on the math. On Advanced Placement (AP) exams, African Americans score an average of 2.11, Mexican Americans 2.68, and Puerto Ricans 2.74 on a scale of 5, compared with 3.05 among white test takers. Across all groups, African-American girls score the lowest on AP exams, with an average of 2.06, while African-American boys are second-lowest at 2.21. Some of the gender disparity reflects a more selective population of males (more lower achieving girls than boys take AP exams) who constitute only 35 percent of African-American test-takers overall. African Americans likewise score the lowest among racial minorities on admissions tests to both law school and medical school. If current trends continue, African-American children now in kindergarten will be only half as likely and Hispanics one-third as likely as their white classmates to have completed college by the time they reach age twenty-nine.[60]

Another way to examine achievement differences between white and minority students is to compare statewide data with figures drawn from urban school districts that include significant populations of minority students. In Illinois, for example, while nearly two-thirds of the state's third graders in 2001 met the state standards on the prescribed reading test, barely more than one-third of the students in Chicago met that standard. The average Connecticut fourth grader that year was four times as likely as the average fourth grader in Hartford to meet the statewide goal on all three of the state's mastery tests (math, reading, and writing). The percentage of fourth graders scoring at "basic" or higher on the 1998 National Assessment of Educational Progress reading test, in urban and nonurban districts, respectively, was 47 and 75 percent in New York, 41 and 72 percent in Minnesota, and 44 and 65 percent in Maryland.[61] Add these statistics to the compelling figures on crime, dropout rates, drug abuse, teenage pregnancy, and homicide, and the educational needs of minority urban youth reach crisis proportions.

Researchers continue to debate the roots of academic failure and particularly the achievement gap between white and minority students. Aside from societal forces, much of the blame has fallen on the "residual racism" that continues to characterize many public schools. Poor facilities, inadequately trained teachers, and low expectations historically have maintained African Americans and Hispanics as an underclass in society.[62] These problems reach heightened proportions among the inner-city poor. Nevertheless, among racial minorities academic failure goes beyond poverty and the limitations of urban public schools. For reasons that have confounded educators and researchers, it shows up not only in cities but also in rural areas and even in middle-class and affluent suburbs. In Prince George's County, one of the wealthiest predominantly African-American suburban communities in the nation, the combined average SAT I score for African-American students in 2000 was 845, 30 points below average scores for Hispanics and 227 points below those of white students.[63]

Obviously something other than institutional failure or indifference is operating here. Some associate the problem with student motivation as it collides with conflicting expectations between the larger and more immediate cultures. According to the psychologist Claude Steele, part of the blame goes to the inability of public schools to develop and constantly reaffirm what he calls "academic identification"—that is, the belief that school achievement is a promising basis for self-esteem. The real culprit Steele says, is stigma—"the endemic devaluation many blacks face in our society and schools." And once "disidentification" occurs, he warns, "it can spread like the common cold. The pressure [from peers] to make it a group norm can evolve quickly and become fierce. . . . One's identity as an authentic black is held hostage, made incompatible with school identification." For Steele, the problem is not inextricably tied to poverty but cuts across social class and even race. He suggests that the sort of stigmatization suffered by African Americans also impedes the achievement of other groups in society, including lower-class whites and Hispanics, as well as women in such male-dominated fields as mathematics. He attributes their classic deficits in standardized test performance at least partially to what he calls "stereotype threat"—the risk of confirming or being judged by a negative societal stereotype about their group's intellectual ability and competence.[64]

Researchers and educators have long recognized that the sex appropriateness of academic learning varies with social class. Although success in school has gradually moved from male-identification to a more gender-neutral position among the middle and upper classes, it continues to be sex-typed as female among poor and working-class populations. This dichotomy is particularly problematic for adolescents who are in the process of trying to forge an identity. As they experiment with various "possible selves," they tap into their surrounding environment for role models, including parents and other family members, peers, and perhaps teachers and members of the community. In the normal course of events, the marginally different perceptions of these individuals will sort themselves out.

Adolescents growing up in poor minority neighborhoods, however, often receive dissonant messages that make it difficult for them to establish a stable identity. For many of them, learning to adopt the attitudes and academic practices of the school is negatively equated among their peers with "acting white." That perception places an especially heavy burden on boys for whom successful role models in the professions are rare, causing them to resist academic striving to avoid rejection from within their own community. They effectively buy into an oppositional peer-group culture that discourages academic effort. Research has shown that primarily among African-American boys, and to a lesser extent African-American girls and Hispanic boys, the correlation between self-esteem and achievement dramatically decreases over the four years of high school. Although students' self-esteem remains consistently high, their declining achievement suggests that they have developed an "imperviousness" to poor school performance and so draw their self-worth from something other than academic success. Whatever identity they form in these crucial years bears significant consequences for their adaptation to adult society and to their future life choices. Adolescents who fail to see themselves as academically competent are far less likely to have high educational and career aspirations.[65]

With differing social dynamics operating within disadvantaged minority groups, African-American boys in particular may succumb to peer pressure as well as perceived social stigma and low expectations. In doing so, they increasingly identify with other aspects of their self-concept, such as popularity and athletics. Again, in the everyday world that many African-American boys inhabit, academic engagement is frowned upon by their peers, while athletic expertise and sexual experience gain the utmost respect. Within this counterculture, hypermasculinity serves as a form of defiance and protest. At the same time, these self-defeating priorities perpetuate the myth that African-American male students are athletically superior but academically inferior. And although many minority girls do, in fact, appreciate the value of education and express lofty goals, far too many find initial identity in teen motherhood and/or marginal employment as social pressures derail their plans.[66]

The root causes of the achievement gap obviously are multifaceted. Nevertheless, the data make clear that the convergence of race, culture, and class present a complex set of social factors that reach well beyond the conventional girl-boy arguments. This combination of forces creates challenges that have proven resistant to conventional educational approaches and suggest that educators and policymakers need to consider more innovatively bold measures to effectively address the problem.

## BEYOND DIFFERENCE

The question of who is "winning" and who is "losing" in the academic race is indeed a complicated one, with multiple twists and turns that defy simple conclusions on both the "what" and the "why." Sex differences in performance are subject to wide interpretation depending on the data examined and the measures used. Gender gaps cut both ways on a wide range of indicators. Nonetheless, even those of us who feel passionately about women's equity cannot deny a simple fact. While girls still have difficulty reaching the top of the academic ladder or moving into technologically based careers, these realities, though troubling and in need of continued attention, as a matter of social policy pale in comparison to the escalating academic downslide that has caught in its reach many economically disadvantaged students, especially boys.

We should not fail to recognize that some of the lingering gender differences in school performance are attributable not merely to biology or socialization but to the more resistant academic and social problems that characterize certain groups of students whose life experiences within a given subculture work against academic achievement. The fact that the average eleventh-grade boy writes with the proficiency of the average eighth-grade girl, or that nearly two-thirds of African-American and Hispanic fourth graders are functionally illiterate, or that the dropout rate among males is 12 percent and a stunning 27.8 percent among all Hispanic students, or that males make up only 44 percent of today's college students—all these data have major implications for society. These startling numbers underscore how race, culture, and social class intersect with gender in a most particularized and magnified way that too often gets lost in the heated debate over gender and schooling.[67]

Beyond these troubling facts, research efforts to determine the precise magnitude and source of gender differences in cognitive abilities are still very much a "work in progress" despite significant advances in neuroscience, technology, and statistical techniques. Yet as popular books now display lengthy lists of "innate" sex-linked traits based in tentative research findings, there is an almost irresistible temptation to accept these assertions as scientific "truth." By focusing on the differences between girls and boys, however, we tend to ignore the variation within each group. A considerable amount of the differences observed draws from mean scores. On any given attribute, each sex falls on a normal distribution. Although the mean for one group may be higher than for the other, depending on the specific trait, there is substantial overlap between the two and the differences are small. A more recent reworking of the data used in the studies examined by Maccoby and Jacklin, for example, revealed that gender accounted for only 5 percent of the variance in spatial ability. At the same time, methodologists warn that relatively small mean differences can produce rather large differences at the tails or extremes of the distribution, which may partially account for the large proportions of males at the top and at the bottom of the achievement ladder.[68]

The obvious danger in this whole exercise is that differences in academic performance can simply be dismissed as purely a function of biology. That dismissal would surely shortchange both girls and boys, relegating each to a predestined, limited, and gender-locked future while ignoring the larger and diverse social contexts in which children are raised and educated. There is also the risk of interpreting "different" as "deficient," an approach that in the not so distant past worked to the educational and social disadvantage of women who presumptively could not measure up to the norm of "maleness."

If we take a measured approach to the available research, it appears that there are indeed some biological differences between females and males that seem to affect learning. But it also appears that educational programming can mediate to a significant degree between these differences and the equally powerful forces of sociological conditioning. Genes do not dictate our destiny but rather define a range of possibilities. The potential for realizing those possibilities can be quite large, given appropriate attention. Consequently, rather than focus on achievement test scores, a more promising approach for educators might be to examine the stages at which sex differences typically develop, all the while remembering that there are variations within each sex group. It then becomes a matter of how to improve the differential performance and maximize the potential of different populations of girls and boys across the schooling experience and across curriculum areas without falling into the pitfall of harmful stereotypes and gender essentialism. Here is where educational policy and specific intervention strategies come into play. And here is where the question of separating students by sex becomes a significant factor in the discussion.

# 6
# Legal Narratives

The policy debate over single-sex schooling versus coeducation ebbed and flowed over two centuries of women's participation in formalized schooling. Not until the second half of the twentieth century was the question gradually transformed into a series of legal conflicts. At that time, the Supreme Court's unanimous and far-reaching decision on racial segregation in *Brown v. Board of Education* became a guiding force in breaking down social and political barriers that historically excluded certain groups, including women, from equal opportunity.[1]

Over the following two decades, *Brown* inspired the civil rights and women's movements and laid the groundwork for broadscale congressional action that lent additional legal weight to the decision's promise of equality for all. Title IX of the Education Amendments of 1972 more fully realized that mandate and, together with the Fourteenth Amendment equal protection clause, became the primary vehicle for advancing equality for women in the educational arena. The symbolic and real impact of these two provisions dealt single-sex education a near-fatal blow until urban school reformers and minority communities unexpectedly revived the approach as a tool for leveling the educational playing field for boys and girls, in different ways.

In the mid-1990s the Supreme Court's decision striking down the all-male admissions policy at the Virginia Military Institute further muddied the waters in what was fast becoming a contentious debate over gender separation and equal educational access. Ultimately the interconnection between constitutional and statutory standards, confounded with competing views on sameness and difference and the arguably inherent inequality of separation, framed a tenuous political compromise over single-sex schooling. It also left the constitutional question in a state of suspended animation. As the century came to a close, *Brown*'s unequivocal statement that "separate is inherently unequal" in the context of race came to fuel the opposition to single-sex schooling.

The road between *Brown* and the present-day aftermath of the VMI decision has been fraught with peril for school districts interested in experimenting with single-sex schools or classes. Civil rights groups have used the Constitution, Title IX, and other antidiscrimination laws in an attempt to stop these efforts dead in their tracks. Leading the charge with unshakable resolve are the American Civil Liberties Union and the National Organization for Women, together with their local chapters. The resulting court orders and agency rulings, while strikingly limited in number and jurisdictional scope, have had a profound effect on educational policy, setting school districts across the country on a roller-coaster ride of aborted starts and veiled attempts.

A thoughtful examination of that small but seemingly impenetrable maze of judicial ambiguities, administrative inconsistency, and legislative gridlock brings the current legal and policy dispute into bold relief. The distinct narratives presented, particularly in several seminal court decisions, speak volumes about the uneven quest for gender equity, programmatic diversity, and appropriate education for girls and boys, both rich and poor.

## DRAWING ON THE LEGACY OF *BROWN*

Opponents of single-sex programs base their most foundational legal claim in the equal protection clause of the federal Constitution. That argument takes on two casts. The first focuses on separation itself: separating girls from boys in public schooling is intrinsically unequal and therefore unconstitutional. The less absolutist argument looks for equal treatment: offering a particular type of education—single-sex—to one group while denying it to the other violates the constitutional rights of the group denied. The first leads to a blanket prohibition; the second invites a case-by-case comparison of the programs provided to both sexes.

Both of these views are grounded in legal events whose details, though forgotten in history, help us understand more clearly the depths of current opposition and the ground rules for resolution. *Brown* was the culminating point in a litigation strategy developed by NAACP lawyers to incrementally whittle away at the "separate but equal" doctrine passed down in the now infamous case of *Plessy v. Ferguson*.[2] In *Plessy*, the Supreme Court upheld a state law requiring separate accommodations for blacks and whites in railway trains on the basis that "separate" was not necessarily unequal. The Court progressively repudiated this doctrine in a series of higher education cases beginning in the 1930s, recognizing that separate facilities denied African Americans certain intangible benefits that are critical to the equality calculus. Two of these decisions bear particular weight in the debate over single-sex schooling.

The first case grew out of the efforts of Lloyd Gaines, an African American, to gain admission into the University of Missouri School of Law. The year was 1935 and the state's system of racially segregated higher education was still in full force. In response, the university bluntly and unapologetically informed Gaines that it was "contrary to the Constitution, laws and public policy of the State to admit a Negro as a student in the University." With no separate law school for African Americans, the state offered him financial aid to pursue the study of law in a neighboring state. Represented by the NAACP, Gaines took his case to court. The state made a lame attempt to justify its failure to open a law school for African Americans by arguing that there simply was a limited demand for legal education among them. Here the Court laid down two principles that continue to resound through contemporary legal discourse on single-sex education. First, the justices made clear that a constitutional right did not depend on the number of persons asserting it. Second, the state had to provide Gaines, within its borders, a legal education that was "substantially equal" to the one afforded to whites. But state officials resisted; rather than admit Gaines to the University of Missouri, they pressured Lincoln University, the state's black public college, to quickly establish a law school.[3]

Gaines never enrolled at Lincoln. In fact, he disappeared, despite repeated attempts of NAACP lawyers to keep him engaged. They tried to press the case further on the grounds that the Lincoln program was grossly inadequate. But with the plaintiff gone from sight, the Court dismissed the case. This deeply disappointed Thurgood Marshall and his NAACP colleagues. Nevertheless, he later recalled that the case "produced the victory, the legal precedent" that the organization used to "wipe out Jim Crow" in Oklahoma, Texas, Louisiana, and other states. In *Gaines,* he noted with satisfaction, the NAACP "dragged the federal courts one more step away from 'separate but equal.' "[4]

Notwithstanding that positive start, it took more than another decade for the NAACP to push the doctrine to the edge of the abyss. In *Sweatt v. Painter* the organization challenged the very remedy that the Court had ordered in *Gaines.* The state of Texas had created a shadow Jim Crow law school that met the "separate but equal" doctrine. At the same time, the state denied African Americans admission to the more prestigious University of Texas at Austin School of Law. Here the Court reaffirmed and more clearly defined the "substantial equality" standard, underscoring not only such tangible factors as library holdings but those intangible qualities that are incapable of objective measurement—the position and influence of alumni, traditions, and institutional prestige. As the justices saw it, these intangibles were even "more important" than the tangible resources. Again, as in *Gaines*, the Court emphasized that the number of black applicants was irrelevant. Limited demand was not an acceptable justification for unequal treatment.[5] The stage was set for *Brown* and its driving principle that "separate is inherently unequal," a principle that civil rights groups continue to invoke as their mantra whenever the state separates individuals based on certain group characteristics.

Whether the principle on its face applies to single-sex education is currently the subject of much dispute. But the analogy itself is seriously flawed. In the case of racial segregation, the state denied African Americans access to mainstream society based on the invidious belief that they were inferior as a group. The Court in *Brown* explicitly addressed the question of separating children "solely" because of their race and how it "generated a feeling of inferiority as to their status in the community." The state could offer no pedagogical justification for segregation. There the Court was examining a deeply entrenched segregated system that operated under the "sanction of law," which, the Court noted, had a "tendency to [retard] the educational . . . development" of African-American children. The objective was to preserve racial separation throughout society.[6] *Brown* suggests that when government policy forces a historically disadvantaged group to remain separate from the dominant group, it stigmatizes its members and conveys a message that they are of lesser intrinsic worth. From that vantage point, the decision implies a principle of not just antidiscrimination but also antisubordination.

Now it is undeniable that the history of women's education, similar to that of racially segregated schools, is tainted with the mark of subordination. Many prestigious academic institutions explicitly denied entry to women based on the implicit belief that they were intellectually inferior to men. And even where separate schools were available, these schools perpetuated gender stereotypes while the educational program and facilities offered to women were often of lesser quality or rigor. To fully understand and objectively assess contemporary single-sex education proposals, therefore, we must first disengage them from these past indignities and recognize both the subtle nuances and the sharp distinctions between then and now. In the current context, attendance is typically voluntary. More important, neither the intent nor the effect is to "generate a feeling of inferiority" but rather to help students realize their full potential. In contrast to the racial and gender segregation of the past, the purpose is to provide access, not to deny it, and to mainstream students into the larger society, not to perpetually segregate them—to empower and not disempower them. This is not segregation as an end in itself but rather as a means to provide appropriate education to students who may benefit from this particular approach at certain points in their schooling.

Rather than violate *Brown*'s core holding, these programs arguably fulfill the decision's very promise. *Brown* was about one's self-esteem and self-worth based on how one is perceived and respected in the more immediate community and in the larger society. The Court noted the importance of education as "the principal instrument in awakening the child to cultural values, in preparing him for later professional training, and in helping him to adjust normally to his environment."[7] This language supports one of the primary goals that school districts have tried to achieve in establishing single-sex schools and classes especially for disadvantaged students. What I am referring to here is "cultural socialization"—that is, preparing students for the roles they will assume as adults, both in mainstream society and in their communities.

There also are fundamental differences between race and sex. Race is a social construct; sex is irreducibly biological with an overlay of social considerations that define gender. There are circumstances where we, in fact, allow segregation by sex based on the biological differences between men and women. For example, we permit separate teams for contact sports such as football and hockey to protect women's safety. We also accept separate public restrooms for women and men based on cultural norms of privacy and appropriateness. The same would be denounced as morally unjust in the case of race. More fundamentally, unlike the history of separate but equal that weighed upon the period from *Plessy* to *Brown*, the division of labor enforced in the ideology of separate spheres for men and women was not fixed in "fear or loathing" but rather in "romantic paternalism." That ideology, however limiting in the end, arguably granted women such protections as maximum working hours and exclusion from military service. Yet it would defy rationality to defend the institution of slavery or any form of racial segregation for that matter on the grounds that it granted benefits to African Americans.[8]

The Supreme Court has recognized these differences. In view of the long and painful history of racial subjugation and its lingering effects, the Court most carefully examines racial classifications, applying an exacting standard of review, or what is commonly known as "strict scrutiny." Whenever government draws racial distinctions, the program or policy must be "strictly" necessary to achieve a "compelling" government interest. On the other hand, although women have suffered a history of political exclusion and powerlessness, the Court has not placed that history on a par with the harms suffered by racial minorities, and rightly so. The Court, therefore, holds sex classifications to a somewhat lesser standard of scrutiny than race classifications, without affording them the presumption of constitutionality typical of other social and economic policies.

Over the past three decades, the Court has repeatedly drawn these distinctions, most recently in the case against the Virginia Military Institute, where the justices further reaffirmed the standard of "substantial equality" and thereby addressed both the absolutist and more moderate claims against single-sex programs. But before discussing VMI, I shall digress into several lower-court cases that have defined the legal issues and shaped both political discourse and the public perception of single-sex schooling over the past two and a half decades. I also examine the Supreme Court decision that laid the immediate groundwork for VMI.

## THE PHILADELPHIA STORY: A BITTERSWEET VICTORY

One of the key legal disputes that loom large over single-sex schooling took place in Philadelphia, the City of Brotherly (but not, it seems, sisterly) Love. Philadelphia, like many urban school districts in the East, had a long and much-revered history of single-sex schools for academically talented students. By the mid-1970s other school systems, including those in Boston, Baltimore, and New York, had started converting such schools into coeducational institutions in the wake of Title IX and in response to market demands and pressure from women's rights advocates. Over the previous decade, the movement toward coeducation had been overwhelming. Particularly remarkable was the change in private institutions that embraced coeducation without the prodding of constitutional and statutory prescriptions. Between the mid-1960s and the mid-1970s the percentage of coeducational elementary and secondary private schools grew from 38 to 66 percent.[9]

But somehow Philadelphia had gotten caught in a time warp. Central High School for Boys, founded in 1836 by an act of the Pennsylvania legislature, remained a selective all-boys school whose academic standing and reputation as a training ground for community leaders had gained national recognition. The Philadelphia High School for Girls, founded in 1848 as Girls Normal School, was for much of its history a training school for public school teachers. There were no similarly selective coeducational counterparts. Philadelphia's resistance to change would ultimately draw the district through two rounds of litigation, first in federal and then in state court, in the end yielding a bittersweet victory for women.

The Philadelphia story began in 1974, when Susan Vorchheimer, a junior high honors student, set about to challenge the system of gender separation and unequal educational access that Philadelphia imposed on academically talented females. She had visited Girls' High, her only selective academic option within the city system, and sat in on one of the classes. From that experience she concluded that attendance at the school would cause her "harm," although later at trial she presented no specific evidence to directly support that belief.[10] In any event, she set her sights on Central High. Clearly meeting the academic admissions standards, Vorchheimer applied to the school. Predictably, school officials rejected her application solely on the basis of her sex. Not to be so easily rebuffed, she and her parents took their case to federal district court in a class action suit. She contended that the system denied her and similarly qualified female students equal educational opportunity.

The district court found that the education available at Girls' High was "comparable" despite Central's concededly superior science facilities and its substantial private endowment, unique among the city's schools. But the court was not looking for parity between the two schools to begin with. Rather, it was looking for an equivalent mixed-sex alternative, and there was none in the city. With no coeducational high school offering the range of courses or the highly capable student body available at Central or Girls' High, Philadelphia could not justify excluding girls from Central, not even as a means for providing students with alternatives.[11] For academically superior students like Susan Vorchheimer, the choice was illusory. There were no comparable alternatives outside of the two single-sex schools, while members of each sex were eligible for only one.

The appeals court was far less sympathetic to Vorchheimer's arguments. As the court read the record, all she claimed was a mere preference for Central High School without any evidence that single-sex schooling was in fact harmful. Employing a "separate but equal" analysis, the court concluded that the opportunities and facilities at Girls' High were equivalent to those at Central. "If there are benefits or detriment in the system," the court noted, "they fall on both sexes in equal measure." But the court did not stop at comparability. Rather it drew a distinction between race, where there are no inherent differences, and gender, where differences between the sexes may in "limited circumstances" justify separate treatment. And in the end, the court bowed to localism with some lip service to family choice. School officials had the discretion to initiate innovative methods and techniques. At the same time, students and their parents had the freedom to choose public single-sex education for their children. For the appeals court, this was a case of "equal benefit and not discriminatory denial."[12]

Noticeably absent from the court's rationale was any regard for the right to choose coeducation on a comparable level. Yet that was the precise factor that had driven the lower court's decision. In distinct contrast with the contemporary political debate, the appeals court placed the burden on the challengers to prove the harms of single-sex schooling rather than on the supporters to prove its benefits. In the first case, the approach is presumptively good. In the second, it is presumptively evil.

As the case progressed to the Supreme Court, the plaintiffs acquired additional legal representation from the American Civil Liberties Union Foundation. In briefs presented to the Court, appearing first on the list of ACLU attorneys was Ruth Bader Ginsburg, who, as a sitting Supreme Court justice two decades later, was to speak for the Court in the Virginia Military Institute case. In the brief supporting its petition for Court review, the ACLU took the same hard line that it has maintained to the present day. According to the attorneys, "Even if the facilities of Girls' High approached the theoretical 'separate but equal' model, the claim of Susan Vorchheimer and the class she represents would be well-founded. The very names assigned to the two schools tell the story; they are symbolic of a larger inequality identical facilities would not cure." In other words, in the area of sex as in race, "separate is inherently unequal."

The ACLU brief quoted from Christopher Jencks and David Riesman's *Academic Revolution*. According to the two noted sociologists, "The all-male college would be relatively easy to defend if it emerged from a world in which women were established as fully equal to men. But it does not. It is therefore likely to be a witting or unwitting device for preserving tacit assumptions of male superiority—assumptions for which women must eventually pay."[13] Embracing that perspective, later echoed in Justice Ginsburg's opinion in the VMI case, the brief unequivocally stated, "In the context of the subordinate place so long assigned to women in society, no school 'sister' to Central can supply an educational experience genuinely equal in character, quality, and effectiveness."[14]

No amount of legal expertise or novel argument, however, could save Susan Vorchheimer's case from its paltry trial record. An "equally divided" Supreme Court issued a brief statement affirming the appeals court judgment. Without a majority opinion from the justices, the decision had no legal effect nationwide. Nevertheless, it inadvertently placed a symbolic judicial imprimatur on publicly supported single-sex schooling, at least for the time being. After *Vorchheimer*, the separate-but-equal doctrine rejected two decades earlier as to race seemed constitutionally permissible in the realm of gender.

In the following years, Philadelphia's three remaining nonselective single-sex high schools moved to coeducation, while Central and Girls' High continued untouched. But the coeducation tide was rising too fast to insulate the city from its sweep much longer. In the early 1980s three Girls' High students, Elizabeth Newberg, Pauline King, and Jessica Bonn, applied to Central for admission in their junior year. School officials rejected all three on the basis of their sex. This time the plaintiffs took their class action to state and not federal court. This time they did so from the start with the legal advice of seasoned attorneys from the American Civil Liberties Union and the Women's Law Project who knew how to ferret the facts and frame the legal arguments to build a winning case. And this time they went sufficiently armed with the Pennsylvania Constitution's Equal Rights Amendment, a clearer reading from the U.S. Supreme Court on gender discrimination under the federal Constitution, and a mound of damaging evidence that proved fatal to the school district at trial.

In *Newberg v. Board of Education,* the attorneys presented before the state trial court a striking picture of gross inequalities between Central and Girls' High. Some of these were more quantifiable than others, but all proved clearly compelling. A Central graduate who had passed all major subjects beyond the ninth grade received a bachelor of arts degree under a legislative act going back to 1849; a Girls' High graduate received a high school diploma. There were two and a half times as many Ph.D.s and one and a half times as many teachers with twenty-one years or more of teaching experience at Central than at Girls' High. Central's campus was almost three times as large, while its library contained almost twice the number of books and was housed in a more attractive setting. Central had twice as many computers and a separate computer room. Central's "mentally gifted" program offered thirty-eight courses and seminars, while a comparable program at Girls' High listed only seven courses and three seminars.

The disparities in inputs and outputs continued. Girls' High students almost invariably scored lower on the Preliminary Scholastic Aptitude Test/National Merit Qualifying Test, an initial filter for college scholarships. The same was true for the Scholastic Aptitude Test for college admission. Girls' High students received fewer than half the overall scholarship dollars awarded to Central students. Between the two schools, 64 percent of the students taking Advanced Placement examinations over a four-year period came from Central. Almost thirteen times as many Central students as Girls' High students took the physics B test. Central received a higher per-student allocation, including an athletic allotment of $7,000 annually, as well as funds from a private endowment. Girls' High students had to raise supplemental revenue from annual magazine subscription sales. Added to these qualitatively measurable differences, there was the intangible quality of Central's impressive and widely recognized reputation, built on a lengthy list of illustrious graduates and further enhanced by frequent and favorable media publicity that Girls' High had never attracted. As the attorneys laid the evidence before the court, Susan Vorchheimer's instincts about the inequities between the two schools finally became vindicated almost a decade after her unsuccessful lawsuit. Basing its decision on both the federal and state constitutions, the state court enjoined the Philadelphia school district from refusing to admit students to Central High School solely on the basis of their sex.[15]

Obviously, the court did not have to stretch too far to find that the two schools were "materially unequal" in a concrete and measurable way. What remained unanswered, however, was whether gender separation in public schooling, like racial separation, is in and of itself unequal, as modern-day oppositionists continue to argue. In its discussion of the Pennsylvania Equal Rights Amendment, with its highly exacting level of judicial scrutiny, the court stated that sex classifications are "inherently suspect." It did not state, however, that they produce "inherently unequal" institutions. The court's conclusion under the Fourteenth Amendment equal protection clause was somewhat more guarded. Nonetheless, the court found that there was no "important governmental objective" to be served by maintaining Central and Girls' High as separate single-gender schools. At trial, the district had offered merely a "vague, unsubstantiated theory of single-gender schooling": that adolescents study more effectively in single-sex schools. As far as the state court was concerned, the means employed—gender separation—was not "substantially related" to that theory.[16]

The ruling sent shock waves throughout the city, where underlying anxieties and intense feelings became played out in the local press. The *Philadelphia Inquirer* hailed the decision, denouncing publicly supported single-sex schools as "anachronisms" that work against "all that has been accomplished in long struggles to eliminate discrimination."[17] Central's alumni were far less enthusiastic. The alumni association board overwhelmingly adopted a resolution urging the board of education to appeal the decision. But to fully understand the alumni's opposition, as the press explained, one had to understand what Central represented for "generations of the city's brightest boys—boys who grew up to dominate the Philadelphia bar and hold office in the top echelons of the city's power structure." Central High School was "their fraternity, their public prep school, the last bastion . . . of quality public education for boys."[18]

Meanwhile, the faculty, students, and well-organized alumnae association of Girls' High were equally concerned that the litigation had cost their school considerable capital. In an effort to mitigate the damages, they joined the opposition. Alumni of both schools made an impassioned plea before the school board to appeal the court decision. For Common Pleas Court Judge Lisa Richette, a Yale Law School graduate and one of Girls' High's most distinguished alumnae, the court's comparison of the two schools was "invidious." She warned board members that to let "this bad law stand" would do "a disservice to . . . the girls at Girls' High, who have been told that they're going to an inferior school because it's female." For her, as for many others, the school had been a "turning point" in her life, the "very core of affirmative action."[19]

Both alumni groups insisted that the two schools were academically equal, that their academic excellence was inextricably bound to their single-gender enrollments, and that at the very least, the district should maintain the option of single-sex education for students who could not afford private schooling. Mayor William Green, on the other hand, had a different view. He resoundingly endorsed the decision. He too called the separate system an "anachronism," despite the fact that he himself sent his daughters to a private all-girls school. On that count, the principal of Girls' High took the mayor to task. "The result," she retorted, "is that only the rich who can afford private school will have the option of single-sex education."[20] After six weeks of tense deliberations, the school board voted 5 to 3 not to appeal the ruling. In the meantime, more than a dozen girls had been attending Central since school began. And while the judge had specifically enjoined the school district from denying girls admission to Central High based solely on gender, implicit in the court's ruling was a similar prohibition against Girls' High's all-female admissions policy. Not surprisingly, though, no boys sought admission to Girls' High.

The board's decision seemed rational in view of the circumstances. One can easily speculate that the striking disparities between the two schools had a chastening effect on school officials. How could they possibly defend such indicting evidence? What educational justification could they offer? Of course, they could have argued that the numbers were merely "form over substance." Neither a Ph.D. nor twenty-plus years of teaching necessarily makes for an effective classroom teacher. Besides, part of Central's campus size was attributable to the football field and lawn space, neither of which added to the academic capital of the school. The football team, in fact, consumed at least part of Central's additional funding. Moreover, Girls' High did in fact offer academic opportunities that Central did not, including two years of both biology and physics, compared with Central's one, as well as Advanced Placement classes in Spanish and French, neither of which Central offered. And, of course, Girls' High was academically successful. More than 95 percent of its students went on to college, many of them to the most prestigious institutions in the country.

But school officials were hard-pressed to make a convincing argument on the record. Once the lawsuit put the tangible discrepancies into the public domain, the numbers assumed a life of their own and reaffirmed the perception long held by Philadelphians that all-male Central High was the "jewel in the crown" of the city school system. Moreover, aside from the differences in resources, the recent success of selective schools like Boston

Latin in moving toward coeducation severely undercut the district's argument that single-sex schooling was a matter of academic necessity.

The students and staff of Girls' High met these events with outrage and dismay. They would not readily accept defeat and quickly mobilized, "trying like hell to maintain [their] school," as the dean of students put it. To their credit, school officials and staff used the long list of inequalities recited by the court as leverage to obtain more resources. From the district, that meant additional teaching staff and $40,000 worth of computer equipment. It also meant increased financial support from alumnae. The students showed similar initiative. They mounted a public relations campaign, writing letters, and passing out leaflets extolling the virtues of Girls' High. They volunteered to recruit prospective students from the elementary and junior high schools throughout the city. Several Girls' High and Central students and graduates who had submitted an *amicus* brief to express their concerns before the court desperately tried to mount an appeal or intervene as defendants in the case, but the court refused.[21]

From the perspective of outsiders not caught up in this life-size drama, the court's decision might have seemed a sweeping victory for the young women of Philadelphia. For those seeking formal equality, it certainly was a major triumph. Yet for those who embraced the difference principle, it was a painful defeat. As one alumna lamented in a letter to the press, "The American Civil Liberties Union . . . can gloat over having killed us off in the promotion of their 'cause.' " In the course of the litigation, the principal of Girls' High expressed a sentiment that continues to echo throughout the single-sex schooling debate. "What the three girls [who brought the litigation] are doing is not helping women," she mournfully stated. "They're just destroying another opportunity for [them]."[22] Subsequent history has proven that the ACLU and the Women's Law Project did indeed have a cause, however well-intentioned, to completely dismantle single-sex schooling. And the divisions they created in the Philadelphia litigation have painfully deepened with time among supporters of women's educational equity.

In the end, Girls' High has remained practically if not technically single-sex. Over the years, it has maintained its all-girls status through "a fragile blend of tradition, informal district policy, and success in warding off the handful of boys who express interest."[23] Meanwhile, Central High School, with its tangible and intangible benefits, subsequently proved far more attractive to women and swiftly evolved a gender-balanced population. But in the end, the lawsuit also presented a downside for at least some of the boys in the city. Although girls within the Philadelphia public school system can now choose between an academically rigorous education that is either single-sex or coeducational, that option is in a real sense closed to boys.

Of course, one can argue that the court order merely tracked the market. By the early 1980s boys in particular had begun to find single-sex schooling far less appealing than coeducation. At the time of the litigation, Central's enrollment was only 55 percent of capacity. One can reasonably speculate that most of Philadelphia's academically talented boys welcomed the transition. Only 10 percent of Central's student body actively protested the admission of girls. Nevertheless, no court order could undo the sobering fact that for more than a century Philadelphia had denied women the same academic and ultimately life opportunities offered to men. If the Philadelphia community historically viewed Central as the city's preeminent academic high school, with Girls' High as the less-than-equal alternative for girls, the litigation carved that perception into stone. Central still attracts a somewhat higher percentage of academically strong students, who still perceive it as the more prestigious of the two institutions. The significant difference the litigation made was that it gave girls the option to tap those resources. Many girls do, but then again, many others still prefer the unique environment of an all-girls school, in particular, Girls' High School. And Girls' High, with a more equitable resource allocation than its prelawsuit days, and despite a student population that is increasingly poor and minority, still sends nearly 98 percent of its graduates on to college.

From a legal perspective, the Philadelphia case is not an easy one to reconcile as one moves through the various layers of the court's decision. What exactly was the constitutional violation? Was it the striking inequality or the insufficiently justified gender separation itself? The state court seemed to indicate that it was the separation, while using the inequality to support its decision. Nevertheless, the court's focus on both tangible and intangible factors provided a caliper for measuring equality, a key element in the contemporary debate. In that sense, the court's careful examination of the facts presented a useful paradigm for school administrators, courts, and federal enforcement officials to follow in the future.

In hindsight, the state court decision would appear to have limited value as precedent, and the whole case might seem like a mere curiosity in the history of educational equity. Nevertheless, the facts surrounding the litigation, and the decision itself, with all its ambiguities, invariably enter legal discussions on single-sex schooling. Perhaps the significance of the case is more symbolic than legal. The image of girls storming open the doors of a school like Central High after a century of feigned equality certainly is a powerful one. But there is more to it. On a policy level, the ghost of those inequalities continues to haunt the wider debate as opponents of single-sex schooling argue that, based on history, gender separation for whatever purposes inevitably results in unequal and diminished resources for women's education. The Philadelphia case has come to embody that proposition, while the compelling "then and now" arguments get tossed aside.

Central High was a prototype of a first-generation single-sex school, an academically prestigious institution that operated for the sole benefit of males. It was established in a time when the prevailing belief among educators was that women were not fit for this level of intellectual endeavor nor was it appropriate for them to pursue the careers for which the school prepared its graduates. These archaic attitudes seemed to underlie the district's policies and practices through the course of the following century and a half. A decade and beyond the dismantling of single-sex education at Central and similar all-male public secondary schools, the ACLU and the National Organization for Women have continued to challenge single-sex programs even absent the taint of similar spending inequities or invidious intent, where officials are trying to enhance educational opportunities for such previously excluded groups as women and racial minorities.

## DETROIT: A CIVIL RIGHTS DILEMMA

In the late 1980s urban school officials and community leaders became increasingly alarmed over the apparent failure of public education to raise the educational achievement and social well-being of minority students. They were particularly concerned with the plight of African-American males, who, according to press reports, were becoming an "endangered species—unemployed, imprisoned, and murdered in disproportionate numbers."[24] In cities across the country African-American boys proved to have dramatically higher suspension, expulsion, retention, and dropout rates and dramatically lower grade point averages when compared with other students.

At that time, Dr. Spencer Holland, an educational psychologist in the Baltimore public schools, conceived of a radical approach to addressing the problem—creating all-male classes taught by male teachers, in kindergarten through third grade. In this way, Holland argued, the schools could prevent the development of negative attitudes toward academic achievement prevalent among inner-city boys. His rationale was as follows: African-American girls are exposed early in their academic careers to literate and consistent African-American female teachers who offer an alternative to the role models encountered elsewhere in the community. Something happens to girls in their early years that "makes them see an alternative to the life Mama lives." African-American boys, on the other hand, do not come into contact with positive male role models until the upper grades, if at all, according to Holland. By then it is too late to make a difference. Up to that point, their only role models are males who have already rejected academic achievement. For Holland, all-male classes headed by male teachers could make a profound difference, especially in the inner city.[25]

To put his idea into the stream of discussion, Holland published several articles targeted at the educational establishment. In 1988 he devised Project 2000, a program that used male volunteers from the corporate world and local colleges and universities. They worked with students in the schools, accompanied them on field trips, and agreed to continue mentoring them from first grade through high school. He originally envisioned the program as an adjunct to single-sex classes. By 1994, however, he realized that legal forces were working against him and decided to give up trying to institutionalize single-sex programs in organized educational systems and instead work directly with children. As he now recalls, "I didn't have the rest of my life to fight this battle with the ACLU and NOW."[26] He expanded Project 2000 into Washington, D.C., where it now operates a separate after-school program for inner-city students, about two-thirds of them boys, from seventh through twelfth grades.

In the meantime, back in the late 1980s, Holland engaged the *Washington Post* columnist William Raspberry, who provided him a national forum for circulating his ideas.[27] As Raspberry began spreading the "gospel according to Holland" through his syndicated column, he set the organizational wheels spinning in urban school districts across the country. Over the following years, a number of school systems, including Dade County, Baltimore, Detroit, and Milwaukee, established committees to examine the status of African-American males. These committees bought into Holland's formula but added an Afrocentric twist. They recommended separating boys and girls, hiring not just males but African-American males to serve as teachers and role models, and reorganizing the curriculum to enhance racial pride and self-esteem. Dade County and Baltimore experimented with single-sex classes. Officials hoped to counteract the social and environmental factors that typically diminish the prospects of African-American males to achieve academically. Milwaukee and Detroit went even further, planning Afrocentric immersion schools that were all male and effectively segregated by race.

These programs touched off a national debate in which gender and race became conflated. The Milwaukee proposal provoked a critical response from the National Association for the Advancement of Colored People (NAACP) Legal Defense and Educational Fund (LDF), which saw the approach ultimately as a threat to an integrated society. In the view of LDF staff and members, the plan posed a real danger of racial resegregation. It also undermined efforts to eliminate the pervasive isolation of black males in special education classes and in separate schools for students with disciplinary problems.[28] In the case of Dade County, the federal government stepped in. There a program for kindergarten and first grade boys established in 1987 closed after the first year even though attendance rates had risen by 6 percent, test scores had increased by 6 to 9 percent, and the students' social behavior had noticeably improved. These impressive gains were of little consequence to the federal Office for Civil Rights in Atlanta. Officials there rejected the district's proposal to continue the program, on an experimental basis, with a control group of students in coed classes as basis for comparison.[29]

The Detroit plan ultimately proved the most divisive, propelling school officials into federal court, where they defended their well-intentioned plan against the onslaughts of civil rights groups. In 1991 a district court in Michigan preliminarily enjoined Detroit school officials from opening three Afrocentric academies for at-risk boys. The case never went to trial for a full hearing, and the ruling has limited jurisdiction. Nevertheless, *Garrett v. Board of Education* quickly defused a movement that was gaining increased momentum in urban school districts nationwide.[30] In a disquieting way, the case acquired the gloss of the "definitive word" on the legality of all-male programs for African-American youth.

The Detroit saga began in August 1989 with a report published by the United Community Services of Detroit, documenting the devastating educational and social problems facing young African-American males. The following March, an ad hoc group of concerned citizens from Detroit Public Schools Area B organized a conference, attended by more than five hundred people, to specifically address these issues. The outcome was a resolution charging Detroit officials to convene public hearings on "the crisis of the African-American male." In response, one of the district's principals, Clifford Watson, prepared a proposal entitled "Boys Developmental Academy," which he forwarded to the superintendent of schools. After some discussion, the district established a task force of educators and community leaders to gather data and formulate a plan.

The group understandably was concerned about the legal implications of what it was setting out to do. And so it enlisted the aid of Robert Sedler, a constitutional law professor from Wayne State University. Sedler had litigated a number of race and gender equity cases for the ACLU and the NAACP. He later prepared a legal opinion that lent credibility to the group's final recommendations. In the meantime, Detroit school officials ignored an unsolicited warning letter from the Michigan state education agency's sex equity coordinator. The letter stated unequivocally that Title IX "clearly prohibits" such a "sex-segregated school."[31]

The task force report, echoing the 1989 document, presented a frightening portrait of growing up male in the inner city. The data and conclusions bore a stark resemblance to a similar document prepared by the Milwaukee task force. In Detroit, for example, the public school population was 90 percent African American, and 70 percent of the children were being raised by single mothers. In the 1989–90 school year, 54 percent of African-American males dropped out of school before graduation, compared with 45 percent of African-American females, while males accounted for 66.4 percent of the short-term suspensions. Only 39 percent of high school graduates were male. Among Detroit's male high school students, 70 percent had grade point averages below 2.0. Of those children receiving special services for substance abuse, mental health problems, or special education, 67 percent were male.

The data on crime revealed a similar pattern. Eighty percent of those admitted to the county youth home were minority males, while 80 percent of males in the criminal justice system were public school students. Sixty percent of the drug offenses in Wayne County were committed by eighth- and ninth-grade dropouts. The number of young minority men in the county who were within the criminal justice system was greater than the total number of minority men of all ages enrolled in college. At the time of the report, as now, the leading cause of death among African-American males between the ages of twelve and twenty-four was homicide—189 deaths in one year in Detroit alone.[32]

In an attempt to address this crisis, the task force recommended that Detroit explore the concept of the all-male academy on an experimental basis. The program would provide a pilot setting for evaluating the effectiveness of curricula and guidance strategies directed toward meeting the educational, emotional, and social needs of urban minority male students. Admission technically would be open to all males regardless of race, although the Afrocentric curriculum realistically would attract few if any non-African-American students. The Detroit school board approved the proposal in February 1991 and two months later passed a resolution authorizing the creation of the Malcolm X, Marcus Garvey, and Paul Robeson Academies the following fall. The three academies would serve boys from preschool through grade five and would phase in grades six through eight in subsequent years. They would offer special programs, including an Afrocentric curriculum, a class entitled "Rites of Passage," mentors, Saturday classes, individualized counseling, extended classroom hours, and student uniforms. The public response was overwhelming. The district received more than 1,200 applications for 560 seats.

The idea of single-sex programs was not new to Detroit. For at least ten years the district had been operating all-female and all-male programs, including three schools for pregnant girls and one for boys at risk of expulsion. None of these had ever been challenged in court or subject to public scrutiny. In fact, the idea of single-sex schools was not new to the African-American community in general. The notion of using separate schooling to promote self-esteem and the economic and social welfare of African-American students harkens back to the establishment of separate schools for girls in the early 1900s. The Daytona Literary and Industrial School for Negro Girls, founded in Daytona Beach, Florida, in 1904 by Mary McLeod Bethune, and the National Training School for Negro Girls founded by Nannie Helen Burroughs in Washington, D.C., in 1909 were the most noteworthy examples of that movement.[33] These historical initiatives shared with their contemporary counterparts a belief in gender-specific conduct and instruction.

Yet times had changed. In the intervening years a civil rights movement had promised to lift the shackles of forced segregation, and a women's movement had resolved to place women on an equal social and political plane with men. The task force recommendation unleashed within Detroit a firestorm of controversy that reverberated nationwide. More immediately, the General Superintendent's Cabinet raised serious concerns about segregating students by race and gender. In the end, it rejected the report.

Reaction to the proposal among Detroit parents was sharply divided. Some of the strongest supporters were African-American mothers. For Tandrea Black, the plan was an answer to her prayers. She feared that her son would become "one of those negative statistics." This program gave her hope that he would be among the "few that make it to college, . . . that turn out to be productive human beings." Marsha Cheeks, a single mother, well understood why boys were being singled out for special treatment. "[My] daughter . . . sees me as a positive role model," she told the press. "By the same token, I'm not a male, so I cannot show [my son] the way a man should be. There are few positive role models that he can look at and say, 'Well, Ma, I want to be like him.'"

Nevertheless, mothers like Shawn Garrett, whose daughter would be attending the Detroit schools the following year, saw it differently. As far as these mothers could see, the Detroit schools were failing their daughters. Only 60 percent among them would end up with a high school diploma. Garrett wanted her daughter to understand that "she's a person also, [that] she has choice."[34] The district soon found itself in court, facing off against the American Civil Liberties Union of Michigan and the National Organization for Women Legal Defense and Education Fund (NOWLDF). The ACLU and its affiliates would persistently and aggressively oppose single-sex programs of any stripe throughout the next decade. The NOWLDF would later hand the mantle over to NOW and its local chapters.

The position taken by both groups was part of a coherent philosophy that each had voiced in previous litigation, and it went beyond education. That history made it all the more politically problematic for them to give the issue a "fresh look," despite disagreements within their ranks. The views expressed were reminiscent of the arguments both organizations had advanced in *amicus* briefs before the U.S. Supreme Court in the late 1980s. There they had challenged a state statute that required employers to grant women temporarily incapacitated from pregnancy up to four months unpaid leave while the statute omitted other disabilities. Roundly rejecting the stereotypes reflected in "protective legislation," the ACLU had argued, and the NOWLDF had agreed, that "legislative distinctions drawn on the basis of sex (and pregnancy) are inherently dangerous even when they purport to confer advantages."[35] That argument has since become a fixed plank in the legal and political platforms of both groups.

In the case of Detroit, the distinction conferred educational advantages on male students but denied the same advantages to females. At least that is what the civil rights attorneys contended. They enlisted two mothers to carry the case into court on behalf of themselves and their school-age daughters: Shawn Garrett and her four-year-old daughter Crystal, and an unidentified mother and her eleven-, six-, and five-year-old daughters. Both women charged that their children were ineligible, solely on the basis of their sex, to apply to the academies.

The animosity that most African-American women felt toward NOW made both Garrett and her coplaintiff "Nancy Doe" vulnerable and susceptible to accusations of racist betrayal. Shawn Garrett's enthusiasm for joining the fight soon waned. As is common in such highly emotional controversies, she had fallen victim to harassing phone calls, hostile criticism, and threats from community members. Before the August 1991 court hearing, she withdrew herself and her daughter from the lawsuit. The anonymous mother and her daughters held steadfast and successfully challenged a subpoena to appear in court. With one mother silenced and the other hiding in the shadows, the ACLU and the NOWLDF became the voice and face of the African-American girls of Detroit. Yet the lead attorney for neither organization was African American, and the ACLU attorneys were all male.[36]

The legal claims were multifaceted, including violations of the Fourteenth Amendment equal protection clause, Title IX of the Education Amendments of 1972, and the Equal Educational Opportunities Act of 1974. The district presented a mound of statistics to support its argument that male students were particularly at risk and needed specialized programming. School officials argued that the program was experimental and designed to combat high homicide, unemployment, and dropout rates among African-American males. The court concluded that these numbers, while indeed troubling, did not demonstrate that the exclusion of girls was substantially related to the program's objective. Although it was clear that coeducational programs had failed black males, the court could not find that coeducation was the cause. There simply was no evidence that the system was failing males because of the presence of females; in fact, the system was also failing females.

The court found unconvincing the district's argument that girls were not expressly prohibited from attending the academies. In the court's view, the name Male Academies and the descriptive literature clearly excluded females from "real participation in the program."[37] It also found unpersuasive the argument that the program was experimental and would gather useful data on meeting the needs of African-American boys in the inner city. The court relied on two earlier rulings from the federal Office for Civil Rights. One was in response to a 1988 request from the Dade County Public School system for permission to continue its kindergarten and first-grade class for African-American boys as a two-year pilot program. The other ruling responded to a 1990 inquiry from the Wisconsin Department of Public Instruction in which state officials sought legal guidance on projected plans for a proposed African-American all-male school in Milwaukee. In both instances, federal officials made clear that the segregation of students in all-male classes or schools violated the Title IX regulations.[38] In the end, the court concluded that the plaintiffs were likely to succeed on their constitutional and Title IX claims.

A group of three hundred supporters protested the decision outside the federal court building in Detroit. At the same time, the NAACP Legal Defense and Educational Fund publicly supported the position of the NAACP and threatened to join the lawsuit if school officials appealed the judge's ruling. After some initial wavering, the school board agreed to admit girls rather than risk further litigation that it believed it was almost certain to lose. A trial on the complex legal, social, and educational issues raised in the case would have cost the district an estimated one million dollars.[39] Nine days after the court ruling, the board entered into a settlement agreement with the ACLU and the NOWLDF. The board agreed to allocate 136 of the 560 available seats to girls.

The initial response from Detroit families was less than enthusiastic. A community coalition urged parents of girls to boycott the program. On the first day of school, there were only 19 girls enrolled in the academies. By the end of the first semester, that figure had risen only to 39. Gradually enrollment became more gender-balanced. In recent years, the schools have continued to offer an African-centered curriculum to an approximately equal number of girls and boys chosen by lottery, with priority given to siblings.[40]

The Milwaukee plan for two all-male schools met a similar fate. School officials transformed both of them into coeducational African-American immersion schools.

Similar to the lawsuit challenging Philadelphia's Central High, the political impact of the Detroit decision has been overwhelmingly disproportionate to its legal importance. The ruling has no binding precedence outside the eastern district of Michigan. The case never went to trial, nor did it reach a final decision on the merits. It merely concluded in a preliminary injunction. Nevertheless, it has given symbolic force to the opponents of single-sex education who have wielded the decision against school systems considering similar programs for males or females alike.

The legal arguments challenging the Detroit and other all-male Afrocentric programs focused on sex discrimination against females. In their briefs and in court, the ACLU and NOW lawyers used race merely to demonstrate by analogy the illegality of gender segregation. In reality, race was a nonissue. The public school population in these communities was predominantly if not totally African American, and admission technically would have been open to males of all races. More importantly, if we consider typical class assignment patterns in urban schools nationwide, the notion that it is unconstitutional to segregate African-American males appears absurd at best and disingenuous at worst. As the former Detroit schools superintendent Deborah McGriff pointed out at the time, "If you'll look at special education classes in this country where they label children as emotionally disturbed, most of these students are African-American males and neither one of these organizations [ACLU and NOW] came forward to petition or protest that. . . . But when we say as a school system that we want to do something positive, we want to establish an experimental program to see if we can discover ways to educate all children, we are challenged."[41]

The political controversy, nevertheless, centered on the legacy of racial segregation and set local and national African-American leaders on opposite sides of the divide. The plan brought to the surface competing desires for integration and segregation that have alternately tugged at the African-American community since slavery set upon the nation's shores almost four centuries ago. The very concept of officially created racially identified schools sent shock waves throughout the civil rights network. The wounds of segregation ran so deep that the mere suggestion of racial separation, even for arguably benign reasons, raised the specter of Jim Crow in the eyes of many. As one commentator later observed, this was a "desperate remedy for desperate times," one that reflected the "grim state of American race relations" four decades after *Brown v. Board of Education*.[42]

The proposal proved particularly offensive to leading scholars and others who had labored in the fields of the civil rights movement to break down racial barriers. Among the harshest criticism was that of Kenneth Clark, whose pioneering research into the harmful effects of segregation on African-American children gave theoretical support to the "separate is inherently unequal" principle of *Brown*. Clark viewed these schools as a "damaging psychological procedure," a "shameless" and "flagrant" "violation" of the decision.[43] To his mind, they constituted "academic child abuse."[44] Charles Willie of Harvard University echoed Clark's concerns. "This is a way of stigmatizing, . . . a way of saying [these youngsters] are more dangerous today than they have been in the past."[45] James Comer, the noted psychiatrist and director of the Child Study Center at Yale University, feared that the schools might increase the sense of isolation felt by many of these young men and consequently make it difficult for them to cope with the larger society.[46]

Just before the court's decision, the NAACP at its annual convention in Houston reaffirmed the position taken the previous year by the LDF. The organization officially adopted a policy proclaiming its "historical opposition to school segregation of any kind." In lieu of single-sex schools, the resolution urged school districts to create "workable alternatives to the proposed segregated education for African-American males."[47] It made no mention of African-American females. But the Detroit delegates to the convention disagreed. They opposed the resolution during floor debate, and local African-American leaders shared their concerns. As the executive director of the NAACP Detroit branch explained, all-male schools were "a level of redress and a response to discrimination."[48] The president of the Detroit Urban League captured the critical nature of the problem for African Americans when he noted that "prisons are the male academies that we already have."[49] Judging from the unanticipated number of applications received, many Detroit parents seemed to agree.

As the arguments on both sides make clear, the issues underlying all-male classes, and particularly the all-male Afrocentric academies, are sensitive and controversial. The ACLU and NOWLDF focused their legal arguments on sex, using the race analogy merely as a strategic prop. The NAACP, on the other hand, placed the race issue center stage, resurrecting a century-old debate within the African-American community about the relative merits of separateness and integration. In doing so, the group evoked painful memories of government-enforced racially segregated and unequal schools. Perhaps a more accurate picture emerged from the more contextual bipolar dispute that erupted among Detroit parents. There the educational needs of African-American males collided head on with those of African-American females.

Obviously these were not merely single-sex programs of a generic nature. The immersion schools, in particular, promoted a particular approach and content in which social consciousness played a key role. For its supporters, the incorporation of Afrocentric materials into the curriculum directly attempted to reconcile the conflicting influences of the African-American and dominant American cultures.[50] Yet despite the unique aspects of these proposals, the controversy over all-male programs became caught up in the debate that was simultaneously swirling through educational circles about the educational needs of girls. The Detroit ruling soon became another weapon in the oppositionist arsenal against single-sex education of any nature.

## THE LEGAL AND POLITICAL FALLOUT

In the aftermath of Detroit, other urban school systems revised or retreated from similar plans. Milwaukee's African-American Immersion School opened admissions to all races and both sexes following an agreement with the Office for Civil Rights (OCR). New York City revised its original proposal to establish an all-male experimental high school, the Ujamaa Institute (*Ujamaa* being the Swahili word for family), to appease civil rights groups who claimed the plan was racist and sexist. Like Detroit and Milwaukee, New York opened the school to any student interested in an African-centered learning experience.[51]

At the same time, and in an unconnected way, the general concept of separating students by sex was gaining new currency in the wake of now controversial findings that schools were shortchanging girls. School systems across the country began to experiment with separate classes for girls or boys or both. Some went underground, hiding from the press and using ambiguous titles to avoid legal challenge. A 1996 report from the U.S. General Accounting Office cited numerous examples of such programs nationwide. But the information not included in the report was as revealing as what it included. Government researchers intentionally failed to identify specific programs for fear of placing them at risk. If their identity had been made public, OCR surely would have closed them down.[52]

Each new program invited threatening noises from civil rights groups who refused to budge from the position they had taken in Philadelphia and Detroit. Various initiatives also invited an occasional administrative warning from OCR. Both tactics forced schools to either offer admission to members of the opposite sex or terminate the project. In Presque Isle, Maine, and Ventura, California, officials nominally opened all-girl math classes to boys when faced with a Title IX challenge. In one, the class was renamed "Algebra I with an Emphasis on Women's Contributions in Mathematics." In the other, a more guarded nomenclature, "Math PLUS" (Power Learning for Underrepresented Students), still failed to attract any boys.

The formality nevertheless insulated both programs from federal administrative action. In Irvington, New Jersey, a new superintendent shut down separate boys' and girls' classrooms in the middle schools on the advice of state officials who warned that the classes violated Title IX. The fact that girls in particular benefited—honor roll numbers were up and discipline problems were down—could not save the program. In Des Moines, Iowa, state officials closed the door on single-sex classrooms operating on a voluntary basis in two public schools for part of the day.[53] Philadelphia, threatened with a lawsuit by the ACLU, canceled a first-grade class for twenty boys with learning problems. Here again, nine of the boys had made the honor roll.[54]

As school districts tossed about between the fallout, both real and perceived, from the Philadelphia and Detroit court decisions and the administrative roadblocks that OCR had set up under Title IX, it was not long before local frustration spilled over into the halls of Congress. The legal uncertainty began to weigh heavily on the increasingly visible needs of certain student populations and the interest of school districts in testing the effectiveness of single-sex programs as a workable approach to meet those needs. In response to what was fast becoming a legal and political impasse, Senator John C. Danforth of Missouri in 1994 introduced an amendment to the Elementary and Secondary Education Act that would have allowed public school officials to establish single-sex programs on a limited experimental basis. The Danforth amendment directly addressed both the decision in the Detroit case and OCR's interpretation of the Title IX law and regulations. In his remarks before the Senate, Senator Danforth noted the chilling effect of ACLU threats and OCR action. Some programs had buckled under, while others continued in "near secrecy for fear of discovery by lawyers and government officials intent on shutting them down in the name of equality."

To many the proposal seemed quite modest. It neither challenged OCR's interpretation of the law nor suggested amending the regulations. Instead, it allowed the Department of Education to waive Title IX enforcement and permit local school officials to voluntarily establish such programs for low-income educationally disadvantaged students. Under the plan, the department would have awarded ten five-year grants to school districts for the design and operation of educational opportunity single-sex classes for both males and females, provided there was a comparable coeducational option. Introducing the bill, Senator Danforth invoked research studies supporting the positive effects of single-sex schooling on achievement among girls and minority boys. Citing grim statistics of academic failure among black and Hispanic young people—high dropout rates, low literacy rates, and high retention rates amid widespread poverty—he made an impassioned plea to his colleagues, appealing to their sense of justice and fair play. He reminded them of the numerous private schools in Washington, D.C. Some of these schools were single-sex and most of them educated many of the senators' own children. Echoing throughout Danforth's presentation was the notion of family choice—available to the rich but not to the poor.

The Equal Educational Opportunity Program garnered support from prominent educators, researchers, lawyers, and government officials including Elizabeth Fox-Genovese and David Reisman, who both later testified on behalf of VMI, as well as the historian Diane Ravitch and Senator Dianne Feinstein, both graduates of single-sex schools. Nevertheless, some members of Congress feared that at least some school districts in need of funds would use the program as a cash cow without making any commitment to single-sex schooling. Perhaps they were prescient on this count, at least judging from the subsequent fate of California's dual-academy initiative in the late 1990s. The state offered substantial funds for school districts to open separate schools for girls and boys. Yet when the state seed monies disappeared, only one of the six funded programs remained.

To save the essential idea, Senator Danforth agreed to eliminate the funding provision from his proposal. The program would simply allow the secretary of education to select a limited number of school districts that were experimenting with single-gender classes and insulate them for a limited period of time from Title IX and other federal laws prohibiting sex discrimination. The purpose was to collect data to determine the effectiveness of these programs in educating educationally disadvantaged children.

Those limits and purposes, however, did not satisfy some members of Congress, particularly Senators Edward Kennedy and Carol Moseley-Braun. To them, even a limited experimental program might lead to further racial segregation and might ultimately shortchange women. More broadly, the amendment would set a dangerous precedent for the Education Department to grant similar waivers from other civil rights laws. Joining the opposition were the American Association of University Women, the National Coalition of La Raza, the ACLU, the Anti-Defamation League, the NAACP, and NOW.[55] The revised proposal passed the Senate by a vote of 66 to 33 but was not included in the House version of the legislation. Senator Danforth made a last-ditch effort to convince House-Senate conferees that his proposal had merit, but it nevertheless failed.

## FEMALE NURSING SCHOOLS: THE DANGERS OF SOCIAL STEREOTYPES

With the Danforth amendment set aside and the momentum in Congress broken, the issue of single-sex schooling was tossed back into the murky and turbulent waters of OCR enforcement and intermittent threats of litigation. Federal officials wielded a heavy enforcement stick and local school officials were risk averse. They feared the financial and political costs of going the distance to the U.S. Supreme Court on an issue that was deeply dividing the civil rights and feminist communities. Yet the Court had already begun laying the foundation for such a decision in a rather remote case that had the barest factual connection to what was generating so much controversy.

In 1982 the Court struck down the all-female admissions policy of Mississippi University for Women School of Nursing, where the issue was not sex separation per se but comparability. Joe Hogan had applied to the school because he resided in Columbus, Mississippi, where MSU is located, and the state maintained no other nursing program within reasonable traveling distance from his home. The options available to him were either to commute or leave his long-standing job and relocate his family in closer proximity to another school. For Hogan, the harm suffered was not that he was separated from the opposite sex but that the state was constructively denying him an educational benefit available in his locality only to women. In reality, this was more than mere personal inconvenience. It was denial of an equal educational opportunity.

Despite a decision that on its face signaled a victory for men, and language that was decidedly gender-neutral, the Court appeared particularly sensitive to the constraining and harmful effects of traditional paternalism toward women. For Justice O'Connor and a bare majority of her colleagues, gender separation potentially bore harmful social consequences for women. As the justices pointed out, the all-female admissions policy tended to "perpetuate the stereotyped view of nursing as an exclusively woman's job" and made that view a "self-fulfilling prophecy." In language that was to dominate the Virginia Military Institute decision more than a decade later, the Court made clear that government agencies could not base policies on "fixed notions concerning the roles and abilities of males and females." Gender classifications had to be grounded in an "exceedingly persuasive justification"; that is, at the very least they had to be "substantially related to an important governmental objective." The majority rejected outright government policies intended to "exclude or 'protect' members of one gender because they are presumed to suffer from an inherent handicap or to be innately inferior."[56]

The state tried to justify the policy as "educational affirmative action," the purpose being to compensate for discrimination against women. But there was no evidence that women actually suffered discrimination in nursing; in fact, they dominated the field. In 1981 women constituted 96.5 percent of the registered nurses nationwide. At the same time, however, the Court acknowledged that a compensatory purpose might be permissible if it "intentionally and directly assists members of the sex that is disproportionately burdened" and who "actually suffer a disadvantage related to [their gender]."[57] The inference here was that at least some single-sex programs could find support in antisubordination values.

In the end, *Hogan* left open the door to publicly supported single-sex education, at least for compensatory purposes, as long as neither the intent nor the effect was to promote archaic and stereotypic views on the roles and abilities of females and males. These limited parameters generated uncertainty in the years to come, as single-sex schooling gained increased interest while popular and judicial support for affirmative action began to wane. The Court left unanswered the more difficult question as to what governmental interest, other than compensation for those actually suffering a disadvantage, could possibly support single-sex education. And what did the Court mean by a "disadvantage"? Although it did not explicitly preclude biological differences between the sexes and merely expressed skepticism toward the mechanical application of traditional gender roles, the tone of the decision suggested a socially constructed burden, which almost inevitably applies to women. Yet the opinion merely mentioned women specifically in a footnote, recollecting that they had historically been excluded from "particular areas" simply because they were thought to be "less than men." Nor did the Court resolve the larger question, not presented in the case, of whether gender classifications, like racial classifications, are inherently suspect. There was no separate facility for men that the Court could reject as "inherently" unequal despite tangible measures of equality, a fact that the Court acknowledged.[58]

But before leaving *Hogan*, one final point needs to be addressed. The state attempted to rely on Title IX to justify excluding men from the nursing school. Section 901(a) of the statute exempts the admissions policies of undergraduate public institutions "that traditionally and continually from [their] establishment [have] had a policy of admitting only students of one sex."[59] On this count the Court made clear that Congress, in enacting Title IX, could not "restrict, abrogate, or dilute" rights that are guaranteed by the Fourteenth Amendment.[60] Not only did the Court thus cast doubt on the exemption for traditionally single-sex public colleges, but it laid the foundation for scrutinizing other Title IX exemptions, including the one covering the last stronghold of male educational exclusivity—state military colleges.

## THE CITADEL: UNDOING MALE PRIVILEGE

In the decade following *Hogan*, the debate over single-sex education seemed to shift ground. With the last of the prestigious all-boys public secondary schools opened to girls in Philadelphia in 1984, women's rights advocates redirected their energies toward documenting gender inequities within the coed classroom. At the same time, largely to address the seemingly intractable needs of disadvantaged minority students, a small but growing number of school districts around the country became passionate defenders of single-sex programs. In this odd twist of events, suddenly single-sex education was no longer the violation but a remedy to denial of equal educational access. Yet while public school officials consistently avoided pushing the question to the Supreme Court, for the state military academies in South Carolina and Virginia, the sole remaining all-male public colleges in the country, the stakes were much too high to refuse the challenge. In both cases, the defense was sufficiently organized, powerful, and determined not to retreat in what it considered a "life or death" struggle for survival.

That struggle goes back to the 1970s, when a confluence of forces moved Congress to open the federal military academies to women. The end of the draft, declining respect for the military in the aftermath of Vietnam, and an organized and foreseeably successful movement to achieve equality for women all compelled that decision. On a practical level, both congressional members and academy leaders realized that women could help meet the demand for career officers, who in turn would attract more women recruits to fill the military's dwindling ranks. By 1976 West Point, the Air Force Academy, and the Naval Academy had moved toward coeducation. So had most state colleges and prestigious Ivy League institutions.

Despite this dramatic transformational wave throughout higher education and military education in particular, the Citadel in South Carolina and the Virginia Military Institute tenaciously held on to their all-male status for another two decades until forced to yield by the U.S. Supreme Court. By the late 1980s both institutions started feeling the strains of social change. At that time, both came under increased pressure from women's rights advocates and young women themselves who saw them as symbols of gender exclusion and perpetuators of harmful stereotypes that undermined women's social and economic progress. The only effective way to change that, the critics felt, was to force open the schools' doors to women. To their students, alumni, and state officials, on the other hand, the institutions represented manliness and tradition. Caught between these two opposing views, VMI and the Citadel soon found themselves in the vortex of a contentious dispute over the educational merits and legal permissibility of single-sex education. As the drama unfolded in southern courtrooms and in the press, the fate of the two institutions became gradually joined and ultimately cast forever in the VMI decision. In turn, despite its factual limitations and interpretational haziness, VMI set the stage on which the debate over single-sex education would subsequently search for resolution.

Over the course of several years, the VMI and Citadel litigation alternately marched in tandem through federal trial courts in Virginia and South Carolina, although Virginia started the journey on its path and eventually concluded it. Yet the two cases followed somewhat different routes into court. In the VMI case, the U.S. Department of Justice initiated the lawsuit on the complaint of a female who remained nameless and faceless. In the Citadel case, a female who had been denied admission took the college to court herself, with the Justice Department subsequently intervening as a party. This lawsuit produced a real but tragic heroine (or villain, depending on your perspective) in the person of Shannon Faulkner. Her compelling story and the indignities she suffered at the hands of angry and mean-spirited cadets, tacitly encouraged by a resistant administration, have been well documented. Just as the case against VMI set the course for legal interpretation, so the case against the Citadel provided a personal backdrop for understanding the underlying issues and concerns. It also opened a window onto the glaring distinctions between these extreme examples of traditional first-wave single-sex schools and the second-wave programs now passionately promoted by some of the most vocal opponents of the first.

Shannon Faulkner's quest to join the Corps of Cadets unfolded in the American eye through intermittent news reports, leaving even her staunchest supporters completely bewildered and disheartened, especially as the case came to a crashing climax. As summed up by one critic reviewing Catherine Manegold's compelling book *In Glory's Shadow,* "It's probably safe to say that many feminists . . . gave Shannon Faulkner the same kind of grimacing endorsement that we would accord to, say, prostitutes. We supported Ms. Faulkner's right to be what she wanted to be. . . . At the same time, we wondered why on earth anyone would want to pursue such an unpalatable vocation in the first place." As Manegold reveals, the Citadel was conceived originally in white fear of antebellum slave uprisings. It was designed to house a private army that would guard the white elite. It took a century and a half and the determination of one young woman to finally uncover how those same forces of violence and white male supremacy continued to shape its culture.[61]

This is the story of a high school honors student who defied single-handedly what she initially perceived as inexplicable inequality but came to understand as an emblem of southern tradition and a relentless and sometimes brutal male culture. What began as a youthful challenge turned into a political cause with stakes higher than this teenager from rural South Carolina ever could have imagined. What initially piqued her interest was a class discussion of a *Sports Illustrated* article featuring the institution. She decided to submit an application for admission to the 1993 entering class.

With her high school guidance counselor complicit in the ruse, all references to her gender were "whited-out" from her school transcripts, while the attached school appraisal spoke completely in gender-neutral terms. She soon received an acceptance letter with the opening: "Dear Mr. Faulkner." The admissions office had mistaken her for a male. But as news of the error traveled through the grapevine, the Citadel unapologetically rescinded the acceptance.

Citadel alumni later called Faulkner a "pawn" of the National Organization for Women and spoke of a feminist plot. Yet Shannon Faulkner was not a likely "feminist poster girl."[62] Nor was she a trailblazer. She was merely amazed and indignant that the trail was closed to begin with. Coming from a generation of young women unaccustomed to such blatant inequality, she found herself willingly in court, surrounded by a flock of New York City lawyers, including attorneys from the ACLU Women's Rights Project and the prestigious firm of Shearman and Sterling, as well as the president of the South Carolina chapter of NOW.

For the next two and a half years, as her lawsuit ground through the courts, she was taunted, vilified, and humiliated. She received telephone death threats and hate mail. Her car was pelted with eggs. The Citadel newspaper dubbed her "the Divine Bovine" and "Mrs. Doubtgender." "Die Faulkner" was scrawled across a billboard in Charleston, and a local radio station made her the subject of parodies in song. Her parents' home was sprayed with obscene epithets. Women stopped her on the street and berated her for trying to destroy a tradition. The Citadel's lawyer argued in court that she was setting about to impose a "unisex worldview" on the Constitution.[63] Meanwhile, Citadel officials dragged their feet on devising a remedy even after the appeals court governing the Citadel had found the Virginia Military Institute's identical policy in violation of the Constitution. They persistently argued that there simply was no demand for a Citadel-type institution or program for women. They made it clear that Shannon Faulkner would never be accepted to the powerful network that she was fighting to join. In fact, in their view, she would more likely destroy it. They fought her and her lawyers down to the wire and beyond.

While one side consistently argued that Faulkner should be admitted pending court resolution, the other side repeatedly sought delays of preliminary orders and asked the Supreme Court to intervene. In a compromise measure ordered by the district court, the Citadel allowed her to attend day classes with cadets for a year and a half but barred her from all other activities and from living on campus or wearing a uniform until the court resolved the case on the merits. She was a lone woman among more than 1,900 men, most of whom hostile at best toward her presence. When she spoke up in class, they hissed. In the hallways, they bumped into her and called her offensive names. When she reported these incidents to school officials, the invariable reply was, in essence, that boys will be boys.[64] Yet outside the institution she was a heroine, at least in some circles. In July 1994 she received a Woman of Courage award at NOW's national conference, where she delivered a keynote speech that was carried on C-SPAN. That month, after a bench trial, the district court ordered the Citadel to admit her into the Corps of Cadets. For the court, the school's assertion that there was no demand among women as a group was unproven and therefore could not justify denying Shannon Faulkner her individual right under the Constitution. The court also ordered the school to develop a plan to admit additional women.

Days before classes were to begin, officials won a stay, pending appeal. The following April, a divided appeals court affirmed the district court ruling ordering the Citadel to admit Faulkner unless they could develop an acceptable alternative plan by the opening of school the following August. School officials hastily engaged Converse College, a private women's school in Spartanburg, to launch the South Carolina Institute for Leadership (SCIL), a parallel cadet program for women. It was a win-win deal for the struggling liberal arts school. The Citadel offered a nonrefundable $5 million startup check and promised an additional $3.4 million from the state. The twenty-two students entering the first class received scholarships worth the full value of their college costs. But as far as Faulkner's lawyer was concerned, the program was a "glorified Girl Scout program."[65] The women wore civilian clothes and ate meals in a dining room decorated with crystal chandeliers, in striking contrast to the austere and somewhat abusive dining conditions of Citadel "knobs," so called because of their shaved heads. At SCIL, the military component consisted primarily of Reserve Officer Training Corps (ROTC) training at nearby Wofford College and, unlike the Citadel, there were few strict rules and no harsh discipline.

Just days before the beginning of yet another academic year, the Citadel's attorneys were again back in court. They were seeking another stay until the court decided whether the parallel program was an acceptable alternative to admitting women to the school. The lower courts denied the request, and two U.S. Supreme Court justices refused to intervene, stopping this desperate ploy to prevent Shannon Faulkner from entering the Corps of Cadets. But Citadel attorneys were unrelenting. Down to the wire, they argued to no avail that she did not meet the weight requirements and had a bad knee. They threatened to shave her head like other knobs, while attorneys for the Department of Justice argued that it would "deny her female identity."[66] The school's lawyers ultimately backed off for fear of appearing mean-spirited. On 12 August 1995 Faulkner reported to the Citadel as the first female cadet in the school's 152-year history. But unlike West Point's first coed class of 120 women who had entered with each other's support and a clear mandate from Congress, Faulkner was a solitary pioneer accompanied only by her parents and four U.S. marshals. The sheer emotional strain from that isolation soon brought her project to a crashing halt.

Predictably, no warm welcome awaited her. In fact, she was treated as a pariah. She lasted but one week, mostly in the infirmary, ostensibly suffering from heat exhaustion but in reality caving in under the intense scrutiny and pressure of the previous two and a half years, magnified by the animosity of her peers and the devastating isolation. Nevertheless, as she later recalled, "hell week" was nothing compared to what she had endured on her way there. She had gained fifty pounds and felt as if she had aged ten to twenty years. She was battle worn. By late afternoon on day six, despite her lawyers' desperate urging that she could make it, she announced that she was withdrawing from the school. The response from the Corps of Cadets was quick and unequivocal: sheer celebration and pandemonium. The young men whooped and howled and "ran in circles chanting slogans, arms raised in victory." Her final encounter with the Citadel came as she exited the gates in a jeep to the strains of "Hey, hey, the witch is dead," sung by three dancing cadets in soaking uniforms. Their euphoria underscored the institutional ethos—that only "real men" could survive the rigors of the Citadel's program. The fact that thirty male cadets had also withdrawn within the first week could not discredit this pervasive belief.[67]

Shannon Faulkner had won the battle but lost the war, at least her own personal war. For her lawyers, it was admittedly a bitter victory. Although her departure weakened their case, their primary goal had been to get her admitted in the first place, and they had succeeded. As Val Vojdik, one of the lead attorneys, proclaimed, "This is not about Shannon Faulkner, this is about discrimination. Just think back to the battles over segregation. It was never just one individual. It took a lot of people fighting for justice for a long time to succeed." In the meantime, the Citadel had given a $5 million dollar nonrefundable check to Converse College for a parallel program never approved by the court, while the legal fees owed to Faulkner's attorneys and the school's legal team had mounted to millions of dollars. Shearman and Sterling later gave the ACLU Women's Rights Project more than $1 million of the $4.5 million it received and established a fund with the remainder to litigate other causes that advance women's economic rights. Yet it was still not over. The judge allowed the attorneys to substitute a new female candidate's name in the case. When an unusually high number of upper-class students did not return after Christmas break, Citadel officials realized the high toll the litigation had taken on the institution.[68]

In the end, it was the Supreme Court's decision in the case against the Virginia Military Institute the following June that forced coeducation on the

Citadel. Within two months of the Court's ruling, Citadel officials acquiesced and submitted to the district court a twenty-one-page plan to admit women. The plan included sexual-harassment sensitivity training for all cadets. The following September, four women officially entered the Corps of Cadets without any overt signs of opposition. But even an edict from the highest court in the land could not change such a deeply embedded institutional culture, or at least not with sufficient speed to integrate women without incident. By January two of the women had filed harassment complaints and withdrawn from the school. Their claims may have proven shocking and even unthinkable in another setting. Their fellow cadets had sprayed them with nail polish remover and set them on fire, had washed their mouths out with cleanser, and had kicked them and subjected them to unwelcome sexual advances.

Fourteen male cadets were punished in the wake of the allegations. Two of them were dismissed and three resigned. Both women subsequently sued the Citadel, one of them ultimately settling for $100,000 and the other for $33,750, although the school admitted no wrongdoing. In the meantime, the Justice Department again engaged the federal court. The Citadel agreed to enroll at least twenty women the following fall. They further agreed to make administrative changes that would expedite the recruitment and integration of women students. The incidents, nevertheless, had placed the institution's hidden culture of violence and cruelty under intense public scrutiny. A *Washington Post* editorial urged the school's leaders to "make a judgment about how this worse-than-fraternity nonsense prepares their students for military service or life in the real world."[69]

The Faulkner litigation and its aftermath obviously left Citadel officials with more problems than they had anticipated. Yet they seemed to accept the fact that they would have to recruit more women into an institution whose dwindling enrollments pointed out that it was becoming understandably less appealing even to sensible men. Throughout this ordeal, the state of South Carolina had advanced an old segregationist argument reminiscent of one pursued almost a half-century earlier in the South and shot down by the Supreme Court in the *Gaines* case. State officials had doggedly insisted that there was no demand for a Citadel-type program for women. But this fact was impossible to ascertain because the institution had kept no records of inquiries from women, at least up until the time of trial. It also was irrelevant that the South Carolina Commission on Higher Education had received no requests for a women's program in the twenty years since the all-female Winthrop College, a state-supported school, had become coeducational.

Shannon Faulkner and her attorneys never made it to the Supreme Court. They were preempted by the Justice Department and the VMI litigation. Despite her valiant and persistent efforts, she will not officially go down in legal history as the young woman who broke barriers that seemed totally impenetrable to women. Nor will her name grace the pages of law texts and treatises as a symbol of gender equality. Nevertheless, she was a heroine in her own right. That point was perhaps best made by Pat Conroy, a Citadel graduate and author of *The Lords of Discipline,* a novel set at an all-male southern military school much like his alma mater. To his mind, Faulkner "never had a chance." Having studied the Citadel for thirty-two years, Conroy later told her, "The most courageous person ever seen to enter was Charles Foster, the first black cadet. Not anymore. Now, the bravest person I have ever seen enter the Long Gray Line wore a dress."[70]

It is reasonable to speculate that Shannon Faulkner's story had an unspoken effect on the ultimate outcome in the VMI litigation. The public nature of her painful ordeal to gain entrance into the Citadel propelled her and her legal claims into the public eye and gained for her the sympathy of many observers who could not "wrap their minds" around the impersonal and abstract arguments emerging from the VMI case. As the two cases wove in and out of each other through the federal courts, the dramatic events surrounding her efforts and the images that flashed across television screens and appeared in newspapers nationwide set the real-world backdrop for the Court to sort through the complex legal and policy issues ultimately presented in the VMI litigation.

So to say that Sharon Faulkner never made it to the Supreme Court is a half-truth. In a technically legal sense, she played no part in the deliberations. But her story surely must have haunted the justices as they handed down one of the Court's most textured decisions on gender equity.

# 7
# Reconciling the Law

In the modern-day struggle to achieve gender equity in education, 1972 and 1996 stand out as hallmark years. The first marks congressional enactment of Title IX. The second brought the Supreme Court's ringing affirmation of women's equality in the case against the Virginia Military Institute (VMI). In the intervening years, the law governing single-sex elementary and secondary programs had gradually evolved as a patchwork quilt of lower court decisions and Office for Civil Rights rulings and warnings. None of these alone or combined provided satisfactory guidance, while the facts presented in *Hogan,* the case challenging the all-female nursing school, proved somewhat idiosyncratic. Nonetheless, each legal encounter gave a faint glimpse into the underlying social and political tensions. When the issue of single-sex education again reached the Court in the VMI case, it carried with it a quarter-century of federal enforcement, changed social norms, and the still unresolved conflict between sameness and difference. And similar to *Hogan,* it arrived cloaked in a set of facts that bore but a bare resemblance to current single-sex initiatives.

An unanticipated turn of events characterized the decade between *Hogan* and the VMI case, in particular. Some urban school districts had become ardent defenders of single-sex programs. School officials were moving ahead with fragmented support from segments of the civil rights and women's rights communities. The situation was slowly turning inside out. In some circles, at least, single-sex education was no longer a barrier but a remedy to achieving equal educational access. In the meantime, the Court had gained among its members a leading champion of women's rights who was not only eager to make inroads on gender equity, but sufficiently persuasive to bring a sizable Court majority into agreement. For all these reasons, the VMI case presents an interesting study of the Court's grappling simultaneously with a fairly simple text and an extraordinarily complex subtext, all the while mindful of the potentially broad implications of its decision. For the very same reasons, it has presented a challenge to educators, policymakers, and federal authorities, who must now weave together into a seamless web the many constitutional strands of the VMI case and the seemingly conflicting requirements of Title IX, particularly its regulations.

## VMI AND SKEPTICAL SCRUTINY

In the Citadel litigation, state officials tried persistently but unsuccessfully to convince the courts that there was simply no demand for a Citadel-type program for women. If that argument rang hollow for South Carolina, it found even less credibility in the state of Virginia; the school's own records showed just the opposite. In fact there apparently was a demand not only for a VMI-type education for women but for coeducation at VMI itself. In the two years before the litigation started, VMI had received 347 inquiries from young women who, one could only assume, were testing the system's long-standing exclusionary policy. The institution responded to none of them. One of these women, a northern Virginia high school student whose identity has remained shielded from the public, was not so easily dismissed. In early 1989 she sent a letter to the Department of Justice in Washington, where attorneys in the Civil Rights Division, eager for the opportunity, initiated an inquiry into VMI's all-male admissions policy.

When the school's justification proved unsatisfactory, the department threatened to bring suit if the school failed to change its policy. But in a preemptive strike, and to the dismay of Justice attorneys, in February 1990 both the state attorney general and the VMI Foundation beat the federal government to the courthouse. Each brought a separate suit in the federal district court in Roanoke, where they were more certain to get a sympathetic hearing. They challenged the federal encroachment on the state's system of higher education and asked the court to declare the institute's admissions policy constitutional. The following month, the Civil Rights Division brought its own suit in the same court. The government argued that VMI's policy excluding women violated the equal protection clause of the Fourteenth Amendment.[1]

VMI officials had long anticipated legal action, and when it finally came, the reaction was visceral. To many VMI loyalists, this was an issue of "states' rights vs. federal intrusion, Southern tradition vs. Northern self-righteousness." For some it even evoked images of the Civil War, when

VMI had trained officers for the Confederacy. Buried deep within the institution's collective memory was the devastation that Union troops had wreaked on VMI's buildings, including its library and scientific collections.[2]

This was not the first time that the legal system had called the state of Virginia to task for its discriminatory education policies against women. Two decades earlier, a federal court had pushed the state to admit women to the University of Virginia at Charlottesville, the state's flagship institution. At that time, the court declined to address the state's four other single-sex colleges, specifically noting that one of them (VMI) was "military in character." "Are women to be admitted on an equal basis, and if so, are they to wear uniforms and be taught to bear arms?" the court pondered in 1970, as it unknowingly sat on the cusp of a feminist revival that was soon to transform America.[3] In the following years, many women did in fact don uniforms, enter the federal military academies, and slowly move up the officers' ranks. They also learned how to bear arms and eventually experienced combat. Fast-forward to 1990 and that same military college found itself fiercely defending its right to exclude women based on archaic generalizations of their capabilities and tendencies. Over the next five years, VMI went through two rounds of litigation in the lower courts, the first to determine whether the policy violated the Constitution, and the second to determine the appropriate remedy.[4]

The thorny legal and social issues raised in the VMI litigation are best understood when viewed against the backdrop of history. Like the Citadel's, the Virginia Military Institute's male-only policy was a relic of an era when society considered women unfit for higher education and particularly unfit for military service and leadership. In 1839 the state of Virginia established VMI as one of the country's first military colleges. Initially the school assigned cadets to guard the state militia arsenal in Lexington, where the school is located. Many of them were young men, as young as sixteen, drawn from the lower classes of rural Virginia. Some were poorly educated. Despite VMI's attempts to model itself after West Point, in its early years the institute functioned, by an 1842 act of the legislature, as the state's first normal school, training teachers to improve Virginia's appalling educational system. VMI quietly abandoned this role after the Civil War, when schoolteaching came to be viewed as women's work, carrying low prestige and low pay. In an attempt to prove its value in rebuilding the economy of the state, VMI redefined a new mission for itself, offering a baccalaureate degree that emphasized science and engineering. By the close of the century, it had expanded its engineering curriculum, raised academic standards, opened its doors to out-of-state students, and improved the credentials of its faculty.[5]

Over the next hundred years, VMI gradually gained a reputation of prestige, not only throughout Virginia but nationally. Yet unlike the federal military academies, which prepare cadets for service in the armed forces, VMI primarily trained its students for leadership roles in the corporate world and in government. By the early 1990s only 15 percent of its graduates pursued military careers, an even smaller number than the 30 percent at the Citadel. As former United States Senator Harry F. Byrd, a VMI alumnus, observed in the 1970s, "The military, the most conspicuous feature of the Institute, often creates the impression that training men to be soldiers is the main objective." For Byrd, that merely masked other "vital aspects" of a program designed for "drawing out the man."[6] At the time of the Court's decision, VMI was the only remaining single-sex public college, male or female, in Virginia—the sole remnant of a system where most of the public colleges were single-sex institutions.

VMI's academic offerings in the liberal arts, sciences, and engineering were available at other public colleges and universities in the state. What made the institute special within the state system was its unique mission "to produce educated and honorable men, prepared for the varied work of civil life . . . ready as citizen-soldiers to defend their country in time of national peril."[7] Like the Citadel, the way it carried out this charge was through an "adversative" or doubting model of education. As described by the district court, the key features of this model were "physical rigor, mental stress, absolute equality of treatment, absence of privacy, minute regulation of behavior, and indoctrination in desirable values."[8] The underlying purpose was to strip cadets of their individuality in a way that built a sense of camaraderie and bonding.

Yet unlike the Citadel, which couched its legal argument in the vague administrative language of student demand and institutional autonomy, VMI directly and stridently placed great weight on the adversative approach to justify the exclusion of women. Throughout the litigation, VMI attorneys argued with certitude that women were unfit to withstand its rigors. They made it clear that this was a "highly specialized program for the distinctive physiological and developmental characteristics of males."[9] They insisted that if forced to admit women, VMI would have to modify the program which inevitably would destroy its success. From their arguments one would never suspect that almost 50 percent of the new male cadets regularly failed the physical fitness test and were offered remedial training, while 2 percent graduated without ever having passed it.[10]

More important, the school's arguments masked the truth behind the most physically demanding and unremittingly brutal aspects of the VMI experience. Many of these practices were not part of the school's physical education program, nor official policy of the institution, but merely a hazing system of arbitrary tests that upper-class cadets imposed on the "rats" (first-year cadets) and to which the institution historically gave silent consent. A group of high-ranking military women best captured the core of that experience in a brief submitted to the Court. As they described it, this was "an abusive method of imposing stress on cadets, but . . . an artificial stress, not a real-life or combat-type stress."[11] Meanwhile, the United States held fast to its position that the appropriate remedy was for VMI to admit women.

Here was an institution that touted Stonewall Jackson as a past professor and its "patron saint." It therefore was not surprising that school officials and alumni deeply resented change of any kind, particularly when forced upon them by outsiders. They especially feared that women would shatter the vaunted "VMI experience." Meanwhile, a majority of the faculty did not share this sentiment. In a poll taken by the head of VMI's history department in March 1990, 62 percent favored the admission of women. For some, coeducation was a way to raise academic standards and to improve the quality of an applicant pool with less than stellar SAT scores. For others, it was simply a matter of equality.[12] Those in the "trenches" apparently had a keener sensitivity to what was going on at the institution and in society. They were also less wedded to VMI's "cult of masculinity." Perhaps their insider's view had given them a real sense of its dark side.

Before trial, the district court permitted both the VMI Foundation, which has the largest per-student endowment of any undergraduate college nationwide, and the VMI Alumni Association to intervene as defendants in the litigation despite objections raised by the federal government. At the same time, the court released Governor Douglas Wilder, also named as a defendant, and granted the state attorney general permission to withdraw from representing any party. In response to the complaint, Wilder had stated unequivocally that "the failure to admit females to [VMI was] against [his] personal philosophy," and that "no person should be denied admittance to a state supported school because of her gender." The governor nevertheless assured the court that he would abide by whatever decision it reached. The Commonwealth of Virginia itself obtained a stay of proceedings while the court considered the state's liability.[13]

By the time the case ultimately reached the Supreme Court, a changed administration with more supportive views toward VMI allowed a new attorney general to represent the state's interests. In the meantime, with the state's lawyer removed from the picture at least during the liability phase, the interests of the remaining public defendants—VMI, its superintendent, and the Virginia State Council of Higher Education—were so closely aligned with one another and with the private interveners that they all shared the same attorneys. For that purpose, the VMI Foundation drew on its wealth of resources to assemble a high-powered and politically positioned legal team, with Griffin Bell, the former U.S. attorney general and then a partner in the Atlanta firm of King and Spalding, as lead counsel. And so at least on the initial question of liability, the legal theories, factual analysis, and institutional vision presented to the court were shaped not by the state but primarily by the private interests of the alumni, the foundation, and the Board of Visitors. And by law, at least seventeen of the board's members had to be VMI graduates. The alumni thus effectively carried the weight of defending the constitutionality of VMI's admissions policy. Their unswerving loyalty, determination, and perspective reverberated throughout the litigation, for better or for worse.

As the case worked its way through two rounds in the trial court, both sides bolstered their legal arguments with testimony from experts in the social sciences, higher education, and gender studies. In the first round, the appeals court found that the VMI program violated the Fourteenth Amendment equal protection clause and offered the state three options as remedies. That ruling for the time shifted the debating ground away from liability to the question of an appropriate remedy. VMI could admit women, establish a separate parallel institution for women, or forgo state support and pursue its own policies as a private institution. This last option proved especially appealing to many alumni, although others saw privatization as institutional suicide. At that point, VMI was receiving $8.4 million a year from the state, a sizable sum that undoubtedly gave even the school's most ardent supporters serious pause.

In response, the state of Virginia proposed a separate all-female program, the Virginia Women's Institute for Leadership (VWIL), which later served as a model for the women's program initiated by the Citadel. The women's institute would be established at Mary Baldwin College, a private liberal arts college for women located about thirty-five miles northeast of VMI. Mary Baldwin established a task force to develop the VWIL plan, which the college's faculty approved by a vote of 52 to 8. The promise of a generous $5.5 million permanent endowment from the VMI Foundation, plus an annual state allocation of $5,900 for each Virginia student enrolled, made this an offer Mary Baldwin officials could not refuse.

When the parties returned to the trial court, the programmatic aspects of VMI and VWIL took center stage. As the attorneys on both sides pounded the witnesses and turned their testimony upside down on cross-examination, it became an evidentiary war between the forces of sameness and of difference. The VMI lineup of experts, including David Riesman, professor emeritus at Harvard, and Elizabeth Fox-Genovese, the noted feminist historian from Emory University, offered numerous generalizations about the distinct abilities and proclivities of males and females.

The eighty-two-year-old Riesman, whose testimony appeared before the court on videotape, clearly noted the "undisciplined nature of many men" and the "overdisciplined, oversubdued, self-mistrustful nature of many women." Yet he conceded that he had "known and . . . worked with many women who do not fit this picture at all." For anyone familiar with his scholarship, his position supporting the school was indeed perplexing. In 1968 the distinguished sociologist had portrayed the "all-male college" as "a witting or unwitting device for preserving tacit assumptions of male superiority—assumptions for which women must eventually pay." He admitted at that time that he "did not find the arguments against women's colleges as persuasive as the arguments against men's colleges." At the height of the civil rights movement, he pointedly rejected "the pluralistic argument for preserving all-male colleges [as] uncomfortably similar to the pluralistic argument for preserving all-white colleges." That initial characterization from almost three decades earlier resurfaced in the Court's discussion of VMI.

In his testimony from the first trial, Professor Riesman had given some abstract mention to the negative effects of coeducation and even surprisingly stated that "for many boys, a single-sex school . . . is optimal." He noted, in fact, his earlier "misgivings" about single-sex male colleges but attributed these to the circumstances of that time, when all the Ivy League schools except Cornell were all-male. He also suggested that the negativity expressed in these remarks reflected more decidedly the view of his coauthor than his own. Yet his remarks to the court at this stage seemed less a testament to all-male colleges than a critique of college-age males and their need for VMI's uniquely punishing educational approach. Perhaps he simply believed that VMI was not denying women anything worth their wanting. Fox-Genovese lent particular credibility to the state's parallel program for women. She testified that adolescent girls lag in self-confidence and so, unlike boys, they do not need the adversative method to beat the "uppityness and aggression" out of them. In her view, the leadership experiences offered in the VWIL program would produce young women who can "imagine themselves as leaders."[14]

The government countered with testimony from, among others, Carol Nagy Jacklin, dean of social sciences and communication at the University of Southern California and coauthor of the 1974 classic *The Psychology of Sex Differences*. Basing her testimony on more than two decades of research, Jacklin maintained that there are greater learning differences within than between genders. When asked on cross-examination whether she was aware of any educational authorities supporting the "adversative methodology for the education of women," Jacklin responded, "No, nor for men."[15]

The government also brought in Alexander Astin, director of the Higher

Education Research Institute at the University of California at Los Angeles. Both VMI and the district court in the first trial had placed considerable weight on Astin's 1977 book *Four Critical Years,* in which he had touted the academic benefits of all-male colleges. Displeased with what he considered the misuse of his research, Astin subsequently published a clarification of his findings, suggesting that because the student and faculty at all-male colleges arguably might have changed in the intervening years (the original colleges were elite institutions), his original finding could not be used to justify an all-male VMI.

The issue in the second trial, however, was not the merits of single-sex education but whether the VWIL program was an appropriate remedy. In his testimony, Astin maintained that it was not in fact comparable to the program offered at VMI. As far as he could see, VWIL could not measure up, especially on such important intangible benefits as the power of VMI's peer group network and its effect on student outcomes. The VMI program, with all its military rigor and trappings, would attract a different type of student than the program at Mary Baldwin, and the experience would produce a different type of graduate. Astin, like Jacklin, could not recall any authoritative support for the adversative method, whether for women or for men.[16] The state remained unmoved by the implied suggestion that the method itself might be inappropriate for any students, regardless of sex. The trial court agreed and upheld the VWIL program. The Department of Justice again appealed.

The details of the Mary Baldwin program made it clear that the experience for women would scarcely resemble that of the VMI cadets. The proposed objective was to maintain the VMI mission to produce citizen-soldiers by using an approach that the program's organizers considered more appropriate to women, or at least to the type of woman who might apply to such a program at Mary Baldwin College. This was not intended to be a "women's VMI" but rather a program for women "utilizing . . . a structured environment emphasizing leadership training." The Corps of Cadets would be little more than ceremonial, while the ROTC program would provide the main military experience. VWIL students would not live in barracks, would not wear uniforms, and would not eat all meals together. Training in self-defense and self-assertiveness through a Cooperative Confidence Building Program would replace the VMI adversative approach. The dean of students at Mary Baldwin drew out the distinction. "The VMI model," she explained, "is based on the premise that young men come with inflated sense of self-efficacy that must be knocked down and rebuilt in a more meaningful way." College officials believed that "women had that leveling experience already in their lives" and thus did not need any more in college.[17]

Aside from organizational and philosophical differences, there were clear disparities in the quality of the educational program. The VWIL curriculum did not offer the advanced math, engineering, and physics courses available at VMI. If a VWIL student wanted to pursue an engineering degree, she could attend Washington University in St. Louis for two years and pay the tuition at the private school rate. Only 68 percent of Mary Baldwin's faculty held Ph.D.s, compared with 86 percent at VMI. And there was no comparison between the facilities of the two campuses, particularly in athletics. As one commentator called it, this was "VMI-lite," the place where girls went because "they just [were] not cut out to take the real tough, manly citizen-soldier leadership training."[18]

From the perspective of sex equality, there was something even more deeply troubling about the plan. It was in fact a testament to the enduring power of separate-spheres ideology, a striking example of "gender essentialism." The underlying premise was that sex (denoting biologically determined physical characteristics) and gender (denoting attitudinal and cultural characteristics coded as feminine or masculine) are coextensive. In other words, the plan left no room in either the VMI or the VWIL program for women or men who departed from the culturally gendered norms of the respective sexes. The two program models existed as bipolar extremes: adversative vs. cooperative, leveling vs. self-esteem building, and so on.[19]

The dangers and fallacies inherent in this view became crystallized in a brief submitted to the appeals court by Carol Gilligan and the Program on Gender, Science, and the Law at Columbia University. The brief challenged VMI's use of Gilligan's research to support the argument that gender-based differences justified state-supported single-sex education for men. It made clear that her findings suggested just the opposite, that a coeducational environment might have a "salutary effect" at VMI if the presence of women would challenge stereotypes that prove harmful to both sexes. The brief nevertheless drew an exception for those who face "systemic impediments" to their education similar to those experienced by women (perhaps a nod to single-sex programs for minority boys). Gilligan had confronted a similar misinterpretation in the Citadel litigation. There she had filed an affidavit explaining, as she did here, that her "observations about psychological development patterns that are generally associated with gender are not based on any premise of inherent differences between the sexes, but solely on the different nature of their experiences."[20]

The VWIL proposal provoked sharp disagreement between the parties over what an acceptable program should offer. The United States looked for equal inputs. The separate program for women would have to be a mirror image of VMI. The government knew that, by its own definition, equality could not be found even if the tangible qualities were equal, which they clearly were not. A newly minted parallel program for women could never offer VMI's intangible features, including its powerful alumni network, its stellar reputation, its prestige, and its traditions, all built on more than a century and a half of history. Virginia, on the other hand, looked for comparability of outputs—that is, a state-supported female college that would attain an outcome comparable to the one achieved for the male cadets at VMI.[21]

The appeals court tried to place some parameters on comparability but also seemed to elide that concept with inputs. It warned that the state had to "mitigate the effects" of gender classification by offering both men and women benefits that were "comparable in substance, but not [identical] in form or detail."[22] In other words, the programs need not be the same, dot for dot, dash for dash. Disparities could reflect differences in needs between men and women as long as they did not tend to lessen the dignity or societal regard of either sex. Applying this notion of "substantive comparability" and taking a position that seemed far more deferential toward the state's choice of means than the Supreme Court had suggested in *Hogan*, a divided appeals court found the parallel program constitutionally permissible. Senior Circuit Judge J. Dickson Phillips, a Carter appointee from North Carolina, disagreed in a sharply worded dissent. His characterization of the VWIL program as "but a pale shadow of VMI" would later guide the Supreme Court opinion, as would much of his rationale. For him the two programs were not "substantially equal" in view of the tangible and especially the intangible inequalities.[23] These fine, and not so fine, distinctions between equality and comparability, both substantive and formal, perhaps trivial at first glance, are indeed significant and have come to dominate legal discussion on single-sex education in the following years.

The first class of forty-two women entered the VWIL program in August 1995, within days of Shannon Faulkner's painful departure from the Citadel.[24] Meanwhile, the Justice Department was not about to let the case rest. It had gone this far and the stakes were too high to admit defeat. Department attorneys first tried for a rehearing before the full membership of the appeals court. With that request denied, they petitioned the Supreme Court for consideration.[25] As far as they could determine, the two programs were not in fact equal. The VWIL at Mary Baldwin College lacked the resources and prestige of the nation's oldest military college. The differences between the two programs were "substantial" and "deliberate," the government argued. They also were constitutionally unacceptable because they were premised on "explicit and archaic sex-based stereotypes" that merely served to "reinforce patterns of historical discrimination." On a larger scale, the United States tried to use the case to chart new terrain in the law of sex equality, entreating the Court to apply to sex classifications the level of "strict scrutiny" review traditionally applied to race.[26] VMI's all-male admissions policy should stand, government attorneys argued, only if it was "narrowly tailored" to serve a "compelling" state interest.

The case elicited an onslaught of amicus briefs, many signed by a long list of individuals and interest groups from across the political spectrum. The litigation had clearly struck a nerve in American culture, while the complex issues apparently had forged a number of unanticipated alliances. Some amici enthusiastically endorsed VMI and its mission. Others were more guarded. Though they did not necessarily support the institution, they feared the impact that a negative ruling might have on the broad landscape of single-sex schooling, from elementary through higher education, both public and private. Still others absolutely opposed single-sex education in any form. Among the VMI supporters were a number of conservative organizations, including the Family Research Council, Concerned Women for America, Phyllis Schlafly and the Eagle Forum, and the Independent Women's Forum, whose president, Anita Blair, was a member of the VMI Board of Visitors. The states of Pennsylvania and Wyoming argued that VMI had a valid interest in protecting diversity and experimentation. Other states saw it differently, showing less concern for state autonomy and more for individual rights. For Hawaii, Maryland, Massachusetts, Nevada, and Oregon, VMI had absolutely no legitimate interest in refusing to admit women.

Three amicus briefs seem to have carried special weight with the Court. The first came from the American Association of University Professors. Leading scholars in gender studies, among them Carol Gilligan, challenged the "time-worn" generalizations threaded throughout the trial record. These generalizations, they argued, depicted "women as passive, men as aggressive; women as peaceful, men as violent; women as cooperative, men as competitive; women as insecure, men as confident." Gilligan and her colleagues pointed out, "While it is undoubtedly true that there are average differences between the sexes, even Virginia concedes and the trial court recognized that many individuals of both sexes do not conform to the 'average' for their sex." More specifically, they noted how experts on both sides of the single-sex schooling question conceded that the data supporting the approach were unconvincing, except perhaps for minority boys.[27]

The second brief that resonated with the Court came from the International Coalition of Boys' Schools and a diverse group of individuals, including Cornelius Riordan whose research on single-sex schooling and minority students has proven pivotal in the debate. Some of the signatories had reservations about the VMI philosophy, yet they all shared a concern with the potential consequences of the Court's decision for single-sex education. Included among the group were representatives of urban school districts that had established or were thinking of implementing single-sex programs. Also included were representatives of private single-sex schools who feared the fallout of a negative decision on their institutions, in particular the loss of federal or state aid.[28] The third influential brief spoke for a group of private women's colleges expressing similar concerns. They specifically emphasized the educational benefits that single-sex higher education historically has offered women. Their views resurfaced in a key footnote to the Court's opinion.[29]

In June 1996, seven years after the anonymous student had filed her complaint with the Department of Justice, the Supreme Court, in a seven-to-one decision, ruled that VMI could no longer operate as a publicly funded single-sex institution. Justice Clarence Thomas, whose son was a student at VMI at the time, recused himself from the case. The Court's spokesperson was Justice Ruth Bader Ginsburg, a seasoned veteran of the gender wars. She had served as general counsel and founding director of the ACLU Women's Rights Project, the same organization that more recently had joined in representing Shannon Faulkner in her case against the Citadel.[30]

In a carefully and forcefully crafted opinion, Justice Ginsburg stressed the narrowness of the decision, the unique facts presented, and the historical background of women's exclusion against which the facts had arisen. Citing several groundbreaking cases that she herself had argued and won before the Court in the 1970s, she restated and applied the *Hogan* standard—that classifications by sex must be "substantially related" to an "important governmental interest" and must be supported by an "exceedingly persuasive justification." By emphasizing this last requirement and reinforcing it with stronger language than used in previous Court decisions, she seemed to give it more teeth. The opinion tells us that courts must apply "skeptical scrutiny," taking a "hard look" at "generalizations or tendencies" based on gender. Once a violation is found, the remedy must closely fit it, placing the claimants in "the position they would have occupied in the absence of [discrimination]."[31] The real significance of this language is still to be tested. It is nevertheless clear that the Court was relying on both antidiscrimination and antisubordination understandings of the equality principle.

The state of Virginia again offered two justifications for the exclusion of women from VMI: to provide diversity to an otherwise coeducational state system of higher education, and to preserve the educational benefits of VMI's unique "adversative" approach. The Court recognized the "Commonwealth's prerogative evenhandedly to support diverse educational opportunities." The state's actions, however, were anything but "evenhanded." Virginia effectively had denied women a unique educational opportunity available solely at the state's "premier military institute." Justice Ginsburg recounted in detail the history of higher education, replete with pervasive exclusionary policies against women even into the recent past. She counseled that the all-male college, set against that backdrop, is very likely to be a device for "preserving tacit assumptions of male superiority." Here she was quoting the observation made almost three decades earlier by the state's own witness, David Riesman, a quotation which she herself had incorporated into a brief submitted by the Women's Rights Project in the case against the all-boys admissions policy at Central High School in Philadelphia.[32]

Justice Ginsburg warned that even "benign" justifications would not necessarily support categorical exclusions. Nevertheless, she implied that exclusions based on sex might pass constitutional muster if grounded in an important and genuine purpose but not if conceived merely to meet the exigencies of litigation. Looking back over VMI's history, it was clear that diversity had not driven the decision of its founders, nor had it played a part in continuing to exclude women. But her suggestion that a conscious effort to promote educational diversity through single-sex schools might be permissible if backed by a commitment to promote equal educational opportunity carries broad implications for current single-sex initiatives.[33]

The Court dismissed outright Virginia's arguments supporting the second justification—to preserve the benefits of the adversative method which the state claimed was critical to the program's success although other military institutions had rejected it. More important, expert testimony had established that some women were "capable of all the individual activities required of VMI cadets." The district court had recognized in fact that "some women . . . would want to attend [VMI] if they had the opportunity."[34] It was not a question of whether women should be forced to attend VMI. Rather it was a question of whether the state of Virginia could categorically exclude from a unique benefit those women who did have the ability and capacity merely because most women did not.

Justice Ginsburg recalled how similar arguments had been used in the past to exclude women from the practices of law and medicine. Citing *Hogan*, she warned that "state actors controlling gates to opportunity . . . may not exclude qualified individuals based on 'fixed notions concerning the roles and abilities of males and females.'"[35] In sum, there was insufficient evidence that the admission of qualified women would effectively destroy the adversative method that VMI so prized. The implication was that women could enter VMI without any significant modifications in the program. That is precisely how VMI officials would ultimately sell coeducation to a most reluctant group of alumni and students.

The Court in the VMI case stopped short of renouncing all gender-based classifications, leaving open the door to single-sex schools under certain conditions. Nor did it claim that men and women must be treated exactly the same under all circumstances. Here we see Justice Ginsburg cautiously navigating a middle course between competing visions of absolute sex equality or equal treatment, on the one hand, and the recognition that women should be compensated for socially imposed disabilities or accommodated for different educational needs on the other. Unlike race, for which the law recognizes no differences, she tells us, the "inherent differences, between men and women" are "cause for celebration, but not for the denigration of members of either sex or for artificial constraints on an individual's opportunity." As the legal scholar Cass Sunstein has noted, the problem was not that Virginia had recognized a difference between women and men, but that it effectively "turned that difference into a disadvantage." For the Court, the equality principle meant that the state could not use sex differences as a justification for depriving either men or women of equal educational opportunities. Sex classifications, the Court held, "are permissible where they "advance the full development of the talent and capacities of our Nation's people." They may not be used, however, "as they once were . . . to create or perpetuate the legal, social, and economic inferiority of women."[36]

This broad language, taken as a whole, could translate into an oblique bow to single-sex schools for inner-city minority students, including boys. At least in some contexts, equal might of necessity mean different. Yet the closing qualification also sets the outer limits and suggests a particular apprehension of discrimination against women. That inference and the underlying fear are both quite reasonable when we consider that the Court was not writing on a blank slate. Justice Ginsburg cast her decision against the historical exclusion of women from educational opportunities and the harmful stereotypes upon which that exclusion was grounded. She acknowledged both the reality of difference and its potentially harmful misapplication. Officially recognized distinctions traditionally had placed women in a less advantageous position vis à vis men, while inherent differences could be misapplied to artificially constrain the opportunities of either sex.

This "badge of inferiority" or second-class citizenship, and the consequences that flow from it, appeared most troublesome to the Court. Even in *Hogan,* in which the Court upheld the right of a male to attend an all-female nursing school, the justices were more than incidentally mindful that the all-female policy had a harmful impact on women, if not in fact then at least in principle. Rather than compensate women for "discriminatory barriers" that they faced, the exclusion of men from the nursing school "perpetuated the stereotyped view of nursing as an exclusively woman's job."[37]

The state of Virginia repeatedly cast the case in court and in the public eye as having all to do with single-sex education, a strategy intended to give the school a broader base of support. The Justice Department attorneys, on the other hand, cast it as a question of gender equality, which is how the justices in the majority played it out. Yet they could not responsibly avoid the single-sex question without placing existing programs in serious jeopardy, something they apparently were not inclined to do. So they dismissed outright any concerns over the decision's impact on single-sex education as "see[ing] fire where there is no flame," making clear that the United States did not challenge the district court's finding that men and women could both benefit from single-sex education.[38]

To underscore that point, Justice Ginsburg directly affirmed the position taken in the amicus brief submitted by a group of private women's colleges. In words that would both lend support to single-sex education and at the same time arguably define its contours, she recognized "the mission of some single-sex schools to 'dissipate, rather than perpetuate, traditional gender classifications.' " And while she made clear that the Court was not addressing the question of whether states could provide "separate but equal" undergraduate institutions, she nevertheless opened a window on to what courts might consider in judging the equality of separate programs. Drawing on *Sweatt v. Painter*, the case that desegregated the University of Texas School of Law in 1950, she counseled that equality must be measured by both tangibles and intangibles. Following that rationale, the Mary Baldwin program was merely a "pale shadow of VMI" in terms of curricular and extracurricular choices, the stature of the faculty, funding, prestige, library resources, and alumni support and influence.[39]

"Substantial equality," the Court maintained, was preferable to the more deferential "substantial comparability" test used by the appeals court.[40] This linguistic distinction carries serious weight. By emphasizing equality rather than comparability, together with *Sweatt's* specific factors, the Court suggested an objective inputs standard (based on tangibles and intangibles) even if not palpable and measurable with a degree of certainty—one that would allow the institution less discretion, but also lend itself to less abuse.

Chief Justice William Rehnquist voted with the majority but wrote a separate concurring opinion. He was concerned that the Court had ratcheted up the standard for reviewing sex-based classifications. He also acknowledged more expressly and conclusively that a state may have a "valid interest in promoting [single-sex education]" simply because "considerable evidence" demonstrates that it benefits students pedagogically. The lone dissenting voice on the Court was that of Justice Antonin Scalia, who attacked the majority's opinion as "politics smuggled into law." To his mind, the Court had distorted judicial precedent, denied the real differences between women and men, and in the end even threatened the vitality of private single-sex schools, whose tax-exempt status and government funding were now placed in jeopardy. He predicted that the decision would render single-sex public education "functionally dead," and that experiments such as the all-male schools in Detroit would not be tried again.[41] History ultimately proved him wrong, although the decision initially did have an undeniable chilling effect on new initiatives.

For Justice Ginsburg, the VMI case vindicated her entire legal career. As Mark Tushnet, then dean of the Georgetown University Law School, summed it up, "This is the opinion she had hoped the Court would one day arrive at when she first started arguing cases of discrimination in the 1960s." She herself later likened it to *Vorchheimer v. School District*, the lawsuit challenging Philadelphia's all-male Central High School. "To me," she recalled, "it was winning the *Vorchheimer* case twenty years later." The language, reasoning, and spirit of her opinion in the VMI case drew heavily from the brief she had prepared for the ACLU Women's Rights Project in that earlier litigation.[42]

Like the Citadel, the Virginia Military Institute adamantly maintained that education was at the heart of the debate. Both institutions argued that states should be left to their own judgment in allocating their educational resources based on need. Underneath it all, however, both conflicts were only marginally related to education. As the concurring judge in the appeals court decision from the Citadel case had observed, "They instead [had] much to do with wealth, power, and the ability of those who have it now to determine who will have it later." Despite institutional protests that maleness was merely a proxy for interest and ability, at the core of both cases was a "cult of masculinity" and the potential threat to male privilege that the presence of women represented. It was not VMI's (or the Citadel's) single-sex basis per se that offended the Constitution, but more profoundly the role the institution played in "preserving a haven for a dominating and anti-female understanding of men and masculinity."[43]

Just two days following the Court's decision against VMI, the Citadel announced that it would "enthusiastically accept qualified female applicants into the Corps of Cadets." It took VMI another three months to arrive at the same decision. During that time, VMI alumni explored privatization while school officials thought through the possibility of coeducation. The administration quickly appointed an executive committee and eight subcommittees to "map a future that was in keeping with the past." The plan that emerged the following year covered a broad range of issues, some seemingly peripheral but nonetheless important to the entry of women. Haircuts, jewelry, class rings, dating, club sports, uniforms, privacy, and sexual harassment all had to be addressed. Unlike the federal academies that had made significant changes to accommodate and integrate women cadets over the years, change at VMI would be the least possible. Women would have to assimilate into the existing program with minimum accommodations.[44]

Throughout those three months of deliberation, passions ran high both within and without the institution. Some saw privatization as a national cause, with stakes much larger than VMI itself. Phyllis Schlafly of the Eagle Forum captured the depths of those feelings in an open letter sent to VMI's alumni and posted on their unofficial website. As far as she was concerned, the "massive government lawsuit against VMI wasn't about 'ending sex discrimination' or 'allowing women to have access to the same educational benefits' that men have at VMI. It was a no-holds-barred fight to feminize VMI waged by the radical feminists and their cohorts in the Federal Government." Schlafly knew her audience well. She challenged their masculinity and warned them, "If you allow Ginsburg et al. to do what Pat Schroeder et al. have done to the United States Navy, you are not the exemplars of manhood we thought you were. And that goes for Citadel alumni too."[45] The message was clear and the danger was imminent; they could soon fall in defeat at the hands of powerful women.

Just a week following the Court's decision, VMI Superintendent General Josiah Bunting III insisted that schools such as VMI and the Citadel would be "radically transformed" if they became coeducational, and in ways that he did not believe would prove "useful." The changes would be "seismic, profound." He lamented that the Court's decision was a "bitter, bitter blow" for VMI alumni who helped pay the $14 million in legal fees brought on by the litigation.[46] He reluctantly moved his staff toward planning to admit females in the event that the Board of Visitors gave the go-ahead. With the cost of going private estimated to fall between $100 million and $400 million, the Board voted nine to eight to open VMI's doors to women. In a surprising twist of events, most of the yes votes came from those who had graduated before 1970.

In hindsight, General Bunting and other VMI officials later conceded that the admission of women did not create the cataclysmic changes they had feared. In fact, the move to coeducation was far less painful than the Citadel experience. That ease, however, came with the advantage of not being first, along with a $5.1 million state grant to renovate the barracks and a year to thoughtfully plan the transition. Three years later, when the first class of women reached senior year, VMI named its first female battalion commander, one of only two students chosen out of a class of 298 to lead the institution's 1,200 cadets. At the same time, Bunting even admitted to feeling "elegiac and enthusiastic." "In the end," he allowed, "VMI has changed very little."[47]

*United States v. Virginia* was indeed a landmark case in the quest for gender equity and equal educational opportunity for women. It was also typical of cases where the Court strains to resolve complicated legal issues that bear on conflicting social norms and understandings. In that sense, it left a trail of questions for scholars to ponder, school districts to struggle with, and federal civil rights officials and the judiciary ultimately to address head on. These questions raise issues of compensatory purposes and affirmative action, gender differences and stereotypes, girls' versus boys' programs, the inherent limitations of "comparability," the meaning of "substantial equality," and the permissible bounds of Title IX.

## TITLE IX IN A WEB OF CHANGED REALITIES

One of the arguments leveled against single-sex programs that receive any federal monies is that they violate Title IX. To fully understand the implications of the law, we have to look back to its beginnings three decades ago. By 1970, as the women's movement started gaining momentum, congressional attention turned to the pervasive discrimination against females in educational opportunities. Extensive hearings by the House Special Subcommittee on Education in the summer of 1970, together with research gathered by the Senate Labor and Public Welfare Committee, reaffirmed these concerns. Most of the data addressed higher education, including admissions to selective schools, financial aid awards, and sex disparities in faculty salaries and in the number of graduate professional degrees awarded.[48] The resulting legislative package that included Title IX laid the groundwork for an administrative structure to investigate educational institutions, process complaints by individuals, and initiate enforcement proceedings. The package also incorporated Title IV of the Civil Rights Act of 1964 authorizing the attorney general to bring suit against educational institutions that engaged in sex discrimination in their policies and practices. The intent was to create a broad-based mechanism to root out sex discrimination as far as the federal dollar could reach.

Title IX is a briefly worded statute. It states that "No person in the United States shall, on the basis of sex, be excluded from participation in, be denied the benefits of, or be subjected to discrimination under any education program or activity receiving Federal financial assistance." As currently configured, the Office for Civil Rights (OCR) within the Department of Education serves as the main federal agency enforcing Title IX. (Before 1980, when Congress established the Department of Education, education fell under the authority of the former Department of Health, Education, and Welfare [HEW]). The statute authorizes OCR to issue rules and regulations based on congressional intent. It also authorizes the agency to enforce the law by terminating funds from educational institutions found in noncompliance, and by "any other means authorized by law."[49]

There is little evidence in the legislative history of either strong political support or organized lobbying leading up to Title IX.[50] It was primarily the product of skilled drafting and bargaining on the part of its two sponsors, Representative Edith Green of Oregon and Senator Birch Bayh of Indiana. As Senator Bayh saw it, Title IX was designed to be "a strong and comprehensive measure [that would] provide women with solid legal protection from the persistent, pernicious discrimination which is serving to perpetuate second-class citizenship for [them]."[51]

The real battles over Title IX did not begin until it was time for OCR to draft implementing regulations. Nevertheless, as the bill wended its way through congressional committees and full floor debate, opposing interests were voiced, and some were accommodated. The law's express and implied exceptions reflect these concerns. In drafting Title IX Congress attempted to defer to local decision making and institutional autonomy wherever feasible. The House version would have exempted all undergraduate institutions. Much to the dismay of Representative Green, however, the law as passed focused on those cases in which, as Senator Bayh explained, there was "no justifiable reason to discriminate against one sex or the other"—namely, graduate and professional higher education (where discrimination against women historically denied them access to the most prestigious academic institutions and where their numbers were still disproportionately low) and vocational schools (where programs promoted invidious stereotypes of women and charted them into a narrow range of low-paying careers).[52]

The current legal debate over single-sex programs and Title IX involves two issues: the admissions policies of single-sex schools and single-sex classes in coeducational schools. Each raises distinct questions. First, consider single-sex schools, a concept that has generated much disagreement in urban school districts across the country. With regard to admissions, the statute applies "only to institutions of vocational education, professional education, and graduate higher education, and to public institutions of undergraduate higher education." It expressly exempts religious educational institutions whose tenets are inconsistent with the law, military training schools (such as the Citadel and VMI), and undergraduate public institutions of higher education that traditionally and continually had a policy of admitting only students of one sex at the time that the statute was enacted (such as the Mississippi University for Women School of Nursing). The statute is silent on admissions to private undergraduate colleges (such as Smith and Wellesley), as well as to public and private elementary and secondary schools, other than vocational schools. In 1975 OCR adopted regulations that reflect these inclusions, exclusions, and omissions.[53]

Opponents have drawn on the Detroit case to strengthen their Title IX claim. In granting a preliminary injunction against the all-male Afrocentric academies, the district court reasoned that the explicit and implicit exemptions for admission policies were "applicable primarily to historically pre-existing single-sex schools and not as an authorization to establish new single-sex schools."[54] Neither the language of the law nor the debates preceding its enactment, however, support that interpretation. A more reasonable reading is that Title IX implicitly excludes the admissions policies of all institutions not expressly covered—for example, all nonvocational single-sex public and private elementary and secondary schools. The legislative history suggests that Congress exempted these schools because it did not fully understand the "manner, extent, or rationale" of separate education below the college level and therefore could not foresee what effect a total ban might have had on them.[55]

Remarks by Senator Bayh confirm this conclusion. In presenting the proposed legislation to Congress, he focused on institutions of higher education, making only a passing reference to elementary and secondary schools. And though he believed that "[as] a matter of principle, our national policy should prohibit sex-discrimination at *all* levels of education," he recognized that, particularly in the private sector, "a change such as requiring a sex-neutral admission policy would be disruptive both in terms of the academic program and in terms of psychological and financial alumni support." Senator Bayh recommended that Congress require the Commissioner of Education to conduct a study, with open hearings, on admissions policies in general and specifically on single-sex high schools and make recommendations to Congress the following year. He was "amazed" that the Office of Education did not maintain statistics on "how many elementary and secondary schools—even public schools—are restricted in admission to one sex." He noted that "no one even knows what special qualities of the schools might argue for a continued single sex status."[56] He wisely understood that Congress could not politically justify a blanket prohibition without first assessing the pervasiveness of the practice, its merits as compared with coeducation, and the implications of undoing it.

It must be remembered that the year was 1972 and private single-sex secondary schools were just beginning to embrace coeducation more broadly. There were also a number of public single-sex schools, many of them academically selective, particularly in such large eastern cities as Boston, Baltimore, New York, and Philadelphia. To wipe the slate clean of these schools with one stroke from Washington would have proven not just radically un-popular but politically impossible. Impassioned cries of federalism, local autonomy, and individual privacy would have reverberated straight up the northeast corridor. Nevertheless, Senator Bayh's implicit reference to both public and private schools in the same breath is noteworthy. Here the Sen-ate sponsor of the legislation specifically noted that the admissions policies of schools not expressly covered in the legislation would be "temporarily exempted." And though he believed that many of the exemptions would not survive further study and discussion, his congressional colleagues in the House either did not share that view or perhaps feared that it might become a reality. In conference, the Senate yielded to the House amendment, which made no mention of the proposed study.[57] The study was never under-taken, the hearings were never held, and the original exemption presump-tively remains in place.

It is not surprising that in the following years Congress took no further action to eliminate any of the exemptions or to further extend the law's reach. In fact, the events that unfolded proved quite the opposite. The cli-mate in Washington remained at best resistant to sex equity. That resis-tance showed signs of hostility as the reality of Title IX's potential impact began to sink in. Throughout that period, there was a small but persistent movement in Congress to limit the law's coverage. A failed amendment that would have exempted revenue-producing sports from Title IX was a wake-up call to HEW officials that they had better validate the law with de-tailed rules. In June 1974 the agency issued proposed regulations.

Later that year, Congress enacted additional exemptions to Title IX. These amendments excluded social fraternities and sororities, Boy Scouts, Girl Scouts, the YMCA, the YWCA, Camp Fire Girls, and other voluntary youth organizations. The mood in Washington had become so threatening that women's groups formed a coalition to persuade Congress to approve the final regulations, which would serve as a bulwark against further at-tempts to amend the statute. The regulations went into effect in 1975. The following year, Congress was back at the drawing board once again, whit-tling away at the law, this time exempting boy or girl conferences, father-son and mother-daughter activities, and scholarships awarded as prizes for beauty pageants. With congressional attention diverted to these peripheral issues, along with the continuing and far more contentious controversy over athletics, the question of admissions policies within elementary and secondary programs simply fell off the Washington radar screen. When it reappeared almost two decades later, it carried an unexpected twist and an equally unanticipated split in the women's coalition. Throughout the inter-vening years, revenue-producing sports dominated the discussion while women's equity advocates fought to maintain the status quo and prevent backsliding.[58]

From the legislative language and subsequent history of Title IX, we can reasonably conclude that neither the statute nor the regulations cover the admissions policies of public elementary and secondary schools. The Title IX regulations, however, limit that exclusion, and that critical condition lends itself to a range of interpretations. According to what is commonly known as the "comparability" requirement, a local school district cannot exclude any student from admission to a school unless it makes available to the student, "pursuant to the same policies and criteria of admission, courses, services, and facilities [that are] comparable."[59] This proviso applies only to public school districts, an understandable accommodation to the numerous private single-sex schools that existed at the time the federal government adopted the regulations.

Aside from single-sex schools, the debate over Title IX has a second dimension. Here the focus is on single-sex classes within coeducational schools. In this case, the arguments turn solely on the Title IX regulations that seemingly present a broad prohibition against segregated course offerings. A public school cannot "provide any course or otherwise carry out any of its education program or activity, . . . or require or refuse participation" to any of its students on the basis of sex.[60] Nonetheless, the regulations incorporate a number of exceptions that recognize gender differences in the interest of maintaining privacy and safety but also with a view toward protecting girls' opportunities to compete on an equitable basis. For example, schools can maintain separate teams for contact sports, can group students in physical education activities according to their individual abilities, can conduct separate portions of classes that extensively address human sexuality, and can organize separate musical choral groups based on a particular vocal range or quality.[61] School districts also can establish separate programs for pregnant students, as long as participation is voluntary and the program is comparable to the one offered to nonpregnant students.[62] These narrow exceptions do not cover any of the core academic subjects, such as math and science, or computers, all of which have been the focal point of recent single-sex class initiatives for girls.

The Title IX regulations contain yet another provision that has proven significant for single-sex programs. The language allows school districts to take "affirmative action" to "overcome the effects of conditions which resulted in limited participation . . . by persons of a particular sex." Remedial programs of this sort are permissible even where neither the Department of Education nor a court has made formal findings that the school or district has engaged in sex discrimination.[63] This provision brings the notion of compensation into play. It suggests that single-sex programs of some nature might be permissible for certain populations if justified by a compensatory or remedial purpose. This is the premise on which such school districts as Dade County and Baltimore implemented single-sex classes and Detroit proposed separate schools for African-American boys in the early 1990s. It is also the basis on which school districts like New York and Chicago have justified all-girls schools while other school systems across the country have opened separate classes for girls in math, science, and technology.

## RECENT DEVELOPMENTS

For more than two decades, the Office for Civil Rights appeared to take an absolutist position on the Title IX regulations and their relation to single-sex programs. In the process, the agency fed the opposition through a short list of agency letters and warnings directed at school districts. The early single-sex programs that provoked OCR responses were typically complicated with racial separation. More recent enforcement efforts have targeted both single-sex schools and classes, even absent the racial factor.

As one former OCR insider noted, the single-sex question is probably the most complex gender issue that the agency has faced over the years. Next to women's athletics, it is probably the most politically charged. In the years immediately following the VMI case, OCR seemed to have tempered its position. The agency appeared to be searching for a more flexible approach that could address contemporary problems and at the same time gain consensus among competing views within the agency and with Justice Department attorneys. Just weeks after the Court's decision, Norma Cantú, then assistant secretary for civil rights in the Department of Education, stated in a press interview that Title IX does not prohibit separate schools by gender as long as the facilities and offerings are "comparable." She also noted that the majority of the Court "was very clearly speaking to the VMI case. It was silent on any other program around the country."[64] But OCR's qualified articulation of the law was not simply the result of the Court's ruling. Urban school districts, in particular, were clamoring for a definitive go-ahead, while the charter school movement was fast creating a fertile field for testing the merits of alternative educational approaches, including single-sex education. Most important, the question at hand addressed separate schools and not separate classes, and there was no suggestion of intentional racial identification as in past cases where the agency had threatened to enforce the law.

In February 1999 OCR issued a brief response to concerns raised in a Senate Appropriations Committee report. The agency stated that it was "examining whether there is a legal basis for interpreting Title IX to permit single-sex classrooms as well as schools where they are justified on educational grounds *and* do not involve stereotyping or stigmatizing students based on gender *and* where comparable educational opportunities are afforded to students of both sexes."[65] The report estimated that if changes in the regulations were necessary, a notice of proposed rulemaking would be published in the spring or summer of 1999. That never occurred.

In May 2000 OCR issued civil rights guidelines for charter schools. The guidelines merely restated the Title IX regulations on single-sex programs. Single-sex schools were permissible as long as the school district offered "comparable courses, services, and facilities" to students of the excluded sex and applied the same admissions policies and criteria. The guidelines permitted single-sex classes and programs where they were "necessary to remedy discrimination found by a court or OCR" or where they responded to "conditions that have limited participation by sex." The guidelines also stated that the department was reviewing the Title IX regulations on single-sex programs and schools.[66]

OCR's foot-dragging on the single-sex question did not sit well with some members of Congress, where proposals to make an end run around the Title IX quagmire continued to surface in the years following the VMI decision. With the defeat of the Danforth amendment in 1994 and the subsequent retirement of its sponsor, Senator Kay Bailey Hutchison of Texas took up the charge. The political strategy, however, readjusted itself through trial and error. The Danforth Amendment would have suspended the operation of Title IX, a risky proposition for civil rights, while later proposals would have amended Title IX itself.

Senator Hutchison repeatedly sponsored legislation that would have allowed school districts to use federal education reform funds for programs that provide "same gender schools and classrooms, if comparable educational opportunities are offered for students of both sexes." The proposal as originally worded met resistance from the American Association of University Women, who opposed any amendments to Title IX, and from attorneys at the National Women's Law Center, who saw the comparability standard as a marked retreat from the "substantial equality" of the VMI decision. They feared that it could "open the door to sex-segregated programming based on harmful stereotypes." The final and ultimately successful version, proposed as part of the No Child Left Behind Act, dropped the comparability language and explicitly permitted programs that provide "same gender schools and classrooms, consistent with applicable law." Signed into law in January 2002, the amendment gave the Department of Education 120 days to issue guidelines to school districts.[67]

The shift in language removed any potential threat to existing civil rights laws, and that proved politically significant in garnering bipartisan congressional support. Senator Edward Kennedy, who chaired the Senate Committee on Education and Labor, expressly endorsed the proposal. This was a sharp turnaround from his firm opposition in 1994 to the Danforth Amendment. The revisions also brought on board Senator Hillary Rodham Clinton, herself a graduate of an all-women college. Joining as a cosponsor, she noted how "single-sex schools and classes can help young people, boys and girls, improve their education." Her enthusiastic endorsement was about as strong as it could get, stating unequivocally that "public school choice should be expanded as broadly as possible," that "there should not be any obstacle to providing single-sex choice within the public school system."[68]

Providing federal funds for single-sex programs was an important step in the right direction. It placed the congressional imprimatur on the core approach, leaving the federal courts to determine the outer bounds under the Constitution. It also signaled to the Office for Civil Rights that it had to affirmatively address the Title IX regulations, a politically volatile exercise that the agency had persistently avoided despite repeated signals in recent years that it was planning to do so. What perhaps made sense in the 1970s, when OCR had drafted the original regulations, had since become a matter of regulatory misjudgment, obsolescence, and even overkill. At that time, OCR was responding to blatant gender inequities throughout education, and widespread gender stereotyping in course offerings. The agency was operating against the vivid memory of doors having been closed to women at the most prestigious institutions, and the recent dismantling of racially segregated school systems.

As a matter of policy, those circumstances compelled a hard line on gender separation. A quarter-century down the road, changed realities and understandings demanded more local flexibility, along with a strong measure of vigilance to prevent backsliding. OCR staff members themselves had come to realize that something had to done to bring the Title IX regulations in tune with the times or at the very least to resolve the ambiguities within the law. The congressional mandate to issue guidelines for implementing the new funding program forced the issue.

In May 2002 OCR issued the requisite guidelines, which laid out for school districts the agency's official interpretation of the existing Title IX regulations. In doing so, the agency made several significant points. First, Title IX did not prohibit single-sex elementary and secondary schools, other than vocational programs. The only limitation was that they meet the "comparability" requirement—that is, where a school district established a single-sex school for one sex, it had to provide comparable courses, services, and facilities to the other. Second, according to "longstanding [OCR] interpretation, policy, and practice," the "comparable school" had to be a single-sex school. Third, single-sex classes were permissible only if they constituted remedial or affirmative action, although the guidelines left these terms undefined. And finally, although OCR could not question the justifications underlying single-sex schools, which technically are exempt from Title IX, school districts might base their justification in remedial or "affirmative action" purposes. The guidelines warned school districts, however, that even if they conformed to these ground rules, Supreme Court rulings, particularly in *Hogan* and the VMI case, might still leave them open to constitutional challenge in court.[69]

Both the tone and the message made clear that OCR had reached a critical juncture. Not only were the regulations, and OCR's interpretation, out of sync with Congress's new federal funding program, but they were also on a collision course with constitutional developments on the Court. OCR seemingly had no choice but to reconcile the law and to do it speedily, smoothly, and unequivocally.

With time being of the essence, OCR simultaneously published a separate notice of intent informing the public that the agency was planning to propose amendments to the Title IX regulations that specifically would allow "more flexibility for educators to establish single-sex classes and schools at the elementary and secondary levels." The notice presented certain broad policy objectives that the agency was trying to achieve: encouragement of local innovation, expansion of parental choice, an increase in educational diversity, and promotion of equal educational opportunity, while at the same time avoiding sex-role stereotypes. Meanwhile, the agency was eager to gather a wide range of expert information and competing views before beginning the redrafting process. The notice invited the public to submit comments on a series of questions addressing several key issues that continued to divide supporters and opponents of single-sex schooling. Specifically the agency was looking for guidance on the research or other evidence that school districts should offer to justify single-sex classes, the question of whether a single-sex class or school for one sex requires a single-sex school for the other, and whether the regulations should apply "comparability" or an alternative standard when comparing programs offered to each of the sexes.[70]

It remains to be seen how and when OCR finally will resolve these questions. In the meantime the agency has received more than 170 comments and proposals from across the political spectrum. For OCR this is both a challenge and an opportunity to develop a clear and cohesive position on Title IX that responds to contemporary social and legal realities.

## RESOLVING THE AMBIGUITIES

Public attention is now focused on Title IX and the process of re-designing the regulations. But this is no free-wheeling exercise. Nor is it an easy task. And while the Court's decision in the VMI case has receded from the public eye, OCR must take its cues not only from the underlying purposes of Title IX itself but also from the constitutional parameters set by the Court in that case and others. As a matter of law, OCR must now find sufficient interpretative room in the Title IX law to justify amending the regulations. Given the ambiguities and silence in the statute on a number of key issues, the regulations must at the least prove to be a reasonable interpretation of the intent of Congress when it originally passed Title IX in 1972. Otherwise, the Court could strike them down on the grounds that the agency has overstepped its bounds. More fundamentally, the revisions must agree with constitutional principles. If not, then even the most permissive statutory language and flexible enforcement scheme could still leave school districts vulnerable to a constitutional challenge in court. Both the Virginia Military Institute and the Mississippi University School of Nursing learned that painful lesson. Title IX explicitly exempted the admissions policies of both institutions, yet neither could survive an attack on equal protection grounds.[71] The ultimate legality of single-sex schools and classes clearly depends, therefore, on weaving constitutional norms into the regulations.

Despite all its rhetorical flourishes, the Court's decision in the VMI case resolved one fundamental issue which seems to have fallen on deaf ears among the most absolutist opponents of single-sex schooling. The VMI decision did not sound the death knell for single-sex education. In fact, it left considerable room for well-designed programs with clearly stated and non-biased objectives. The decision actually gave renewed life to the approach, effectively decoupling sex from race and making clear that, in the context of gender, separate is not inherently unequal. Unlike race, which the law absolutely rejects as a basis of innate traits, here the Court tells us that "'inherent differences' between men and women . . . remain cause for celebration."

Meanwhile, although single-sex programs are not per se unconstitutional, the opposite is also true. All single-sex programs are not per se or presumptively constitutional. From the VMI case we can rightly conclude that coeducation is still the norm in public schooling. School districts, nevertheless, may depart from the norm as long as they have an "important governmental interest" in mind, the program is "substantially related" to that purpose, and the overall justification is "exceedingly persuasive." The Court suggested that a sufficiently "important" governmental interest might be to "advance the full development of the talent and capacities of our Nation's people," provided that the program is not based in "overbroad generalizations" and does not perpetuate sex stereotypes.[72]

One has to read between the lines and behind the historical pages of the Court's decision to figure out how all this plays into the contemporary interest in single-sex schooling. The case, in fact, has little in common with recently established elementary and secondary school programs. VMI was analogous to the first generation of elite single-sex institutions that excluded women from unique educational opportunities based on stereotypical notions of their capabilities. The Court concluded that VMI, in doing so, was perpetuating the "inferiority of women" and the superiority of men. The more recent vintage of programs has just the opposite intent and projected effect. These new public school initiatives do not imply any inherent deficiencies among the categorically excluded sex, as was the case with VMI, but address the specific educational needs of the included sex, whether those needs are socially or biologically constructed. In the end, these programs attempt to level the playing field rather than exclude on the basis of negative stereotypes.

The Court also tells us in the VMI decision that government-run programs cannot be based in "fixed notions concerning the roles and capabilities of males and females." This point obviously opens to question the permissibility of all-girls schools and classes that focus on math, science, and technology. Aren't they based on stereotypes about girls' underachievement? Don't they suggest after all that girls are deficient in some way, that perhaps they lack a math or science gene? The response turns in part on the underlying purpose and the way that school officials present it. These programs undeniably rely, to some degree, on generalizations about females and males. Some of the generalizations, however, are not necessarily "overbroad" but are increasingly gaining ground in scientific research combined with anecdotal evidence from professional reports, attitudinal surveys, and classroom observations.

We are now coming to understand that there may in fact exist small cognitive differences in the overall rate at which boys and girls, as distinct groups, develop specific verbal and spatial skills relative to each other. But there is also research indicating that these differences are not carved into stone, that they diminish and disappear over the course of childhood and adolescence, and, most important, that they respond to training and experience. We also have available data on achievement, participation levels, and student attitudes that indicate a greater willingness on the part of some girls to take intellectual risks in the absence of boys.

These generalizations are not intended to exclude such girls from the fabric of society, but ultimately to weave them into that fabric without restricting opportunities for men. The same can be said for programs that address the slower maturational rate of young boys when compared with girls and their slower verbal development. In the case of VMI, in contrast, the institution used broad generalizations about the specific inabilities of women in order to foreclose them from valuable opportunities afforded only to men. The Court rejected such generalizations "about the way women are" because they denied an opportunity to those whose "talent and capacity" placed them "outside the average description."

That again contrasts with what we find in currently contested initiatives. Here single-sex programs are not excluding girls or boys who would like to be included but who fall outside the average description or norm for their group, as at VMI, but rather including them on a voluntary basis because they fall within a normative assessment for their group. Nor are these programs excluding the other sex on the basis of stereotypical notions about their inferior capabilities but rather on the basis of growing evidence of what might be more effective in addressing specific observed sex-related differences in performance. Moreover—and this is an important distinction—the generalizations made by VMI officials were generalizations about men and women and not about boys and girls who are still in the process of maturing and developing. In this case, certain differences may be real at different stages as students move from childhood through adolescence and into adulthood. By the time individuals reach higher education, we can assume that gender-based developmental differences have disappeared and therefore are no longer relevant to educational programming.

It all boils down to the fit between the program's means and ends, and to its context. If the program is designed to expand opportunities and not to limit them, then the justification becomes more persuasive. The effect, however, must also support the intent. No matter how benign the intent, a program cannot perpetuate a sense of inferiority among its beneficiaries or in the eyes of the general public. School officials must exercise extreme diligence in monitoring the program's explicit and implicit messages and assessing its cognitive and affective outcomes on an ongoing basis. And the federal Office for Civil Rights can play a key role in monitoring compliance with the letter and spirit of the law.

Given these clear directives that emerge from the VMI decision, there are three provisions in the current Title IX regulations that demand reexamination: first, the comparability standard; second, the affirmative action exception; and third, the sweeping prohibition against single-sex classes.

### Comparability Versus Substantial Equality

The first provision, and the one most directly linked to the Court's decision, addresses the standard used to compare programs offered to each sex. The current Title IX regulations speak only to single-sex schools and require that the program offered to one sex must be "comparable" to that offered the other. Women's groups have argued that the comparability standard is too deferential and that it has been overridden by the VMI case. On this count they are correct. The VMI decision tells us that the two programs must be "substantially equal" as measured by tangible and intangible factors. In fact, the Court expressly rejected the appeals court's use of "substantial comparability" (similar to the comparability standard in the Title IX regulations) as showing too much deference to state officials.[73] The difference is more than simple semantics. As already noted, the language of "equality," along with the Court's specific defining features or factors, puts more teeth into the measure than mere comparability.

More important, and what seems to go unnoticed, is that neither the terminology nor the implicit standard originated with the VMI decision. Rather, both draw on firm and long-standing judicial precedent going back more than a half-century to the Supreme Court's decision in *Missouri ex rel. Gaines v. Canada* and later affirmed and more clearly defined in *Sweatt v. Painter*. These early race desegregation cases laid the foundation for the equality principle articulated in *Brown v. Board of Education*. Both Title IX and the VMI decision grow out of and give force to that very principle. The Court explicitly relied on *Sweatt* in concluding that the all-male VMI program and the parallel women's program established at Mary Baldwin College were not "substantially equal" based on various measures of equality, including faculty credentials, course offerings, alumni influence, and overall institutional prestige.[74] Given this solid grounding in constitutional law, and the reaffirmation of the VMI decision in the context of gender and particularly single-sex education, it seems unquestionable that the same standard should be incorporated into the Title IX regulations.

The question then remains as to whether "substantial equality" can be met only within another single-sex program or whether a program operating within an existing coeducational school or class could suffice. In other words, if a school district establishes a single-sex school or class for girls, must it also establish one for boys, or in the alternative, may it offer a substantially equal program in a coeducational setting? The factual background of the VMI case does not provide a direct answer. The uniquely "totalistic" educational approach used at VMI contrasts sharply with the typically student-centered and ability-focused elementary or secondary school curriculum. Nevertheless, there is no indication in the Court's decision that the two programs had to be identical in order to pass constitutional scrutiny. The Court recognized "inherent" sex differences. It also used broad language that looked toward developing the "talents and capacities" of students. The Court's core concern was that school officials allocate equal resources to both programs and that neither program promotes stereotypical notions of group capabilities or tendencies that might limit life opportunities.

Together with the Court's prohibition against such "overbroad generalizations," the substantial equality standard, reasonably interpreted and applied, strikes a balance between equal educational opportunity and local discretion. Focusing on inputs, it provides guidelines (tangible and intangible elements) that establish minimal safeguards against the inequitable allocation of resources based on sex. At the same time, it allows local officials and educators flexibility in the short run to develop educational programs based on informed professional judgment. In so doing, it permits them to initiate educational reform incrementally and to assess programmatic interests among students and their parents. Where a school district, for example, opens a single-sex school for girls, it can offer equal educational opportunities to boys in a coed setting such as a comprehensive high school or a magnet school, as long as the admissions criteria (for example, grades, achievement test scores, residency) are the same and the educational offerings and facilities are substantially equal in substance and quality.

It may be that a given community has no desire for a single-sex school or particular classes for girls but overwhelmingly supports either or both for boys or vice versa. If participation is truly voluntary, which it undoubtedly should be, then school officials cannot force the approach on unwilling clients, but then again, neither can they deny opportunities to those who desire them merely because members of the other sex do not. And although a school district might choose to establish parallel schools for girls and boys in the same or adjacent facilities—"dual academies," as they have come to be known—that model should not be a sine qua non under the law. As a practical matter, to interpret the substantial equality requirement as "separate but identical," or to a lesser degree "separate but single-sex," would place unnecessary hurdles in the way of school communities and inevitably dissuade at least some of them from moving forward. Even in the context of parallel schools or classes, an identical curriculum could undercut some of the gender-specific benefits that single-sex programs are intended to provide beyond mere separation.

A more crabbed interpretation of "substantial equality" would particularly hobble charter school initiatives. The charter school concept allows school districts as well as outside groups to organize schools that are essentially public but freed from many of the usual hiring restrictions and other state and local regulations. Now numbering about twenty-seven hundred nationwide, these schools provide a most appropriate context for exploring alternative and innovative approaches to educating diverse populations. Experience has proven that most charter schools serve poor and minority students, who, as research suggests, may benefit the most from single-sex education. Given the start-up costs of such schools and the difficulties in raising sufficient funds for capital expenses, however, it defies logic and practical realities to require charter school sponsors to simultaneously establish a school for one sex as a condition to establishing one for the other. Such a "single-sex only" rule would hold organizers hostage to local public school officials or to the chartering agency who may have other resource priorities or who may see no clear community demand. On the other hand, mere "comparability" could easily lend itself to widespread inequities.

### Affirmative Action Exception

The second—and perhaps more contentious—issue that demands serious reconsideration relates to affirmative action. This point relies not only on the VMI decision but on more general trends in the Court's thinking. The Title IX regulations as originally written suggest, as some qualified supporters argue, that single-sex classes in particular are permissible only where they have a compensatory purpose. The question remains, compensation for what? For limiting conditions imposed by society, or by the school district, or from biological differences? On this count the VMI decision offers little direct instruction. Although the Court noted that sex classifications are permissible when used "to compensate women 'for particular economic disabilities [they have] suffered,'" compensation was neither part of the school's rationale nor its intent.[75]

More clearly, however, and in the context of the specific facts, the VMI decision requires a "persuasive" or convincing educational justification but not necessarily a compensatory one. Research findings on the math, science, and technology gap for girls, the compelling social and academic data on inner-city minority students, favorable anecdotal reports on the single-sex experience, and more recent writing on the educational and emotional needs that boys share as a group may prove exceedingly persuasive as a means to fully develop the "talent and capacities" of particular students while avoiding reliance on a compensatory rationale. The only way to assess whether single-sex programs can effectively address any of these problems is to allow school districts to explore various models and to gather empirical and anecdotal data that can be shared nationwide. In recent years, lower courts have upheld even the use of race in public elementary school admissions for the exact purpose of generating and disseminating research findings. It therefore seems reasonable to allow the use of sex for similar purposes.[76]

Aside from the fact that the VMI decision apparently offers a broader perspective on programmatic purposes, there are other compelling legal and practical arguments that work against adopting the compensatory rationale. As a matter of policy, compensatory purposes lock single-sex programs into a "victimization" mode that has proven politically polarizing. The word *compensatory* is a loaded term, implying that the program is "making up" for some deficiency that is either inherent or externally created. To imply that males or females are "deficient" (as contrasted with "different") in some ability vis à vis each other obviously evokes the same negative stereotypes that the Court roundly and correctly rejected in the VMI case. As a matter of law, to ascribe deficiency to social neglect, negative attitudes, or historical discrimination runs into potential conflict with recent Supreme Court decisions. In the context of race, it appears that a majority of the justices would recognize group-based classifications only as a means to remedy identified illegal or unconstitutional discrimination but not to compensate for the effects of broader discrimination in society.[77] And while the Court has drawn a distinction between race and sex that could lower the constitutional bar somewhat in the case of single-sex schooling, it is reasonable to assume that at least a slim majority on the Court might likewise require some evidence of specific discriminatory policies or practices even where separation of the sexes is being used for benign and not invidious purposes.

From a practical perspective, if single-sex programs could be justified only on compensatory grounds, unreasonable obstacles would be placed in the way of local initiatives. Here, the school district would bear the burden of proving that it had in fact engaged in sex discrimination, which it hoped to remedy through single-sex schooling. Realistically speaking, how many school officials would travel down that perilous road of self-incrimination? At worst, the compensatory model places them in a lose-lose situation. At best, it pushes them to devise compensatory objectives merely to avoid enforcement action. That exercise in itself feeds into stereotypical notions of gender which the Court rejected in the VMI decision.

Getting back to the VMI case, we should not overlook that the facts arose in the context of higher education and not elementary and secondary education. The Court has afforded considerable deference to elementary and secondary school officials and parents, repeatedly stating that education is a matter of state and local control, especially in curriculum matters. Moreover, while *different* has generally been a "euphemism for 'worse'" in the arena of race, the justices have found "different" treatment to be a core feature of equality in nonrace contexts. The Court has held, for example, that merely providing linguistic minority students "with the same facilities, textbooks, teachers, and curriculum . . . effectively foreclos[es] [them] from any meaningful education." Similar reasoning should hold with respect to the use of sex as a standard for similar purposes.[78]

We can therefore rescue single-sex education from affirmative action discourse and from the constraints of the racial analogue by shifting the operative paradigm from compensatory education to appropriate education. Affirmative action applied to job opportunities and college admissions often entails preferential treatment, which is not a zero-sum game. The beneficiaries win an important economic advantage, while others who have sought the benefit, who arguably have met objective qualifications, and who can also profit from it, lose. Single-sex education, on the other hand, rises to a benefit only for those for whom it is educationally appropriate, similar to gifted and talented programs, special educational services, or English as a second language classes. It merely offers a particular approach to education based on what we know empirically and experientially about the academic, social, and developmental needs of students who fall within certain group norms. At the same time, it does not in and of itself deny other students an appropriate education.

Different treatment therefore does not necessarily imply preferential treatment, which lies at the heart of the legal and political opposition to affirmative action. For some students, different treatment merely suggests that single-sex programs may, for whatever reason, provide an environment that is more conducive to learning than coeducation. Such treatment does not unavoidably evoke negative stereotypes, particularly where participation is voluntary, the resources and opportunities offered to both groups are substantially equal, the educational program is sound, as measured by conventional standards, and the overt and subtle messages convey individual fulfillment and empowerment rather than group deficiency. The language of appropriateness is more neutral, less politically polarizing, and, most important, more accurate than that of compensation. It fits well with an understanding of gender in which, as David Kirp and Mark Yudof have insightfully pointed out, "differentiation and diversity retain considerable normative appeal when attributable to personal volition, and where 'better,' 'worse,' and 'identical' do not exhaust the universe of alternatives." It thus reaffirms the ideal set forth in *Brown* of equality based on equal dignity and respect, concerning itself more with "constrictions on choice" than with the "desirability of sameness."[79]

### Single-Sex Classes

There is one final provision within the Title IX regulations that begs for reexamination: the apparent prohibition against single-sex classes. The regulations ban schools from offering a course "separately on the basis of sex," with few enumerated exceptions. On this point the VMI decision is useful only in the sense that it does not prohibit single-sex classes as a matter of constitutional law. But again, neither does it permit them. The problem here is that the blanket prohibition on single-sex classes is difficult to reconcile with the Title IX statute. It must be remembered that there was no accompanying House or Senate report on Title IX. And so not only is the statute silent on the question of single-sex classes, but there is scarce evidence in the legislative history that the question was thoroughly considered. As a result, both the debate surrounding Title IX's enactment and the various enumerated statutory exemptions, taken together, suggest that Congress did not intend to impose a sweeping ban on all single-sex education.

Introducing the legislation in the Senate, Senator Birch Bayh made an isolated statement that federal agencies enforcing the law could permit "differential treatment by sex" only in "very unusual cases" where such treatment was "absolutely necessary to the success of the program."[80] Nevertheless, in the years immediately following the law's enactment, Congress itself adopted additional exceptions, including fraternities and sororities, boy or girl conferences, and father-son and mother-daughter activities that would hardly meet the "absolutely necessary" threshold. And so it seems that Congress, broadly speaking, did not share the sponsor's near-absolute ban on single-sex activities. As former insiders have suggested, it was only after OCR had drafted proposed regulations to the law that Congress finally began to comprehend what Title IX meant and how it could change longstanding policies and practices. At that point even Representative Edith Green, the House sponsor of Title IX, started working to mitigate the impact of the law that she had worked tirelessly to get passed.[81] Moreover, the fact that OCR itself incorporated into the regulations specific exceptions to the prohibition against separate course offerings demonstrates that the Title IX statute does not preclude the agency from expanding the list of exceptions to include other types of single-sex activities or programs for similar important educational and social purposes. The VMI decision presents the same view under the equal protection clause so long as programs are voluntary, do not impose gender stereotypes, do not limit opportunities, and provide substantially equal services to both groups.

The statute itself implicitly permits a school district to establish an entire school, other than a vocational school, that serves students of one sex as long as comparable services are provided to the other group. Though it appears that Senator Bayh believed the exception was only temporary, pending further study, his congressional colleagues apparently were of a different mind. Because single-sex schools therefore have remained permissible, it would force an incoherent and unreasonable reading of the statute as a whole to ban a coeducational school from merely offering certain classes on the basis of gender.

When drafting the original Title IX regulations, OCR staff had little background material to guide them in interpreting the law. That fact could account, at least in part, for apparent inconsistencies and possible overreaching. One can also understand the concerns that led them to take such an extreme stand on single-sex classes at that point in time. Most of the congressional debate leading up to Title IX's enactment centered on higher education. Whatever discussion was afforded to elementary and secondary education focused on vocational education, where schools commonly separated girls and boys, and on the more general but related issue of sex stereotyping in the curriculum. Vocational programs historically were highly gendered, training girls for jobs in fields like cosmetology and food handling, which were less lucrative than the opportunities offered to boys in auto mechanics and television repair. At the time Title IX was enacted, a study examining one city's vocational schools, for example, found that the expected wages for the occupations open to girls were 47 percent lower than the average salary for the trades in which schools were offering training to boys. Some school districts further offered a much wider range of vocational courses to boys than to girls. And so from that vantage point, it may have seemed reasonable to draft a general rule eliminating all single-sex classes with few exceptions. Yet with the absence of any congressional discussion of this topic, the mere fact that Congress officially approved the regulations carries little weight. No one in 1975 could foresee the current issues that now drive the debate.[82]

At first blush it may still seem prudent to maintain constraints on separate classes in vocational programs as a protection against backsliding, especially in view of the long and continuing pattern of sex discrimination in this area. Yet on closer examination, coeducation apparently has not been completely effective in breaking down all the barriers even after almost thirty years of Title IX enforcement. Vestiges of discrimination and sex stereotyping remain. A recent study from New York City undeniably gives cause for concern and reflection. Researchers found that coeducational vocational schools are still identifiably and predominantly boys' or girls' and clearly reinforce updated sex-role stereotypes in their course offerings—cosmetology, medical assistance, and fashion for girls; computer repair, mechanical engineering, and computer electronics for boys. The study also found that schools that are predominantly male still offer a wider selection of courses and Advanced Placement classes, while recruiting methods and school names send strong messages to students that certain programs are more appropriate for girls or boys.[83]

Admittedly, student choices rather than overt discrimination account for at least some of these imbalances. Yet this may be one of those cases in which choice is not totally free but is constrained by circumstances. Some girls may not enroll in certain courses or schools dominated by boys because they feel uncomfortable as a minority, especially in trades traditionally defined as male. The same might hold for boys in classes or schools dominated by girls. Another way of looking at the problem is that perhaps single-sex classes, offered very selectively and on an optional basis within coeducational schools—for example, an all-girls class in auto mechanics— might in fact offer students a broader range of vocational training and ultimately of career options. The Title IX regulations already make an exception for separate classes and teams in contact sports. The logic here is that girls' smaller size and muscle strength on the average would prevent them from competing against boys on an equal basis, shut the majority of girls out from competitive athletics, and thereby deny them equal educational opportunities. A similar rationale, considering gender differences on the average, could justify offering optional separate classes in other curriculum areas.

## THE NEXT STEP

When Congress enacted Title IX in 1972, it essentially voted on a "general principle of equality" without affording that principle any clear definition. Few congressional members seem to have understood the specific implications of their action until the proposed rules were laid before them.[84] Lawyers within what was then the Department of Health, Education, and Welfare drafted and fine-tuned the regulations based on their understanding of the legislative debates both before and after the law was passed, the concerns raised by women's groups, and the general mood of the times. Much has happened, however, in the intervening years. Social realities and understandings have changed dramatically. Meanwhile, the knowledge base on child and adolescent development, learning, and achievement has broadly expanded, while the interconnections among them are now far more apparent. Those transformations now impel OCR to revisit Title IX, affording the statute a more reasonable reading and reconciling the regulations with constitutional developments, including the Supreme Court's VMI decision.

The blanket prohibition against single-sex classes needs to be loosened. The affirmative action rationale for such programs may have run its course, while a broader array of educational objectives may prove more legally justifiable and more politically palatable. Meanwhile, there is no doubt that the "substantial equality" test, bolstered with the Court's clear prohibitions against sex stereotyping and the commands of equal educational opportunity, should be a guiding force behind any revisions to the Title IX regulations. Indeed, the VMI decision commands that it be so. Beyond that, OCR must establish enforcement guidelines to ensure that programs comply with the standard. Obviously, the agency must carefully weigh the assignment of evidentiary burdens in the process. The regulations should require school districts to demonstrate from the outset that the program, whether a single-sex school or class, adheres to three key principles: first, it does not offer a "unique" or "extraordinary" opportunity to one sex that is not available to the other in a "substantially equal" program which need not be single-sex; second, it is intended and designed to expand and not to constrain the participants' opportunities; and third, the decision to limit participation to one sex or the other has some grounding in research findings, though these findings need not necessarily be conclusive. The regulations should further allow school districts the opportunity ultimately to demonstrate over time that the program has produced positive educational or other broadly defined outcomes.

Nonetheless, however OCR ultimately resolves the sensitive issues before it, the regulations must remain true to the overall vision of Title IX's drafters, that it would help realize for women the right "to attend the schools of their choice, to develop the skills they want, and to secure the jobs of their choice."[85] How to carry out that broad vision and lift the constraints on choice, as we now understand them, is the challenge facing OCR. But resolving the legal standard does not end the debate. There is still one critical issue that needs to be addressed, and it is one that seems to defy conclusive resolution. The weight of the legal and policy evidence supporting single-sex schools and classes finally rests in empirical research supported by anecdotal reports documenting the academic, social, and developmental benefits that at least some students may derive from single-sex schools or classes.

# 8
# The Research Evidence

The presumption in favor of coeducation runs not only in the law but just as deeply in the hearts and minds of most Americans. As single-sex education slowly gains interest and appeal in wider circles, policymakers, educators, and advocates continue to search for empirical findings to legitimize this apparent departure from the prevailing norm.

Recent developments in Washington promise to give public school districts some breathing space, within certain guidelines. Nevertheless, at the bottom line, the Supreme Court's VMI decision still requires school officials and charter school organizers to present "an exceedingly persuasive justification" for separating students on the basis of sex. That standard implicitly requires not only a rationale based in students' needs but also some confirmation on the outputs end. And although private schools are not constrained by these legal requirements, they are in fact sensitive to a highly competitive market. Informed parents, some of them understandably skeptical, demand evidence that single-sex schooling produces academic and social benefits for their children. What seems to get lost in the rush for definitive proof, however, is that the exact nature of the benefits is highly contextual. It depends in large part on the individual students and their particular backgrounds, abilities, and needs. It also depends on what the stakeholders are looking for in the end.

Those who support single-sex programs typically offer both short- and long-term rationales. For girls, the arguments primarily point to educational equity: improving overall academic achievement; developing interest and competency in math, science, and technology; enhancing self-esteem;

opening access to nontraditional careers; providing leadership opportunities. Urban school reformers place special emphasis on overcoming and preventing the social and educational disadvantages confronting inner-city minority youth, both males and females. With all else having failed, they look to single-sex schools and classes as a strategy for decreasing the rate of drug abuse, violence, dropping out, and teen pregnancy, and for increasing academic achievement among this population. Related to that project is cultural socialization—that is, preparing students for the roles they will assume as adults, both in mainstream society and in their communities. All-male Afrocentric academies, as well as separate classes for African-American boys, have clearly built on this last objective.

Educators within the more elite independent boys' school network maintain that separation better accommodates the slower maturational rate, shorter attention span, and higher energy level especially evident among young boys. They offer convincing arguments that, similar to girls' programs, single-sex schools enable boys throughout the grades to experience a broader range of academic and extracurricular options, including those traditionally considered female, such as foreign languages and the arts. Yet there are other proponents who simply view single-sex schooling within the larger context of family choice and educational diversity. Political and social perspectives often govern at this fundamental level.

The Supreme Court's broad language in the VMI case arguably supports each of these objectives to a greater or lesser degree, although academic performance obviously is the easiest to measure empirically. The question then becomes whether we can make more than an educated guess that separating students by sex produces positive educational and social outcomes, however we may choose to evaluate them.

Research on single-sex education has focused principally on the possible benefits to females, although with global attention now placed on the academic failure among boys, more recent studies, especially from abroad, often include male students in the analysis. Up to this point, the findings have been mildly and qualifiedly supportive, though by no means conclusive. This lack of certainty or finality is not surprising given the wide diversity in objectives, pedagogical approaches, organizational structures, and cultural and political settings among these programs, the various ways in which success has been measured, both empirically and anecdotally, and the inherent limitations of the research enterprise itself. Many of the studies from outside the United States raise questions of internal validity regarding selection bias. Single-sex schools in these settings traditionally have drawn brighter students from more privileged backgrounds. Even in countries like England, where single-sex schools were common in the state sector until the early 1970s, those that remain are primarily private. Not only do these students self-select, but the schools also engage in an academic weeding-out process. So it is difficult to determine whether the differing outcomes are attributable primarily to gender organization or to differences in the student populations themselves. A 1983 report commissioned by the Equal Opportunities Commission in the United Kingdom made exactly that point.[1]

Some researchers have attempted to isolate this factor more directly and successfully than others. But this is not pure science. Unlike the true random assignment used in scientific experimentation, researchers do not place students in "treatment" groups but simply take the groups or classes as they come. Some studies have addressed this problem by utilizing large databases, generally selecting schools or students randomly from among a cross-section of the population. To dilute the potential effects of preexisting student differences, researchers apply various statistical procedures. The availability of new computer software for multilevel modeling of data has enabled more accurate comparisons. Yet methodologists still sometimes disagree among themselves about which procedures are the most appropriate or effective in analyzing any given set of data.

With few exceptions, the research on single-sex schooling has also failed to consider within-school-type differences among students. Only in recent years have researchers considered the possibility that either single-sex or coeducation might prove more beneficial to some students than to others. Yet they still cannot control the environment to adequately screen out other factors that might influence the outcome. Institutional characteristics including class size, the percentage of female and male faculty, teaching styles (collaborative or competitive), the overall curriculum, and the strength of particular courses such as science and mathematics all have significant bearing on student learning and achievement. Single-sex schools tend to provide an academically rigorous and largely uniform curriculum for all students, and often, but not always, class size tends to be small. It is therefore hard to determine whether students fare better in these schools because of the single-sex environment itself or because of some other elements thrown into the mix.[2]

Most of the studies that have framed the debate also present problems concerning their external validity. Some of the earlier studies examined the world of higher education and the elite women's colleges of a bygone era, although more recent ones have included a broader representation of institutions. Meanwhile, studies examining elementary and secondary programs have explored settings that are geographically, culturally, or religiously different from current public school initiatives in the United States. Findings do not always translate well across educational norms and traditions. Opponents of single-sex schooling are quick to point out these distinctions and limitations. As one commentator has noted, findings are a mix of "passionate conviction and rather ambiguous research results."[3] But what educational approach can present results free of ambiguities?

Coeducation has become so deeply ingrained in our social psyche, and single-sex schooling so ideologically tied to racial segregation, that even setting aside legal presumptions, we demand far more of it than we do of other equally uncertain educational approaches. Part of the problem lies not in the findings themselves but in conflicting reports of the findings, tinged with each commentator's political perspective or preference for certain statistical methods. As a result, the evidence on single-sex education at times takes on an "eye of the beholder" quality. Scholars, educators, and news reporters selectively invoke this diffuse body of research to support positions from both sides of the debate line. Nonetheless, with so much of the public discourse weighted on these studies, we should objectively scrutinize and thoughtfully replicate them rather than dismiss them outright, as some opponents suggest.

In the following discussion, I attempt to cut through the subjective analysis and intellectual backbiting that has all but paralyzed the search for research evidence supporting single-sex schooling. In doing so, I explore recurrent themes in this broad mix of findings while remaining fully cognizant of its limitations. As much as I have carefully mined the field, I am nevertheless certain that there are studies that have escaped my eye. But I have also exercised a measure of discretion. Aside from anecdotal reports, I include only those studies published in peer-reviewed journals or presented as scholarly papers at professional conferences. I do not cover the numerous masters' theses and doctoral dissertations that have addressed the topic in recent years. In the discussion of elementary and secondary education, I include only studies published since 1980, as these are more likely to examine programs that reflect contemporary views on sex roles. I focus on attitudes and achievement and only peripherally touch on self-esteem, a construct subject to varying definitions. And though the discussion at times may seem to dig too deep into methodology, much of the controversy over the ultimate findings has focused precisely on that point.

I also give what some might consider undue attention to the research on women's colleges. My reasoning is that the findings of that research have fallen victim to such reductionism that important subtleties have been lost. These studies beg for clarification if we are to fully appreciate how they initially laid the groundwork for subsequent research on single-sex schooling and the discourse on educating women. They also raise interesting methodological questions that can prove useful to researchers now embarking on similar studies of elementary and secondary school programs.

I urge particular caution in reading the findings from developing countries. In these settings, while boys' schools generally represent a cross-section of the population, the same is not true for girls' schools. By and large fewer girls attend school, and those who do so typically come from more privileged backgrounds. That selectivity tends to skew the findings arguably in favor of girls' schools. And finally, we should fully recognize that the scope of most studies has been predominantly academic. The resulting picture could change dramatically if we considered less conventional measures of programmatic success, such as dropout and teen pregnancy rates or more long-term college and career choices.

## WOMEN'S COLLEGES

Policy arguments supporting single-sex schooling at times draw from higher education. The research is rooted in the 1970s, when the tide of coeducation sweeping the country proved a particular threat to women's colleges. During the previous decade, public institutions had begun expanding at breakneck speed to offer affordable quality education to the post–World War II baby boom generation. Fearful of being left behind in the dust of that frenetic whirl, private single-sex institutions tried to remain academically competitive by becoming coeducational. Thus the push toward coeducation was driven largely by market forces wrapped in the rhetoric of what was "natural" and "equal." Between 1960 and 1972 about half of the existing women's colleges opened their doors to men or closed down completely. During the six-month period between June and December 1968, an astounding sixty-four institutions met one or the other fate. By 1986 single-sex colleges had become an "endangered species."[4] The majority of those that survived were church-affiliated, primarily Roman Catholic. By 1993 the number of women's colleges had dwindled to seventy-six from a 1960 high of about three hundred.[5] The ones that held fast to their core mission were hard-pressed to justify their existence to a postfeminist generation of young women eager to prove themselves equal to men. Coeducation, many of them believed, presented the academic path to full equality and assimilation.

This perspective had merit in a society that had long denied women equal status and opportunity. Yet it was still unproven whether coeducation could fully measure up to the expectations of females flocking to its doors. As Catharine Stimpson has insightfully observed, coeducation was originally conceived "to educate men and women in the same space, although rarely for the same place."[6] Researchers set about injecting reasoned judgment into a movement that seemed to have taken off on its own steam. Some initially looked at the comparative effects of attending women's and coeducational colleges on attaining educational and professional success.

Others compared the personal experiences of women at single-sex and coed institutions. Subsequent efforts focused on isolating the institutional features that support success among women students. The potential, limits, and applicability of this research have provoked sharp disagreement between proponents and opponents of single-sex education, clouding the details and significance of the findings in overstatement and oversimplification. Some of the reporting and interpretation has been incomplete, inaccurate, or misleading.

The academic discussion begins three decades ago. In 1973 the Carnegie Commission on Higher Education published a study that captured the prevailing concerns over the education of women in a time of social and institutional flux. The report was intended to identify certain factors that colleges should consider when moving toward coeducation. It presented data from the late 1950s and 1960s indicating that women's colleges were awarding undergraduate degrees to women in the physical sciences and mathematics at a higher rate than coeducational institutions, and graduates of women's colleges were continuing on to graduate school and completing Ph.D.s in disproportionate numbers. The commission recognized that the selective policies at some women's colleges had a skewing effect on the data. Nevertheless, it ascribed the differences at least in part to the advantages of attending a women's college, including increased leadership opportunities and the comfort of participating in class discussion without fear of losing one's "feminine appeal."[7]

The Carnegie study reported on the work of M. Elizabeth Tidball, who first published her findings in 1970 and later presented them at the national meetings of the American Association for the Advancement of Science.[8] A graduate and former trustee of Mount Holyoke College and currently professor emerita of physiology at George Washington University, Tidball was struck by the dramatic increase in the number of women attending college throughout the twentieth century. From the early 1900s to the early 1970s, the number of women college graduates had risen from 4,500 to a quarter of a million, with projections of up to 400,000 by the mid-seventies. Despite these encouraging figures, however, Tidball sensed that access alone was not an adequate measure of gender equality; the quality and not merely the quantity of the educational program needed to be examined. She also believed that male students in coeducational colleges presented a distraction to women. To her mind, the presence of men constantly reminded women that their primary task was to find a "suitable mate," preventing them from exploring and developing their talents and capabilities.

In a series of studies working backward from random samples of women listed in *Who's Who of American Women,* Tidball correlated graduation from a women's college with career achievement. In two early studies, she found that for the decades covering 1910 to 1960 and later 1966 to 1971, women's colleges produced almost twice as many "achievers" as coeducational schools. And the higher the ratio of male to female students at coeducational schools, the lower the percentage of women achievers among their graduates. Tidball attributed these differences to two factors: women's colleges had twice the proportion of women faculty members, and their male faculty demonstrated more accommodating attitudes than those at coeducational institutions. Tidball then moved on to examine other measures of success. She looked at women who had earned doctorates between 1920 and 1971, as well as later graduates from the 1970s, who had enrolled in medical school or received doctorates in the natural sciences. She confirmed her earlier findings. Among the more recent graduates, she found that formerly all-male colleges did not produce as many female achievers as formerly women's colleges, while those colleges that had remained single-sex continued to outrank both. Tidball questioned whether the presence of men in the formerly women's colleges had negatively affected the interests of women students to pursue traditionally masculine fields of study.[9]

From the beginning, leaders in women's education relied on Tidball's research to validate the merits and continued existence of women's colleges. More recently, proponents have drawn on her findings to support single-sex schools on the elementary and secondary levels. Her research, nevertheless, has also attracted sharp criticism. Researchers have challenged her conclusion that women's colleges are more productive of women achievers than are coeducational institutions. Opponents of single-sex education have focused on findings from one study, reexamining Tidball's medical school data from 1976, to refute her central thesis. Yet the investigators themselves urged caution in interpreting their data, which were seventeen years old at the time of publication, and which failed to account for the changing demography of women's colleges in the intervening years. There were also significant differences in methodology that make comparisons between the two studies unreasonable. In response, Tidball reanalyzed her own data and again found differences between women's and coeducational colleges of comparable selectivity similar to those she had found earlier.[10]

More recently Tidball has collaborated with others to update her research. Examining college graduates from the 1970s who received their doctorates by 1991, she found that although women's colleges overall were less selective than other institutions, they were by far the most productive in graduating women who later completed doctorates. She concluded that even among the most prestigious and productive private and public institutions in the country, "what works for women has not been incorporated into the campus environment and program." What exactly drives the differences? For Tidball, it is the *"wholeness* of the environment"—from the mission statement to the existence of a "critical mass" of women throughout the institution—that creates a "community" where women "have a clear sense of ownership" and know that they "make a difference."[11]

Tidball's research laid the groundwork for much of the debate over the comparative effects of single-sex and coeducation. Scholars have cited, dissected, challenged, and attempted to replicate her work with almost unprecedented frequency. The Institute for Scientific Information selected her 1973 article as a "Citation Classic" based on the number of citations it had received in other scholarly publications. More recently her findings have been invoked widely both in political commentary and in the literature applauding the renaissance of single-sex education.

Tidball used what is referred to as universe data, examining the entire field of *Who's Who of American Women* honorees. Other researchers have used longitudinal data to explore possible correlations between institutional type and later career success. One such study found that while attending a women's college has no significant net impact on early-career attainment, it may in fact socialize women in a way that enhances their self-esteem. That short-term effect may ultimately improve their success in certain professional careers such as medicine and science rather than affect the occupational status of their particular job. The benefit of attending a women's college may take time to manifest itself. If so, then perhaps Tidball's use of data from *Who's Who* is a more accurate measure of this long-term influence than early-career success. Other research similarly has found that single-sex education leads to greater income. Graduates of women's colleges earned on the average 20 to 25 percent more than women graduates of coeducational institutions.[12]

One of the most carefully controlled studies comparing the effects of women's and coeducational colleges was conducted by the sociologist Cornelius Riordan, who is best known for his research on elementary and secondary single-sex schools. Using data collected over a seven-year period (1972–73 to 1978–79) for the National Longitudinal Study of the High School Class of 1972, Riordan found that more than 90 percent of women who attended a women's college had successfully completed the program, compared with 50 percent of women from coeducational schools. They also demonstrated higher self-esteem and a higher sense of control over their own environment. Although women from coeducational schools were significantly more likely to obtain a graduate degree, graduates of women's colleges were more likely to hold higher-prestige jobs and earn higher incomes than their coeducational counterparts.[13] This may suggest that, for reasons of public perception, educational quality, or student motivation, the women's college degree had greater purchasing power in the career marketplace.

Alexander Astin drew similar conclusions in his comprehensive and widely cited research on the effects of college. Using data from the Cooperative Institutional Research Program (CIRP), an ambitious ongoing study conducted jointly by the American Council on Education and the University of California at Los Angeles, Astin confirmed his earlier findings that women attending women's colleges are more likely to complete their undergraduate degrees and to develop strong academic and leadership skills. They are also more likely to have a strong diversity orientation, to demonstrate concern for social change, and to plan on attending graduate school. The women's movement in the intervening years apparently had not diluted these differences between women's and coeducational institutions. According to Astin, most of these findings were directly attributable to attending a women's college.[14]

These studies measured academic and professional outcomes. Others have examined specific student experiences to provide a sense of institutional process in achieving positive effects. These typically rely on student self-reporting. One study used two national student data sets from 1987 and 1991 college student surveys sponsored by the American Council on Education and the Higher Research Institute at UCLA, as well as data from a 1989 national faculty survey. Based on responses at the beginning and end of college, students attending women's colleges rated themselves more highly on academic ability and social self-confidence at graduation than their coeducational counterparts. However, they rated themselves lower on career and job preparation skills, even though they showed no statistically significant differences in their preparation for graduate or professional school. The researchers attributed the higher reported academic ability to the fact that students at women's colleges not only experience fewer distractions but also find themselves surrounded by peers who see themselves as intellectually able. This, too, suggests that women's colleges provide a long-term benefit. The social self-confidence and academic ability gained may provide a foundation for ultimately achieving career and professional success.[15]

A study conducted through a series of questionnaires administered over the course of the four-year college experience (1984–88) at four small liberal arts colleges supports the view that women's colleges provide a different set of experiences. Students attending the women's college reported that they had more women faculty as role models, participated more actively in classroom discussion, held more leadership positions in campus activities, perceived college personnel as more concerned with their needs, and enrolled in more courses emphasizing women's issues. They also gained more in self-satisfaction, which was primarily associated with taking courses in women's studies. The researchers concluded that a curriculum that puts women "at the center" is "an important mechanism whereby women students learn to value themselves."[16]

Similar results emerge from a study of women students participating in 1986 college entry and 1990 follow-up surveys. Here the women attended equally selective private four-year colleges. The researchers found that as compared with similar coeducational institutions, women's colleges provided an environment that promoted a high level of academic involvement, which in turn created greater student satisfaction and success. Students believed that the institution cared about them and their learning, about civic involvement, and about multiculturalism. At the same time, colleges that were perceived to hold these values were more likely to have students who were involved in campus activities and successful in achieving their personal goals.[17]

In light of these studies, women's colleges appear to offer a positive educational experience to their students and to produce positive career and professional outcomes for their graduates. These effects appear strong even in recent years, when the student bodies of these institutions have become more socioeconomically diverse. The data on professional achievement bear this out. Among women's college graduates from the classes of 1967 and 1977, nearly half surveyed in the mid-1980s held traditionally male-dominated jobs, such as lawyer, physician, or manager, and nearly three-quarters were in the workforce. According to data gathered by the Women's College Coalition, in the early 1990s, among Business Week's list of fifty women who were rising stars in corporate America, 30 percent had received their baccalaureate degrees from women's colleges, even though women's college graduates accounted for less than 4 percent of college-educated women. One-third of the women board members of the 1992 Fortune 1,000 companies held degrees from women's colleges. Add to that list fifteen of the seventy-three women members of Congress (21 percent) and 20 percent of the women identified by Black Enterprise Magazine as the twenty most powerful African-American women in corporate America.[18]

It cannot be denied that women currently at the peak of their careers constitute a select group. Some of them attended women's colleges in the years when prestigious male institutions refused to admit them. But many also rode into college on the 1970s crest of coeducation. The data still show that a disproportionate number in this transitional generation attended women's colleges. Only time will tell whether subsequent classes of women's college graduates will achieve a similar level of comparative success. Meanwhile, the research evidence drawn from what may have been the golden years of these institutions offers us a focused view on the critical factors that contribute to a supportive and effective academic climate for women. Whether these factors can be transplanted onto coeducational soil and whether they have a similar effect on younger females at a different developmental period of their lives have become hotly contested questions as the debate over single-sex education has shifted to elementary and secondary schools.

## ACADEMIC CLIMATE AND THE ADOLESCENT SUBCULTURE

The research on women's colleges has focused in part on the overall institutional environment. That issue becomes more problematic but perhaps even more salient when we shift to precollege education. Here the discussion on single-sex programs, specifically for girls, has centered on middle and secondary schools, where the preadolescent and adolescent years each present distinct social and developmental challenges. As young people in these age groups struggle to chart their own identity and gain emotional independence, the way they experience these school years has an enormous impact on their future life options. The school dynamic is therefore a critical factor contributing to the success or failure of that enterprise, both in the short term and in the long term. Undoubtedly the social and academic climates of single-sex as compared with coeducational schools demonstrate marked differences that draw in part from the absence or presence of the other sex. Some of the basic arguments supporting single-sex education underscore these differences and their potential effects on academic achievement and attitudes.

Four decades ago, the sociologist James Coleman was one of the first American researchers to question the environment of coed secondary schools. In his book *The Adolescent Society,* Coleman challenged the conventional wisdom on adolescent education—that it was "better" for boys and girls to be in school together during this period of their lives. Coleman, on the contrary, boldly suggested that at least in some high schools, "coeducation may be inimical to *both* academic achievement *and* social adjustment." Having examined the value systems of adolescents in ten schools and communities, he found that many more students would rather be good athletes or leaders in extracurricular activities than brilliant students. He concluded that the "youth culture" in secondary schools exerted a negative effect on intellectual pursuits. In the "competition for adolescent energies," he explained, the coeducational organization of at least some high schools contributed to a system of adolescent values that emphasized popularity rather than academic achievement. The "cruel jungle of rating and dating," he warned, proved particularly harmful to girls who were overly concerned with making themselves into "desirable objects for boys." In no area of adult life could a woman survive so successfully merely on "personal attractiveness, an enticing manner, and nice clothes."[19]

Twenty years later, John Goodlad's A Place Called School echoed Coleman's earlier findings, that coeducational schools promote popularity based on physical attractiveness for girls and athletic ability for boys. Meanwhile, similar results from studies in New Zealand, Canada, and the United States underscored the more academic orientation of single-sex schools. Single-sex students spent more time on homework and more frequently expressed a desire to be remembered for their academic abilities rather than their social popularity or leadership in student activities.[20]

In the years since Coleman made his troubling observations, the educational picture has changed considerably. The women's movement and particularly Title IX have broadened the horizons and interests of adolescent girls. They now participate in sports in far greater numbers than Coleman reported, technology consumes more of their leisure time, though not necessarily in the same way as it does for boys, they can reasonably aspire to a wider range of careers and life plans, and they appear to be surpassing boys on most measures of academic performance. Yet in other respects the picture has remained distressingly the same. Much of what Coleman found in values, climate, and status ascription rings true of contemporary high schools and even middle schools. Popular culture, in particular hip hop culture, has fostered a school climate in which teens suggestively display their bodies, engage in sexually explicit talk, and freely touch each other, creating an environment conducive to sexual harassment and making girls feel uncomfortable and powerless. Young women still struggle to gain male acceptance in educational settings that are by many accounts still cruel jungles of rating and dating. Being pretty and sexy—but not too sexy—makes a girl a social "winner," while being an A student most often does not. At the same time, young males battle the forces of a subculture that values sports, competitive superiority, sexual "scoring," and social popularity above academics.[21]

Describing the adolescent social ethic of American high schools, the author Judy Mann notes that "football players are still the heroes—watch who gets the lion's share of cheers at a high school commencement—and the homecoming festivities are still focused on football games, with no thought of alternating between football and, say, girls' soccer."[22] This phenomenon plays itself out in more extreme and different ways across the educational and economic spectra, from wealthy suburban and private day schools, where expensive cars, alcohol, and sex are the valued currency, to public schools in the inner city, where minority students of both sexes fall victim to a distinctly damaging social climate of violence, drugs, crime, and teen parenthood. In many but not all privileged communities, some of the academic distraction is tempered by the high value that families and peers place on academic achievement and college placement. As we move progressively down the socioeconomic ladder, those mitigating forces gradually disappear among both rural and urban poor.

Although Coleman's conclusions may have been somewhat overstated, his book received wide acclaim in academic circles and has since become a classic in the literature on adolescence. *Science* magazine hailed him for having "looked under the rock on which the school system is built." *Saturday Review* commended him for equipping "the educated parent and layman alike to ask the necessary questions" of themselves and of school officials. Yet despite the accolades and the intuitive appeal of its findings, the book's implicit challenge to coeducation was perhaps too subtle. In fact, it remained largely unnoticed. Launched just as modern-day feminism was about to burst on to the political scene, Coleman's message waited more than two decades to gain salience. In 1990, on the cusp of the current single-sex revival, Coleman himself lamented how the force of changed conventional values in previous decades had dissuaded sociologists from examining the intellectual, psychological, and social consequences of attending single-sex or coeducational schools.[23] Yet in an unanticipated but understandable way, his findings have resurfaced in recent years to support single-sex education, particularly for girls and minority boys. The argument suggests that at least for some adolescents, coeducation fosters nonacademic values and heightens social pressures that distract students from the academic work of the school.

In the meantime, in an odd twist of events, the same social and economic values that pushed Coleman's thesis into the background soon energized and became validated in competing findings from England and Wales. In a three-volume work that has become a mainstay in the literature on schooling, *Mixed or Single-Sex School?*, Reginald Dale turned Coleman's thesis on its head. Dale administered questionnaires to thousands of students, former students, and teachers in British secondary grammar schools, and found that "mixed-sex" schools proved positive in school environment and social structures. Both teachers and students tended to prefer coeducation, both girls and boys derived some social advantage from the approach, and boys in particular seemed to gain academically. In direct contrast to Coleman, Dale hailed the coeducational model as a "microcosm of society incorporating within it all the essential features of life in the world outside school and preparing children to take a place in the community of men and women." To his mind, coeducation created greater happiness because it was less "unnatural."[24]

Dale's work has gained wide recognition for the proposition that coeducation is "better" than single-sex schooling. On more careful analysis, however, that proposition begins to crumble under its own weight. First of all, the students in Dale's study "preferred" coeducation because, as they saw it, single-sex schooling overemphasized academic work and academic success. Depending on how you interpret these findings, they could in fact support Coleman's thesis that coeducation diverts student energies from the academic enterprise which is the primary work of the schools. Furthermore, Dale himself conceded that coeducation accentuated the polarization of interest in academic subjects, with boys showing a stronger interest in math and science and less interest in French and girls showing the direct opposite. His findings, in fact, initiated that very debate over the gender-polarized curriculum. Dale tried to reconcile these results with his earlier observations that coeducated girls performed comparatively well in mathematics, suggesting that the presence of boys might have seemingly conflicting effects on girls. On the one hand, it might cause them to doubt their ability and consequently express less interest in math. On the other hand, it might teach them new ways to solve problems and even make them more competitive.

Nevertheless, as he reviewed the major research studies covering almost fifty years, Dale found that while coeducational schools produced significantly higher performance among boys, single-sex schools overall worked a slight academic advantage for girls. Dale tried to explain away the findings by pointing out that the coeducated girls were younger, dropped fewer weaker subjects, and tended to be of lower social class. He argued that the girls were more conscientious and therefore may have positively influenced the coeducated boys. He suggested that a "friendly rivalry" between the sexes in mixed-sex schools caused both groups to work harder, although the boys apparently reaped higher rewards. In an alarming stroke of the pen, he simply collapsed the boy-girl evidence and concluded that, "the advantage . . . lies with the co-educational school."

As one British commentator put it, Dale's overall interpretation of his findings was a "sexist programme in the extreme." He effectively traded off girls' academic achievement for overall satisfaction, "better adjustment," and a "more mature attitude" toward members of the opposite sex despite obvious sex-role stereotyping and the potential constraints on women in the long run. That is not surprising as Dale's outlook on sex differences was quite conservative. In a separate paper, he used an analogy that infuriated Britain's feminist community. Here he compared aggression in men to the "bull who is master and defender of the herd while the cows peacefully graze and look after their offspring." Dale examined particular schools during a particular period of time—British grammar schools between 1947 and 1967—schools with a distinct academic and class ethic that departed from most state secondary schools. He made certain assumptions about what was ."natural," and from that vantage point he built the case for coeducation.[25] Yet educators and researchers remained unaware of these critical shortcomings or simply refused to acknowledge them. His work consequently provided a widely touted research base for the move toward coeducation in the years that followed.

## OERI VERSUS AAUW: WHO'S WRONG? WHO'S RIGHT?

For most of the twentieth century there was little interest or opportunity for researchers in the United States to compare the effects of single-sex and coeducation. In the world of private independent schools, single-sex schooling was considered a perfectly legitimate option and even the norm particularly among denominational schools. Meanwhile, coeducation reigned in the public sector with few exceptions. Operating against this limited backdrop, renewed interest in single-sex schooling since the 1980s has generated repeated analysis and discussion of research findings that draw primarily from two contexts: private and government-operated schools abroad, some from non-Western countries, and Catholic schools in the United States. Both settings present cultural, socioeconomic, and institutional distinctions that cast some doubt on the applicability of the findings to current initiatives. More recently, researchers have begun to focus attention on single-sex classes, particularly in math and science for girls, as well as on the concept of the dual academy or coinstitutional approach, which some consider a reasonable compromise between single-sex and coeducation. Much of the evidence, at least from the United States, is anecdotal.

But before considering individual studies, it would prove useful to examine two comprehensive reports which, despite substantially similar findings, had strikingly different impacts on political and academic discourse. That difference was due in no small measure to the specific position espoused by each of the sponsoring entities, one a government agency and the other a women's interest group. It was also a matter of pure timing. The first was a two-volume report commissioned by the Office of Educational Research and Improvement (OERI) of the U.S. Department of Education during the first Bush administration and known only within a small circle of educators. The second was a highly controversial and much-publicized 1998 study issued by the American Association of University Women.

In 1992 Diane Ravitch, who was then assistant secretary of education for educational research and improvement, convened a group of federal officials, scholars, and educators to examine the academic and social-affective effects of single-sex education on students. A graduate of coeducational public schools and Wellesley College, Ravitch has been a passionate and vocal defender of the choice and diversity that marked her own educational experience. Troubled by the reality that single-sex education had to prove itself when there were so many failing coeducational schools, she wanted to explore whether American society should reexamine its received attitude that single-sex education is "antiquated and irrelevant."[26]

The OERI meeting resulted in the publication of a two-volume report. The first volume presented an overview of twenty studies on single-sex schooling. Many of those from abroad did not control for student and family background characteristics, including socioeconomic status, parents' education, prior achievement scores, and curriculum track. The second volume consisted of nine papers prepared by researchers and practitioners, including several heads of all-boys and all-girls schools, both independent and Catholic. Among the contributors were M. Elizabeth Tidball; Valerie Lee and Cornelius Riordan, two researchers whose work has played a pivotal role in the debate; and Richard Hawley, the headmaster of the University School, founding director of the International Coalition of Boys' Schools, and a fervent advocate of separate schooling for boys. All the participants supported the concept of single-sex education.[27]

The report found that, despite inconclusive findings, there was sufficient empirical evidence to suggest that single-sex schools may produce positive outcomes, particularly "for girls and those who are less educationally successful and stand outside the white, male culture that has traditionally dominated U.S. society." The countervailing evidence was not sufficiently convincing. The report nevertheless acknowledged that existing studies were limited in scope and methodologically weak, and so it presented a list of pointed recommendations for future research. Specifically it suggested that researchers draw data from larger samples, examine the effects of single-sex classes and not just schools, explore the effects of different educational practices within particular types of schools, and control for individual student differences. It also suggested that researchers examine a broader set of outcomes, such as dropping out of school and teen parenthood, and compare the effects of different models and practices on different racial and ethnic groups. The report sounded a clear warning: unless researchers extended and refined the existing findings, there would be little opportunity to learn from single-sex schools because few of them would survive.[28]

Here was a government document challenging the conventional wisdom of coeducation, a position that should have provoked a storm of discussion and research. Yet it made barely a blip on the education and media radar screens. By the time OERI published the report in 1993, the Bush appointees who had commissioned the study had left the Department of Education. At that point apparently no one in Washington wanted to hear what the report had to say; federal officials, school reformers, and news reporters pointedly or inadvertently turned a deaf ear. It was also likely that the report's tentative and cautious tone made the supporters of single-sex schools too uneasy to publicly discuss its findings. In any event, it disappeared from view except as an occasional bibliographic entry in subsequent studies.

Five years later, in March 1998, a very different phenomenon occurred. A similar report, including papers presented by several of the same researchers participating in the OERI project, examined much of the same research but within an expanded database. In striking contrast to the OERI analysis, this report did in fact ignite a firestorm of controversy in the popular press and sent shock waves throughout the educational community. But this time it was the American Association of University Women who was voicing its opinion. This was the same group whose series of reports in the early 1990s had sparked a similar debate over coeducation for girls. But the conclusion this time was that "separating by sex is not the solution to gender inequity in school."[29] As so often occurs, only a select group of educators and researchers read the full report. The group's press release thus became the defining piece of evidence in the court of popular opinion. The release listed the following among the report's findings: that there was "no evidence *in general* that single-sex education works or is better for girls than coeducation," and that there was "no significant improvement in girls' achievement in single-sex classes" (emphasis added).

The media ran with these two findings but, oddly enough, ignored or underplayed a third, that "some kinds of single-sex programs produce positive results for some students, including a preference for separate math and science classes among girls." News accounts also disregarded specific findings in the full report, particularly the fact that while some studies had found no differences in achievement attributable to school type, others had shown positive effects from single-sex schools. In the days following the report's release, newspaper headlines read: "All-Girl Schools Questioned as a Way to Attain Equity"; "Report Casts Doubt on the Value of Single-Sex Schooling"; and "Separate and Unequal? A Study Finds No Evidence That All-Female Classes Are Better, But Some Girls Are Happy on Their Own." There was an obvious disconnect in the reporting. As the *Washington Post* columnist William Raspberry summed it up: "There's hardly anything in the AAUW study to support the news reports." That the organization had issued an embargo against releasing the report prematurely suggested significance, according to Raspberry. "Reporters naturally think it their duty to find that significance and not get lost in inconsistencies. But in this case, the inconsistencies may be the heart of the story."[30] And indeed they were.

As the report swirled through the media, AAUW officials emphatically underscored those inconsistencies. At the same time, they publicly drew a definitive conclusion in favor of coeducation through a series of nationally publicized sound bytes. In a commentary published in the *Chicago Tribune,* Maggie Ford, president of the AAUW Educational Foundation, stated flatly, "Single-sex education does not solve the problem of gender inequality." Appearing on the *Today* show, AAUW President Janice Weinman reaffirmed that conclusion. "Separating by sex is not the solution," she stated. "Good education is. What the study showed was that, in general, you cannot conclude that separating by sex makes a difference." In an interview with the *Houston Chronicle,* she was more directly critical: "Girls cannot be put in situations in which they're seen as the exception to the rule. They need to be seen as part of the rule."[31]

For those who remembered the AAUW's opposition to the proposed Danforth amendment in 1994, these statements were not surprising. They were nonetheless troubling to supporters of single-sex education and above all to educators within the girls' school network. The likelihood of negative fallout was obvious. The syndicated columnist Ellen Goodman speculated that the report would "leave anyone skeptical about putting too much of the public hope or education money into P.S. Mars and P.S. Venus." *Newsweek* warned that it "could dampen some of the enthusiasm for single-sex schools in the rest of the country."[32]

The National Coalition of Girls' Schools (NCGS) immediately fired off a press release to counter the deceptively negative implications. Particularly striking was the subtle but important disconnect between the AAUW's blanket assertions rejecting single-sex education as "the solution" to gender inequities and the conclusion drawn by the AAUW's own experts that "there is insufficient data to make a definitive judgment." The NCGS shot back with data supporting the proposition that all-girls' education does work. In 1997 NCGS students scored on average almost one hundred points above the national mean for the SAT, receiving 594 on the verbal and 575 on the math components as compared with scores of 503 and 494 among girls nationwide. Seventy-seven percent of NCGS students taking Advanced Placement examinations scored a 3 or higher, while 7.8 percent were National Merit semifinalists and another 13 percent received letters of commendation.[33]

In considering these figures one should not lose sight that these schools educate a select group of students who typically come from more affluent and educated families than the larger student population. Meanwhile, the schools themselves generally have greater resources to provide the small class size, enrichment programs, and range of course offerings that lead to academic success, compared with schools nationwide, most of which are in the public system. A more meaningful assessment would compare girls' school students with girls attending private independent coeducational schools. Nevertheless, the numbers proved at the very least that single-sex schooling was in no way harming girls. To the contrary, in some measure it was producing positive academic outcomes.

On the more general question, the NCGS statement hit the mark. A careful reading of the AAUW report, in fact, belies the sweeping negative conclusions that emerged from the association's press release, subsequent press reports, and public statements. Of the four roundtable presentations included in the report, only one flatly rejected single-sex education. The other three suggested that either it works for certain populations or that the educational and research communities should define more clearly the specific practices that fall under the rubric and proceed with caution before investing additional public resources in a concept that begs for further empirical support. The report summarized suggestions, made by various participants, for further research. The implication was that single-sex education merits additional attention. Yet judging from their public posture, AAUW officials seemed to view it as a dead issue.

Where positive effects were found, the report speculated that perhaps it was not the single-sex setting itself that yielded the benefits, at least for some students, but certain organizational features that typically characterize single-sex schools. Included among these were small classes, a strong academic curriculum, parental involvement, orderly classrooms, and nonsexist teaching practices. The gist of the report was that the remedy for gender inequity is not to separate girls from boys but to transport these elements into coeducational schools. Yet at the same time it admittedly questioned whether one could effectively do so with the same results.

The OERI report had yielded essentially the same findings. But the clear sense of that report, in contrast, was that single-sex education might be one approach that produces positive outcomes especially for groups of students who have failed academically in the past. The "inconconclusivity" of the findings was seen as an opportunity for further study, while the AAUW report treated it as a decided liability. The different spin on each report had as much to do with choice of language and above all with perspective as it did with empirical findings. Where one starts out in analyzing the data can determine where one winds up. In the end, the AAUW report created far more heat than light, leaving policymakers, educators, and parents in the dark over the very issue that it purported to clarify. As the *Wall Street Journal* pointed out, this was a case study of how "politics trumps policy."[34]

## SINGLE-SEX SCHOOLS ABROAD

The reports of both the OERI and to a larger extent the AAUW discussed a number of studies conducted in countries where separating girls and boys historically had been the norm rather than the exception. Some of these studies examined single-sex schools and others specific single-sex classes in coeducational schools. Although the two strategies share overlapping rationales, they also offer significantly distinct social and academic environments that presumably bear on educational outcomes. And so I will examine each of them separately in their many forms and various places of origin.

Much of the research from abroad has looked at the effects of single-sex schools on achievement and attitudes toward particular academic subjects. One of the arguments advanced in favor of single-sex schooling is that it creates attitudes toward certain subject matter that are less gender-polarized than those typically found in coeducational schools. Part of the discussion centers on the much-debated gender gap in math and science and the fact that high school math is a "critical filter" to later opportunities and options. The conventional wisdom is that girls in particular may consider mathematics as a masculine subject. That perception may negatively influence both their achievement and their decisions to enroll in advanced math and science courses. In turn, these courses open the gates to certain careers most of which men have traditionally dominated.[35] Some studies have also raised an increasingly articulated and equally troubling concern that boys tend to demonstrate less interest and ability in such stereotypically female subjects as language arts and foreign languages. Arguments supporting single-sex education as an antidote to this perceived problem have found mixed empirical support in different cultural settings. Some of the studies have been referenced many times in the literature. Others are of more recent vintage and are relatively unknown.

Research conducted in Nigeria and Thailand, controlling for student and school background characteristics, found that girls in single-sex schools demonstrated higher achievement levels and held less stereotypical views of math than did girls attending coeducational schools. Boys fared better in coeducational schools. In a similar study of government-funded schools in Jamaica, girls in single-sex schools showed the highest achievement in chemistry and biology, followed by boys in single-sex schools and coeducated boys, with coeducated girls coming in last.[36]

Research from more developed countries has generally found that although girls tend to have less gendered and more positive attitudes toward math and science in single-sex schools, which may influence their subsequent course enrollment and career choices, that advantage does not necessarily pay off in the short run in achievement gains. For example, research on secondary schools in New Zealand (English, math, and science) and Australia (physics) yielded no significant differences in achievement. The Australian study confirmed earlier findings that female students from single-sex Australian schools were more likely to prefer science subjects. They also rated their achievement high in science and mathematics as compared with females from coeducational schools. At the same time, male students in single-sex schools rated their English achievement higher than their counterparts in coed schools.[37]

A more general survey of thirteen- and fourteen-year-olds attending British public schools also found that single-sex-educated boys were more favorably inclined toward drama, biology, and languages, while physics held greater appeal for the girls educated in single-sex schools. A comparable study comparing fourteen- and fifteen-year-olds attending select English schools made similar observations. Girls in the single-sex school were more likely to choose mathematics as an A-level course, preparatory to testing for university admission, in the sixth year, while girls in the coeducational school chose English. At the same time, more boys from the single-sex school chose A-level languages, as contrasted with coeducated boys, who were more apt to choose physics. Even more striking data on course selection come from a comprehensive English study of students at year eleven. Researchers found that boys in coed schools were virtually avoiding modern foreign languages, with only 8 percent enrollment as compared with 23 percent among students at all-boys schools.[38] Findings from Northern Ireland, where single-sex schools are less uniformly privileged and the racial and cultural mix between school types is more balanced, present a somewhat different picture. There studies have shown no significant advantage to attending a single-sex school in terms of participation in science A-level courses or in science achievement. In fact, the findings have run, to a small degree, in favor of coeducation. Similarly nonsignificant differences in performance emerge from a study of nonselective government-maintained schools in England, Wales, and Northern Ireland.[39]

A recent study from Canada, however, suggests that social context may play a role in the effects of single-sex schooling. Comparing junior and senior high school girls attending both public and private single-sex and coeducational schools, researchers found the lowest attitudes and achievement-related self-perceptions toward math at senior high level among girls attending coed private schools. The reason offered is that within the more demanding and competitive private school academic environment, created in part by higher student selectivity, the attitudes of teachers and high-performing boys may strengthen the cumulative negative impact of repeated social comparisons between girls and boys. On the other hand, in public or nonselective schools, where there is generally less pressure to perform and where high-achieving students are not in the majority, social comparisons between girls and boys might not be as salient. These findings suggest that girls may experience particular difficulty in overcoming traditional attitudes in subjects like math in more academically pressured coed environments. They also support other data showing that girls lose most at the highest levels of academic achievement.[40]

Other studies that have examined more general measures of academic performance have highlighted the selectivity of single-sex schools as an important factor contributing to higher achievement. Researchers from the Republic of Ireland examining student performance in the Junior Certificate (around age fourteen) and the Leaving Certificate (around age sixteen) ascribed the significant differences found between schools to the type of students attending them and the way the schools assigned them to classes rather than the gender organization. One study from New Zealand, where single-sex schools are common in both the public and private sectors, found that differences in English, math, and science achievement between girls attending single-sex and coed schools disappeared when adequate controls were placed on student ability levels and social and ethnic backgrounds.[41]

There is no doubt that single-sex schools tend to be more selective in the families and students that they attract, a policy that reasonably has some bearing on student achievement. Nevertheless, several recent large-scale studies from English-speaking countries call the arguments on selectivity into serious question. Each of these studies found significant advantages to single-sex schooling even after adjusting for student background differences. An ambitious longitudinal study of New Zealand students from birth to age eighteen found that students in single-sex schools demonstrated significantly higher rates of achievement in the School Certificate exams taken in the third year of secondary school. They also showed longer school retention and lower unemployment rates than students in coeducational schools. A report prepared by the Australian Council for Educational Research revealed similarly positive results. The findings were based on several studies, including a six-year analysis of Year 12 student achievement. Among 270,000 students, boys and girls from single-sex environments scored an average of 15 to 22 percentile points higher than their co-educated counterparts on fifty-three subjects required for the Victorian Certificate of Education. And while the particular classroom (implicitly the teacher) proved more significant than school effects, the report concluded that there is "evidence suggesting that co-educational settings are limited in their capacity to accommodate the large differences in cognitive, social and developmental growth rates of girls and boys between the ages of 12 and 16."[42]

A similar pattern has emerged from the United Kingdom, where there has been considerable debate in recent years over the results of the General Certificate of Secondary Education (GCSE), taken at about age sixteen, and the General Certificate of Education (GCE) A-levels, generally taken two years later. Together they make up the traditional entry route into higher education in England, Wales, and Northern Ireland. Students in single-sex secondary schools routinely earn the highest scores on these exams. In 2001 fifty of the top-ranked British high schools, including all of the top twenty, were single-sex schools. While proponents of single-sex schooling have touted these findings, others have dismissed them as merely a mark of the more privileged population that these schools typically serve. Recent findings from several studies, however, present strong evidence to refute that view. One study examined more than four thousand students in thirty-six schools. The study matched schools on academic selectivity and socio-economic mix, and still found that students attending single-sex schools scored higher in the A-levels. In fact, contrary to conventional wisdom, boys seemed to gain an even greater advantage than girls from the single-sex setting.[43]

A more recent report prepared by the National Educational Research Foundation takes the discussion a step further. Using a national database of individual student data across 2,954 high schools throughout England, researchers found that girls attending comprehensive (nonselective) single-sex schools showed a small but significant advantage in overall achievement on the GCSE exams, with a particularly marked effect on their performance in science. Although there were no differences found among boys in general, those at the lower end of the ability scale derived some benefit from single-sex schooling, while boys at the upper range of ability showed the greatest gains. The study also found that girls' comprehensive schools were most effective in countering traditional sex stereotyping in subject choices. Among students attending selective schools, though the differences favoring girls' schools were small, single-sex schooling appeared to have a significant effect on boys, particularly in English and science, again defying widely accepted perceptions of boys' schools. The most significant finding across gender, however, was that on most outcomes, single-sex schooling seemed to benefit most the students in nonselective schools who were at the lower end of the range of ability and achievement. That important point has particular merit in the discussion of single-sex schooling for disadvantaged students in the United States.[44]

## SINGLE-SEX SCHOOLS IN THE UNITED STATES

Research from abroad using large databases and controlling for student background characteristics is providing new evidence to counter some of the earlier less ambitious studies that have been widely cited in the literature on single-sex schooling. It is also confirming, to some degree, the findings of two researchers from the United States whose highly regarded work has left an indelible mark on scholarly discussion and policy debate across the globe. Beginning in the 1980s Valerie Lee, a professor of education at Michigan State University, and Cornelius Riordan, a sociology professor at Providence College in Rhode Island, separately reported on a series of studies examining the effects of single-sex and coeducation. Both drew their findings from Catholic schools in the United States, although Lee later extended her work into the private independent sector. Both examined a broader set of outcome measures beyond academic achievement. Both used data from random samples extracted from large national databases that they were able to control for selectivity factors. And again, both participated in the 1992 OERI and the 1997 AAUW roundtable discussions. They initially, though not ultimately, reached similar conclusions.

In two widely cited studies of secondary school students and graduates in the mid- to late 1980s, the first with Anthony Bryk and the second with Helen Marks, Lee found positive effects of single-sex schooling for girls but few differences attributable to school type for boys. Both studies used data from *High School and Beyond,* a 1980 national survey. Both studies drew from a sample of 1,015 Catholic schools, thirty-six sophomores from each school surveyed at random, with a follow-up two years later in senior year. They found that girls in all-girls schools expressed a more positive attitude toward academics, spent more time on homework, watched less television, and demonstrated higher achievement gains in reading, writing, and science than their coeducational counterparts. Boys attending single-sex schools, on the other hand, did not show statistically significant gains between sophomore and senior years. Yet they were more likely to enroll in math and science classes and less apt to enroll in vocational classes than students in coeducational schools.

Lee and Bryk also examined self-esteem, which is generally linked to educational achievement. Again the effects seemed to favor single-sex schools and particularly girls' schools, while the findings on boys' schools were "more ambiguous." Subsequent research from abroad presents an inconsistent and more complex picture. An Australian study, in fact, found just the opposite—significantly higher self-esteem among boys from single-sex schools but no differences between girls. Findings from Northern Ireland muddy the waters even further. According to that study, attending a single-sex secondary school led to an increased sense of cognitive competence and a more inner-directed locus of control among both girls and boys. But the effect applied only to students attending more academically oriented schools.[45]

The findings of Lee and Bryk rocked the educational establishment and refueled public discussion on single-sex education. They soon found themselves wrapped in a spirited debate with Herbert Marsh, an Australian researcher who challenged their methodology. He charged that they had failed to control adequately for preexisting differences among the students studied. They countered that the background characteristics of students attending single-sex and coeducational Catholic schools were "reasonably well-balanced," especially in the case of girls, which made the evidence supporting single-sex schools especially strong in their case. They in turn accused Marsh of stacking the deck in favor of coeducation. By relying on sophomore-to-senior-year gains as evidence of school effects, they argued, Marsh failed to recognize that school effects for certain outcomes like absenteeism, homework, and academic interest may occur early on. In an attempt to disprove their findings, Marsh later used the same database, adding information previously unavailable and controlling for seventeen background variables. He found that achievement among girls in single-sex Catholic schools was higher when compared with that of coeducational public school students but that there were no achievement differences between girls attending Catholic coeducational and those in single-sex schools. Marsh concluded that the strongest academic effect came from the greater emphasis on academic course selection in Catholic schools, both single-sex and coed.[46]

Lee continued her study of single-sex education with Helen Marks. The researchers found that the positive effects observed in high school students carried into the college years. Both females and males from single-sex secondary schools were more likely to attend selective four-year colleges and to consider attending graduate school. The effect on girls extended to attitudinal and behavioral outcomes. Female graduates of single-sex schools held significantly less-stereotypical attitudes about women in the workplace, had higher aspirations for attending graduate school in nontraditional disciplines, and demonstrated a higher sense of social responsibility by the end of college. The researchers concluded that the single-sex experience appeared to be "somewhat more empowering for young women than for young men." They suggested that even within coeducational schools, educators should consider all-girls mathematics and science classes taught by female instructors. Lee later recanted that proposal.[47]

Lee and Marks wondered whether it was the "Catholicness" of these schools and not merely their single-sex organization that accounted for the differential effects. When they searched for comparable differences in achievement and attitudes among students attending private independent schools, they hit a "stone wall." Collecting data in 1989 and 1990 from a random sample of sixty independent secondary schools (twenty all-girls, twenty all-boys, and twenty coed), they found no consistent pattern of effects for either boys or girls. Disappointed and perplexed, they decided not to publish the findings. Instead, they expanded the scope of the study and reported on why students and families choose a single-sex school over a coeducational one. They found that academic achievement was the most salient factor for boys, while a safe social environment proved most compelling in the selection of all-girls schools.[48]

That finding in itself was rather benign. But when Lee shifted her focus toward classroom climate and observed eighty-six classrooms in twenty-one of these schools (seven all-girls, seven all-boys, and seven coed), the findings were far more troubling. She found incidents of sexism in nearly half of the classes observed—more in coeducational schools than in boys' schools, and fewest in girls' schools. Most of the sexism in girls' schools occurred in only two cases, where teachers stereotyped girls by shying away from aggressive teaching while male teachers treated them in an overly "chivalrous" manner. This paled in comparison to what she found in boys' schools, where, as she later recalled, the rampant stereotyping and demeaning language concerning females "was actually pretty shocking." It suggested to her that "an all-male environment is not a very good one."

Someone from the independent-school network who was familiar with the study later told me off the record that Lee's randomly selected sample was not representative of single-sex schools in their stereotypical gender orientation, implying that the findings should not be afforded much weight. Sometimes the laws of probability work against random sampling. But Lee's observations also confirmed reports in the literature that all was not well in coeducational schools, where male domination was common, particularly in science classrooms.[49] Obviously we cannot generalize from such a limited and arguably unrepresentative study. Moreover, the findings indicate that although single-sex schooling is not a cure for sexism in the schools, it may contain it to some degree, at least among girls.

Despite the interesting nature of her findings, Lee still could not reconcile the inconsistencies between Catholic and independent secondary schools in achievement and attitudinal effects. She has subsequently proposed several plausible explanations that grow out of a more in-depth book project on Catholic schools. First, she notes that the two sectors serve different populations. Catholic schools seem to offer the promise of social mobility to disadvantaged students for whom they have proven especially effective. Independent schools, on the other hand, generally aim at preserving the privilege already enjoyed among their primarily upper-class students. Girls in particular seek out Catholic schools specifically for the academic opportunities they offer. That is not necessarily the motivating force behind independent school attendance.

Another possible reason goes to the different historical evolutions of these schools. Lee accurately observes that those Catholic schools that have remained single-sex, such as the Jesuit and Sacred Heart schools, are relatively elite institutions, operated by religious orders and as a rule serving students of higher socioeconomic status. (Over the past decade, religious communities have established single-sex schools specifically for poor inner-city students. The Holy Child schools for girls in New York and Boston, for example, follow the Nativity middle school model originally developed by the Jesuits for boys and now used in urban settings nationwide.) Those Catholic schools that have converted to coeducation are typically operated by parishes or dioceses, have fewer resources, and tend to attract more lower- and middle-class students. In the private independent sector, the reverse is true. The most elite and selective tend to be the coeducational schools that were formerly all-boys, the likes of Andover, Choate, Exeter, Groton, and St. Paul's.[50] These differences in student population obviously can skew the achievement findings in favor of single-sex schools within the Catholic sector and in favor of coeducational schools among the independents.

The confused messages emerging from these studies, nonetheless, dampened Lee's enthusiasm for single-sex education and pushed her to dig deeper for answers. She abandoned a book project on single-sex education and shifted her research focus to examine the effects of school organization and climate on student outcomes. Here she found that girls' schools demonstrate many of the organizational characteristics that define "good" schools along parameters of both equity and effectiveness. They tend to be smaller in size than boys' or coeducational schools. Their principals are typically women who, compared with their male counterparts, are inclined to exercise more participatory and democratic management and personal leadership styles. They are in general communally organized in such a way that interactions are more informal and prevalent among administrators, teachers, and students. And their principals are more actively engaged in the school's learning aims, including a conscious concern for social justice.[51]

Meanwhile Lee's research on coeducational schools has revealed some interesting connections between school climate and gender equity. Drawing data from the National Educational Longitudinal Study of 1988 on eighth-grade students, she found that in schools with more positive student-teacher relations, the gender gap favoring males in science and social studies was even larger, increasing by almost half in social studies at more academically oriented schools. At the same time, the usually small gender gap favoring boys in math almost doubled in schools with high parental involvement, while the gender gap favoring girls in reading increased in schools characterized by high socioeconomic status. As we have seen, a more recent Canadian study made a similar observation.[52]

A reasonable conclusion is that gender equity for both girls and boys may be more at risk in schools that demonstrate a strong academic climate. It could also be the case that more educated or privileged parents who send their children to coeducational schools, as well as the schools themselves, are more apt to reinforce traditional beliefs regarding gender-related abilities in certain academic subjects. Perhaps in less-educationally focused or less-affluent communities, schools merely push students to a minimal level of achievement at best without developing their talents in any direction, stereotypical or otherwise. Or as sociological data has shown, boys in low socioeconomic environments gain validation and peer acceptance by excelling in activities outside the academic setting—for example, athletics or social popularity. In that context, girls are free to take the lead academically, at least by default.

Lee did not imply that coeducation was the culprit or that single-sex schooling might yield more favorable results, though the correlation between gender equity and these various factors makes that a question worth exploring. To the contrary, as her research agenda expanded, her skepticism toward single-sex schooling eventually took on the tone of dismissal, dealing the approach a serious blow. One of the leading researchers who had helped define the debate just a decade previously was withdrawing her support. What a difference ten years, even five years, had made in her perspective. In 1992, in her closing remarks to the OERI roundtable, she positively noted that there was "something important going on in some single-sex schools for young women" and urged that society "not allow this option to disappear from the American educational landscape." In 1997, with the results of several more studies behind her, she reassessed that conclusion. In her AAUW roundtable presentation, Lee unequivocally stated that "separating adolescents by gender in secondary schooling is not an appropriate solution to the problem of gender inequity in educational outcomes, either in the short or in the long run."[53]

Even though she still concedes that single-sex schools seldom disadvantage girls, her research has convinced her that they often disadvantage boys. Yet she questions how all-girls schools can be implemented without tipping the gender composition of coeducational schools in favor of boys, a situation that ultimately disserves the interests of the girls who remain. As for gender differences in performance, she warns that single-sex classes, particularly in math and science, are "misguided," often leading to a "soft touch" approach for girls (or "wrapping Calculus in a pink ribbon") that smacks of "sex-role stereotyping" and "embedded discrimination."[54]

Lee apparently recognizes that school gender inequities affect both boys and girls. Her solution, however, is not to separate students but to reorganize schools so that they are effective for all students. That means smaller size, more intimate relations among students and teachers, an academic orientation for all students, active student involvement in the learning process, teacher responsibility for student learning, and the creation of a functioning community. She suggests that the effectiveness of girls' schools hinges on these organizational differences and not on their single-sex composition. But that belief assumes that the critical features she has identified can be transposed into a coeducational setting with the same academic and social effects, both short- and long-term. This assumption is largely speculative and contradicts Tidball's plausible thesis that it is the "wholeness" of the environment that makes single-sex education "work," at least for women. At the same time, while Lee cannot find a solid research base to support single-sex education as a "policy change," she again admits that "separate by gender education may benefit particular students (usually girls), or be beneficial to some in particular settings (perhaps in Catholic schools)."[55] Unfortunately, this more nuanced and arguably equivocal position has been lost in the storm of Lee's more visible retreat from earlier findings and conclusions.

Just as Lee has modified her position and shifted her focus over the years, Cornelius Riordan, the other researcher who has played a major role in the debate, has gradually refined his views while remaining steadfast in his support for single-sex schooling. His research is best known for analyzing the effects of separate schools on African-American and Hispanic students. Riordan admittedly did not set out to validate single-sex education but rather stumbled upon his original findings in the course of examining the effects of Catholic schooling. In fact, realizing how unfashionable the approach was and the professional risk involved if his conclusions were wrong, he was extremely cautious in reporting his early findings.[56] Like Lee and her colleagues, he used the large High School and Beyond database gathered from Catholic single-sex and coeducational schools, adjusting for initial differences between the two groups on ability, home background, school policies, and school environment. He also added two significant dimensions: race and class.

Before looking at the outcome data, one surprising finding from Riordan's analysis is especially noteworthy. Riordan examined the responses of students who rated themselves as members of what Coleman had coined the "leading crowd" in their school. Among this group he found a prevalent adolescent subculture. More than 50 percent had positive attitudes toward athletics, negative attitudes toward good students, and heavy involvement in dating. But in contrast to Coleman's thesis that coeducation reinforced the values implicit in this subculture, Riordan found the strongest evidence in boys' schools. He attributed this in part not only to an expected male emphasis on sports but also to an unexpected higher level of dating among boys in single-sex schools. Yet he also found the weakest evidence of broad subculture values among students attending girls' schools and particularly among minority girls.

As anticipated, girls in coeducational schools were more positively attracted to athletes (assumedly male athletes) and negatively inclined toward good students. At the same time, the girls' school students, like the boys, were more likely to be dating in senior year. It could be that both male and female single-sex students tend to formalize their social interactions with each other in dating situations in the absence of other less formal opportunities. In contrast, coeducational students share daily informal contacts that may encourage more mixed-sex group and fewer one-on-one activities and relationships outside the school setting. These differences, however, had minimal effect on ultimate outcomes when Riordan controlled for this factor. His findings therefore suggest that the influence of school type on student social behavior and values might be more complex than Coleman assumed.[57]

Riordan's data on cognitive and affective measures present even more interesting insights. Comparing performance in sophomore and senior years, he found that white girls and African-American and Hispanic students of both sexes fared better in single-sex schools, while coeducation appeared to benefit white boys. When scores were adjusted for initial ability, school characteristics, and home background, girls and minority boys attending single-sex schools demonstrated higher cognitive achievement, higher self-esteem, higher internal control, and more liberal attitudes toward working women than their counterparts in coeducational schools. The opposite effect held for white boys in single-sex schools, who were surpassed by coeducational students on all cognitive and affective measures used in the study. Although the affective differences were not large, the data seemed to indicate that white males develop healthier attitudes in coeducational schools. Meanwhile, single-sex schools appeared to provide minority males in particular with an environment and set of school policies that fostered the growth of internal mechanisms that in turn strengthened their belief that they were masters of their own destinies. Initially published in the mid-1980s, Riordan's findings lent theoretical support to a movement that was slowly taking shape in urban school districts throughout the country—establishing separate schools and classes for minority boys.[58]

The differential effect of single-sex and coeducation between white and minority males was indeed remarkable. But how could it be explained? Riordan suggests that white males in coeducational schools may gain an advantage by comparing themselves to females who serve as a "negative reference group." In the competitive environment of predominantly white all-male schools, some low-performing males end up serving that function which drives overall achievement scores down. Riordan maintains that several factors offset these forces for minority and white females in single-sex schools. First, low-status students have a "greater receptivity" for school effects. They also derive a greater benefit from same-sex teachers as role models. And again there is what Coleman initially referred to as the "adolescent subculture" of athletics, social life, and dating, which Riordan found strongest among boys in single-sex schools. That factor, along with such school variables as curriculum, coursework, and homework, accounts, he claims, for about 70 percent of the test-score difference between single-sex and coeducational schools among African-American and Hispanic boys and girls. These formal and informal structures apparently have a more significant positive impact on members of minorities than on white males.

Riordan's findings confirm those of previous studies, including Coleman's—that the overall effects of school quality are greater among minorities and among the poor. They also support recent findings from England indicating that students at the lowest end of the ability range, as measured by previous performance, reap the greatest benefits from single-sex schools, assuming that disadvantaged students are most likely to fall into that group.[59]

Riordan's subsequent research on Catholic schools moved him to adjust his original thesis. In his remarks to the AAUW roundtable participants in 1997, he acknowledged findings that at least partially contradict the results obtained in his own studies and those of Lee and Bryk. Data gathered in the 1990s indicated that single-sex Catholic schools were not particularly favorable settings and that any benefits in achievement could be explained by preenrollment differences and prior achievement. These findings were consistent with the conclusions that Lee had drawn from her research on private independent schools.[60] Riordan attributes the convergence to changing demographics among Catholic school students, who, he maintains, became more affluent as a group (or, more accurately, more economically diverse) between the early 1980s, when he gathered his original data, and later studies. He suggests that the effects of single-sex education fall within a hierarchy of low-status characteristics (female, racial minority, low socioeconomic status). The greatest effects are found among African-American and Hispanic females from low socioeconomic homes, with slightly diminished effects among African-American and Hispanic males from low socioeconomic homes, smaller effects still for white middle-class females, and virtually no differential effects among white males or affluent students regardless of race or gender.

Riordan agrees with Lee that certain organizational features, including small school size and a strong academic curriculum, explain the greater academic effectiveness of single-sex schools. Yet in his view they do not totally explain the difference. For him, the keys to the success of single-sex schools are the specific features that flow out of school type itself: the role models, leadership opportunities, diminished youth-culture values, and affirmative pro-academic parent and student choice—what Tidball would call the "wholeness of the environment." These features, Riordan argues, make the approach work best for historically disadvantaged student populations.[61]

Nonetheless, troubled by the inconsistency with early studies conducted abroad, Riordan did not accept his findings as the last word on single-sex schools. Along with several other researchers, he conducted a cross-national study of four countries: Belgium and New Zealand, where the enrollment in single-sex schools was 68 percent and 48 percent, respectively, and Thailand and Japan, where it was 19 percent and 14 percent, respectively. Their findings indicate that as these schools become more common, the achievement differential between them and coeducational institutions may diminish.[62] This may explain the more frequently reported achievement disparities found in the United States. In many of the countries, such as Northern Ireland, where similar studies have found no differences, a more even balance exists between single-sex and coeducational schools, both private and government-operated. In the United States, in contrast, single-sex schools, which are largely private, form a minute and select segment of the country's educational system and seemingly attract different students from those educated in the large coeducational sector. Perhaps in this case single-sex schools represent a decisively pro-academic choice.

This last observation, however, should have little effect on the United States. Given the overwhelmingly strong preference for coeducation, single-sex schools will remain too rare an exception, particularly within public education, to even approach the diminishing differential effects observed in foreign countries. If that is so, then Riordan's findings suggest that single-sex education for low-income minority students, both male and especially female, merits serious thought. It could very well be that single-sex schools are less empowering for those students whose families are already empowered socially and economically. More recently, he has underscored that view, arguing that this approach bears significant consequences for students who are "historically and traditionally disadvantaged—minorities and lower-class and working-class youth (students at risk)." As for white middle-class or affluent students, Riordan suggests that while the outcome is likely to be "neutral," there exists the "possibility" that they may acquire "small gains that are undetectable," but in no sense are they harmed.[63]

## WHAT ABOUT THE BOYS?

Riordan's research pushed the debate into new directions. Not only did he explore issues of class and race, but he expanded the discussion beyond girls and suggested some advantage to minority boys. At the same time, he placed white males at the bottom of his hierarchy of those likely to benefit from single-sex education. Other researchers, including Lee and Bryk, have likewise suggested that coeducation might better serve boys. These conclusions, which are not surprising, represent a general theme running through the literature. In fact, one of the rationales underlying coeducation in the early decades of public schooling was that girls would act as a leavening agent or "civilizing" force to counteract the more rambunctious tendencies of boys.

In recent years Riordan has admitted that he might have sold boys' schools slightly short. Nevertheless, by flagging the needs of disadvantaged minority boys, he placed himself ahead of the curve by a couple of years, inadvertently spearheading a wave of scholarly research and popular literature on the educational and social needs of boys. By the end of the 1990s, he turned his attention more directly to what he termed the "silent gender gap."[64]

Riordan, like Lee, used large existing databases from which he drew his evolving conclusions. In doing so, he was able to manipulate the numbers and control for a variety of factors, beyond school type, that might have influenced student outcomes. In that sense, his findings on disadvantaged boys and single-sex schooling remain unique in the United States. Nevertheless, another study of far less ambitious scope also deserves mention. In this case, a monograph sponsored by the International Coalition of Boys' Schools examined the effects of single-sex schooling on various psychosocial indexes among middle school boys. The researcher was Diane Hulse, the middle school principal at the prestigious Collegiate School in New York City. Hulse compared data gathered from students enrolled in grades five through eight in two "elite" private independent middle schools, one all-boys and the other coeducational, in the borough of Manhattan. It would be reasonable to speculate that the all-boys school was Collegiate. The schools were similar in key institutional features and in student background. Hulse found that students attending the all-boys school were less defensive and less susceptible to social pressures, believed that they had more options available to them in defining their masculinity, and had a greater sense that the school allowed them to appropriately express their aggression. They also felt more comfortable in their relationships with girls and had more egalitarian attitudes toward women's and men's roles in society. Although few of the differences were statistically significant, they nonetheless were important.[65]

The results of this small-scale study reaffirm some of Lee and Bryk's early findings on Catholic school students. They also confirm Coleman's thesis on coeducation and counter Riordan's findings on the more prevalent adolescent subculture found in the all-boys Catholic schools in his study. This is another case in which caution should be exercised in interpreting findings from different research contexts. The variation in the student responses among these three studies could, in fact, simply be a function of how the researchers framed the questions. Perhaps the two schools that Hulse studied were not necessarily representative of schools within their type in terms of institutional gender climate and values. But it could also be that her findings reflect a more contemporary vision of boys' schools, one that has benefited from the research and greater attention afforded over the past decade to the unique issues surrounding boys' development. They may further reflect a general sensitivity toward gender equity acquired over the past three decades.

Beyond these few studies and the more recent findings from abroad, the evidence on boys' schools is largely anecdotal and impressionistic.[66] Researchers have demonstrated scant interest in examining what is popularly considered an educational dinosaur, and especially one that caters to the traditional preferences of the most privileged. At least for the most reform minded, there are simply more pressing public policy issues to address. One such question, as Riordan's research has demonstrated, is the much-publicized failure of coeducational public schools to address the educational, developmental, and social needs of disadvantaged minority boys and the possibility that same-sex schools might yield more favorable results. Regrettably, that proposition was effectively lost in the legal controversies enveloping Detroit, Milwaukee, and New York in the early 1990s.

Reports on minority males therefore come from isolated experimental single-sex classes. Arguments in favor of these programs typically address two problems. First, there is the belief that coeducational classes in inner-city schools are fraught with dangerous manifestations of a youth culture characterized by violence, academic "disidentification," and personal irresponsibility. Second, there is the concern that poor minority males lack positive male role models and that single-sex programs are an effective means for filling that void. Many of these programs have shut down under legal threat despite positive effects on discipline, attendance, and achievement.

What occurred in Florida's Dade County is a good case in point. In 1987 the school district opened two classes for African-American boys with no fathers at home. One was a kindergarten class with an African-American male teacher, the other a first-grade class with a white male teacher. By the end of the school year, ten of the twenty kindergarteners and twenty-two of the twenty-three first graders had perfect attendance. Students in the kindergarten class scored 7 to 11 percent higher on standardized tests of sounds and letters and 8 to 9 percent higher in math than students in the coeducational class. For first-grade students, the differences were 4 to 5 percent higher in reading comprehension and 5 to 7 percent higher in mathematics. There also was a noticeable improvement in student behavior. Unmoved by these promising results, the regional office of the Office for Civil Rights put an abrupt halt to the program on the grounds that it violated federal civil rights laws.[67]

An all-male middle school program serving twenty at-risk African-American boys in grades six through eight in a southern California school district reported similar findings. The staff selected the students based on various school adjustment indicators and assigned them to a self-contained class taught by an African-American male teacher who instructed them in English, math, social studies, and science. Boys participating in the program continued in mainstream classes for physical education and an elective. The emphasis was on collaborative learning, and the curriculum incorporated materials on Africa, African Americans, and good citizenship. When these students were compared with a similar group of boys enrolled in the mainstream program, the data on academic grades and days of suspension favored the single-sex program.[68]

A first-year study of fifth graders attending inner-city public schools in an undisclosed mid-Atlantic community confirms these findings. The two schools in the study used the same curriculum and materials, and both were known for the quality of their teaching staffs. African-American male students enrolled in an all-boys class had higher grades in all subjects and higher attendance than a comparable group of boys enrolled in a coeducational class in the neighboring school.[69]

In the California study, perhaps the most striking findings were in the students' observations. Students rated their own intellectual ability and social competence significantly higher than the mainstream group. They also viewed their classmates and teachers as friendly and accepting of them and their ideas. These perceptions suggest that students supported each other's academic competence, which challenges a widely held belief that peer pressure among African-American males discourages academic achievement.[70] It appears that learning context matters. These findings, taken together, support Riordan's thesis that single-sex programs may prove particularly beneficial to minority males.

## SINGLE-SEX CLASSES AND ATTITUDINAL EFFECTS

Separate classes for minority boys are just a small part of a larger phenomenon quietly changing the educational landscape. The practice of teaching boys and girls in separate classes within coeducational schools is slowly gaining ground in both the public and private sectors. The approach initially emerged in Australia in the 1980s in response to the academic needs of girls. It subsequently took off in Great Britain as a strategy to combat the lower achievement levels of boys in public examinations. In the United States, the main impetus has been the continuing concern over girls' lagging interest and achievement in math and science and more recently in technology. Some school districts, like Baltimore's, have used this strategy evenhandedly to improve academic performance among inner-city girls and boys. Like single-sex schools, these classes have generated controversy among educators and women's advocates. Some contend that they reinforce the view that males and females differ biologically in their cognitive abilities and suggest that females are simply deficient. Supporters nonetheless maintain that they offer girls and boys a "safe space" for learning and taking risks free from the distraction of the other sex while affording them the social advantages of coeducation. They similarly suggest that single-sex classes afford teachers the opportunity to challenge students' gendered perceptions and enhance their self-confidence in nontraditional subjects and careers. By using different teaching methods and materials, proponents believe, single-sex classes raise student motivation, facilitate the learning process, and ultimately improve achievement.

The evidence supporting these classes in the United States is largely anecdotal, much of it reported in the popular press and unpublished conference papers. The limited research findings, primarily from abroad, reveal a dichotomy consistent with some of the research on single-sex schools. Here again there seems to be no differences in achievement, yet girls participating in single-sex classes tend to have more positive attitudes toward math, science, and technology. They also express a level of comfort in classes that are separate from boys.

Reports from Australia, which has provided extensive research on this question, have yielded such results. In the mid-1980s the Australian national government set on a policy course that ultimately encouraged a proliferation of single-sex classes in coeducational schools. Beginning in 1984, the Australian Government's Participation and Equity Program funded several intervention projects that introduced single-sex classes aimed at increasing achievement and enrollment in mathematics among girls. Eight years later, a five-year review of the government's National Policy on the

Education of Girls in Australian Schools expressed qualified support for the approach, even though the initial policy statement itself had discouraged single-sex grouping. At about the same time, the Ministry of Education in Western Australia decided to fund a pilot program of single-sex classes in math and science. Meanwhile, in response to the growing body of international literature documenting how coeducational classrooms were "shortchanging" girls, local schools had begun implementing single-sex classes as an option for students within the public schools. These initiatives have generated numerous research studies examining the effects on math and science achievement and attitudes, primarily among girls. Several of these studies underscore the seeming paradox between these two outcomes.

A three-year longitudinal study in a Western Australian high school found that while single-sex classes in math and science had a minimal effect on achievement for boys or girls, both groups reported feeling more relaxed and comfortable than in their mixed-sex classes. A more recent report on the Western Australian pilot project found that, compared with girls in mixed-sex classes, those in the single-sex group had more favorable attitudes toward math and science. Students also reported that they participated more, were more extroverted, interacted more with the teacher, and were subject to less harassment from other students. The study added an interesting wrinkle to the debate. It concluded that single-sex classes yielded the least benefit for high-achieving students, both girls and boys, suggesting that low-achieving students gained the most. That suggestion has obvious implications for educating inner-city minority students. Participating teachers also noted how the approach provided an opportunity to concentrate on boys' weaknesses, especially in organizational and communication skills, which became more apparent in the absence of girls.[71] But again, caution should be exercised in interpreting these findings, as each of the studies had certain methodological weaknesses. None assigned students randomly to treatment groups, and some used no control group at all but merely relied on student self-reporting.

The one Australian study that researchers have widely cited for its methodological rigor and particularly for its random student assignment ultimately took an unexpected negative turn. In the original study, Kenneth Rowe had reported on a program in Victoria in which middle school girls and boys in single-sex classes had gained significantly in their confidence in learning and using mathematics as compared with students enrolled in mixed-sex classes. Eight years later, Rowe reanalyzed his data and refuted the findings in an article cowritten with Herbert Marsh. The only significantly positive differences that Rowe found on this second look were in fact among girls in mixed-sex classes.[72] It should be remembered that in the

1980s Marsh had attacked on methodological grounds Lee and Bryk's initial findings on American Catholic schools.

As in other countries, the reported gender gap in math, science, and technology has created a renewed interest in single-sex classes in the United States. These programs are still too recent, isolated, and tentative to have generated significant research findings. They have also existed under a legal cloud that has kept most of them hidden from public view. The scattered reports, largely anecdotal, generally affirm that girls-only classrooms create a safe environment in which students can take risks and develop confidence in their math and science ability.[73] Many of these classes technically are open to both boys and girls specifically to insulate them from legal attack. However, they actively recruit female students and send a clear message that "boys need not enroll."

The all-girls college algebra I class at Presque Isle (Maine) High School is an example of this approach. Operating since 1988, the program came under serious threat in 1995 when the regional office of the Office for Civil Rights charged that it violated Title IX because it was excluding boys and it was not voluntary. In response, school officials changed the name to College Algebra with Emphasis on Women and Mathematics and offered it on an optional basis to both male and female students. No male has chosen to enroll in the course. The girls participating in the class are college bound, yet they are not the most academically advanced students who have taken algebra I as eighth graders in middle school. As with other programs, an outside study found no significant impact on achievement. Nevertheless, girls who had taken the class even when enrollment was not voluntary were more likely to improve their scores on the statewide math test from eighth to eleventh grades. School officials report that whereas girls lagged behind boys by 72 points on the statewide assessment in 1991, there are now no significant differences. Anecdotally, students enjoyed the single-sex environment and did not feel that it was "remedial" in any way. If anything, girls in the mixed-sex class seemed to be "envious" of students participating in the program.[74]

A number of private schools across the country have taken a similar route. The Walker School, a private coeducational school in Marietta, Georgia, began separating boys and girls in eighth-grade algebra in 1993. Informed by Gilligan's and the Sadkers' research, school officials realized that only 30 percent of their female students were selecting advanced math and science courses, as compared with almost 100 percent of the males. As the Middle School principal sees it, "Boys seem naturally competitive. They need to be taught to work in cooperative learning groups. They care more about getting the right answer. Girls care more about the process." Nearly all the school's math classes, beginning in the fifth grade and continuing through the eighth grade in middle school, are now single-sex.

Both boys and girls in the program have reported a higher comfort level in these classes. They are less self-conscious about asking questions and participating in cooperative learning groups. They also report that they enter upper-school coed classes with greater confidence in their ability to understand and solve problems in math and science as well as in unrelated subjects. Similar to findings from other countries, the classes have not changed girls' achievement, but they have helped them develop more positive attitudes toward math and science. The number of girls enrolling in upper-level math and science classes has increased to approximately 45 to 55 percent. School officials also report a rise in the number of graduates, especially girls, who choose technology programs in college as well as a dramatic increase in the number of students selected in the Duke University Talent Search. The head of the Rippowam Cisqua School in Bedford, New York, another private coed school that has met similar success with single-sex math classes, best sums it up: "What you can't measure in a quantitative way is how these kids feel about themselves. It's enough to know that I have more girls saying, 'I love math.' "[75]

In recent years, as the gender gap has narrowed in math and science, concern has shifted to technology and the relatively low numbers of girls taking elective computer classes. To address this problem, school districts around the country have initiated a variety of in-school and after-school girls' programs, including clubs and professional mentoring. A strategy increasingly considered is the single-sex class. This approach draws support from research findings that women have performed better on computer tasks in the presence of females rather than males.[76] The idea is to create an environment in which female students experience less computer anxiety and are more comfortable taking risks. A careful look at several of these programs lends credence to that idea.

For the past seven years, Washington Middle School in Olympia, Washington, has offered an all-girls class combining technology skills with subject matter that adolescent girls typically find most interesting—issues such as nutrition, eating disorders, career exploration, and women's self-defense. Before the class was instituted, twice as many eighth- and ninth-grade boys as girls enrolled in technology electives. The ratio has since become more evenly balanced. Funded by a grant from Intel, the program has expanded to four schools within the district, as well as school districts nationwide through its online curriculum. The classes are technically open to girls and boys on a voluntary basis to meet the requirements of Title IX. School officials, however, hold a promotional meeting only for girls when recruiting students for the special class.[77]

In Manchester (Connecticut) High School students can enroll either in a single-sex or a coed section of a course entitled "world of technology," each using the same curriculum. School officials have similarly avoided legal problems in designing the course description: "For female students but open to boys by request." No boy has yet applied. Initially funded with a grant from AT&T through the Connecticut Women's Education and Legal Fund, the program now includes four school districts. According to school officials, the program has enhanced the students' self-confidence and their interest in technology careers. Of the girls in the female-targeted sections, 81 percent report a positive difference in the classroom environment without male students. They ask questions more freely, focus better on their classwork, are less embarrassed about making mistakes, and express relief that there are no boys to overpower classes. The observations of program evaluators not only confirm these perceptions but also reveal that girls in the coed classes rarely ask questions during class and feign ignorance or outwardly express their lack of interest.[78]

From a research perspective, these reports are admittedly subjective and nonscientific. The question of single-sex classes in all their permutations clearly begs for more carefully controlled longitudinal studies. Random assignment of students to each group would be the scientific ideal. But from an ethical and pedagogical perspective, that undercuts the ability of individual students and parents to make a personal decision regarding what is still an untested and controversial approach. As administrators in Presque Isle, Maine, learned, it also can provoke the ire of the Office for Civil Rights. As ultimately happened in that case, however, researchers shy away from settings where they cannot use random selection to control for preexisting student differences. The end result is that particularly within public schools, the legal issues have driven a demand for empirical evidence and at the same time prevented the type of experimentation that could provide it.

In the meantime, the reported outcomes from a small but growing number of existing programs, however inconclusive, continue to expand the discussion of single-sex education beyond achievement gains. Educators involved in these programs, both public and private, consistently report that girls in particular prefer single-sex math and science classes and that they demonstrate greater confidence and willingness to take risks when they later return to mixed classes in these subjects. These programs also push us to consider the initial effects of such short-term attitudinal and behavioral changes on long-term career opportunities and choices. The more recent attention to boys can develop this discussion even further.

## DUAL ACADEMIES

One single-sex educational model that has attracted significant media attention is the dual academy, or what in the past was called the coinstitutional approach. In this case, boys and girls are educated in separate classes, typically within the same or adjacent buildings. They join together, however, for extracurricular activities and perhaps for certain academic subjects. They may also have the opportunity to interact informally before and after school, in between classes, and at lunchtime, depending on the organization of the program. Proponents maintain that this model combines the best features of single-sex and coeducational schools. It offers a "safe haven" for students to flourish academically, free from the tension and distraction of the opposite sex, especially in such traditionally "gendered" subject areas as math, science, English, and foreign languages, while allowing them to develop the social skills they need to function in a mixed-sex world. It also avoids claims of favoritism or preferential treatment toward one sex or the other. Dual academies have existed sporadically within the private independent network in one form or another. During the first half of the twentieth century, they were used in the elementary grades in some urban schools, which still occasionally bear separate designations for boys and girls over their entrances. They were especially popular among Catholic schools in the 1950s.

The most ambitious example of public support for the dual academy model, and the only one systematically studied, comes from California, which initiated a pilot program of grants in 1997–98 primarily to address the needs of at-risk students. At that time, the state awarded $500,000 to each of six school districts for single-gender middle or high school academies. To avoid legal challenge, each district had to divide the grant equally between a boys' and a girls' academy. The program immediately caught the attention of the media. It also appealed to researchers eager for the rare opportunity to gather longitudinal data on the effects of public single-sex schooling in the United States.

Despite its initial promise, a three-year report prepared by outside researchers reveals that the California Single Gender Academies initiative, the brainchild of former Governor Pete Wilson's administration, was doomed from the start. The report represents, in fact, an interesting case study on the politics of school reform as well as a cautionary tale of the pitfalls to avoid in planning and implementing a single-sex program. For the latter reason alone, the findings merit careful consideration. As Wilson noted in his 1996 state of the state address, from the state's perspective this was largely an effort "to provide public school students more options, more choice, and better preparation for real-world opportunities." Although the state raised additional concerns regarding the discipline problems evidenced by boys and the math and science gender gap among girls, these seemed largely peripheral. The California Department of Education made clear that "increasing diversity of choice . . . [was] the primary purpose for establishing single-gender pilot academies," despite express legislative language that the academies should "be tailored to the differing needs and learning styles of boys and girls as a group."[79] From the perspective of school districts, on the other hand, this was essentially an opportunity to benefit from the smaller classes and extra resources that state funds would bring. Neither state nor local officials, therefore, had much apparent interest in single-sex education or a clearly articulated commitment to gender equity.

For an experimental approach, the program lacked all the critical elements to make it work. There was no cohesive structure or any clear forethought. The state provided no funding for staff development or for monitoring program progress. School districts had but a brief planning period to recruit teachers and students and to plan the curriculum. The schools varied in setting (urban, suburban, and rural) and served a diverse population of students in terms of race, ethnicity, and socioeconomic and linguistic background. Four pairs of single-gender academies were at the middle school level and two pairs were high schools. Some were self-contained, while others were schools within a school. Some students, particularly boys, were aggressively recruited because of discipline problems, while others volunteered. Most were low achievers. When the political tide turned and the legislature failed to reauthorize the program for what originally was understood to be a two-year commitment, school districts scrambled to find the funds for year two, and the program began to unravel. Despite positive anecdotal reports on student attitudes and grades, at the end of the second year, four of the districts discontinued the program. By the close of the third year, only one remained.[80] This confused political and organizational backdrop obviously presented the worst circumstances for evaluating the effects of any educational approach.

The three-year report contains a number of negative observations that confirm some of the worst fears of women's advocates. Perhaps the most damaging finding, and the one picked up by the media, was that schools often appeared to reinforce gender stereotypes. Boys were taught in a more traditional fashion and girls in a more collaborative and open environment. This problem assumed a particularly troubling cast in the academies that operated on a single campus. These seemed to foster a dichotomous understanding of gender wherein students and faculty generally considered girls as "good" and boys as "bad." Although girls seemed to find a safe haven from sexual harassment in these schools, they were still subject to unsolicited comments and improper touching in school areas that remained coeducational. There also was a tendency for other students to label the academy students as "bad" kids (because the programs were focused on at-risk or low-achieving students) and even more commonly as "gay."

The report underscores the problems inherent in defining and putting gender equality into practice. It also brings to the fore the various arguments surrounding the sameness-difference tension played out in a single-sex setting. The researchers take issue with the program's initial design to pursue a gender-blind approach in the name of equal opportunity. By setting that goal at the outset, they argue, the program undermined gender equity, implicitly suggesting that girls and boys have different issues that need to be addressed differently. At the same time, however, they criticize the program for reinforcing "essentialized" and traditional perspectives on gender. Teachers presented boys with a definition of masculinity portrayed in terms of "financial and emotional strength," they tell us, while sending girls conflicting messages on femininity. Although the schools overtly placed no limits on girls' potential, they enforced certain expectations regarding girls' clothing and appearance.

Some of these dichotomies, nevertheless, lend themselves to an alternate interpretation. What the researchers viewed as a conflict is also a social reality whose significance can be determined only in the context of this population of students. Perhaps a man's financial responsibility toward his family was not part of the value system of these particular boys and needed to be directly taught and reaffirmed. At the same time, this particular group of girls, many of whom undoubtedly came from single-parent homes, may have understood financial responsibility all too well. But at the same time, they may not have comprehended the importance of clothing and appearance and how they create a certain impression of one's intellectual and professional seriousness. In that sense, the schools were perhaps trying to address some of the social deficiencies of these students and acculturate them into the accepted norms of the larger society.

Yet even conceding that cultural sensitivity and socialization might have driven this duality, teachers and administrators at these schools obviously needed to be more consciously aware of how to navigate the tricky divide between gender stereotyping and gender equity. Perhaps that issue demands more serious consideration in school settings like those described here, where students are expressly classified on the basis of sex. The schools' failure on this count was not necessarily the direct consequence of the single-sex approach itself, but perhaps more a function of inadequate planning, poor staff development, and overall inattention to how "gender equity" might best be played out in a single-sex setting. As one of the researchers commented, "Most of the public single-gender academies [studied] lacked a strong theory of single-gender education that is present in some single-sex private and parochial schools." That problem is symptomatic of most public schools, which seldom have a clearly identifiable sense of mission and purpose.[81]

The report makes one particularly important point, suggesting that the dual-academy approach may itself present its own challenges. It appears that where girls' and boys' schools are located on the same campus and/or staffed by the same teachers, students may be subjected to sex stereotyping, harmful comparisons, harassment, and distractions that might not arise in self-contained single-sex schools. These observations run directly counter to the perceived wisdom among some educators that the dual academy or coinstitutional model provides the best of both single-sex and coeducation, separating the sexes in their core academic pursuits while affording opportunities for social interaction. Yet at least as implemented in California, the approach arguably created a context wherein the immediate goal of gender equity was in fact undercut. Of course, these findings may again have more to do with other institutional factors than with the approach itself, yet the possible connection between the dual-academy model and the failure to effectively promote equity principles deserves further consideration.

In the end the findings caused the researchers "to pause about whether single gender schooling is a wise move in the public sector." Embedded in the report, however, are several positive and important observations that unfortunately got lost in the negative media spin surrounding the report's initial release. The researchers note that when "educators, parents, and students . . . have a strong theory about the purpose of single gender education, single gender schools are more likely to survive." They offer as an example an all-girls public high school in the eastern United States, apparently Western High School for Girls in Baltimore. They recognize that this school, established in the mid-1800s and deeply steeped in tradition, has maintained its single-sex status and its reputation for academic excellence with the support of alumni, teachers, and parents.[82] In contrast, the California dual academies lacked a "strong ideological commitment to single gender education." They also served primarily an academically and socially troubled student population.

The report nevertheless describes a notable positive exception in an unidentified school whose district superintendent firmly believed that this arrangement was particularly important for the boys. Two preliminary papers that the researchers presented in the course of the three-year study more clearly articulate and highlight the success of this school. These papers focus on three specific academies whose stated mission was to serve at-risk students. The one described in the final report had existed as a single-sex middle school for at-risk boys before state funding and subsequently had added a girls' school with initial state support. It has enjoyed a level of local commitment clearly lacking in the other districts. Not surprisingly, it is the sole remaining school in the project.

In these three pairs of schools, the researchers found that the single-sex setting "gave at-risk students an option—an opportunity for another chance at success." They describe how "gender separation facilitated [these students'] academic and personal growth. Freed from the distraction of the other gender, students were able to focus on their lessons." The single-sex setting sheltered girls in particular from pressures related to their appearance and offered them an opportunity to concentrate on their academic work. For teachers, it created a comfortable and appropriate context for teaching social and moral lessons that conveyed gender-specific messages from real-life circumstances on such topics as dating, pregnancy, and careers. The researchers caution that these positive effects were not solely the result of the single-sex program. Even so, they suggest that the single-sex setting can prove particularly effective for at-risk students when combined with caring, proactive teachers, along with sufficient funding for academic and social supports, including small class size.[83]

These earlier observations more narrowly focused on particular schools whose express mission was to serve at-risk students. And so, the California findings, as negative as they appear in the aggregate, may in fact offer a kernel of support for Riordan's thesis that disadvantaged students benefit most from single-sex programs. Unfortunately, this fine point is swamped by a mass of observations culled from a diverse set of programs, four of which did not survive beyond the initial year of the study. In fact, the principal of the one remaining school took issue with some of the studies' characterizations. As he later reported to the press, among the 132 girls and boys enrolled, grades had improved, suspensions were down, and the number of fights had declined. "We think we've managed to get a buy-in from students into what they need to stay in school and into the idea that we want to celebrate and respect differences," he noted.[84] Yet it would be wise to exercise caution in drawing any conclusions on the comparative merits of single-sex or coeducation from this politically misguided, unfocused, and misintentioned venture. The overall program had too many intrinsic and extrinsic strikes against it to seriously advance the ongoing debate. Just as it may be unreasonable to conclude that any benefits gained by at-risk students were solely the result of the single-gender approach, so it is unfair to conclude that the approach was a dominant factor in the stereotypically gendered attitudes and behaviors demonstrated by students and teachers.

One final point needs to be underscored. Educators and policymakers should give serious thought to the potential, although by no means inescapable, problems inherent in the dual-academy model. On this score, the Jefferson Leadership Academies in Long Beach, California, a program that has attracted local and national media attention, present additional insights. There boys and girls share the same teachers and the same classrooms, and the school makes every effort to provide each group with equal resources. School officials maintain that both boys and girls tend to focus better on academics, students participate more actively in class discussion, and parents enthusiastically support the program. By the end of its second year, the school had quadrupled its targeted gains on the California Academic Performance Index, which measures the progress of state schools and districts based on standardized tests, and ranked in the top 20th percentile among schools with similar demographics. Yet the school's academic turnaround was due, no doubt, to a combination of factors and not solely to its new gender organization. In the conversion from coeducation, the school had acquired a dynamic new principal, a cosmetic makeover in the form of new paint and a thorough cleaning, and a new ethos of potential success that generated interest and involvement on the part of parents.[85]

Despite these initially positive outcomes, a first-year study of the program points out some of the challenges that school staff faced, some of them driven by legal constraints, others the result of inadequate resources or merely the inevitable mishaps of charting new ground. Motivated by what school officials believed to be a Title IX mandate, teachers struggled mightily to provide exactly the same curriculum and materials at the same pace to girls and boys. Not surprisingly, the study found, in doing so they failed to accommodate developmental and attitudinal differences between the two groups. They also failed to take into account the higher energy levels of the boys, many of whom had been identified with special needs. Meanwhile, the program design compelled teachers to hold back the girls, who were performing at a higher academic level and presented far fewer discipline problems, in order to keep the curriculum in sync with that of the boys. In the end, the study concluded, neither the girls nor the boys as a group received an education that was appropriate to their particular abilities and learning styles. But again, inadequate staff development, inexperienced teachers, and a school mission that was more focused on raising standardized test scores than consciously addressing the specific educational needs of girls and boys undoubtedly confounded the results. Although the program could in fact claim success in that test scores improved, it apparently missed many opportunities to develop both girls and boys to their full potential.[86]

Nonetheless, notwithstanding these problematic reports on the California experience, the dual-academy approach has much to offer within the range of single-sex models. A number of school districts around the country, in fact, are now experimenting with coinstitutional programs as an alternative to the all-boys and all-girls schools that provoked a legal uproar in Detroit and New York in the 1990s. In September 2002 the Brighter Choice Charter Schools, including separate girls' and boys' academies under the same roof, opened in Albany, New York. This is the first single-sex public elementary school program among the new initiatives. The two academies exist under separate charters, a legal fiction created to meet Title IX's prohibition against single-sex classes within a coeducational school. Like many charter schools, they target disadvantaged students based on eligibility for free or reduced lunch. Beginning with kindergarten and grade one, the program will add a grade each year until it reaches 290 students from kindergarten through fifth grade. The schools provide an extended schoolday and a longer school year. Students wear uniforms to minimize peer pressure, and teachers must also follow a dress code as role models for their students. The curriculum is subject-based, and the same teachers teach both girls and boys. All students learn Spanish, beginning in kindergarten, as a complement to the program's intensive focus on history and world cultures.

In this case, program organizers and staff have carefully designed the curriculum and instructional approach to draw on the distinct advantages of the dual-academy model while trying to avoid the problems evidenced in California. Rather than keeping boys and girls in academic lockstep, teachers are allowed a measure of flexibility in what they teach and how they teach it. Although the boys' and girls' academies benefit from the same resources, and students in both must meet the same standards, it is understood that they may not meet each standard at the same pace. As Thomas Carroll, the Brighter Choice Charter Schools' founder and chairman, explains, "This is a unique way to observe whatever gender differences there are but also to have teachers vary the instruction accordingly for the sake of equity. Boys and girls benefit from single-sex schooling perhaps in different ways. If girls develop reading skills faster, they won't be held back. But we may also provide tutors for boys to help them catch up." Recruitment efforts have far exceeded the expectations of the program's founders. For the initial incoming classes, the schools attracted more than twice the number of applicants for ninety places, most of them from Albany's poorest neighborhoods.[87] Similar dual academies serving at-risk students are in the planning stages in other cities.

Meanwhile, existing inner-city public elementary schools are slowly experimenting, with remarkable success, with separate classes for boys and girls. At Moten Elementary School in Washington, D.C., students achieving at the "advanced" and "proficient" levels on the Stanford 9 test jumped from 49 percent to 88 percent in math and from 50 percent to 91.5 percent in reading within one year of sex-separate classes throughout the schoolday. At Thurgood Marshall Elementary School in Seattle, school officials report a rapid decline in boys' suspensions and a marked improvement in academic achievement following a similar conversion to single-sex classes. As Benjamin Wright, the school's principal, sees it, the elementary grades are the most critical. If you "don't engage students then, all is lost."[88] Obviously, these findings need to be examined carefully in light of other organizational and curricular changes that may have influenced student behavior and achievement in these schools. Nevertheless, these unofficial preliminary reports lend additional anecdotal support to the proposition that single-sex schooling may prove especially beneficial to disadvantaged students. They also point out the critical need for more systematic research on that precise question.

## CHARTING A RESEARCH AGENDA

There is no doubt that the research comparing the relative merits of single-sex and coeducation has not yielded definitive answers. But that admission in itself says less about either approach than it does about educational policy and research. Nonetheless, we can draw several reasonable and useful conclusions from the growing body of research and anecdotal reports on programs operating in Great Britain, Australia, and the United States in particular.

First of all, there is no clear indication that single-sex schooling harms students academically, and any negative effects on boys' social development are speculative. On the other hand, there appears to be strong evidence that single-sex schools and classes develop in students more positive attitudes toward certain traditionally male or female subjects, whether math, science, and technology for girls or foreign languages, English, and the arts for boys. These changed attitudes, in turn, may lead to more advanced course taking and ultimately broader career options. Furthermore, earlier findings that separate schooling may prove considerably more favorable to girls than to boys seem to be undercut by more recent research pointing to the benefits gained by certain populations of male students. And finally, there is a growing body of data pointing to the academic and social benefits that disadvantaged minority students above all might derive from single-sex programs.

These observations, concededly, are tentative and suggestive. The more recent empirical findings supporting single-sex education generally come from abroad. Nevertheless, the growing number of anecdotal reports from the United States, especially from urban public schools, is becoming increasingly persuasive. As single-sex schooling gains legal and educational legitimacy, these findings in the aggregate provide researchers with useful direction in establishing a broad and varied research agenda. That agenda should replicate some of the key studies from the past to compare the effects in a modern-day public school setting in the United States. But researchers also should formulate new research questions that reflect a contemporary view of the gender gaps favoring girls and boys, and should consider a wider range of short- and long-term outcomes beyond school performance and achievement, including changed attitudes and course selection patterns, as well as pregnancy, suspension, and dropout rates, and even long-range effects on college enrollment and career choices.

It would further prove useful to study the effects of single-sex schools and classes on both girls and boys across the grades from elementary through middle and high school, in rural, suburban, and urban contexts, and across socioeconomic, racial, and ethnic categories. Various approaches should be studied, including single-sex classes in math, science, technology, foreign languages, and language arts, as well as single-sex schools and dual academies. Finally, there should be an overarching attempt to gather not just quantitative but also qualitative data to develop a clearer sense of educational process, along with academic outputs. Researchers should examine what takes place in differently organized programs with respect to curriculum content, teaching style, classroom interaction, and overall climate that may influence specific student outcomes. Meanwhile, school systems must make equally vigorous efforts to promote gender equity and improve the academic performance and achievement of girls and boys in coeducational settings. Otherwise, research findings will stand on a thin reed, as we will not be able to isolate gender organization as the critical factor.

A broad but carefully conceived research agenda of this nature will provide educators and policymakers with sufficient knowledge and understanding to make more considered and defensible judgments on the choice between single-sex (in any of its forms) and coeducation for any specific population of students. Just as important, it will arm parents with adequate information to make informed decisions on how best to meet the educational and social needs of their children.

# 9
# Rethinking Single-Sex Schooling

Despite growing popular support for single-sex schooling, both the overwhelming cultural preference for coeducation and the continuing legal and social presumptions against sex separation have kept the approach on the defensive. Whether or not this position is justified, it has set the ground rules for public and scholarly discourse. Nonetheless, the surrounding debate that has filtered through the courts and the press for three decades has come to a critical juncture, presenting both a challenge and an opportunity to educators, policymakers, and society at large. As the pieces slowly fall into place, we should dare to rethink and redefine this seemingly anachronistic approach to meet present-day understandings and realities.

The legal issues appear to be reaching resolution, at least in the abstract. The Supreme Court's 1996 decision striking down on constitutional grounds the all-male admissions policy at the Virginia Military Institute leaves considerable room for well-designed programs with clearly stated and nonbiased objectives. Although commentators continue to ponder the meaning and force of an "exceedingly persuasive justification," we can reasonably conclude that it essentially comes down to the fit between the program and its intended ends, and the context in which the program exists. As long as the program has academic merit, does not promote sex stereotypes or rely on "overbroad generalizations" concerning the abilities or preferences of girls or boys, and does not offer a "unique" or "extraordinary" opportunity that is not available to the other sex in a "substantially equal" setting, then it will pass constitutional muster.

At the same time, recent congressional action promises to end years of aggressive enforcement, administrative foot-dragging, and uncertainty under Title IX. Congress has now placed its imprimatur on single-sex programs, and the Office for Civil Rights has set about the task of clarifying the Title IX regulations. It remains to be seen whether school districts will enthusiastically use federal funds for single-sex schools and classes or for other innovative programs. In any event, that question is now left to local discretion and not federal fiat.

Setting aside the legal issues, however, will not end the debate but merely shift it to other related and equally contentious grounds. The search undoubtedly will intensify for educational justifications that respond to public concerns about the short- and long-term effects of separating students by sex. Yet therein lies the opportunity to reframe the discussion in accordance with what we now know about different populations of girls and boys as they move through the cycle of childhood into adolescence. And therein lies the long overdue chance to thoughtfully assess the evolving landscape of single-sex schooling.

As psychologists have brought attention to the "boy question," they and others have revealed how schools shortchange girls and boys in different ways. The gender gap favoring boys in math and science has narrowed, but girls continue to lag behind them, especially on high-stakes tests like the SAT and Advanced Placement exams. Despite impressive gains in school performance, girls still have difficulty penetrating a "glass ceiling" at the highest levels of academic achievement, particularly in math, science, and technology. At the same time, boys as a group have fallen even farther behind girls in reading and verbal skills. They also demonstrate a much higher incidence of learning disabilities, academic failure, and emotional difficulties, although there is growing evidence that girls may suffer similar problems that go unidentified because of their compliant classroom behavior. Yet while there are fewer girls at the top of the academic performance ladder, there are far more boys at the bottom. These issues are most acute among disadvantaged minority boys whose suspension and dropout rates and incidents of criminal activity have reached alarming proportions. Many of them exist in a subculture that attaches little value to academic achievement for men. That is where we find the real "boy crisis." Meanwhile, the different social dynamics of the same- or mixed-sex classroom affect the learning experience of many students. Boys still tend to dominate classroom discussion and small-group activities, especially in conventionally male subjects. Many girls still shy away from asking questions or challenging others especially in mixed-sex groups. Girls as a group still appear to prefer a collaborative learning environment. Boys more typically like the charge of competition.

The possible reasons for these boy-girl differences in school performance, achievement, and classroom behavior have provoked sharp disagreements among scholars and researchers. Nevertheless, the consensus holds that individuals are shaped both by nature and by nurture. Although biology is not destiny, it appears to set the outer bounds of performance in the absence of focused intervention. There is also widespread agreement that innate abilities respond to outside forces that either reinforce their strengths or offset their weaknesses. Reasonable evidence suggests that social, experiential, and biological factors interact in many of the observed differences between females and males. The small differences in visual spatial skills favoring boys, their slower maturational rate as compared with girls, and the earlier and advanced verbal abilities that girls exhibit are all factors that influence academic performance and interest. Yet society has also established over time certain normative expectations of girls and boys that either enhance or undermine their confidence in such subjects as math, science, and computers (strengths for boys), and English and foreign languages (strengths for girls).

The obvious question is whether separating the sexes at certain points in the educational experience can alleviate to any degree the negative effects of these differences. Unfortunately, much of the research on single-sex schools suffers from methodological flaws or findings from cultural contexts that differ from current initiatives in the United States. Moreover, the evidence itself is not sufficiently weighty to yield definitive conclusions. But inconclusivity is not negativity. There is no significant indication among more recent findings that single-sex programs harm students academically, and any social drawbacks are largely unsubstantiated. To the contrary, a large and scattered body of research from across the globe, combined with a wealth of anecdotal evidence from public and private school programs in the United States, when looked at collectively, reveals recurrent and promising themes that provide positive direction for potential program design and research efforts.

It appears that girls in particular derive academic and psychosocial benefits from single-sex programs. The literature is replete with evidence pointing in that direction. All-girls settings seem to provide girls a certain comfort level that helps them develop greater self-confidence and broader interests, especially as they approach adolescence. Research has found that single-sex schools and classes promote less-gender-polarized attitudes toward certain subjects—math and science in the case of girls and language arts and foreign languages in the case of boys. Although the effect of these programs on achievement gains is not observably clear, they seem to encourage more advanced course taking and may influence students' interest in pursuing nontraditional careers in the long term. Research findings further indicate that disadvantaged minority girls and boys may gain the most in academic identification and achievement from same-sex schooling. It may prove useful to test these findings among poor white students living in rural areas or on the fringes of cities, groups frequently forgotten in the discussion on academic failure.

A smattering of early studies confirmed the conventional wisdom that boys in general derive greater benefits from coeducational schools, although recent findings from English-speaking countries outside the United States have placed doubt on that widely held belief. That conclusion, in fact, results in part from the limited focus of research to date. Most studies, driven by the "girl question," have examined math and science or middle and secondary school programs that are thought to benefit girls. Research at the elementary school level or in such areas as English and foreign languages might yield more favorable outcomes from single-sex programs for boys. Several studies seem to bear this out. Research on child and adolescent development suggests that boys may benefit most from single-sex programs in the early grades, while the middle-school years may be the most critical for girls. Although conclusive support for this proposition remains to be found, it is certainly worth examining.

Some of the findings frequently discussed in the literature are now outdated. Most of these come from private schools and reflect a perspective on single-sex education that has gradually become more the exception than the norm. As public school officials begin to explore single-sex schooling in all its permutations, girls' middle and secondary schools in particular have the advantage of looking toward successful models like the Young Women's Leadership School in New York, Philadelphia's High School for Girls, and Baltimore's Western High School. The Brighter Choice Charter Schools in Albany likewise hold the promise of creating a similar template for dual academies and elementary schooling. Across the country, in rural and urban areas, coeducational schools that have established single-sex classes for girls in math, science, and technology have further developed positive experiences worth pursuing, perhaps in different subject areas. Anecdotal reports from the growing number of separate-sex classes for disadvantaged minority students have similarly proven encouraging.

But much can also be learned from the world of private schools, despite an initial inclination to reject them for the obvious socioeconomic differences. Over the past twenty years and especially over the past decade, single-sex schooling in the private sector has undergone significant changes that undoubtedly affect student learning and attitudes. Through a confluence of forces, including the women's movement, the resulting push for gender equity in schools, and the more recent attention to the emotional needs of boys, single-sex schools in the main are no longer the "girls' finishing schools" or the "bastions of male privilege and exclusion" that they once were considered to be. And unlike the boarding schools of the past, where students were isolated in a pervasively same-sex environment, the vast majority of single-sex schools today are day schools that allow students regular contact with members of the opposite sex in their homes and in their communities. More important, single-sex schooling is not monolithic as an educational approach. Some programs are totally same-sex. Others, in particular secondary schools, are beginning to "partner" with neighboring schools, incorporating curricular and extracurricular programs that engage students in mixed-sex activities of an academic and social nature. Still others maintain separate organizational structures but allow cross-registration between schools in certain subject areas. Such collaborative initiatives are important. Sex separation should not turn into isolation.

The gender composition of faculty at these schools also has changed, offering students the opportunity to relate to both sexes throughout the school day in an environment that more closely replicates the real world. Boys' schools, for example, now include a significant number of women among their teaching staff, particularly in the lower grades, where the atmosphere has become far more nurturing than in the past. This change in the gender mix not only infuses a broader spectrum of views into the school's operation, but it also permits boys to see adult women and men interacting as equals in a common professional pursuit, an invaluable lesson that fosters more positive attitudes toward women. The same can be said for the more frequent presence of male faculty in girls' schools. Boys' schools have now moved women into the administrative ranks so that students learn to respect women in positions of authority. At the same time, just as girls' schools present female teachers as role models in traditionally male subjects like math and science, boys' schools offer the experience of male teachers engaged in intellectual pursuits, such as foreign languages, literature, and the arts, stereotypically considered feminine. The importance of male teachers as role models has proven especially salient in the education of disadvantaged minority boys.

Educators within the boys' school network are quick to point out that as girls' schools over the years have adopted an empowerment philosophy, boys' schools now embrace a sensitivity toward gender issues and boys' development. They note how these schools channel the high physicality of boys in the lower grades rather than contain it as coed schools typically attempt to do. The headmaster of a prominent boys' school remarked how he never hears teachers commenting that a particular boy cannot "sit still," which was a common complaint in the coed schools where he had previously served. It is now common knowledge that girls enter school with better verbal and fine-motor skills, which puts young boys at a disadvantage in coed settings. At coed schools boys are expected to function at the same level as girls, but girls are also sometimes held back so that the boys can catch up. For similar reasons related to developmental differences, schools are increasingly delaying the start of school for boys considered too "immature"—that is, compared with girls of the same age. Many boys eventually do catch up, but in the process others simply give up or are diagnosed as learning disabled. As the lower school principal of a highly regarded boys' school explained, "We avoid a lot of small learning disabilities by giving structure which boys desperately need." At the same time, girls' school educators value their ability in the lower grades to move girls along at a quicker pace in reading and language arts.

As one boys' school administrator observed, coed middle schools can prove unkind and even hostile to the "nerd" or the violinist—boys who do not fit the stereotypical male mold. The all-boys environment provides a protective space where boys can pursue their own path to self-fulfillment free from the distraction of girls, similar to the way the all-girls' environment operates for girls. In the absence of girls, educators say, boys are more willing to explore and openly discuss a broader range of literature beyond the typically male adventure and suspense genres and to willingly engage in literary forms that many adolescent boys would reject outright as "female." As one headmaster put it, "Our boys love to write poetry. It appeals to the musical-lyrical piece of them." And just as girls' schools offer girls leadership opportunities sometimes difficult to attain in coeducational environments—class president, editor in chief of the yearbook, top athlete—boys' schools allow boys a full assortment of experiences beyond athletics to gain recognition and build self-esteem, including such activities as drama, choir, and community service, which girls often dominate in coeducational schools.

In both boys' and girls' schools, by necessity no task can be assigned or identified by sex, whether it is making props or costumes for the school play, playing in a jazz quartet, or running the school newspaper. Here you are likely to experience an entire room of middle school boys playing the violin. Or you can hear an operetta performed by members of an all-boys choir or see high school young men sitting on the floor helping first graders learn to read. You can also enjoy large numbers of girls playing the gamut of musical instruments, including those typically reserved for boys, like the saxophone, the trombone, and percussion. You would be hard-pressed to experience any of these occurrences in a coed school.

Yet amid the enthusiasm to try new approaches where all others have failed, educators and organizers considering single-sex programs must remain mindful that the educational effect, and for public schools the ultimate question of legality, will depend in part on each school's willingness to consciously stretch traditional bounds and shed outmoded views on gender and schooling. The perspectives, values, and practices that constitute both the "overt" and the "hidden" curriculum are critical to the success of any program. At its best, single-sex education can be an effective tool of empowerment and self-realization for some girls and boys. Then again, at its worst, and as history has proven, it can unwittingly become a tool of gender polarization and oppression, perpetuating stereotypical images that produce feelings of inadequacy among girls while reinforcing exclusionary and sexist attitudes among boys. Strategies and materials that appeal to different learning styles or interests between girls and boys should be used with thought and careful attention to individual student needs. That being said, as school officials embark on this old venture turned new, they must make every effort to assure that single-sex programs do not regress into pre–Title IX stereotypes or unequal resource allocations. Nor should they abandon vigorous efforts to promote gender equity throughout the educational system, including coeducational schools, as some women's advocates fear. In the meantime, we can reasonably rely on three decades of gender equity awareness and the legal force of Title IX to provide a strong measure of protection from the remote but nonetheless real possibility of backsliding.

Given what we now know about gender, schooling, and child and adolescent development, it defies reason for government to mandate coeducation for all students enrolled in public schools. Of course, this is not to propose that public officials mandate single-sex schooling in any case. Nor does it suggest that the approach is even appropriate for all students or for all members of certain groups. Enrollment in single-sex schools and classes should be purely voluntary. Nor should we thoughtlessly assume that separating students by sex is the ideal way to prepare girls and boys for adult lives in which they will interact in mutual understanding and respect. But then again, this is not an ideal world. For at least some students, and for reasons that we are just beginning to comprehend, it has become increasingly clear that the most effective way to reach that end is to offer an emotional and developmental "safe haven" apart from the other sex for at least a portion of their education, whether in particular classes, or grades, across the curriculum, or in completely separate schools.

But there is another aspect to the single-sex debate that should not go unnoticed. Single-sex programs also respond to current school reform efforts, including the push for greater local flexibility and educational options and the increasing attention to providing appropriate and not just compensatory education to meet the needs of different student populations. In this particular context, shedding the language of compensation rescues the debate from the divisive and unjustly one-sided discourse of girls' disadvantage, and even worse, victimization. Within single-sex education, moreover, the principles of liberty (in the form of choice) and equality (in the form of equal educational opportunity) are clearly reconcilable and mutually reinforcing despite assertions to the contrary—assertions grounded more in ideology and misplaced fears than in sound pedagogy or reasoned judgment. This argument rings especially true in the case of low-income minority students, for whom three decades of compensatory programs have proven a dismal failure. If equality is truly a fundamental goal of education, then public schools should afford students across the economic spectrum, and with potentially greater personal and social returns, the same choice and opportunity historically enjoyed by those with the means to purchase them in the market of private schooling.

Over the past three decades, the equality ideal has come to mean not just "same is equal" but sometimes "different is equal" and even "more is equal" when applied to various groups, including the economically and educationally disadvantaged, linguistic minorities, and the disabled. The ultimate goal has been to develop each student's full potential by initially leveling the playing field to accommodate individual needs. Why should gender be any different? Girls and boys appear largely the same at the core but also slightly different within a narrow range at the margins, while some within each group depart from the norm.

Given this profile, the road to gender equality should be paved with diverse blends of same and different educational experiences. The exact contours of those experiences promise to take shape over time as schools across the country, both private and now public, serve as laboratories of opportunity and diversity for educating future generations of girls and boys, whether together or separately.

# Notes

## CHAPTER 1. Text and Subtext

1. *United States v. Virginia*, 518 U.S. 515 (1996); *Faulkner v. Jones*, 51 F.3d 440 (4th Cir. 1995).
2. Anne Conners and Norman Siegel, "A School for Girls Only? No, That's Sex Discrimination," *New York Daily News*, 11 November 1997, 63; Rene Sanchez, "In East Harlem, a School Without Boys," *Washington Post*, 22 September 1996, A1; Anne Conners, "All-Girls School for Spanish Harlem? No," *New York Law Journal*, 5 August 1996, 2; *Brown v. Board of Education*, 347 U.S. 484 (1954).
3. Derrick Bell, "Et Tu, A.C.L.U.?" *New York Times*, 18 July 1996, A23.
4. *Faulkner v. Jones*, 859 F. Supp. 552 (D. So. Car. 1994), *aff'd*, 51 F. 3d 440 (4th Cir. 1995).
5. *Choosing a Girls' School: Directory 2001* (Concord, Mass.: National Coalition of Girls' Schools, 2001), 23; *NCGS Member Survey* (Concord, Mass.: National Coalition of Girls' Schools, 2001); Tamar Lewin, "Girls' Schools Gain, Saying Coed Isn't Coequal," *New York Times*, 11 April 1999, Metro Section, 1, 34.
6. National Association of Independent Schools, "Boys Schools Only: Enrollment in Member Schools, 5 Years," table 3A, July 2002.

## CHAPTER 2. A Tale of Three Cities

1. *Choosing a Girls' School: Directory 2001* (Concord, Mass.: National Coalition of Girls' Schools, 2001); International Boys' Schools Coalition, "Our Members: United States of America" <www.boysschoolscoalition.org/members/usa>.
2. Board of Education of the City of New York, *Annual Reports* (Brooklyn, N.Y., 1945–1985).
3. Robert Ingrassia, "Oprah's Words of Hope at Harlem Girls' H.S.," *New York Daily News*, 27 June 2001, 4.

4. Anemona Hartocollis, "Classy Idea for Girls," *New York Daily News*, 17 July 1996, 14.

5. Fred Kaplan, "Storm Gathers over Flowering School," *Boston Globe*, 23 February 1998, 14; Chancellor's Task Force on Sex Equity, *The Gender Gap in New York City Public Schools* (New York: Board of Education of the City of New York, 1994), 16.

6. "The Forbidden School," *Wall Street Journal*, 31 July 1996, A14.

7. Mary W. B. Tabor, "Planners of a New Public School for Girls Look to Two Other Cities," *New York Times*, 22 July 1996, B1.

8. Interview with Ann Rubenstein Tisch, New York City, 3 March 2001; interview with Seymour Fliegel, New York City, 3 March 2001.

9. Telephone interview with John Ferrandino, New York City, 4 December 2001.

10. Administrative complaint, United States Department of Education, Office for Civil Rights, filed by the National Organization for Women—New York City Chapter, the New York Civil Liberties Union, and the New York Civil Rights Coalition, 22 August 1996, 9; Jacques Steinberg, "Central Board Backs All-Girls School," *New York Times*, 22 August 1996, B3.

11. Sheryl McCarthy, "Let This All-Girls School Be All Girls," *New York Newsday*, 18 July 1996, A44.

12. John Leo, "Girls-Only School Is About Leaders, Not Victimization," *Dallas Morning News*, 3 August 1996, 29A; Peggy Orenstein, "All-Girl Schools Duck the Issue," *New York Times*, 20 July 1996, 19; Stephanie Gutmann, "Class Conflict," *New Republic*, 7 October 1996, 12.

13. Scott Baldauf, "Merits, Demerits of Single-Sex Ed Raised in Harlem: Separate but Equal," *Christian Science Monitor*, 4 September 1996, 1; Karen Carpenter Baker and Anemona Hartocollis, "All-Girls School Defended," *New York Daily News*, 17 July 1996, 6; Jacques Steinberg, "All-Girls School Opens to Muffins and Media," *New York Times*, 5 September 1996, B6.

14. Liz Willen, "Girls Learn Together," *New York Newsday*, 9 September 1996, A28.

15. Rene Sanchez, "In East Harlem, a School Without Boys," *Washington Post*, 22 September 1996, A1.

16. Rachel P. Kovner, "Education Dept. Readies Rules to Support Single-Sex Schools," *New York Sun*, 1 May 2002, 1.

17. Jacques Steinberg, "Crew Says No to Compromise on All-Girls Middle School," *New York Times*, 25 September 1997, B3; Jacques Steinberg, "All-Girls School May Violate Rights of Boys, Officials Say," *New York Times*, 18 September 1997, B1; letter from Congressmen Charles E. Schumer, Charles B. Rangel, Thomas J. Manton, Major Owens, and Gary L. Ackerman to Richard Riley, secretary of education, U.S. Department of Education, 6 November 1997; letter from Norma V. Cantú, assistant secretary, Office for Civil Rights, Department of Education, to Congressman Charles B. Rangel, 26 November 1997; interview with Seymour Fliegel, New York City, 3 March 2001.

18. Susan Edelman, "Exception-al Ruling May OK All-Girls School," *New York Post*, 12 February 1998, 26; Kaplan, "Storm Gathers," A1, A5.

19. See Lauren Cowen, "A Class of Their Own," *Chicago Tribune Magazine*, 1 October 2000, 12–17.

20. Board of Education of the City of New York, *Comprehensive Educational Plan, 2001–02: The Young Women's Leadership School* (Spring 2001), 3–4.

21. Young Women's Leadership Foundation, *The Young Women's Leadership School of East Harlem* (New York, 2002).

22. "Bush Push for Single-Sex Schools," *CBSNews*, 9 May 2002, <www.cbsnews.com>.
23. Anemona Hartocollis. "New School Takes the High Road," *New York Times*, 8 January 2002, B1.
24. Karen Hunter, "Single-Sex Schools Work, So Let's Have More of Them," *New York Daily News*, 31 May 2002, 45.
25. Telephone interview with Madeline Moore, 11 November 2001; interview with Kathleen Ponze, New York City, 13 December 2001.
26. Young Women's Leadership Foundation, *Young Women's Leadership School;* Kenneth Lovvett, Clementine Lisi, and Carl Campanile, "Regents-Exam Shocker," *New York Post*, 20 December 2001, 28.
27. Interview with Holly Fritz, New York City, 10 May 2001.
28. David Hogan, "Philadelphia High School for Girls, 1850–1880: Enrollment and Achievement," working paper no. 8 (Philadelphia: Philadelphia High School for Girls); David Hogan, "Philadelphia High School for Girls, 1901–1922: Attendance and Achievement," working paper no. 9 (Philadelphia: Philadelphia High School for Girls).
29. Samantha Stainburn, "All Girls, All the Time," *Teacher* (January 2000), 22–23.
30. Philadelphia High School for Girls, "A Sesquicentennial Celebration," program, 21 November 1998, Philadelphia.
31. Ibid.; Stainburn, "All Girls," 23.
32. Interview with Dimitri Kauriga, Philadelphia, 24 May 2000.
33. Pennsylvania System of School Assessment, 2000 (Pennsylvania Department of Education); website of the Philadelphia High School for Girls, <http://www.phila.k12.pa.us/schools/girlshigh>.
34. *Western High School Past and Present, 1844–1944* (Baltimore: Western High School, 1944); *Western, 150 Years, Tradition, Scholarship, Spirit,* A Commemorative Booklet in Celebration of the Sesquicentennial, 1844–1994 (Baltimore: Western High School, 1994).
35. Traci Johnson Mathena, "Best Western," *Baltimore Sun*, Sunday Magazine, 30 October 1994, 8.
36. *Maryland School Performance Program Report, 2000: School System and Schools, Baltimore City* (Baltimore: Baltimore City Public School System, 2000); *Student Handbook for the 1999–2000 School Year* (Baltimore: Western High School, 2000).

CHAPTER 3. Equality Engendered

1. For a discussion of this perspective, see Richard A. Posner, "Conservative Feminism," *University of Chicago Legal Forum* (1989): 191–217, at 191.
2. See Kimberly M. Schuld, "Rethinking Educational Equity: Sometimes Different Can Be an Acceptable Substitute for Equal," *University of Chicago Legal Forum* (1999): 461–92.
3. Deborah L. Rhode, "Theoretical Perspectives on Sexual Difference," in *Theoretical Perspectives on Sexual Difference*, ed. Deborah L. Rhode (New Haven: Yale University Press, 1990), 1–9, at 3.
4. Feminist scholars have used slightly varying approaches to define developments over the past three decades. Some have identified three stages: equality in the 1970s, difference in the 1980s, and diversity in the 1990s. Martha Chalmers, *Introduction to Feminist Legal Theory* (New York: Aspen Law and Business, 1999), 23.

5. Barbara Welter, "The Cult of True Womanhood: 1820–1860," *American Quarterly*, 18 (Summer 1966): 151–74; Alexis de Tocqueville, *Democracy in America*, ed. Phillips Bradley (New York: Vintage, 1945), 2: 212.

6. *Bradwell v. Illinois*, 83 U.S. 130 (1873)(Bradley, J., concurring).

7. Barbara Deckard, *The Women's Movement* (New York: Harper and Row, 1975), 254–55; Bonnie S. Anderson, *Joyous Greetings: The First International Women's Movement, 1830–1860* (New York: Oxford University Press, 2000), 168–70.

8. Lucy Stone, editorial, *Women's Journal*, 16 July 1870, 220, quoted in Patricia Smith Butcher, *Education for Equality: Women's Rights Periodicals and Women's Higher Education, 1849–1920* (Westport, Conn.: Greenwood, 1989), 41.

9. Nancy F. Cott, *The Grounding of Modern Feminism* (New Haven: Yale University Press, 1987), 19–21.

10. Shari L. Thurer, *The Myths of Motherhood* (New York: Penguin, 1994), 215; Jane Frohock, letter to the editor, *The Lily*, 1 December 1856, 23, quoted in Cott, *Grounding of Modern Feminism*, 19. For an excellent discussion of the women's rights press from 1849 to 1920, see Butcher, *Education for Equality*.

11. Cott, *Grounding of Modern Feminism*, 30.

12. *Lochner v. New York*, 198 U.S. 45 (1905); *Muller v. Oregon*, 208 U.S. 412 (1908).

13. See Barbara A. Brown, Thomas E. Emerson, Gail Falk, and Ann E. Freedman, "The Equal Rights Amendment: A Constitutional Basis for Equal Rights for Women," *Yale Law Journal*, 80 (1971): 871–985, at 924.

14. Deckard, *Women's Movement*, 151–56.

15. Catharine MacKinnon, "Legal Perspectives on Sexual Difference," in Rhode, *Theoretical Perspectives*, 213–25, at 213.

16. William Blackstone, *Commentaries on the Laws of England* (Oxford: Clarendon, 1783), 442–43; Kristen Amundsen, *The Silenced Majority: Women and American Democracy* (New York: Prentice-Hall, 1971).

17. Betty Friedan, *The Feminine Mystique* (New York: Dell, 1963); Simone de Beauvoir, *The Second Sex*, trans. and ed. H. M. Parshley (New York: Alfred A. Knopf, 1952; rpt. Random House, Vintage, 1989).

18. Sarah Grimke, *Letters on the Equality of the Sexes and the Condition of Women* (1838), 10, quoted in Deckard, *Women's Movement*, 253, and cited in Ruth Bader Ginsburg, "Sex Equality and the Constitution: The State of the Art," *Women's Rights Law Reporter*, 14 (1992): 361–366, at 361.

19. *A Matter of Simple Justice: The Report of the President's Task Force on Women's Rights and Responsibilities* (Washington, D.C.: U.S. Government Printing Office, 1970), iii.

20. Bell hooks, *Feminist Theory: From Margin to Center*, 2d ed. (Cambridge, Mass.: South End, 2000), 9.

21. Mary Wollstonecraft, *A Vindication of the Rights of Woman*, ed. Candace Ward (Mineola, N.Y.: Dover, 1996).

22. Alice Rossi, ed., *Essays on Sex Equality* (Chicago: University of Chicago Press, 1970), 41–43, 107, 149, 179; Jane Roland Martin, "The Contradiction and the Challenge of the Educated Woman," *Women's Studies Quarterly*, 1, no. 2 (1991): 6–27, at 6, citing Wendell Robert Carr; Florence Howe, "Why Educate Women?" (1968), in Florence Howe, *The Myths of Coeducation: Selected Essays, 1964–83* (Bloomington: Indiana University Press, 1984), 22–24.

23. *Matter of Simple Justice*, 5.

24. Brown et al., "Equal Rights Amendment," 890, 902–5.

25. Jane J. Manbridge, *Why We Lost the ERA* (Chicago: University of Chicago Press, 1986), 56–59.

26. *Bray v. Lee*, 337 F.Supp. 934 (D. Mass. 1972); *Berkelman v. San Francisco Unified School Dist.*, 501 F.2d 1264 (9th Cir. 1974).

27. Justice Ruth Bader Ginsburg, "The Washington College of Law Founders Day Tribute," *American University Journal of Gender and the Law*, 5 (1996): 1–7, at 3.

28. See, e.g., *Weinberger v. Wiesenfeld*, 420 U.S. 636 (1975) (striking down a Social Security provision whereby benefits were paid to widows and children in their care but only to the children and not to widowers); *Califano v. Goldfarb*, 430 U.S. 199 (1977) (invalidating a federal benefits program whereby survivors' benefits were payable to a widow on the basis of the deceased husband's earnings but paid to a widower only upon proof that he "was receiving at least half of his support" from his deceased wife); Note, "Justice Ruth Bader Ginsburg and the Virginia Military Institute: A Culmination of Strategic Success," *Cardozo Women's Law Journal*, 4 (1998): 541–84, at 545; Ruth Bader Ginsburg, "Gender and the Constitution," *University of Cincinnati Law Review*, 44 (1975): 1–42, at 27. For a discussion of Ruth Bader Ginsburg's approach to equality, see Wendy Williams, *Unbending Gender* (New York: Oxford University Press, 2000), 219–22.

29. *Reed v. Reed*, 404 U.S. 71 (1971) (striking down a state law granting a preference for men over women in the appointment of administrators of estates); *Frontiero v. Richardson*, 411 U.S. 677 (1973) (invalidating a federal law that afforded male members of the armed forces an automatic dependency allowance for their wives but required servicewomen to prove that their husbands were dependent); *Craig v. Boren*, 429 U.S. 190 (1976) (invalidating a state statute that prohibited the sale of 3.2 percent beer to males under the age of twenty-one years and to females under the age of eighteen).

30. *Frontiero v. Richardson*, 411 U.S. 677, 684 (1973).

31. Brief Amici Curiae of the American Civil Liberties Union et al., 17–19, *California Federal Savings and Loan Association v. Guerra*, 479 U.S. 272 (1987); Ruth Bader Ginsburg, "Affirmative Action: An International Human Rights Dialogue," Fifty-First Cardozo Memorial Lecture, *Cardozo Law Review*, 21 (1999): 253–82, at 258.

32. *Geduldig v. Aiello*, 417 U.S. 484 (1974).

33. Herma Hill Kay, "Equality and Difference: The Case of Pregnancy," *Berkeley Women's Law Journal*, 1, no. 1 (Fall 1985): 1–38, 2–3; Sylvia A. Law, "Rethinking Sex and the Constitution," *University of Pennsylvania Law Review*, 132 (1984): 955–1040, at 957, 963–69.

34. Beauvoir, *The Second Sex*, xxii. For a critique of formal equality, see Mary E. Becker, "Prince Charming: Abstract Equality," *Supreme Court Review*, 5 (1987): 201–47. For defenses of equal treatment theory with limited exceptions for biological differences, see Wendy W. Williams, "Equality's Riddle: Pregnancy and the Equal Treatment/Special Treatment Debate," *New York University Review of Law and Social Change*, 13 (1984–85): 325–380; Elizabeth M. Schneider, "The Dialectic of Rights and Politics: Perspectives from the Women's Movement," *New York University Law Review*, 61 (1986): 589–652.

35. Nell Noddings, *Caring: A Feminine Approach to Ethics and Moral Education* (Berkeley: University of California Press, 1984); Jean Baker Miller, *Toward a New Psychology of Women* (Boston: Beacon, 1976); Nancy Chodorow, *The Reproduction of Mothering* (Berkeley: University of California Press, 1978); Adrienne Rich, *Of Woman Born* (New York: Bantam, 1977).

36. Carol Gilligan, *In a Different Voice* (Cambridge: Harvard University Press, 1982).

37. Gilligan, *In a Different Voice*, 7–19; see Lawrence Kohlberg, *The Psychology of Moral Development* (San Francisco: Harper and Row, 1984), 170–205, 345–52; see also Anne Colby and William Damon, "Listening to a Different Voice: A Review of Carol Gilligan's *In a Different Voice*," *Merrill-Palmer Quarterly*, 29, no. 4 (1983): 473–81.

38. Carol Gilligan, "Moral Orientation and Moral Development," in *Women and Moral Theory*, ed. Eva Kittay and Diana T. Meyers (New York: Rowman and Littlefield, 1987), 19–33, at 25.

39. Gilligan, *In a Different Voice*, 2, 3; Carol Gilligan, "Hearing the Difference: Theorizing Connection," *Hypatia*, 10, no. 2 (Spring 1995): 121–27, at 125.

40. Judy Auerbach, Linda Blum, Vicki Smith, and Christine Williams, "Commentary: On Gilligan's *In a Different Voice*," *Feminist Studies*, 11, no. 1 (Spring 1985): 149–60, at 149–50.

41. William J. Turnier, Pamela Johnston Conover, and David Lowery, "Redistributive Justice and Cultural Feminism," *American University Law Review*, 45 (1996): 1275–1300, at 1278.

42. Suzanna Sherry, "Civic Virtue and the Feminine Voice in Constitutional Adjudication," *Virginia Law Review*, 72 (1986): 543–616, at 581, 615.

43. Carrie Menkel-Meadow, "Portia in a Different Voice," *Berkeley Women's Law Journal*, 1 (1985): 39–63.

44. Leslie Bender, "Changing the Values of Tort Law," *Tulsa Law Journal*, 25 (1990): 759–73; Karen Gross, "Re-Vision of the Bankruptcy System: New Images of Individual Debtors," *Michigan Law Review*, 88 (1990): 1506–56; Martha Minow, "Rights for the Next Generation: A Feminist Approach to Children's Rights," *Harvard Women's Law Journal*, 9 (1986): 1–14; Kenneth L. Karst, "Woman's Constitution," *Duke Law Journal* (1984): 447–508.

45. Mary Field Belenky, Blythe McVicker Clinchy, Nancy Rule Goldberger, and Jill Mattuck Tarule, *Women's Ways of Knowing: The Development of Self, Voice, and Mind* (New York: Basic, 1986).

46. Turnier, Conover, and Lowery, "Redistributive Justice and Cultural Feminism," 1287.

47. Carrie Menkel-Meadow, "Excluded Voices: New Voices in the Legal Profession Making New Voices in the Law," *University of Miami Law Review*, 42 (1987): 29–53, at 43 (quoting Beauvoir, *Second Sex*, 153).

48. Debra Nails, "Social-Scientific Sexism: Gilligan's Mismeasure of Man*," *Social Research*, 50, no. 3 (1983): 643–44, at 643; Mary Jo Frug, "Progressive Feminist Legal Scholarship: Can We Claim 'A Different Voice'?" *Harvard Women's Law Journal*, 15 (1992): 37–77, at 48; Joan C. Williams, "Deconstructing Gender," *Michigan Law Review*, 87 (1989): 797–845, at 807, 813; James C. Walker, "In a Diffident Voice: Cryptoseparatist Analysis of Female Moral Development," *Social Research*, 50, no. 3 (Autumn 1983): 665–95, at 690–94; Deborah L. Rhode, *Justice and Gender* (Cambridge: Harvard University Press, 1989), 312; Carol Tavris, *The Mismeasure of Woman* (New York: Simon and Schuster, 1992); Linda J. Nicholson, "Women, Morality, and History," *Social Research*, 50, no. 3 (Autumn 1983): 514–36, at 530–33; Linda K. Kerber et al., "On 'In a Different Voice': An Interdisciplinary Forum," *Signs: Journal of Women in Culture and Society*, 11, no. 2 (1986): 304–33, at 310.

49. Cynthia Fuchs Epstein, "The Difference Model: Enforcement and Reinforcement

of Women's Roles in the Law," in *Social Roles and Social Institutions*, ed. Judith R. Blau and Norman Goodman (New Brunswick, N.J.: Transaction, 1995), 54–71, at 58; Sandra Day O'Connor, "Portia's Progress," *New York University Law Review*, 66 (1991): 1546–58, at 1557; Martha Minow, *Making All the Difference: Inclusion, Exclusion, and American Law* (Ithaca, N.Y.: Cornell University Press, 1990), 20.

50. *United States v. Virginia*, 518 U.S. 515 (1996); Brief Amici Curiae of Professor Carol Gilligan and the Program on Gender, Science, and the Law, *U.S. v. Virginia*, 44 F.3d 1229 (4th Cir. 1995), rpt. *Women's Law Reporter*, 16 (Fall 1994): 1–16, at 14; *EEOC v. Sears Roebuck*, 628 F. Supp. 1264 (N.D. Ill. 1986), aff'd, 839 F.2d 302 (7th Cir. 1988); "Offer of Proof Concerning the Testimony of Rosalind Rosenberg," *Signs: Journal of Women's Culture and Society*, 11 (1986): 757–66.

51. Katha Pollitt, *Reasonable Creatures* (New York: Alfred A. Knopf, 1994), 42.

52. Isabel Marcus and Paul J. Speigelman, "Feminine Discourse, Moral Values, and the Law—A Conversation," *Buffalo Law Review*, 34 (1985): 11–87, at 25; Rhode, *Justice and Gender*, 3, 313; Christine Littleton, "Reconstructing Equality," *California Law Review* 75 (1987): 1279–1337, at 1296; Ann E. Freedman, "Sex Equality, Sex Differences, and the Supreme Court," *Yale Law Journal*, 92 (1983): 913–968, at 965.

53. Catharine A. MacKinnon, *Feminism Unmodified: Discourses on Life and Law* (Cambridge: Harvard University Press, 1987); Catharine A. MacKinnon, *Toward a Feminist Theory of the State* (Cambridge: Harvard University Press, 1989).

54. MacKinnon, *Feminism Unmodified*, 8; Marcus and Speigelman, "Feminine Discourse," 74–75 (statement of Catharine A. MacKinnon); Catharine A. MacKinnon, *Sexual Harassment of Working Women: A Case of Sex Discrimination* (New Haven: Yale University Press, 1986), 117.

55. Martha Minow, "Feminist Reason: Getting It and Losing It," *Journal of Legal Education*, 38 (1988): 47–60; Deborah L. Rhode, "The 'Woman's Point of View,'" *Journal of Legal Education*, 38 (1988): 39–46; Mary Jo Frug, "Sexual Equality and Sexual Difference in American Law," *New England Law Review*, 26 (1992): 665–82.

56. Elizabeth V. Spelman, *Inessential Woman: Problems of Exclusion in Feminist Thought* (Boston: Beacon, 1988), 115; Kimberle Crenshaw, "Mapping the Margins: Intersectionality, Identity Politics, and Violence Against Women of Color," *Stanford Law Review*, 43 (July 1991): 1241–99, at 1244; Trina Grillo, "Anti-Essentialism and Intersectionality: Tools to Dismantle the Master's House," *Berkeley Women's Law Journal*, 10 (1995): 16–30, at 16; correspondence from Berta Hernandez-Truyol, 14 June 2001.

57. Hooks, *Feminist Theory*, 68–71.

58. Angela P. Harris, "Race and Essentialism in Feminist Legal Theory," *Stanford Law Review*, 42 (1990): 581–616, at 591–96; hooks, *Feminist Theory*, 5, 16; Paulette M. Caldwell, "A Hairpiece: Perspectives on the Intersection of Race and Gender," *Duke Law Journal* (1991): 365–96, at 374; Dorothy E. Roberts, "Racism and Patriarchy in the Meaning of Motherhood," *Journal of Gender and the Law*, 1 (1993): 535–72, at 551.

59. Spelman, *Inessential Woman*, 3, 161; Catharine A. MacKinnon, "Reflections on Sex Equality Under Law," *Yale Law Journal*, 100 (1991): 1281–1328, at 1291–97.

60. See, e.g., Susan Estrich, "Sometimes, Single-Sex Schools Educate Best," *Denver Post*, 24 September 1996, B7 (arguing that single-sex education should be an option to help urban students develop their full potential); Deborah L. Rhode, "Single-Sex Schools Can Only Be Way Stations," *National Law Journal*, 18 August 1997, A19 (maintaining that priority should be given to implementing more effec-

tive gender equity policies in coeducational schools rather than establishing separate schools).

61. See, e.g., Rosemary C. Salomone, "Rich Kids, Poor Kids, and the Single-Sex Education Debate," *Akron Law Review*, 34 (2000): 209–29 (arguing that the legal cloud now hovering over single-sex schooling has prevented school districts from gathering empirical and anecdotal data to prove or disprove their academic merit); Denise C. Morgan, "Anti-Subordination Analysis after the *United States v. Virginia:* Evaluating the Constitutionality of K-12 Single-Sex Public Schools," *University of Chicago Legal Forum* (1999): 381–460 (proposing antisubordination theory to undergird public single-sex schools, particularly for girls); Nancy Levit, "Separating Equals: The Educational Research and the Long-Term Consequences of Sex Segregation," *George Washington Law Review*, 67 (1999): 451–526 (arguing that the historical and social significance of sex segregation in American education militates against single-sex schooling); Valerie K. Vojdik, "Girls' Schools After VMI: Do They Make the Grade?" *Duke Journal of Gender Law and Policy*, 4 (1997): 69–100 (maintaining that arguments supporting single-sex schools rely on the same gender stereotypes and generalizations that historically have excluded women from public schooling and traditionally male professions).

CHAPTER 4. Myths and Realities in the Gender Wars

1. Edward Clarke, *Sex in Education; or, A Fair Chance for the Girls* (Boston: Osgood, 1873), 133; Liva Baker, *I'm Radcliffe! Fly Me* (New York: Macmillan, 1976), 77.

2. Carl F. Kaestle, *Pillars of the Republic: Common Schools and American Society, 1780–1860* (New York: Hill and Wang, 1983), 27–28; Maxine Greene, "The Impacts of Irrelevance: Women in the History of American Education," in *Women and Education: Equity or Equality?* ed. Elizabeth Fennema and M. Jane Ayer (Berkeley, Calif.: McCutchan, 1984), 19–39, at 25–28; David Tyack and Elizabeth Hansot, *Learning Together: A History of Coeducation in American Schools* (New Haven: Yale University Press, 1990), 38–43.

3. Bureau of Education, *Coeducation of the Sexes in the Public Schools of the United States*, Circulars of Information, no. 2-1833 (Washington, D.C.: Government Printing Office, 1883), 8.

4. Tyack and Hansot, *Learning Together*, 128; William J. Reese, *The Origins of the American High School* (New Haven: Yale University Press, 1995), 226; Archibald Watson Bain, "Co-Education in the Secondary Schools of the United States," M.A. thesis (Columbia University, 1908), 36, table 7; *U.S. Commissioner of Education Report for 1900–1901*, 1221, cited in Tyack and Hansot, *Learning Together*, 114.

5. F. E. Chadwick, "The Woman Peril in American Education," *Education Review* (February 1914): 109–19; G. Stanley Hall, *Adolescence: Its Psychology and Its Relations to Physiology, Anthropology, Sociology, Sex, Crime, Religion, and Education* (New York: D. Appleton, 1907); G. Stanley Hall, "Coeducation in the High School," *NEA Addresses and Proceedings, 1903*, 446–60, cited in Tyack and Hansot, *Learning Together*, 154–55; A. N. Wheelock, *Segregation of Sexes in the Public Schools*, paper read before the Present Day Club of Riverside, Calif., 23 October 1911 (Riverside, Calif.: Board of Education, November 1911).

6. Diane Ravitch, *Left Back: A Century of Failed School Reforms* (New York: Simon and Schuster, 2000), 55–57, 123–25, 137–40.

7. Board of Education Minutes, 24 February 1909, cited in Letter to Dr. Frank Mac-

chiarola, chancellor, New York City Board of Education, from James Kadamus, assistant commissioner for occupational and continuing education, New York State Education Department, 20 December 1982, 4; John L. Rury, "Vocationalism for Home and Work: Women's Education in the United States, 1880–1930," *History of Education Quarterly,* 24, no. 1 (Spring 1984): 21–44, at 37–39; Karen Graves, *Girls' Schooling in the Progressive Era: From Female Scholar to Domesticated Citizen* (New York: Garland, 1998), xviii.

8. Vernon Loeb, "A Mandate for Equal Access in Conflict with Central's All-Male Tradition," *Education Week,* 2 February 1983, 12; National Association of Independent Schools, *Backgrounder: Single-Sex Independent Schools* (Washington, D.C.: National Association of Independent Schools, 1998); *Jones v. Bd. of Educ.,* 632 F. Supp. 1319 (E.D.N.Y., 1986).

9. Elizabeth Fennema and Julia Sherman, "Sex-Related Differences in Mathematics Achievement, Spatial Visualization, and Affective Factors," *American Educational Research Journal,* 14, no. 1 (1977): 51–71; Elizabeth Fennema and Penelope Peterson, "Autonomous Learning Behavior: A Possible Explanation of Gender-Related Differences in Mathematics," in *Gender Influences in Classroom Interaction,* ed. Louise Cherry Wilkinson and Cora B. Marrett (New York: Academic Press, 1985), 17–35; Jacqueline Eccles and Phyllis Blumenfield, "Classroom Experiences and Student Gender: Are There Differences and Do They Matter?" ibid., 79–114; Jean Stockard, "Sex Inequities in the Experience of Students," in *Sex Equity in Education,* ed. Jean Stockard, Patricia A. Schmuck, Ken Kempner, Peg Williams, Sakre K. Edson, and Mary Ann Smith (New York: Academic Press, 1980), 11–48; Jean Stockard, "Why Sex Equities Exist for Students," ibid., 49–77.

10. Florence Howe, "The Education of Women," in *And Jill Came Tumbling After: Sexism in American Education,* ed. Judith Stacey et al. (New York: Dell, 1976), 64–75; but see Elizabeth Sarah, Marion Scott, and Dale Spender, "The Education of Feminists: The Case for Single-Sex Schools," in *Learning to Lose: Sexism and Education,* ed. Dale Spender and Elizabeth Sarah (London: Women's Press, 1980), 55–66; Dale Spender, *Invisible Women* (London: Writers and Readers Publishing Cooperative Society, 1982), 118–39; Rosemary Deem, *Women and Schooling* (London: Routledge and Kegan, Paul, 1980); Pat Mahoney, *Schools for the Boys? Coeducation Reassessed* (London: Hutchinson, 1985).

11. Carol Gilligan, *In a Different Voice: Psychological Theory and Women's Development* (Cambridge: Harvard University Press, 1982, 1993).

12. Gilligan, *In a Different Voice,* 2; Carol Gilligan, Preface, "Teaching Shakespeare's Sister: Notes from the Underground of Female Adolescence," in *Making Connections,* ed. Carol Gilligan, Nona P. Lyons, and Trudy J. Hanmer (Cambridge: Harvard University Press, 1990), 10, 14.

13. Lyn Mikel Brown and Carol Gilligan, *Meeting at the Crossroads: Women's Psychology and Girls' Development* (New York: Ballantine, 1992), 218; Jill McLean Taylor, Carol Gilligan, and Amy M. Sullivan, *Between Voice and Silence: Women and Girls, Race and Relationship* (Cambridge: Harvard University Press, 1995).

14. Nancy J. Chodorow, *The Reproduction of Mothering* (Berkeley: University of California Press, 1978).

15. Myra Sadker and David Sadker, *Failing at Fairness: How Schools Cheat Girls* (New York: Touchstone, 1994), 42–55.

16. American Association of University Women, *Shortchanging Girls, Shortchanging America: Executive Summary* (Washington, D.C., 1991), 7, 10–11, 14–15.

17. American Association of University Women Educational Foundation, *How Schools Shortchange Girls: The AAUW Report* (New York: Marlowe, 1995); American Association of University Women Educational Foundation, *Hostile Hallways: The AAUW Survey on Sexual Harassment in America's Schools* (Washington, D.C., 1993).

18. American Association of University Women, *Girls in the Middle: Working to Succeed in School* (Washington, D.C., 1996).

19. Peter Schmidt, "The Phony War on Schoolgirls: A Myth Exposed," *The Weekly Standard*, 8–15 July 1996, 22–28; editorial, "A Dreadful Waste of Female Talent," *San Francisco Chronicle*, 13 February 1992, A22; Susan Chira, "Bias Against Girls Is Found Rife in Schools, with Lasting Damage," *New York Times*, 12 February 1992, A1; testimony of Rep. Patricia Schroeder on the Gender Equity in Education Act before the House Education and Labor Subcommittee on Elementary, Secondary, and Vocational Education, 21 April 1993.

20. Peggy Orenstein, *School Girls: Young Women, Self-Esteem, and the Confidence Gap* (New York: Doubleday, 1994); Mary Pipher, *Reviving Ophelia: Saving the Selves of Adolescent Girls* (New York: Ballantine, 1994), 19; Judy Mann, *The Difference: Discovering the Hidden Ways We Silence Girls* (New York: Warner, 1994).

21. Joan Jacobs Brumberg, "When Girls Talk: What It Reveals About Them," *Chronicle of Higher Education*, 24 November 2000, B7–10; Sara Shindler, *Ophelia Speaks: Adolescent Girls Write About Their Search for Self* (New York: Harper Perennial, 1999). See also American Association of University Women, *Voices of a Generation: Teenage Girls on Sex, School, and Self* (Washington, D.C., 1999); Emily Eakin, "Listening for the Voices of Women," *New York Times*, 30 March 2002, B9.

22. National Association of Independent Schools, *Backgrounder: Single-Sex Independent Schools* (Washington, D.C., 1999).

23. Alice Ann Leidel, foreword to AAUW Educational Foundation, *How Schools Shortchange Girls*, x.

24. Christina Hoff Sommers, *Who Stole Feminism? How Women Have Betrayed Women* (New York: Touchstone, 1994), 22–23; Christina Hoff Sommers, *The War Against Boys: How Misguided Feminism Is Harming Our Young Men* (New York: Simon and Schuster, 2000).

25. Sommers, *Who Stole Feminism?* 145–46, 165–66; Sommers, *War Against Boys*, 110.

26. Barbara Ehrenreich, "A Feminist on the Outs," *Time*, 1 August 1994, 61; Megan Rosenfeld, "The Feminine Mistake? Christina Hoff Sommers Sees a Tyranny of the Sisterhood," *Washington Post*, 7 July 1994, C1; Sommers, *Who Stole Feminism?* 138; Sommers, *War Against Boys*, 34; Valerie E. Lee, letter to the editor, "Gender Equity: Pitting Boys Against Girls," *Education Week*, 7 August 1996, 6; Carol Gilligan and David Sadker, letters, "The War Against Boys, Carol Gilligan et al. versus Christina Hoff Sommers," *Atlantic*, 1 August 2000, 6–9; David Sadker, "Where the Girls Are," *Education Week*, 4 September 1996, 49–50.

27. Sommers, *War Against Boys*, 24–33.

28. Sommers, *Who Stole Feminism?* 24–26; Sommers, *War Against Boys*, 62–65, 86–87.

29. Diane Ravitch, "Girls Are Beneficiaries of Gender Gap," *Wall Street Journal*, 17 December 1998, A22; Tamar Lewin, "How Boys Lost Out to Girl Power," *New York Times*, 13 December 1998, section 4, 3; Catherine Manegold, "Gains Aside, Bill Seeks Equality of Sexes in School," *New York Times*, 13 February 1994, section 1, 34.

30. Cornelius Riordan, "Student Outcomes in Catholic and Public Secondary Schools: Gender Gap Comparisons from 1972 to 1992," paper presented at the annual meeting of the American Sociological Association, San Francisco, 21 August 1998, 10.

31. Judith Kleinfeld, "The Myth That Schools Shortchange Girls: Social Science in the Service of Deception," report prepared for Women's Freedom Network, 1998, 13–14; see also Judith Kleinfeld, "Student Performance: Males Versus Females," *Public Interest*, 134 (Winter 1999): 3–20; Valerie E. Lee, Xianglei Chen, and Becky A. Smerdon, *The Influence of School Climate on Gender Differences in the Achievement and Engagement of Young Adolescents* (Ann Arbor: University of Michigan School of Education, 1995, and Washington, D.C.: American Association of University Women).

32. Michael Kimmel, "What Are Little Boys Made Of?" *Ms.*, October–November 1999, 88–91, at 88.

33. Michael Gurian, *The Wonder of Boys* (New York: Jeremy P. Tarcher/Putnam, 1997); Michael Gurian, *A Fine Young Man* (New York: Jeremy P. Tarcher/Putnam, 1999), 50–51; Michael Gurian, *Boys and Girls Learn Differently!* (San Francisco: Jossey-Bass, 2001), 19–33; Michael Gurian, *The Wonder of Girls* (Pocket Books, 2002), 277–79; April Austin, "Is It a Girl's Nature to Nurture," *Christian Science Monitor*, 27 February 2002, 11.

34. William Pollack, *Real Boys: Rescuing Our Sons from the Myths of Boyhood* (New York: Random House, 1998), 239; Dan Kindlon and Michael Thompson, *Raising Cain: Protecting the Emotional Life of Boys* (New York: Ballantine, 1999), 23–24. See also Rob Gilbert and Pam Gilbert, *Masculinity Goes to School* (London: Routledge, 1998); Debbie Epstein, Jannette Elwood, Valerie Hey, and Janet Maw, eds., *Failing Boys? Issues in Gender and Achievement* (Buckingham, England: Open University Press, 1998).

35. R. W. Connell, "Teaching the Boys: New Research on Masculinity, and Gender Strategies for Schools," *Teachers College Record*, 98, no. 2 (Winter 1996): 206–35; Lyn Yates, "Gender Equity and the Boys Debate: What Sort of Challenge," *British Journal of Sociology of Education*, 18, no. 3 (1997): 337–47. See also Madeleine Arnot, John Gray, Mary James, and Jean Ruddick, *Recent Research on Gender and Educational Performance* (London: Office for Standards in Education, 1998); Laura Sukhnandan, *An Investigation into Gender Differences in Achievement* (Berkshire, England: National Foundation for Educational Research, June 1999); *Proceedings of Symposium on Education Attainment and Labour Market Outcomes: Factors Affecting Boys and Their Status in Relation to Girls* (Balmain, Australia: Australian Institute of Political Science, 2000); Epstein et al., *Failing Boys?*

36. American Association of University Women Educational Foundation, *Gender Gaps: Where Schools Still Fail Our Children* (New York: Marlowe, 1999).

37. Letters, "The War Against Boys: Carol Gilligan et al. versus Christina Hoff Sommers," 6–8; Debra Viadero, "Their Own Voices," *Education Week*, 13 May 1998, 34–38. See also Carol Gilligan, *The Birth of Pleasure* (New York: Alfred A. Knopf, 2002), 57–74.

38. Sommers, *War Against Boys*, 122; Christina Hoff Sommers, *Where the Boys Are*, American Enterprise Institute, Bradley Lecture, November 9, 1998, 4–5; Amy Benfer, "Battle of the Celebrity Gender Theorists," *Salon*, 9 March 2001, 3, <www.salon.com/feature/2001/09/sommers>.

39. Valerie E. Lee, "Gender Equity and the Organization of Schools," in *Gender, Equity,*

and Schooling: Policy and Practice, ed. Barbara J. Bank and Peter M. Hall (New York: Garland, 1997), 136–58, at 139.

CHAPTER 5. Who's Winning, Who's Losing, and Why?

1. American Association of University Women Educational Foundation, *Gender Gaps: Where Schools Still Fail Our Children* (New York: Marlowe, 1999).
2. Nicholas Zill, Mary Collins, Jerry West, and Elvie Germino Hausken, *Approaching Kindergarten: A Look at Preschoolers in the United States* (Washington, D.C.: U.S. Department of Education, National Center for Education Statistics, 1995 [NCES 95-280]), 21, 29; Cornelius Riordan, "The Emergent Problems of Boys in School and the Potential of Single-Sex Schools for Both Boys and Girls," paper presented at the International Symposium on Male and Female Education in the Third Millennium, Madrid, September 2001; Christine Winquist Nord, Jean Lennon, Baiming Liu, and Kathryn Chandler, *Home Literacy Activities and Signs of Children's Emerging Literacy, 1993 and 1999* (Washington, D.C.: U.S. Department of Education, National Center for Education Statistics, 2000 [NCES 2000-026]), 2.
3. M. Elizabeth Graue and James DiPerna, "Redshirting and Early Retention: Who Gets the 'Gift of Time' and What Are Its Outcomes?" *American Educational Research Journal*, 37, no. 2 (Summer 2000): 509–34; Office of Special Education Programs, *Twenty-Third Annual Report to Congress on the Implementation of the Individuals with Disabilities Education Act* (Washington, D.C.: U.S. Department of Education, 2002), II-1; National Center for Education Statistics, *The Condition of Education 2001* (Washington, D.C.: U.S. Department of Education, July 2001).
4. Rob McGee and Michael Feehan, "Are Girls with Problems of Attention Unrecognized?" *Journal of Psychopathology and Behavioral Assessment*, 13 (1991): 187–98; Glenn Young, H. Jessia Kim, and Paul J. Gerber, "Gender Bias and Learning Disabilities: School Age and Long-Term Consequences for Females," *Learning Disabilities: A Multidisciplinary Journal*, 9, no. 3 (August 1999): 107–14; Michael L. Wehmeyer and Michelle Schwartz, "Disproportionate Representation of Males in Special Education Services: Biology, Behavior, or Bias?" *Education and Treatment of Children*, 24 (2001): 28–45; Linda Silverman, *What We Have Learned About Gifted Children* (Denver: Gifted Development Center, 2002), <www.gifteddevelopment.com>.
5. Correspondence from Mary Lee Eldon, director, National Geography Bee, 15 October 2001; Lynn S. Liben, Roger M. Downs, and Margaret L. Signorella, "Sex Differences in Adolescents' Success on an Academic Competition in Geography: Explanations and Implications," unpublished paper, 1995.
6. Nancy S. Cole, *The ETS Gender Study: How Females and Males Perform in Educational Settings* (Princeton: Educational Testing Service, 1997), 10–14; Warren W. Willingham and Nancy B. Cole, *Gender and Fair Assessment* (Mahwah, N.J.: Lawrence Erlbaum Associates, 1997); Kate Zernike, "Girls a Distant 2nd in Geography Gap Among U.S. Pupils," *New York Times*, 1 June 2000, A1, B5; Judith Kleinfeld, "The Myth That Schools Shortchange Girls: Social Science in the Service of Deception," report prepared for Women's Freedom Network (Washington, D.C., 1998), 13–14.
7. National Center for Education Statistics, *National Assessment of Educational Progress (NAEP) 2000 Mathematics Report Card* (Washington, D.C.: U.S. Department of Education, 2001); National Center for Education Statistics, *National Assessment of Ed-*

*ucational Progress (NAEP) 2000 Science Report Card* (Washington, D.C.: U.S. Department of Education, 2001).

8. National Center for Education Statistics, *National Assessment of Educational Progress (NAEP) 2000 Report Card, Fourth Grade Reading* (Washington, D.C.: U.S. Department of Education, 1999); National Center for Education Statistics, *Outcomes of Learning: Results for the 2000 Program for International Student Assessment of 15-year-olds in Reading, Mathematics, and Science Literacy* (Washington, D.C.: U.S. Department of Education, 2001); National Center for Education Statistics, *National Assessment of Educational Progress (NAEP) 2000 Report Card, Writing* (Washington, D.C.: U.S. Department of Education, 1999); National Center for Education Statistics, *Trends in Educational Equity of Girls and Women* (Washington, D.C.: U.S. Department of Education, 2000), 18.

9. The College Board, *PSAT/NMSQT Summary Report, National: 2000–01 College-Bound High School Juniors* (New York, 2001); "Gap Narrows on Standardized Test: Girls Improve PSAT Scores, Chances for Merit Scholarships," *Boston Globe,* 15 January 1998, A18; "Changes Forced by FairTest Narrow PSAT Gender Gap; Class of 1999 Girls Will Win More Nat. Merit Scholarships, But Test Bias Still 'Cheats' Many Females," press release, National Center for Fair and Open Testing, 14 January 1998.

10. College Board, *College-Bound Seniors: A Profile of SAT Program Test Takers, National* (New York, 2000).

11. College Board, *Advanced Placement Program 2001, National Summary Reports* (New York, 2001); American Association of Medical Colleges, *MCAT Performance by Sex, Age, Language Status, Undergraduate Major, and Testing History: April 2001* (Washington, D.C.), <www.aamc.org>; Law School Admission Council, *Average LSAT Scores* (correspondence from Robert Carr, senior statistician, Law School Admission Council, 29 August 2001).

12. College Board, *College-Bound Seniors;* National Assessment of Educational Progress, *The Nation's Report Card: Reading 2000* (Washington, D.C., 2001).

13. Cathy Kessel and Marcia C. Linn, "Grades or Scores: Predicting Future College Mathematics Performance," *Educational Measurement: Issues and Practice,* 15, no. 4 (Winter 1996): 10–14; Cathy Kessel and Marcia C. Linn, "Participation in Mathematics Courses and Careers: Climate, Grades, and Entrance Examination Scores," paper presented at the annual meeting of the American Educational Research Association, San Francisco, April 1995.

14. AAUW Educational Foundation, *Gender Gaps;* College Board, *Advanced Placement Program 2001, National Summary Reports* (New York, 2000, 2001); "Survey of Earned Doctorates," *Chronicle of Higher Education,* 9 February 2001, A11.

15. American Association of University Women, *Tech-Savvy: Educating Girls in the New Computer Age* (Washington, D.C., 2000), 7, 41; Rod Corston and Andrew M. Colman, "Gender and Socialization Effects on Computer Competence and Attitudes Toward Computers," *Journal of Educational Computing Research,* 14, no. 2 (1996): 171–83, at 172; Sara Kiesler, Lee Sproull, and Jacquelynne S. Eccles, "Pool Halls, Chips, and War Games: Women in the Culture of Computing," *Psychology of Women Quarterly,* 9 (December 1985): 451–62; Jane Margolis and Allan Fisher, *Unlocking the Clubhouse: Women in Computing* (Cambridge: MIT Press, 2002), 47–48; "Comparison of IT Salaries, by Sex," <computerjobs.com>, 1999. For a general discussion of the issues, see Robert Furger, *Does Jane Compute?* (New York: Warner, 1998).

16. Elizabeth F. Farrell, "Engineering a Warmer Welcome for Female Students," *Chronicle of Higher Education,* 22 February 2002, A31–32.

17. Quoted in Debra Viadero, "Their Own Voices," *Education Week,* 13 May 1998, 34–38, at 38; bracketed interpolation Viadero's.

18. Susan Harter, Patricia L. Waters, and Nancy R. Whitesell, "Lack of Voice as a Manifestation of False Self-Behavior Among Adolescents: The School Setting as a Stage Upon Which the Drama of Authenticity Is Enacted," *Educational Psychologist,* 32, no. 3 (1997): 153–73, at 171; Susan Harter, Patricia L. Waters, Nancy R. Whitesell, and Diana Kastelic, "Level of Voice Among Female and Male High School Students: Relational Context, Support, and Gender Orientation," *Developmental Psychology,* 34, no. 5 (1998): 892–901.

19. Jeffrey W. Burnett, Wayne P. Anderson, and P. Paul Heppner, "Gender Roles and Self-Esteem: A Consideration of Environmental Factors," *Journal of Counseling & Development,* 73 (January–February 1995): 323–26; American Association of University Women, *Shortchanging Girls, Shortchanging America: Executive Summary* (Washington, D.C., 1991), 7–9.

20. See Theresa J. Jordan, "Self-Concepts, Motivation, and Academic Achievement of Black Adolescents," *Journal of Educational Psychology,* 73, no. 4 (1981): 509–17.

21. Kristen C. Kling, Janet Shibley Hyde, Carolin J. Showers, and Brenda N. Buswell, "Gender Differences in Self-Esteem: A Meta-Analysis," *Psychological Bulletin,* 125, no. 4 (1999): 470–500, at 488–90.

22. *Metropolitan Life Survey of the American Teacher 1997: Examining Gender Issues in the Schools* (New York: Louis Harris and Associates, 1997), 40–46, 83, 109.

23. See Dale Spender, "Don't Talk, Listen," *Times Educational Supplement,* 3 November 1978, 19; Dale Spender, *Man Made Language* (London: Routledge and Kegan Paul, 1980); Katherine Clarricoates, "The Importance of Being Earnest . . . Emma . . . Tom . . . and Jane: The Perception and Categorization of Gender Conformity and Gender Deviation in Primary Schools," in *Schooling for Women's Work,* ed. Rosemary Deem (London: Routledge and Kegan Paul, 1980), 26–41; Joann Rossi Becker, "Differential Treatment of Females and Males in Mathematics Classes," *Journal of Research in Mathematics Education,* 12, no. 1 (1981): 40–83.

24. Michael Younger, Molly Warrington, and Jacquetta Williams, "The Gender Gap and Classroom Interactions: Reality and Rhetoric?" *British Journal of Sociology of Education,* 20, no. 3 (1999): 325–41.

25. See generally *Gender Influences in Classroom Interaction,* ed. Louise Cherry Wilkinson and Cora B. Marrett (New York: Academic Press, 1985); Melody D'Ambrosio and Patricia S. Hammer, "Gender Equity in the Catholic Elementary Schools," paper presented at the annual National Catholic Education Association Conference, Philadelphia, April 1996; Joan Swann, *Girls, Boys, and Language* (Oxford: Blackwell, 1992), 68–69.

26. Roberta Barba and Loretta Cardinale, "Are Females Invisible Students? An Investigation of Teacher-Student Questioning Interactions," *School Science and Mathematics,* 9, no. 17 (1991): 306–10; Ellen Rydell Altermatt, Jasna Jovanovic, and Michelle Perry, "Bias or Responsivity? Sex and Achievement-Level Effects on Teachers' Classroom Questioning Practices," *Journal of Educational Psychology,* 90, no. 3 (1998): 516–27; Jasna Jovanovic and Sally Steinbach King, "Boys and Girls in the Performance-Based Science Classroom: Who's Doing the Performing?" *American Educational Research Journal,* 35, no. 3 (Fall 1998): 477–96.

27. Miwha Lee, "Gender, Group Composition, and Peer Interaction in Computer-Based Cooperative Learning," *Journal of Educational Computing Research*, 9 (1993): 549–77.

28. Roger T. Johnson, David W. Johnson, and Mary Beth Stanne, "Effects of Cooperative, Competitive, and Individualistic Goal Structures on Computer-Based Instruction," *Journal of Educational Psychology*, 77, no. 6 (1985): 668–77; Robert S. Chernick, "Effects of Interdependent, Coactive, and Individualized Working Conditions on Pupils' Educational Computer Program Performance," *Journal of Educational Psychology*, 82, no. 4 (1990): 691–95.

29. Younger, Warrington, and Williams, "The Gender Gap and Classroom Interactions," 339; Office for Standards in Education, *Boys and English* (London, 1993), discussed in Joan Swann, "Language and Gender: Who, If Anyone, Is Disadvantaged by What?" in Epstein et al., *Failing Boys?* 150–51; Geoffrey Underwood and Nishchint Jindal, "Gender Differences and Effects of Co-Operation in a Computer-Based Language Task," *Educational Research*, 36, no. 1 (Spring 1994): 63–75; Johnson, Johnson, and Stanne, "Effects of Cooperative, Competitive, and Individualistic Goal Structures," 668–77.

30. Lani Guinier, Michelle Fine, and Jane Balin, *Becoming Gentlemen: Women, Law School, and Institutional Change* (Boston: Beacon, 1997); Elizabeth Mertz, "What Difference Does Difference Make? The Challenge for Legal Education," *Journal of Legal Education*, 48, no. 1 (March 1998): 1–87. Catherine G. Krupnick, "Women and Men in the Classroom: Inequality and Its Remedies," *On Teaching and Learning*, 1 (1985): 18–25; Catherine G. Krupnick, "Meadows College Prepares for Men," in *Gender and Public Policy: Cases and Comments*, ed. Kenneth Winston and Mary Jo Bane (Boulder, Colo.: Westview, 1993), 137–48; Lisa Schorr, "Sex, Lies, and Videotape: A Re-Examination of the Conventional Wisdom About Gender and Class Participation," honors thesis, Harvard University, 1992.

31. Julia Davies, "Taking Risks or Playing Safe: Boys' and Girls' Talk," in *Gender in the Secondary Curriculum*, ed. Ann Clark and Elaine Millard (London: Routledge, 1998), 11–26, at 24.

32. Deborah Tannen, *You Just Don't Understand: Women and Men in Conversation* (New York: William Morrow, 1990); Deborah Tannen, "Teachers' Classroom Strategies Should Recognize That Men and Women Use Language Differently," *Chronicle of Higher Education*, 19 June 1991, B1–B3.

33. Younger, Warrington, and Williams, "The Gender Gap and Classroom Interactions," 325–42; Eleanor E. Maccoby and Carol Nagy Jacklin, "Gender Segregation in Childhood," *Advances in Child Development and Behavior*, 20 (1987): 239–87.

34. Tannen, "Teachers' Classroom Strategies," B3.

35. Becky Francis, *Boys, Girls, and Achievement* (London: RoutledgeFalmer, 2000), 139.

36. Sommers, *War on Boys*; Michael Gurian, *Boys and Girls Learn Differently!* (San Francisco: Jossey-Bass, 2001).

37. Eleanor E. Maccoby, *The Two Sexes: Growing Up Apart, Coming Together* (Cambridge: Belknap, 1998); JoAnn Deak, *Girls Will Be Girls* (New York: Hyperion, 2001); Willingham and Cole, *Gender and Fair Assessment*, 289.

38. Merrill McLoughlin, "Men vs. Women," *U.S. News and World Report*, 8 August 1988, 50–56; Laura Shapiro, "Guns and Dolls," *Newsweek*, 28 May 1990, 56–65; Christine Gorman, "Sizing Up the Sexes," *Time*, 20 January 1992, 42–51; Andrew Sullivan, "The He Hormone," *New York Times Magazine*, 2 April 2000, 46–59,

69–79; Theresa M. Wizeman and Mary-Lou Pardue, eds., *Exploring the Biological Contributions to Human Health* (Washington, D.C.: National Academy Press, 2001), 99–104; Bennett A. Shaywitz et al., "Sex Differences in the Functional Organization of the Brain for Language," *Nature*, 373 (February 1995): 607–9; Georg Gron et al., "Brain Activation During Human Navigation: Gender-Different Neural Networks as Substrate of Performance," *Nature Neuroscience*, 3, no. 4 (April 2000): 404–8; Leonard Sax, "Reclaiming Kindergarten: Making Kindergarten Less Harmful to Boys," *Psychology of Men and Masculinity*, 2, no. 1 (January 2001): 3–12.

39. Eleanor Emmons Maccoby and Carol Nagy Jacklin, *The Psychology of Sex Differences* (Stanford: Stanford University Press, 1974), 94.

40. Maccoby, *Two Sexes*, 116–17.

41. Cole, *ETS Study*, 17; Cornelius Riordan, "The Emergent Problems of Boys in School and the Potential of Single-Sex Schools for Both Boys and Girls," paper presented at the International Symposium on Male and Female Education in the Third Millennium, Madrid, September 2001; Patricia Murphy and Jannette Elwood, "Gendered Learning Outside and Inside School: Influences on Achievement," in Epstein et al., *Failing Boys?* 162–81, at 163; Laura Pappano, "Teen Breakup," *Boston Globe*, 19 May 2002, C13, C16; William Pollack, *Real Boys: Rescuing Our Sons from the Myths of Boyhood* (New York: Random House, 1998).

42. Karen Littleton, "Girls and Information Technology," in *Equity in the Classroom: Towards Effective Pedagogy for Girls and Boys*, ed. Patricia F. Murphy and Caroline V. Gipps (London: Falmer, 1996), 81–96.

43. Henry Jenkins, "Complete Freedom of Movement: Video Games as Gendered Spaces," in *From Barbie to Mortal Combat*, ed. Justine Cassell and Henry Jenkins (Cambridge: MIT Press, 1998), 262–93, at 291.

44. Tor Busch, "Gender, Group Composition, Cooperation, and Self-Efficacy in Computer Studies," *Journal of Educational Computing Research*, 15, no. 2 (1996): 125–83; Marcia C. Linn, "Gender Equity in Computer Learning Environments," *Computers and the Social Sciences*, 1 (1985): 19–27.

45. Thomas P. Carpenter, Patricia Fennema, Megan Loef Franke, Linda Levi, and Susan B. Empson, *Children's Mathematics: Cognitively Guided Instruction* (Portsmouth, N.H.: Heineman, 1999).

46. Elizabeth Femmena et al., "A Longitudinal Study of Gender Differences in Young Children's Mathematical Thinking," *Educational Researcher*, 27, no. 5 (June–July 1998): 6–11; Elizabeth Femmena et al., "New Perspectives on Gender Differences in Mathematics: A Reprise," *Educational Researcher*, 27, no. 5 (June–July 1998): 19–21.

47. James M. Royer, Loel N. Tronsky, Yan Chan, Stanley J. Jackson, and Horace Marchant, "Math-Fact Retrieval as the Cognitive Mechanism Underlying Gender Differences in Math Test Performance," *Contemporary Educational Psychology*, 24 (1999): 181–266; James M. Royer, Kenneth Rath, Loel Tronsky, Horace Marchant, and Stanley Jackson, "Spatial Cognition and Math-Fact Retrieval as the Causes of Gender Differences in Math Test Performance," paper presented at the annual meeting of the American Educational Research Association, New Orleans, April 2002.

48. Paul W. Hill and Kenneth J. Rowe, "Modeling Student Progress in Studies of Educational Effectiveness," *School Effectiveness and School Improvement*, 9, no. 3 (1998): 310–33; Kenneth J. Rowe and Katherine S. Rowe, "Inquiry into the Education of Boys," Submission to the House of Representatives Standing Committee on Em-

ployment, Education, and Workplace Relations, August 2000; Kenneth J. Rowe, "Exploding the 'Myths' and Exploring 'Real' Effects in the Education of Boys," *Boys in School Bulletin*, 3, no. 3 (2000): 10–16, at 13; Madeleine Arnot, John Gray, Mary James, and Jean Ruddick, with Gerard Duveen, *Recent Research on Gender and Educational Performance* (London: Office for Standards in Education, 1998), 27.

49. Arnot, Gray, James, and Ruddick, *Recent Research on Gender and Educational Performance*, 29.

50. National Center for Education Statistics, "Racial/Ethnic Distribution of Public School Students," *The Condition of Education 2002* (Washington, D.C.: U.S. Department of Education, June 2002), appendix 1, 128, table 3–2; Robert C. Johnson and Debra Viadero, "Unmet Promise: Raising Minority Achievement," *Education Week*, 15 March 2000, 1, 17–23; Craig D. Jerald and Bridget K. Curran, "By the Numbers: The Urban Picture," *Education Week*, 8 January 1998 (special issue: Quality Counts '98: The Urban Challenge), 62–63; Jewell Taylor Gibbs, "Young Black Males in America: Endangered, Embittered, and Embattled," in *Young, Black, and Male in America: An Endangered Species*, ed. Jewell Taylor Gibbs (Dover, Mass.: Auburn, 1988), 1–36, at 18–19.

51. Judith S. Musick, *Young, Poor, and Pregnant* (New Haven: Yale University Press, 1993); Stephanie J. Ventura, William D. Mosher, Sally C. Curtin, Joyce C. Abma, and Stanley Henshaw, "Trends in Pregnancy Rates for the United States, 1976–97: An Update," *National Vital Statistics Reports*, 49, no. 4 (Hyattsville, Md.: National Center for Health Statistics, 2001); Children's Defense Fund, *Yearbook 2000: The State of America's Children* (Washington, D.C., 2000); Michele Fine, "Sexuality, Schooling, and Adolescent Females: The Missing Discourse of Desire," *Harvard Educational Review*, 58 (February 1988): 29–53, at 48.

52. Bronwyn Mayden, Wendy Castro, and Megan Annitto, *A Teen Pregnancy Prevention Dialogue Among Latinos* (Washington, D.C.: Child Welfare League of America, 1999), 39.

53. Carlos Salguero and Wendy R. McCusker, "Symptom Expression in Inner-City Latinas: Psychopathology or Help Seeking?" in *Urban Girls: Resisting Stereotypes, Creating Identities*, ed. Bonnie J. Ross Leadbetter and Niobe Way (New York: New York University Press, 1996), 329–36, at 334; Susan A. Basow and Lisa R. Rubin, "Gender Influences on Adolescent Development," in *Beyond Appearance: A New Look at Adolescent Girls*, ed. Norine G. Johnson, Michael C. Roberts, and Judith Worell (Washington: American Psychological Association, 1999), 25–52, at 28; Children's Defense Fund, *Yearbook 2000*, 34.

54. Rebecca A. Maynard, ed., *Kids Having Kids* (New York: Robin Hood Foundation, 1996), 5–10; Jeanne Drysdale Weiler, *Codes and Contradictions: Race, Gender Identity, and Schooling* (New York: State University of New York Press, 2000), 80.

55. Leslie Acoca, "Investing in Girls: A 21st Century Strategy," *Juvenile Justice*, 6, no. 1 (October 1999): 3–13, at 3, 5.

56. Office of Justice Programs, *Juvenile Justice Bulletin, Minorities in the Juvenile Justice System* (Washington, D.C.: U.S. Department of Justice, Office of Juvenile Justice and Delinquency Prevention, 1999); U.S. Department of Justice, Bureau of Statistics, *Criminal Offenders Statistics*, 34, <www.ojp.usdoj.gov/bjs/crimoff.htm> (visited 14 September 2001); Justice Policy Institute, *Cellblocks or Classrooms?* National Summary–Fact Sheet (Washington, D.C., 2000), 3; Centers for Disease Control and Prevention, *National Vital Statistics Reports*, 47 (June 1999), 19, table 8; National Center for Injury Prevention and Control, "Suicide Among Black Youths:

United States, 1980–1995," *Morbidity and Mortality Weekly Report*, 47, no. 10 (March 1998).

57. Nord, Lennon, Liu, and Chandler, *Home Literacy Activities*, 6; Jacquelynne Eccles, "User-Friendly Science and Mathematics," in *Minorities and Girls in School: Effects on Achievement and Performance*, ed. David Johnson (Thousand Oaks, Calif.: Sage, 1997), 65–104, at 73.

58. U.S. Department of Education, "Status Dropout Rates, by Race/Ethnicity," in *The Condition of Education 2002*, 164, appendix 1, table 19-2; Applied Research Center, *Facing the Consequences* (Oakland, Calif., 2000).

59. National Center for Education Statistics, *National Assessment of Educational Progress (NAEP) 2000 Reading Report Card, Fourth Grade Reading*, "Average Fourth-Grade Reading Scale Scores by Race/Ethnicity: 1992–2000" (Washington, D.C.: U.S. Department of Education, 2001); National Center for Education Statistics, *National Assessment of Educational Progress (NAEP) 2000 Mathematics Report Card*, "Average Mathematics Scale Scores by Race/Ethnicity: 1990–2000" (Washington, D.C.: U.S. Department of Education, 2001); National Center for Education Statistics, *National Assessment of Educational Progress (NAEP) 2000 Science Report Card*, "Average Science Scale Scores by Race/Ethnicity, Grades 4, 8, and 12: 1996 and 2000" (Washington, D.C.: U.S. Department of Education, 2001).

60. College Board, *Reaching the Top: A Report on the National Task Force on Minority High Achievement* (New York, 1999); College Board, *College-Bound Seniors;* College Board, *Advanced Placement Grade Distributions by Total and Ethnic Group* (New York, 2001); Law School Admission Council, *Average LSAT and Counts by Ethnic Group*, correspondence from Robert Carr, senior statistician, 29 August 2001; Association of American Colleges, *MCAT Performance by Sex, Racial/Ethnic Group, Age, Language Status, Undergraduate Major, and Testing History* (Washington, D.C., 2001); Johnson and Viadero, "Unmet Promise," 18.

61. Illinois State Board of Education, Data Analysis and Performance Division, *Elementary and Secondary Educational Statistics, 2001*, <www.isbe.state.il.us/research/brochure01.htm>; Connecticut State Department of Education, Division of Evaluation and Research, *Connecticut Mastery Test, Third Generation, 2001*, <www.csde.state.ct.us/public/der/s-t/index.htm>; National Center for Education Statistics, *National Assessment of Educational Progress (NAEP) 1998 Reading State Reports* (Washington, D.C., 1999).

62. See generally *The Black-White Test Score Gap*, ed. Christopher Jencks and Meredith Phillips (Washington, D.C.: Brookings Institution, 1998).

63. Andrea Billups, "Blacks Lag in Academic Scores," *Washington Times*, 2 October 2000, C1.

64. Claude M. Steele, "Race and the Schooling of Black Americans," *Atlantic Monthly*, April 1992, 68–78, at 68, 75; Claude M. Steele and Joshua Aronson, "Stereotype Threat and the Intellectual Performance of African Americans," *Journal of Personality and Social Psychology*, 69, no. 5 (1995): 797–811; Claude M. Steele, "A Threat in the Air: How Stereotypes Shape Intellectual Identity and Performance," *American Psychologist*, 52, no. 6 (June 1997): 613–29.

65. Signithia Fordham and John U. Ogbu, "Black Students' School Success: Coping with the Burden of 'Acting White,'" *Urban Review*, 18, no. 3 (1986): 176–206; Jason W. Osborne, "Race and Academic Disidentification," *Journal of Educational Psychology*, 89, no. 4 (1997): 728–35; George Farkas, Christy Lleras, and Steve Maczuga, "Does Oppositional Culture Exist in Minority and Poverty Peer Groups?" *American*

Sociological Review, 67, no. 1 (February 2000): 148–55; Patricia Gandara, Dianna Gutierrez, and Susan O'Hara, "Planning for the Future in Rural and Urban High Schools," *Journal of Education for Students Placed at Risk*, 6, nos. 1, 2 (2001): 73–93, at 74–75; Steele, "Threat in the Air," 623.

66. James Earl Davis, "Transgressing the Masculine: African American Boys and the Failure of Schools," in *What About the Boys? Issues of Masculinity in Schools*, ed. Wayne Martino and Bob Meyenn (Philadelphia: Open University Press, 2001), 141–53, at 147; R. Patrick Solomon, "Dropping Out of Academics: Black Youth and the Sports Subculture in a Cross-National Perspective," in *Dropouts from School*, ed. Lois Weis, Eleanor Farrar, and Hugh G. Petrie (New York: State University of New York Press, 1989), 79–93, at 82; Roslyn Arlin Mickelson, "The Attitude-Achievement Paradox Among Black Adolescents," *Sociology of Education*, 63 (1990): 44–61.

67. National Center for Education Statistics, "Status Dropout Rates by Race/Ethnicity," in *The Condition of Education 2002*, 165, table 19-2; ibid., "Trends in Graduate/First: Professional Education," section 1, 48.

68. Janet Shibley Hyde, "How Large Are Cognitive Gender Differences?" *American Psychologist*, 36, no. 8 (1981): 892–901, at 894–97.

CHAPTER 6. Legal Narratives

1. *Brown v. Bd. of Educ.*, 347 U.S. 484 (1954).
2. *Plessy v. Ferguson*, 163 U.S. 537 (1896), overruled by *Brown v. Bd. of Educ.*, 347 U.S. 483 (1954).
3. *Missouri ex rel Gaines v. Canada*, 305 U.S. 337 (1938).
4. Quoted in Carl T. Rowan, *Dream Makers, Dream Breakers: The World of Justice Thurgood Marshall* (Boston: Little, Brown, 1993), 77–78.
5. *Sweatt v. Painter*, 339 U.S. 629 (1950).
6. *Brown*, at 494.
7. Ibid., at 493.
8. Kathleen M. Sullivan, "Constitutionalizing Women's Equality," Justice Ruth Bader Ginsburg Distinguished Lecture on Women and the Law, Association of the Bar of the City of New York, *Record*, 56, no. 1 (Winter 2001): 22–37, at 26; Erin Daly, "The Limits of the Constitutional Imagination: Equal Protection in the Era of Assimilation," *Widener Law Symposium Journal*, 4 (1999): 121–66, at 145 n. 89.
9. National Association of Independent Schools, *Backgrounder: Single-Sex Independent Schools* (Washington, D.C., 1999).
10. Testimony of Susan Vorchheimer, cited in *Vorchhemier v. School Dist. of Philadelphia*, 400 F. Supp. 326, 328 (E.D. Pa. 1975).
11. *Vorchheimer*, at 333.
12. *Vorchheimer v. School Dist. of Philadelphia*, 532 F.2d 880, 886–88 (3d Cir. 1976), aff'd by an equally divided court, 430 U.S. 703 (1977).
13. *Petition for Writ of Certiorari to the United States Court of Appeals for the Third Circuit, Vorchheimer v. School Dist. of Philadelphia*, 532 F.2d 880 (3d Cir. 1976), aff'd by an equally divided court, 430 U.S. 703 (1977) at 17–18 (quoting Christopher Jencks and David Riesman, *The Academic Revolution* [New York: Doubleday, 1968], 297–98).
14. Ibid., at 25.
15. *Newberg v. Bd. of Public Educ.*, 26 Pa. D. & C. 3d 682 (Phil. Cty. 1983).
16. Ibid., at 707. Between the court decisions in *Vorchheimer* and *Newberg*, the U.S. Supreme Court had more clearly articulated an intermediate level of judicial scru-

tiny for gender classifications, most forcefully in *Mississippi Univ. for Women v. Hogan*, 458 U.S. 718 (1982).

17. Editorial, "It's Time to End Sex Bias in Public High Schools," *Philadelphia Inquirer*, 1 September 1983, A22.

18. Vernon Loeb, "The Question at Central: Can Separate be Equal?" *Philadelphia Inquirer*, 18 September 1983, F1.

19. Vernon Loeb, "No Appeal of Ruling on Central," *Philadelphia Inquirer*, 12 October 1983, B1; Vernon Loeb, "Enroll All Qualified Girls," *Philadelphia Inquirer*, 22 September 1983, A1.

20. Loeb, "Question at Central," F1 (statement of Marion L. Street, principal, Girls' High School).

21. Kathy Hacker, "A Good Fight for Girls' High," *Philadelphia Inquirer*, 15 October 1983, D1; *Newberg v. Bd of Public Educ.*, 478 A.2d 1352 (Pa. Super. Ct. 1984).

22. H. Ruth Dean, letter to the editor, *Philadelphia Inquirer*, 11 October 1983, A10; Vernon Loeb, "A Mandate for Equal Access in Conflict with Central's All-Male Tradition," *Education Week*, 2 February 1983, 12 (statement of Marion L. Street, principal, Girls' High School).

23. Mary B. W. Tabor, "Planners of a New Public School for Girls Look to Two Other Cities," *New York Times*, 22 July 1996, B2.

24. This reference originated in Walter Leavy, "Is the Black Male an Endangered Species?" *Ebony*, August 1983, 41.

25. William Raspberry, "Male Teachers for Inner-City Boys," *Washington Post*, 2 March 1987, A11 (quoting Spencer Holland).

26. Telephone interview with Spencer Holland, 6 June 2002.

27. Spencer H. Holland, commentary, "A Radical Approach to Educating Young Black Males," *Education Week*, 22 March 1987, 24; Spencer H. Holland, "Fighting the Epidemic of Failure," *Teacher Magazine* (September–October, 1989): 88; telephone interview with Spencer Holland, 6 June 2002; William Raspberry, "All-Boy Classes? The Feds Say No," *Washington Post*, 15 September 1989, A31.

28. NAACP Legal Defense and Educational Fund, *Reflections on Proposals for Separate Schools for African-American Male Pupils* (Washington, D.C., 1990), 9.

29. Belle S. Whelan, "Making Public Education Work for Black Males," paper prepared for the 1991 National Conference on Preventing and Treating Alcohol and Other Drug Abuse, HIV Infection, and AIDS in the Black Community, 16, ERIC document 347 260 (U.S. Department of Education, Office of Educational Research and Improvement, 1991); Millicent Lawton, "2 Schools Aimed for Black Males Set in Milwaukee," *Education Week*, 10 October 1990, 1, 24.

30. *Garrett v. Bd. of Educ.*, 775 F. Supp. 1004 (E.D. Mich. 1991).

31. Memorandum to Arthur M. Carter, interim deputy superintendent for community confidence, Detroit Public Schools, from Robert A. Sedler, professor of law, Wayne State University and legal consultant to the Detroit Public Schools on the Male Academy (7 May 1991); letter from Jo Jacobs, coordinator, Office for Sex Equity in Education, Michigan Department of Education, 7 February 1990.

32. Detroit Public Schools, *Male Academy Grades K-8: A Demonstration Program for At-Risk Males* (Detroit, 1991), 3–4.

33. Audrey T. McCluskey, "The Historical Context of the Single-Sex Schooling Debate Among African Americans," *The Western Journal of Black Studies*, 17 (1993): 193–201, at 194.

34. *Nightline*, ABC News, 15 August 1991 (transcript), 2–3.

35. Brief Amici Curiae of the American Civil Liberties Union et al., 10, 16, *California Federal Savings and Loan Association v. Guerra*, 479 U.S. 272 (1985) (agreeing with employer's argument that state statute was preempted by federal law but suggesting that job-protected leave should be extended to all disabled workers); Brief Amici Curiae of the National Organization for Women et al., 2 n. 3, *California Federal Savings and Loan Association v. Guerra*, 479 U.S. 272 (1987) (referring to the ACLU brief as to the harmful effects of a sui generis approach to pregnancy).

36. For a thoughtful discussion of how the case marginalized African-American females see Menah Adeola Eyaside Pratt, "Where Are the Black Girls? The Marginalization of Black Females in the Single-Sex School Debate in Detroit," Ph.D. diss., Vanderbilt University, 1997.

37. *Garrett*, 775 F. Supp. at 1012, citing Mich. Comp. Laws Ann. §380.1146 (West. 1988).

38. Letter from Jesse L. High, regional director, Office for Civil Rights, to Joseph Fernandez, superintendent of schools, Dade County, Fla., 31 August 1988 (noting that the "proposal to assign students on the basis of sex, even though voluntary on the part of the boys who would participate, is not an exception allowed for by [Title IX]," while the "Title VI regulation admits of no exception to the requirement that a recipient may not subject an individual to 'segregation' or 'separation' on the basis of race"); letter from Cathy Lewis, Office for Civil Rights, to the Cultural and Equity Section, Wisconsin Department of Public Instruction, 18 May 1990 (stating that under Title IX "it would not be acceptable to separate the students on the basis of sex," while to "intentionally segregate students on the basis of race" would violate Title VI).

39. Michigan State School Code of 1976, §380.1146; Amy Harmon, "300 Rally in Support of All-Male School," *Los Angeles Times*, 22 August 1991, A4; Ron Russell, "Board Hopes to Avert Trial on All-Male Schools," *Detroit News*, 5 November 1991, 2B.

40. Telephone interview with Elysa Robinson, assistant director of community and business partnerships, Detroit public schools, 3 April 1998. For a description of the Detroit and Milwaukee programs, see Ronnie Hopkins, *Educating Black Males: Critical Lessons in Schooling, Community, and Power* (Albany: State University of New York Press, 1997): 41–55.

41. Statement of Deborah McGriff, former superintendent, Detroit Public Schools, *Dayna Eubanks Show*, August 1991, quoted in Hopkins, *Educating Black Males*, 14.

42. Larry Cuban, commentary, "All-Male African-American Public Schools: Desperate Remedies for Desperate Times," *Education Week*, 20 November 1991, 36, 37.

43. Quoted in Janet Wilson, "Expert Dislikes All-Male Schools, Consultant Says They Harm Black Students," *Detroit Free Press*, 24 February 1992, 1B.

44. Quoted in Tom Dunkel, "Self-Segregated Schools Seek to Build Self-Esteem," *Washington Times*, 11 March 1991, E1.

45. "Separate Equals Better?" *MacNeil-Lehrer NewsHour*, 1 May 1991 (transcript 4023).

46. Charles Whitaker, "Do Black Males Need Special Schools?" *Ebony*, 46, no. 5 (March 1991): 17.

47. "All African-American Male Schools," *NAACP Resolutions on Education, 1970–1993* (Baltimore, 1991).

48. Ron Russell, "Legal Arm of NAACP Threatens to Join Lawsuit Blocking All-Male School," *Detroit News*, 21 August 1991, 1A.

49. Ron Russell, "NAACP Fund Might Join In Opposing All-Male Schools," *Detroit News*, 21 August 1991, 1.

50. See Kevin Brown, "Do African-Americans Need Immersion Schools? The Paradoxes Created by Legal Conceptualization of Race and Public Education," *Iowa Law Review*, 78 (1993): 813–81.

51. For a discussion of the Milwaukee African-American Immersion Program, see Marcia L. Narine, "Single-Sex, Single-Race Public Schools: A Solution for the Problems Plaguing the Black Community," ERIC document 348 423 (U.S. Department of Education, Office of Educational Research and Improvement, April 1992). For a general discussion of programs for African-American male students, see Carol Ascher, "School Programs for African American Male Students," Trends and Issues no. 15, ERIC document 334 338 (U.S. Department of Education, Office of Educational Research and Improvement, May 1991); Stephanie Gutmann, "Class Conflict," *New Republic*, 7 October 1996, 12, 13.

52. U.S. General Accounting Office, "Public Education: Issues Involving Single-Gender Schools and Programs," no. B-27125 (Washington, D.C.: May 1966).

53. Mark Walsh, "Ruling's Effect on Single-Sex Classes Mulled," *Education Week*, 10 July 1996, 1, 31.

54. William Raspberry, "No Offense, But What Have They Learned?" *Washington Post*, 17 March 1994, A23.

55. *Congressional Record*, daily ed., 1 August 1994, S.10163–74.

56. *Mississippi Univ. for Women v. Hogan*, 458 U.S. 718, 729, 724–25 (1982).

57. Ibid. at 730, 728–29.

58. Ibid. at 726, 724 n. 9.

59. Education Amendments of 1972, 20 U.S.C. § 1681(a)(Supp. 2001).

60. *Hogan*, at 732, citing *Katzenbach v. Morgan*, 384 U.S. 641, 651, n. 10 (1966).

61. Maureen Corrigan, "Invading a Citadel of Hostile Attitudes," review of Catherine S. Manegold, *In Glory's Shadow: Shannon Faulkner, the Citadel, and a Changing America* (New York: Knopf, 2000), *New York Times*, 1 March 2000, E7; Judy Mann, "Marching Orders," review of Manegold, *In Glory's Shadow*, *Washington Post*, 6 February 2000, X9.

62. Susan Faludi, "The Naked Citadel," *New Yorker*, 5 September 1994, 62–81, at 74.

63. Claudia Smith Brinson, "Shannon Faulkner," *Ms.*, January 1996, 48.

64. Ibid.

65. *Faulkner v. Jones*, 858 F. Supp. 552 (D. So. Car., 1994), aff'd, 51 F.3d 440 (4th Cir. 1995); Manegold, *In Glory's Shadow*, 200.

66. Motion of the United States for Reconsideration of Approval of Defendant's Contingency Plan and Disapproval of Plaintiff's Proposed Remedial Plan or Alternately for Stay of Disputed Provisions of Defendant's Plan Pending Appeal, 6 n. 1, *Faulkner v. Jones*, 858 F. Supp. 552 (D.So.Car. 1994) (No. 2:93-0488-2).

67. Debbi Wilgoren, "The Citadel Reasserts Its All-Male Tradition," *Washington Post*, 20 August 1995, A3; Manegold, *In Glory's Shadow*, 271–76; Catherine S. Manegold, "Female Cadet Quits the Citadel, Citing Stress of Her Legal Battle," *New York Times*, 13 August 1995, A1.

68. Manegold, *In Glory's Shadow*, 279, 292–93; American Civil Liberties Union, "Legal Fees from the Battle to Admit Shannon Faulkner Will Go to Women's Rights Project," press release, 4 October 2000.

69. Editorial, "Not Training, Bullying," *Washington Post*, 16 January 1997, A20.

70. Pat Conroy, letter to the editor, *Charleston Post and Courier*, 27 August 1995, A19; Pat Conroy, *The Lords of Discipline* (New York: Houghton Mifflin, 1980).

1. Philippa Strum, *Women in the Barracks: The VMI Case and Equal Rights* (Lawrence: University Press of Kansas, 2002), 92–98. The court's jurisdiction was invoked under Title IV of the Civil Rights Act, 42 U.S.C. §2000c-6, which permits the United States to bring actions alleging discrimination in violation of either the United States Constitution or other federal statutes.

2. Laura Fairchild Brodie, *Breaking Out: VMI and the Coming of Women* (New York: Pantheon, 2000), 11.

3. *Kirstein v. Rectors and Visitors of the Univ. of Virginia*, 309 F. Supp. 184 (E.D. Va. 1970).

4. *United States v. Virginia*, 766 F. Supp. 1407 (W.D. Va. 1991), *rev'd and remanded*, 976 F.2d 890 (4th Cir. 1992), 852 F. Supp 471 (E.D. Va. 1994), *aff'd and remanded*, 44 F.3d 1229 (4th Cir. 1995), *rehearing en banc denied*, 52 F.3d 90 (1995).

5. Diane Avery, "Institutional Myths, Historical Narratives, and Social Science Evidence: Reading the 'Record' in the Virginia Military Institute Case," *Southern California Review of Law and Women's Studies*, 5 (1996): 189–386, at 231–68.

6. Harry F. Byrd, Jr., foreword to H. A. Wise, *Drawing Out the Man: The VMI Story* (Charlottesville: University Press of Virginia, 1978), xiv.

7. *Virginia*, 766 F. Supp. at 1425 (quoting Mission Study Committee of the Virginia Military Institute Board of Visitors, Report, May 16, 1986).

8. Ibid. at 1421.

9. Brief for Appellee at 20, *United States v. Virginia*, 976 F.2d 890 (4th Cir. 1992).

10. Brief for Petitioner at 29, *United States v. Virginia*, 518 U.S. 515 (1996); *Virginia*, 766 F. Supp. at 1438.

11. Brief of Amicus Curiae Lieutenant Colonel Rhonda Cornum et al., at 11–12, *United States v. Virginia*, 518 U.S. 515 (1996).

12. Brodie, *Breaking Out*, 19.

13. *Virginia*, 976 F.2d at 894.

14. *United States v. Virginia*, 766 F. Supp. 1407 (E.D. Va. 1991), transcript of proceedings at 37–39, 74 (testimony of David Riesman); *United States v. Virginia*, 852 F. Supp. 471 (E.D. Va. 1994), transcript of proceedings on remand at 489–90 (testimony of David Riesman); ibid. at 251, 253 (testimony of Elizabeth Fox-Genovese); Christopher Jencks and David Riesman, *The Academic Revolution* (Garden City, N.Y.: Doubleday, 1968), 297–98; see also Elizabeth Fox-Genovese, *Feminism Without Illusions: A Critique of Individualism* (Chapel Hill: University of North Carolina Press, 1991).

15. Eleanor E. Maccoby and Carol Nagy Jacklin, *The Psychology of Sex Differences* (Stanford: Stanford University Press, 1974); *United States v. Virginia*, 852 F. Supp. 471 (E.D. Va. 1994), transcript of proceedings on remand at 857–58, 894 (testimony of Carol Nagy Jacklin).

16. Ibid., transcript of proceedings on remand at 1243–44, 1247–48 (testimony of Alexander William Astin); Alexander W. Astin, *Four Critical Years: Effects of College on Beliefs, Attitudes, and Knowledge* (San Francisco: Jossey-Bass, 1977); Alexander Astin, "VMI Case Dramatizes Basic Issues in the Use of Educational Research," *Chronicle of Higher Education*, 24 July 1991, A36.

17. *Virginia*, 44 F.3d at 1234; Jeffrey Rosen, "Like Race, Like Gender?" *New Republic*, 19 February 1996, 21.

18. Lucinda Finley, "Sex-Blind, Separate But Equal, or Anti-Subordination? The Uneasy Legacy of *Plessy v. Ferguson* for Sex and Gender Discrimination," *Georgia State University Law Review*, 12 (1996): 1089–1128, at 1107.

19. Mary Anne Case, "Two Cheers for Cheerleading: The Noisy Integration of VMI and the Quiet Success of Virginia Women in Leadership," *University of Chicago Legal Forum* (1999): 347–80, at 354–55.

20. Brief Amici Curiae of Professor Carol Gilligan and the Program on Gender, Science and Law, 14, *United States v. Virginia*, 51 F.3d 440 (4th Cir. 1995), *reprinted in Women's Law Reporter*, Fall 1994, 1–16, at 15; Affidavit of Carol Gilligan, filed 7 January 1993, *Faulkner v. Jones*, 10 F.3d 226 (4th Cir. 1993).

21. *Virginia*, 518 U.S. at 540–41.

22. *Virginia*, 44 F.3d at 1240.

23. Ibid. at 1242, 1250 (Phillips, J., dissenting).

24. Peter Baker, "Green and Gutsy and Full of Gumption: Leadership Institute Welcomes 42 Women in Its Charter Class," *Washington Post*, 23 August 1995, D1.

25. *Virginia*, 52 F.3d 90 (4th Cir. 1995).

26. Petitioner's Brief on Writ of Certiorari to the United States Court of Appeals for the Fourth Circuit at 21, *United States v. Virginia*, 518 U.S. 515 (1996).

27. Brief Amici Curiae in Support of Petitioner by the American Association of University Professors et al., *United States v. Virginia*, 518 U.S. 515 (1996), 9–10; 25–28.

28. Brief Amici Curiae of Women's Schools Together, Inc., et al., *United States v. Virginia*, 518 U.S. 515 (1996).

29. Brief of Twenty-six Private Women's Colleges as Amici Curiae, *United States v. Virginia*, 518 U.S. 515 (1996).

30. Chief Justice William Rehnquist wrote a concurring opinion, and Justice Antonin Scalia wrote a sole dissent.

31. *Virginia*, 518 U.S. at 517, 547, 565 (1996), quoting *Milliken v. Bradley*, 433 U.S. 267, 280 (1977).

32. Justice Ginsburg had used this quotation in a brief presented to the Supreme Court in the case of *Vorchheimer v. School Dist. of Philadelphia*, 532 F.2d 880 (3d Cir. 1976), *aff'd by an equally divided court*, 430 U.S. 703 (1977), *Petition for Writ of Certiorari to the United States Court of Appeals for the Third Circuit*, at 17–18.

33. *Virginia*, 518 U.S. at 534–36; Cass R. Sunstein, *One Case at a Time: Judicial Minimalism on the Supreme Court* (Cambridge: Harvard University Press, 1999), 164.

34. *Virginia*, 766 F. Supp. at 1412, 1414.

35. *Virginia*, 518 U.S. at 541, quoting *Mississippi Univ. for Women v. Hogan*, 458 U.S. at 725.

36. Sunstein, *One Case at a Time*, 165; *Virginia*, 518 U.S. at 533–34.

37. *Hogan*, 458 U.S. at 729.

38. *Virginia*, 518 U.S. at 535 n.8.

39. Ibid. at 534 n.7, quoting Brief of Twenty-six Private Women's Colleges as Amici Curiae, 5; *Sweatt v. Painter*, 339 U.S. 629 (1950) (declaring unconstitutional the separate law school established by the state of Texas for black students based on inequalities in both tangible and intangible features as compared with the state's flagship University of Texas School of Law); *Virginia*, 518 U.S. at 553.

40. *Virginia*, 518 U.S. at 554–55.

41. Ibid. at 564 (Rehnquist, J., concurring); ibid. at 595–98 (Scalia, J., dissenting).

42. Robert Marquand, "Court Bolsters Protections for Women in Virginia Case," *Christian Science Monitor*, 27 June 1996, 1; *Vorchheimer v. School District*, 532 F. 2d

880 (3d Cir. 1976), aff'd by an equally divided court, 430 U.S. 1977; Strum, *Women in the Barracks*, 285.

43. *Faulkner v. Jones*, 51 F.3d 440, 451 (4th Cir. 1995) (Hall, J., concurring); Mary Ann Case, "Two Cheers for Cheerleading," 358; Finley, "Sex-Blind," 1127.

44. Michael Janofsky, "Citadel, Bowing to Court, Says It Will Admit Women," *New York Times*, 29 June 1996, section 1, 6; *V.M.I. Assimilation Plan* (Executive Version), 13 August 1997; Brodie, *Breaking Out*, 43.

45. Brodie, *Breaking Out*, 59.

46. "The Pros and Cons of Single-Sex Education," *U.S. News Online*, 7 July 1996, <http://www.usnews.com/usnews/issue/8symp.htm>; Peter Schmidt, "Gloom Pervades VMI Campus as Cadets Learn Their Ranks May Soon Include Women," *Chronicle of Higher Education*, 5 July 1996, A26.

47. Lynn Rosellini, "A Leader Among Men," *U.S. News and World Report*, 10 April 2000, 46–47.

48. Fact sheet accompanying the summary of amendment no. 874 to the Higher Education Bill, S. 659, *Congressional Record*, 118 (28 February 1972), S5808–9.

49. Education Amendments of 1972, 20 U.S.C. §§ 1681(a), 1682 (Supp. 2001).

50. Anne N. Costain and Douglas Costain, "The Women's Lobby: The Impact of a Movement on Congress," in *Interest Group Politics*, ed. Allan J. Cigler and Burdett A. Loomis (Washington, D.C.: Congressional Quarterly, 1981).

51. *Congressional Record*, 118 (15 February 1972), S3935.

52. Ibid., S3936–37.

53. Education Amendments of 1972, 20 U.S.C. §1681 (a) (1–5).

54. *Garrett v. Bd. of Educ.*, 775 F. Supp. 1004, 1009 (E.D. Mich. 1991).

55. *Congressional Record*, 118 (28 February 1972), S2744; Alexandra Polyzoides Buek and Jeffrey H. Orleans, "Sex Discrimination—A Bar to a Democratic Education: Overview of Title IX of the Education Amendments of 1972," *Connecticut Law Review*, 6 (Fall 1973): 1–37, at 16.

56. *Congressional Record*, 118 (15 February 1972), S3935–37; *Congressional Record*, 118 (28 February 1972), S5804.

57. S. Rep. No. 798, 92d Cong., 2d Sess., reprinted in 1972 *U.S. Code and Administrative News* 2698, 2672; *Congressional Record*, 118 (July 20, 1972), S24683-4.

58. Education Amendments of 1972, 20 U.S.C. §1681 (a) (6–9); Rosemary C. Salomone, *Equal Education Under Law* (New York: St. Martin's, 1986), 125. See generally Andrew Fishel and Janice Pottker, *National Politics and Sex Discrimination in Education* (Lexington, Mass.: Lexington, 1977).

59. 34 C.F.R. §106.35 (2001).

60. 34 C.F.R. §106.34 (2001).

61. 34 C.F.R. §106.34 (b–f) (2001).

62. 34 C.F.R. §106.40 (a) (3) (2001).

63. 34 C.F.R. §106.3 (b) (2001).

64. Mark Walsh, "Ruling's Effect on Single-Sex Classes Mulled," *Education Week*, 10 July 1996, 1, 31.

65. S.Rep. No. 105-300 at 258–59, Report of the Senate Appropriations Committee on S. 2440, the 1999 Omnibus Appropriations Act (1998); Report to the Senate Appropriations Committee on Review of Title IX Regulations and Policies Regarding Single-Sex Programs, U.S. Department of Education (February 1999).

66. Applying Federal Civil Rights Laws to Public Charter Schools, U.S. Department of Education, Office for Civil Rights (May 2000), 7.

67. Equal Opportunity Demonstration Program, 103d Cong., 2d Sess., *Congressional Record*, 140 (1 August 1994), S10163–72; American Association of University Women, letter from Sandy Bernard, president, to members of the Senate Appropriations Committee, 2 September 1998; National Women's Law Center, letter from Marcia D. Greenberger, copresident, and Leslie T. Annexstein, senior counsel, to members of the U.S. Senate, 2 September 1998; Better Education for Students and Teachers Act, S4342, chapter 3, §5331(b)(1)(L)(2002).

68. No Child Left Behind Act, Pub. L. No. 107-110, 115 Stat. 1425, §5131 (a) (23), 107th Cong., 1st Sess.; *Congressional Record*, 147 (7 June 2001), S5943–44 (statement of Senator Hillary Rodham Clinton).

69. Department of Education, Office for Civil Rights, "Notice—Single-Sex Classes and Schools: Guidelines on Title IX Requirements," *Federal Register*, 67, 89 (8 May 2002), 31102–3.

70. Department of Education, Office for Civil Rights, "Proposed Rule—Nondiscrimination on the Basis of Sex in Education Programs or Activities Receiving Federal Financial Assistance," *Federal Register*, 67, 89 (8 May 2002), 31098–99.

71. *Chevron USA, Inc. v. Natural Resources Defense Council, Inc.*, 467 U.S. 837 (1984) (ruling that where a statute is silent or ambiguous on a specific issue, the court will inquire whether the agency's interpretation is a permissible one); *City of Boerne v. Flores*, 521 U.S. 507 (1997) (holding that Congress cannot define the substantive scope of the Fourteenth Amendment).

72. *Virginia*, 518 U.S. at 533–34.

73. Ibid., at 555.

74. *Missouri ex rel. Gaines v. Canada*, 305 U.S. 337 (1938); *Sweatt v. Painter*, 339 U.S. 629 (1950); *Brown v. Bd. of Educ.*, 347 U.S. 484 (1954); *Virginia*, 518 U.S. at 554–57.

75. *Virginia*, 518 U.S. at 533, quoting *Califano v. Webster*, 430 U.S. 313, 320 (1977) (per curiam).

76. Ibid. at 553; *Hunter v. Regents of the Univ. of California*, 190 F.3d 1061 (9th Cir. 1999), cert denied, 531 U.S. 877 (2000).

77. See Alison Jones and Susan Jacka, "Discourse of Disadvantage: Girls' School Achievement," *New Zealand Journal of Educational Studies*, 30, 2 (1995): 165–75; *City of Richmond v. J. A. Croson Co*, 488 U.S. 469 (1989); *Adarand Contractors, Inc. v. Pena*, 515 U.S. 200 (1995).

78. *Hazelwood School Dist. v. Kuhlmeier*, 484 U.S. 260, 273 (1988) (upholding the authority of high school officials to remove articles from a student newspaper based on legitimate pedagogical concerns); *Lau v. Nichols*, 414 U.S. 563 (1974) (striking down an all-English educational program for students of Chinese ancestry under Title VI of the Civil Rights Act of 1964, 42 U.S.C. §2000(d)).

79. David L. Kirp, Mark G. Yudof, and Marlene Strong Franks, *Gender Justice* (Chicago: University of Chicago Press, 1986), 87.

80. *Congressional Record*, 118 (15 February 1972), S3937 (statement of Senator Birch Bayh).

81. Fishel and Pottker, *National Politics*, 114, 132.

82. Cleveland Amory, "Trade Winds," *Saturday Review*, 20 March 1971, 16; Andrew Fishel and Janice Pottker, "Sex Bias in Secondary Schools: The Impact of Title IX," in *Sex Bias in the Schools*, ed. Janice Pottker and Andrew Fishel (Cranberry, N.J.: Associated University Presses, 1977); telephone interview with Jeffrey Orleans, former staff attorney, Office of the General Counsel, Department of Health, Education and Welfare, 24 June 2002.

83. National Women's Law Center, letter from Marcia D. Greenberger, copresident, Leslie T. Annexstein, counsel, and Kathleen M. Keller, counsel, to Harold O. Levy, chancellor, New York City Board of Education.

84. Fishel and Pottker, *National Politics*, 132.

85. *Congressional Record*, 118 (15 February 1972), S3938 (statement of Senator Birch Bayh).

CHAPTER 8. The Research Evidence

1. Ann Bone, *Girls and Girls-Only Schools* (Manchester, England: Equal Opportunities Commission, 1983).

2. Fred A. Mael, "Single-Sex and Coeducational Schooling: Relationships to Socio-emotional and Academic Development," *Review of Educational Research*, 68, no. 2 (Summer 1998): 101–29.

3. Judith Gill, "Re-Phrasing the Question About Single Sex Schooling," in *Critical Issues in Australian Education in the 1990s*," ed. Alan Reid and Bruce Johnson (Adelaide, South Australia: Centre for Studies in Educational Leadership, University of South Australia, 1993), 90–99, at 90.

4. Alice S. Rossi, "Coeducation in a Gender-Stratified Society," *Educating Men and Women Together: Coeducation in a Changing World*, ed. Carol Lasser (Urbana: University of Illinois Press, 1987), 11–34, at 11.

5. Carnegie Commission on Higher Education, *Opportunities for Women in Higher Education* (New York: McGraw-Hill, 1973), 70; M. Newcomer, "Number of Women's Colleges, 300 in 1960, Down to 146," *Chronicle of Higher Education*, 7 May 1973, 3; Pauline Tompkins, "What Future for Women's Colleges?" *Liberal Education*, 58, no. 2 (May 1972): 298–303; Irene Harwarth, Mindi Maline, and Elizabeth DeBra, *Women's Colleges in the United States: History, Issues, and Challenges* (Washington, D.C.: U.S. Department of Education, 1997), 46.

6. Catharine R. Stimpson, "New Consciousness, Old Institutions, and the Need for Reconciliation," in Lasser, *Educating Men and Women Together*, 155–64.

7. Carnegie Commission on Higher Education, *Opportunities for Women*, 72–73.

8. M. Elizabeth Tidball, "Educating Women for Achievement," paper presented at the annual meeting of the American Association for the Advancement of Science, Section on Education, Washington, D.C., 27 December 1972.

9. M. Elizabeth Tidball, "Perspective on Academic Women and Affirmative Action," *Educational Record*, 54 (Spring 1973): 130–35, at 132–33; M. Elizabeth Tidball, "The Search for Talented Women," *Change*, 6 (1974): 51–52, 64; M. Elizabeth Tidball and Vera Kistiakowsky, "Baccalaureate Origins of American Scientists and Scholars," *Science*, 193 (August 1976): 646–52; M. Elizabeth Tidball, "Baccalaureate Origins of Entrants into American Medical Schools," *Journal of Higher Education*, 56, no. 4 (July–August 1985): 385–402; M. Elizabeth Tidball, "Baccalaureate Origins of Recent Natural Science Doctorates," *Journal of Higher Education*, 57, no. 6 (November–December 1986): 606–20.

10. Faye Crosby, Brenda Allen, Tonya Culbertson, Catherine Wally, Jennifer Morith, Renee Hall, and Bobbe Nunes, "Taking Selectivity into Account, How Much Does Gender Composition Matter? A Re-Analysis of M. E. Tidball's Research," *NWSA Journal*, 6, no. 1 (Spring 1994): 107–18; Mary J. Oates and Susan Williamson, "Women's Colleges and Women Achievers," *Signs: Journal of Women in Culture and Society*, 3, no. 4 (1978): 795–806; M. Elizabeth Tidball, "Women's Colleges and

Women Achievers Revisited," *Signs: Journal of Women in Culture and Society,* 5, no. 3 (1980): 504–17.

11. M. Elizabeth Tidball, Daryl G. Smith, Charles S. Tidball, and Lisa E. Wolf-Wendel, *Taking Women Seriously: Lessons and Legacies for Educating the Majority* (Phoenix: Oryx, 1999), 49–53, 140.

12. Judith L. Stoeker and Ernest T. Pascarella, "Women's Colleges and Women's Career Attainments Revisited," *Journal of Higher Education,* 62, no. 4 (July–August 1991): 394–411; Joseph C. Conaty, Nabeel Alsalam, Estelle James, and Duc-Le To, "College Quality and Future Earnings: Where Should You Send Your Sons and Daughters to College?" paper presented at the 84th annual meeting of the American Sociological Association, San Francisco, 1989.

13. Cornelius Riordan, "Single- and Mixed-Gender Colleges for Women: Educational, Attitudinal, and Occupational Outcomes," *Review of Higher Education,* 15, no. 3 (Spring 1992): 327–46.

14. Alexander W. Astin, *Four Critical Years* (San Francisco: Jossey-Bass, 1977); Alexander W. Astin, *What Matters in College: Four Critical Years Revisited* (San Francisco: Jossey-Bass, 1993).

15. Mikyong Kim and Rodolfo Alvarez, "Women-Only Colleges: Some Unanticipated Consequences," *Journal of Higher Education,* 66, no. 6 (November–December 1995): 641–68.

16. Leslie Miller-Bernal, "Single-Sex Versus Coeducational Environments: A Comparison of Women's Students' Experiences at Four Colleges," *American Journal of Education,* 102 (November 1993): 23–54; Leslie Miller-Bernal, *Separate by Degree: Women Students' Experiences in Single-Sex and Coeducational Colleges* (New York: Peter Lang, 2000).

17. Daryl K. Smith, Lisa E. Wolf, and Diane E. Morrison, "Paths to Success: Factors Related to the Impact of Women's Colleges," *Journal of Higher Education,* 66, no. 3 (May–June 1995): 245–66.

18. Women's College Coalition, Professional Achievements <http://www.womenscolleges.org> (15 October 2002); *'67/'77: A Profile of Recent Women's College Graduates* (Washington, D.C.: Women's College Coalition, February 1985); "50 Top Women in Business," *Business Week,* 8 June 1992, 80; Cassandra Hayes, ed., "20 Black Women of Power and Influence," *Black Enterprise,* August 1997, 60–80.

19. James S. Coleman, *The Adolescent Society: The Social Life of the Teenager and Its Impact on Education* (New York: Free Press of Glencoe, 1961), 51.

20. John Goodlad, *A Place Called School* (New York: McGraw-Hill, 1984), 75; J. Charles Jones, Jack Shallcrass, and Cathy C. Dennis, "Coeducation and Adolescent Values," *Journal of Educational Psychology,* 63, no. 4 (1972): 334–41; Frank W. Schneider and Larry M. Counts, "The High School Environment: A Comparison of Coeducational and Single-Sex Schools," *Journal of Educational Psychology,* 4, no. 6 (1982), 898–906; Edison J. Trickett, Penelope K. Trickett, Julie J. Castro, and Paul Schaffner, "The Independent School Experience: Aspects of the Normative Environments of Single-Sex and Coed Secondary Schools," *Journal of Educational Psychology,* 74, no. 3 (1982): 374–81.

21. Rosalind Wiseman, *Queen Bees and Wannabees* (New York: Crown, 2002), 247; Barbara J. Bank, "Introduction: Some Paradoxes of Gender Equity in Schooling," in *Gender, Equity, and Schooling: Policy and Practice,* ed. Barbara J. Bank and Peter M. Hall (New York: Garland, 1997), 15.

22. Judy Mann, "Boys and Girls Apart," *Washington Post,* 20 October 1996, C1.

23. William Peterson, "Rock 'n' Roll" (book review), *Science,* 134 (13 October 1961): 1061–62, at 1061; Max Birnbaum, "Teen-Age Subculture" (book review), *Saturday Review,* 16 September 1961, 74–75, at 75; James S. Coleman, Foreword to Cornelius Riordan, *Girls and Boys in School: Together or Apart* (New York: Teachers College Press, 1990), x.

24. Reginald R. Dale, *Mixed or Single-Sex School?* 3 vols. (London: Routledge and Kegan Paul, 1969, 1971, 1974), 3: 37.

25. Jennifer Shaw, "Schooling for Girls, or Mixed Schooling: A Mixed Blessing," in *Schooling for Women's Work,* ed. Rosemary Deem (London: Routledge and Kegan Paul, 1980), 66–75, at 69; Reginald R. Dale, "Education and Sex Roles," *Educational Review,* 27, no. 3 (1975): 240–48, at 241; Madeleine Arnot, "A Cloud over Co-Education: An Analysis of the Forms of Transmission of Class and Gender Relations," in *Gender, Class, and Education,* ed. Stephen Walker and Len Barton (London: Falmer, 1983), 69–91, at 83; Bone, *Girls and Girls-Only Schools,* 8–10.

26. U.S. Department of Education, *Single-Sex Schooling,* vol. 1, *Perspectives from Practice and Research* (Washington, D.C.: Office of Educational Research and Improvement, 1993), ii; Michael Ruhlman, *Boys Themselves: A Return to Single-Sex Education* (New York: Henry Holt, 1996), 352, quoting Diane Ravitch.

27. U.S. Department of Education, *Single-Sex Schooling,* vol. 2, *Proponents Speak* (Washington, D.C.: Office of Educational Research and Improvement, 1993).

28. *Single-Sex Schooling,* 2: 35–37, 72.

29. American Association of University Women Educational Foundation, *Separated by Sex: A Critical Look at Single-Sex Education for Girls* (Washington, D.C., 1998).

30. Tamar Lewin, "All-Girl Schools Questioned as a Way to Attain Equity," *New York Times,* 12 March 1998, A12; Beth Reinhard, "Report Casts Doubt on the Value of Single-Sex Schooling," *Education Week,* 18 March 1998, 8; Connie Leslie, "Separate and Unequal? A Study Finds No Evidence That All-Female Classes Are Better, But Some Girls Are Happy on Their Own," *Newsweek,* 23 March 1998, 55; William Raspberry, "Same-Sex Schools Work—Sometimes," *Washington Post,* 16 March 1998, A21.

31. Maggie Ford, "Report Has Value," *Chicago Tribune,* 25 March 1998, 18; interview with Janice Weinman, president, American Association of University Women, *Today,* 13 March 1998 (NBC News transcript).

32. Ellen Goodman, "Separating Boys, Girls in School Hasn't Been a Panacea," *Boston Globe,* 12 March 1998, A21; Leslie, "Separate and Unequal?" 55.

33. National Coalition of Girls' Schools, "Girls' Schools Offer Valuable Lessons for Education Reform," press release, 11 March 1998.

34. Editorial, "Schools of Girls," *Wall Street Journal,* 13 March 1998, A16.

35. Lucy W. Sells, *High School Math as the Critical Filter in the Job Market,* research report no. SEO16576, University of California, Berkeley, ERIC document 080 351 (U.S. Department of Health, Education, and Welfare, National Institute of Education, 1973).

36. Valerie E. Lee and Marlaine E. Lockheed, "The Effect of Single-Sex Schooling on Achievement and Attitudes in Nigeria," *Comparative Education Review,* 34, no. 2 (May 1990): 209–31; Emmanuel Jimenez and Marlaine E. Lockheed, "Enhancing Girls' Learning Through Single-Sex Education: Evidence and Policy Conundrum," *Educational Evaluation and Policy Analysis,* 11, no. 2 (Summer 1989): 117–42;

Winifred Mallam, "Impact of School-Type and Sex of the Teacher on Female Students' Attitudes Toward Mathematics in Nigerian Secondary Schools," *Educational Studies in Mathematics*, 24, no. 2 (1993): 223–29; Marlene A. Hamilton, "Performance Levels in Science and Other Subjects for Jamaican Adolescents Attending Single-Sex and Co-Educational High Schools," *Science Education*, 69, no. 4 (1985): 535–47.

37. Richard Harker, "Achievement, Gender, and the Single-Sex/Coed Debate," *British Journal of Sociology of Education*, 21, no. 2 (2000), 203–18; Deidra J. Young, "Single-Sex Schools and Physics Achievement: Are Girls Really Advantaged?" *International Journal of Science Education*, 16, no. 3 (1994): 315–25; Judith E. Gilson, "Single-Gender Education Versus Coeducation for Girls: A Study of Mathematics Achievement and Attitudes Toward Mathematics of Middle-School Students," paper presented at the annual meeting of the American Educational Research Association, Montreal, April 1999; Anne E. Foon, "The Relationship Between School Type and Adolescent Self-Esteem, Attribution Styles, and Affiliation Needs: Implications for Educational Outcome," *British Journal of Educational Psychology*, 58 (1988): 44–54.

38. Andrew Stables, "Differences Between Pupils from Mixed and Single-Sex Secondary Schools in Their Enjoyment of School Subjects and Their Attitudes to Science and to School," *Educational Review*, 42, no. 3 (1990): 221–30; Lynne Lawrie and Rupert Brown, "Sex Stereotypes, School Subject Preferences, and Career Aspirations as a Function of Single/Mixed Sex Schooling and Presence/Absence of an Opposite Sibling," *British Journal of Educational Psychology*, 62 (1992): 132–38; Yuan Cheng, Joan Payne, and Sharon Witherspoon, *Science and Mathematics in Full-Time Education After 16*, Youth Cohort Report no. 36 (London: Department of Education and Employment, 1995), 11.

39. Peter Daly, "The Effects of Single-Sex and Coeducational Secondary Schooling on Girls' Achievement," *Research Papers in Education*, 11, no. 3 (1996): 289–306; Alex McEwen, Damian Knipe, and Tony Gallagher, "The Impact of Single-Sex and Co-educational Schooling on Participation and Achievement in Science: A 10-Year Perspective," *Research in Science and Technological Education*, 15, no. 2 (1997): 223–33; John Bell, "A Comparison of Science Performance and Uptake by Fifteen-Year-Old Boys and Girls in Co-Educational and Single-Sex Schools: AOU Survey Findings," *Educational Studies*, 15 (1989): 193–203.

40. Carole Vezeau, Thérèse Bouffard, and Roch Chouinard, "The Impact of Single-Sex Versus Coeducational School Environment on Girls' General Attitudes, Self-Perceptions, and Performance in Math," *Journal of Research and Development in Education*, 34, no. 1 (Fall 2000): 49–59.

41. Damian F. Hannan, Emer Smyth, John McCullagh, Richard O'Leary, and Dorren McMahon, *Co-Education and Gender Equality: Examination Performance, Stress, and Personal Development* (Dublin: Oak Tree, 1996), 197; Harker, "Achievement, Gender, and the Single-Sex/Coed Debate," 203–18.

42. Lianne J. Woodward, David M. Fergusson, and L. John Horwood, "Effects of Single-Sex and Coeducational Secondary Schooling on Children's Academic Achievement," *Australian Journal of Education*, 43, no. 2 (1999): 142–56; Kenneth J. Rowe, "Girls' and Boys' Learning Experiences and Outcomes of Schooling Throughout Their Primary and Secondary Years: Examining the Evidence for What Mattters and the Strategies That Work," background paper to keynote address presented at

the Diocesan Principals' Conference, Longreach, Queensland, 18 April 2002; Australian Council for Educational Research, "Boys and Girls Perform Better at School in Single-Sex Environments," media release, 17 April 2000.

43. Graham Able, "The Academic Benefits of Boys' Schools," unpublished; Graham Able, "British A-Level Results and Single-Sex Education," *International Boys' School Coalition*, series 2, no. 2 (January 2000).

44. Thomas Spielhofer, Lisa O'Donnell, Tom Benton, Sandie Schagen, and Ian Schagen, "The Impact of School Size and Single-Sex Education on Performance," National Foundation for Educational Research, Local Government Association Report 33 (Slough, England, July 2002).

45. Valerie E. Lee and Anthony S. Bryk, "Effects of Single-Sex Secondary Schools on Student Achievement and Attitudes," *Journal of Educational Psychology*, 78, no. 5 (1986): 381–95; Foon, "The Relationship Between School Type and Adolescent Self-Esteem, Attribution Styles, and Affiliation Needs: Implications for Educational Outcome," 44–54; Ed Cairns, "The Relationship Between Adolescent Perceived Self-Competence and Attendance at Single-Sex Secondary School," *British Journal of Educational Psychology*, 60 (1990): 207–11.

46. Herbert W. Marsh, "Effects of Attending Single-Sex and Coeducational High Schools on Achievement, Attitudes, Behaviors, and Sex Differences," *Journal of Educational Psychology*, 81, no. 1 (1989): 70–85; Valerie E. Lee and Anthony S. Bryk, "Effects of Single-Sex Schools: Response to Marsh," *Journal of Educational Psychology*, 81, no. 4 (1989): 647–50; Herbert W. Marsh, "Effects of Single-Sex and Coeducational Schools: A Response to Lee and Bryk," *Journal of Educational Psychology*, 81, no. 4 (1989): 651–53; Herbert W. Marsh, "Public, Catholic Single-Sex, and Catholic Coeducational High Schools: Their Effects on Achievement, Affect, and Behaviors," *American Journal of Education*, 41 (1991): 320–56.

47. Valerie E. Lee and Helen M. Marks, "Sustained Effects of the Single-Sex Secondary School Experience on Attitudes, Behaviors, and Values," *Journal of Educational Psychology*, 82, no. 3 (1990): 578–92.

48. Valerie E. Lee and Helen M. Marks, "Who Goes Where? Choice of Single-Sex and Coeducational Independent Secondary Schools," *Sociology of Education*, 65 (July 1992): 226–53.

49. Valerie E. Lee, Helen M. Marks, and Tina Byrd, "Sexism in Single-Sex and Coeducational Independent Secondary School Classrooms," *Sociology of Education*, 67 (April 1994): 92–120; Ruhlman, *Boys Themselves*, 350 (quoting Valerie Lee).

50. Valerie E. Lee, "Gender Equity and the Organization of Schools," in Bank and Hall, *Gender, Equity, and Schooling: Policy and Practice*, 135–58. For a discussion of more general findings on Catholic schools, see Anthony S. Bryk, Valerie E. Lee, and Peter B. Holland, *Catholic Schools and the Common Good* (Cambridge: Harvard University Press, 1993).

51. Lee, "Gender Equity and the Organization of Schools," 152.

52. Valerie E. Lee, Xianglei Chen, and Becky A. Smerdon, *The Influence of School Climate on Gender Differences in the Achievement and Engagement of Young Adolescents* (Washington, D.C.: American Association of University Women Educational Foundation, 1996), 32–33; Vezeau, Bouffard, and Chouinard, "Impact of School Environment."

53. Valerie E. Lee, "Single-Sex Schooling: What Is the Issue?" in U.S. Department of Education, *Single-Sex Schooling*, 2: 44; Valerie E. Lee, "Is Single-Sex Secondary

Schooling a Solution to the Problem of Gender Inequity?" in AAUW Educational Foundation, *Separated by Sex*, 45.

54. Lee, "Gender Equity and the Organization of Schools," 154–55.

55. Ibid., 151–56.

56. Ruhlman, *Boys Themselves*, 353 (interview with Cornelius Riordan).

57. Cornelius Riordan, *Girls and Boys in School: Together or Separate* (New York: Teachers College Press, 1990), 79.

58. Ibid., 91–106.

59. Ibid., 147–48; Shaw, "Education and the Individual: Schooling for Girls or Mixed Schooling—A Mixed Blessing?" 66–75; James S. Coleman et al., *Equality of Educational Opportunity* (Washington, D.C.: Government Printing Office, 1966); Barbara Heynes, *Summer Learning and the Effects of Schooling* (New York: Academic Press, 1978); Andrew M. Greeley, *Catholic High Schools and Minority Students* (New Brunswick, N.J.: Transaction, 1982); Thomas Hoffer, Andrew M. Greeley, and James Coleman, "Achievement Growth in Public and Catholic Schools," *Sociology of Education*, 58 (April 1985): 74–97; Spielhofer et al., "The Impact of School Size."

60. Paul C. LePore and John Robert Warren, "A Comparison of Single-Sex and Coeducational Catholic Secondary Schools: Evidence from the National Educational Longitudinal Study of 1988," *American Educational Research Journal*, 34 (1997): 485–511.

61. Cornelius Riordan, "The Future of Single-Sex Schools," in AAUW Educational Foundation, *Separated by Sex*, 53–62; Cornelius Riordan, "Single-Gender Schools: Outcomes for African and Hispanic Americans," *Research in Sociology of Education and Socialization*, 10 (1994): 177–205.

62. David B. Baker, Cornelius Riordan, and Maryellen Schaub, "The Effects of Sex-Grouped Schooling on Achievement: The Role of National Context," *Comparative Education Review*, 39, no. 4 (1995): 468–82.

63. Cornelius Riordan, "What Do We Know About the Effects of Single-Sex Schools in the Private Sector? Implications for Public Schools," in *Gender in Policy and Practice: Perspectives on Single-Sex and Coeducational Schooling*, ed. Amanda Datnow and Lea Hubbard (New York: RoutledgeFalmer, 2002), 10–30, at 14, 18.

64. Cornelius Riordan, "The Emergent Problems of Boys in School and the Potential of Single-Sex Schools for Both Boys and Girls," paper presented at the International Symposium on Male and Female Education in the Third Millennium, Madrid, September 2001, 20; Cornelius Riordan, commentary, "The Silent Gender Gap: Reading, Writing, and Other Problems for Boys," *Education Week*, 17 November 1999, 46, 49.

65. Diane J. Hulse, *Brad and Cory: A Study of Middle School Boys* (Hunting Valley, Ohio: University School Press, 1997).

66. See, e.g., Richard A. Hawley, "A Case for Boys' Schools," in U.S. Department of Education, *Single-Sex Schooling*, 2: 11–14; Pat Mahony, *Schools for Boys? Co-Education Reassessed* (London: Hutchinson, 1985); Ruhlman, *Boys Themselves*; Richard A. Hawley, "About Boys' Schools: A Progressive Case for an Ancient Form," *Teachers College Record*, 92, no. 3 (Spring 1991): 433–44.

67. Willie J. Wright, "The Endangered Black Male Child," *Educational Leadership*, 49, no. 4 (December 1991): 14–16.

68. Carol Ascher, "School Programs for African-American Males . . . and Females," *Phi Delta Kappan*, June 1992, 777–82.

69. Kusum Singh and Claire Vaught, "Single-Sex Classes and Academic Achievement in Two Inner-City Schools," *Journal of Negro Education,* 67, no. 2 (1998): 157–67.
70. See, e.g., Susan Tift, "Fighting the Failure Syndrome: A Radical Proposal for Black Boys: Separate Classes," *Time,* 21 May 1990, 83; Cynthia Hudley, "Assessing the Impact of Separate Schooling for African American Male Adolescents," *Journal of Early Adolescence,* 14, no. 1 (1995): 38–57; Cynthia A. Hudley, "Issues of Race and Gender in Educational Achievement of African American Children," in Bank and Hall, *Gender, Equity, and Schooling,* 113–33, at 124.
71. Lesley Parker and Leonie Rennie, *For the Sake of the Girls? Final Report of the Western Australian Single-Sex Education Pilot Project: 1993–1994* (Perth, Australia: Perth Education Department of Western Australia, 1995), cited in Lesley Parker and Leonie Rennie, "Single-Sex Grouping: Issues for School Administrators," paper presented at the annual meeting of the American Educational Research Association, New York, April 1996; Lesley H. Parker and Leonie J. Rennie, "Teachers' Perceptions of the Implementation of Single-Sex Classes in Coeducational Schools," *Australian Journal of Education,* 41, no. 2 (1997): 119–33, at 124.
72. Kenneth J. Rowe, "Single-Sex and Mixed-Sex Classes: The Effects of Class Type on Student Achievement, Confidence and Participation in Mathematics," *Australian Journal of Education,* 32, no. 2 (1988): 180–202; Herbert W. Marsh and Kenneth J. Rowe, "The Effects of Single-Sex and Mixed-Sex Mathematics Classes Within a Coeducational School: A Reanalysis and Comment," *Australian Journal of Education,* 40, no. 3 (1996): 147–62.
73. See e.g., Janice L. Streitmatter, *For Girls Only: Making a Case for Single-Sex Schooling* (Albany: State University of New York Press, 1999), 127.
74. Telephone interview with Frank Keenan, principal, Presque Isle High School, Maine, 8 June 2001; Richard A. Durost, "Single Sex Math Classes: What and for Whom? One School's Experiences," *Bulletin,* February 1996, 27–31; LynNell Hancock and Claudia Kalb, "A Room of Their Own," *Newsweek,* 24 June 1996, 76; Bonnie Wood and Lorrie A. Brown, "Participation in an All-Female Algebra I Class: Effects on High School Math and Science Course Selection," *Journal of Women and Minorities in Science and Engineering,* 3 (1997): 256–77; Kathleen Hudson and John Stiles, "Single-Sex Classes: A Plus for Preadolescent Girls," *Principal,* 78, no. 2 (November 1998): 57–58; telephone interview with Bonnie Wood, professor, University of Maine at Presque Isle, 5 July 2001.
75. Nancy Calhoun, "Single Gender Classes Within a Coed School," *Educational Equity Report* (American Association of University Women of Georgia), 8, no. 1 (Fall 1999): 1, 3; telephone interview with Nancy Calhoun, principal, Middle School, the Walker School, Marietta, Georgia, 8 June 2001; Jeff Archer, "Private Coed Schools Find Benefits in Single-Sex Classes," *Education Week,* 8 April 1998, 6 (statement of Eileen Lambert, head of school, Rippowam Cisqua School, Bedford, New York); telephone interview with Eileen Lambert, 2 July 2001.
76. Rod Corston and Andrew M. Colman, "Gender and Social Facilitation Effects on Computer Competence and Attitudes Toward Computers," *Journal of Educational Computing Research,* 14, no. 2 (1996): 171–83.
77. Mary Ann Zehr, "Computer Classes Aren't Just for Boys Anymore," *Education Week,* 21 January 1998, 1, 17; telephone interview with Mary Piper, teacher, Washington Middle School, Olympia, Washington, 8 June 2001.
78. *The World of Technology Evaluation Report: Fall 1999–Spring 2000* (Hartford: Connecticut Women's Education and Legal Fund, 2000); telephone interview with

Don Sierakowski, administrator, Manchester High School, Connecticut, 8 June 2001.

79. Amanda Datnow, Lea Hubbard, and Elisabeth Woody, "Is Single Gender Schooling Viable in the Public Sector? Lessons from California's Pilot Program," final report, 20 May 2001; California Education Code, §58520; fact sheet, "Single Gender Academies Pilot Program," California Department of Education, 16 September 1997, 1.

80. Kerry A. White, "Separate Worlds," *Education Week*, 25 November 1998, 20–24.

81. Heather Sokoloff, "Single-Sex Schools Reinforced Gender Stereotypes: Study, Experiment in Public Education Fails," *National Post*, 25 May 2001, A13 (statement of Amanda Datnow); see also Lea Hubbard and Amanda Datnow, "Are Single-Sex Schools Sustainable in the Public Schools?" in Datnow and Hubbard, *Gender in Policy and Practice*, 109–32, at 121.

82. Datnow, Hubbard, and Woody, "Is Single Gender Schooling Viable?" 52–53, 63–64, 72.

83. Lea Hubbard and Amanda Datnow, "Do Single Gender Schools Address the Needs of At-Risk Students? The Case of California's Single Gender Academies," paper prepared for presentation at the annual meeting of the American Sociological Association, Washington, D.C., August 2000, 25–27; Lea Hubbard, Amanda Datnow, and Elisabeth Woody, "Assumptions and Realities of Single Gender Public Schooling," paper prepared for presentation at the annual meeting of the American Educational Research Association, Seattle, April 2001, 4.

84. Debra Viadero, "Study Cites Flaws in Single-Sex Public Schools," *Education Week*, 30 May 2001, 9 (statement of William P. Duncan, principal, San Francisco 49ers Academy).

85. "Your School and the Law," *LRP Publications*, 29, no. 19 (12 October 1999); Ian Hanigan, "School Splits Genders, Thrives," *PressTelegram*, 18 May 2002, 1; interview with Jill Rojas, principal, Jefferson Leadership Academies, Long Beach, Calif., 4 January 2001.

86. Kathryn Herr and Emily Arms, "The Intersection of Educational Reforms: Single-Gender Academies in a Public Middle School," in Datnow and Hubbard, *Gender in Policy and Practice*, 74–89.

87. Sara Foss, "Interest in Charter School is High," *Daily Gazette*, 6 February 2002, B4; telephone interview with Thomas Carroll, founder and chairman, Brighter Choice Charter Schools, 9 July 2002.

88. Justin Blum, "Scores Soar at D.C. School with Same-Sex Classes," *Washington Post*, 27 June 2002, A1; Valerie Strauss, "Spotlight on Single-Sex Schooling," *Washington Post*, 14 May 2002, A9.

# Index

civil rights movement, 3, 38–39, 46, 47, 116–20, 133, 156
Civil War, 151–52
Clark, Kenneth, 137
Clarke, Dr. Edward, 65; *Sex in Education*, 65
classroom verbal interaction, 73–74, 95–101; collaborative learning, 97–98; elementary and secondary schools, 95–98, 100; gender biases, 73–74, 77, 78, 95–101; higher education, 98, 99–101; reasons for sex differences, 95–101
class size, 190, 206, 232
Clinton, Bill, 17
Clinton, Hillary Rodham, 17, 18, 174
Coalition of 100 Black Women, 22, 24, 40
coeducation, 1–6, 12, 50, 64–71, 95, 121, 127–28, 135, 143, 188, 200–202, 243; adolescence, 71–80; boy problem, 15–16, 36–37, 67–71, 80–84; harm to girls, 67, 68, 70–71; history, 65–71; private school, 121, 225–26
cognitive differences, in academic achievement, 80–81, 86–92, 101–3
Coleman, James, 198–202, 216–18, 221; *The Adolescent Society*, 198
collaborative learning, 97–98
college, 7, 16, 21, 22, 24, 30, 31, 32, 44, 65, 90, 91, 98, 190; all-male military academies, 142–49, 151–67; classroom interaction, 98, 99–101; race and, 111; Title IX and, 168–69; women's, 49–50, 66, 192–98; women's exclusion from, 49–50, 142–67
Community School District (CSD), East Harlem, New York, 10–25
compensation, 41, 182, 243–44
computers and technology, 91–92, 96–97, 104–5, 223, 226–27
Congress, U.S., 18, 48, 75, 77, 142, 143; Danforth Amendment, 139–40; Title IX, 168–70, 173, 176, 184, 185, 186, 238
Conners, Anne, 2
Conroy, Pat, 149
Constitution, U.S., 117, 124, 146, 174, 267n1
Cooperative Institutional Research Program (CIRP), 196
Cortines, Ray, 12

Cott, Nancy, 43
coverture, 46
Crew, Rudy, 13
criminal justice system, 45, 109–10, 132
cult of true womanhood, 43
culture, 4, 8, 24, 28, 39, 72, 75, 107–14; peer-group, 112–13; schooling and, 107–14; teenage pregnancy, 108–9, 113
Cuomo, Mario, 13
curriculum, 9, 20, 30, 50, 96, 190; Afro-centric, 132, 135, 138; classroom interaction, 95–97; dual-academy, 227–35; gendered, 68–71, 74; *see also specific courses and subjects*

Dade County, Florida, 130, 131, 135, 172, 221–22
Dale, Reginald, *Mixed or Single-Sex Schools*, 200–201
Danforth, John C., 139–40
Danforth Amendment, 139–40, 173, 174
Declaration of Sentiments, 43
Department of Education, 15, 28, 167–68
Detroit, 2, 3, 8, 107, 129–38, 165, 169, 172, 221; *Garrett v. Board of Education*, 131–38; legal and racial issues in single-sex education, 129–38; male Afro-centric academies, 129–38, 169
difference equality, 38, 39, 40, 41, 47, 53–58, 59, 62, 71–72
different "ways of knowing," 41
diversity, 39
domesticity, cult of, 42–43
domination theory, 59–60, 62
dropout rates, 3–4, 11, 31, 34, 67, 72, 86, 109, 110, 111, 129, 132, 134, 139, 189
drugs, 78, 110, 111, 132, 189, 199
dual academies, 180, 227–35
dyslexia, 86, 109

eating disorders, 72
economic class, 50, 60–61, 72, 75, 79, 87, 94, 96, 107–14, 205, 214–15, 218, 240
Educational Testing Service, 87, 103
*EEOC v. Sears Roebuck*, 58
elementary school, 65, 74, 79, 86, 105, 190, 240; academic redshirting, 86; classroom interaction, 95, 100; coed,

Hopper, Grace, 91
hormones, 102–3
hours of work, women's, 45
Hulse, Diane, 220–21
Hutchison, Kay Bailey, 173

immigrants, 67, 68, 82, 110
Independent Women's Forum (IWF), 77
industrialization, 45, 68
(in)essential equality, 41, 60–61, 62
inner-city schools. *See* urban schools
International Coalition of Boys' Schools, 160, 203, 220
IQ-testing movement, 68
Ireland, 208, 209, 210

Jacklin, Carol Nagy, 100, 103, 115, 156
Jamaica, 207
Japan, 82, 219
Jefferson, Thomas, 66
Jefferson Leadership Academies, Long Beach, California, 232–33
Jencks, Christopher, *Academic Revolution*, 123
Jews, 27
jury duty, 46, 62
Justice Department, 17, 144, 148, 151, 157, 159, 161, 164

Kennedy, Edward, 140, 174
Kindlon, Dan, 81; *Raising Cain*, 81
Kirp, David, 183
Kleinfeld, Judith, 79–80, 88
Kohlberg, Lawrence, 54–55
Krupnick, Catherine, 98, 99

labor laws, 45–46
law school, 98, 99–101, 118–19
learning disabilities, 4, 78, 86–87, 88, 109, 110, 242
Lee, Valerie, 77, 80, 84, 203, 211–18, 220, 221, 225
legal conflicts, and single-sex education, 116–49. *See also specific cases*
liberal equality, 46–53, 59, 62, 70
Lowell High School, San Francisco, 50
Lyon, Mary, 66

Maccoby, Eleanor, 100, 103, 115
MacKinnon, Catharine, 59–60, 61

Manchester (Connecticut) High School, 226–27
Manegold, Catherine, *In Glory's Shadow*, 144
Mann, Judy, 199; *The Difference*, 76
Marks, Helen, 211, 212
marriage, 66
Marsh, Herbert, 212, 224–25
Marshall, Thurgood, 118
Mary Baldwin College, VWIL program at, 155–59, 164
math, 3, 4, 5, 138, 188, 190, 207–9, 238; cognitive differences, 87–91; as "critical filter," 207; fact retrieval, 106; gender differences, 12, 13, 17, 20, 30–34, 74, 78–80, 87–91, 96, 97, 104–6, 207, 223, 225; racial differences, 108, 111, 112
maturational rates, 4
McGriff, Deborah, 136
McLaurin, Landa, 33
media, 8, 14, 39, 82, 102, 203, 223; on boy question, 82; on gender bias in schools, 75–78, 83; single-sex school debate in, 15, 125, 204–6, 229–31. *See also specific publications*
mental health problems, 132
metal detectors, 26
middle school, 73–76, 80, 121, 190, 240, 242; adolescent subculture, 198–202; classroom interaction, 96–97, 100; race and, 222; Title IX and, 169–71, 174, 177
Mill, John Stuart, 47, 48; *The Enfranchisement of Women*, 48; *The Subjection of Women*, 48
Milwaukee, 3, 8, 11, 130, 135, 136, 138, 221
minority students, 3, 5, 8, 9, 27, 28, 67, 68, 79, 93, 95, 99, 107–14, 200, 238, 239, 244; achievement gap, 110–13; affirmative action and, 181–83; male Afro-centric academies in Detroit, 129–38; males, and single-sex schools, 220–22; research, 216–19, 220–22; at Western High School (Baltimore), 32–35; at Young Women's Leadership School (New York), 10–25. *See also* race; *specific minorities*

Preliminary Scholastic Aptitude Test (PSAT), 89, 90

Presque Isle (Maine) High School, 225, 227

principals, turnover in, 22–23

prison, 45, 109; minorities in, 109–10, 132

private schools, 5, 7, 21, 67, 70, 121, 126, 169, 202, 214; coed, 121, 225–26; dual academy model, 228

Project 2000, 130

property rights, 42, 44

protectionist laws, 45

Protestantism, 66

public assistance, 13

public schools, 3, 5; dual academy model, 228–35; No Child Left Behind Act, 173–74; race and, 107–14; urban, 6, 7–37, 107–14, 121–24, 129–40

Puritans, 65–66

race, 3, 5, 8, 9, 27, 28, 39, 40, 41, 46, 47, 60–61, 63, 69, 72, 75, 79, 82, 86, 93, 96, 107–14, 203, 267n1; academic identification, 112–13; achievement gap, 110–14; affirmative action and, 181–83; equality and, 60–61; legal conflicts, and single-sex schooling, 117–21, 130–38; male Afro-centric academies in Detroit, 129–38, 169; research on single-sex schools, 216–19, 220–22; schooling and, 107–14; teenage pregnancy, 108–9, 111, 113. See also minority students; racial segregation in education; specific groups

racial segregation in education, 32, 82, 117–20, 191, 265n38; Detroit and, 130–38; differences compared to sex separation, 119–21; history of, 117–20

Rangel, Charles, 13

Raspberry, William, 130, 204

Ravitch, Diane, 12, 79, 140, 202–3

reading and writing, 4, 17, 80, 103, 104, 207, 238; boys' reluctance in, 104, 106–7; cognitive differences, 86, 87–88, 89, 106; race and, 110, 111

Regents exams, 24

Rehnquist, William, 164

religion, 7, 27, 28, 41, 168, 192, 211–19

research evidence, 4, 54, 102, 188–236, 239; adolescent subculture and academic climate, 198–202, 216–17; African-American and Hispanic students, 216–19, 220–22; charting an agenda, 235–36; dual academies, 227–35; OERI vs. AAUW, 202–6; single-sex classes, 202–6, 223–27; single-sex schools abroad, 206–10; single-sex schools in U.S., 210–19; women's colleges, 192–98

Richette, Lisa, 125–26

Riesman, David, 140, 155–56, 162; Academic Revolution, 123

Riley, Richard, 17

Riordan, Cornelius, 79, 195, 203, 211, 216–22, 232

Rosenberg, Rosalind, 58

Rossi, Alice, 48

Rowe, Kenneth, 224

Sadker, David and Myra, 73–74, 77, 78, 79, 80, 92, 95, 99; Failing at Fairness, 73

sameness and difference, 40, 41, 53, 60, 101–7; boys' reluctance to read, 104, 106–7; brain research, 102–3; computers and technology, 104–5; difference equality, 53–58; math, 101, 104–6; pastimes and hobbies, 103–4; risk-taking, 106; verbal processing, 106; visual-spatial ability, 103, 105

San Francisco, 50, 110

Scalia, Antonin, 164–65

Schlafly, Phyllis, 160, 166

Scholastic Aptitude Test (SAT), 22, 34, 80, 86, 89–90, 106, 112, 124, 205, 238

Schroeder, Patricia, 75, 165

science, 3, 4, 5, 152, 188, 190, 238; cognitive differences, 87–91; gender differences, 12, 13, 17, 20, 30–34, 69, 71, 74, 78–80, 87–91, 96, 97, 101, 104–6, 207, 223, 225; racial differences, 108, 111

Scott, Janet, 23

second-generation all-girls' schools, 9

Sedler, Robert, 131

181; single-sex classes, 168, 171, 172, 183–86; guidelines, 173–75; VMI case and, 173, 175, 176–87; vocational education, 168–69, 174, 185–86
tradition and ritual, 36–37
Tushnet, Mark, 165

Ujamaa Institute, 14, 138
uniforms, schools, 19
*United States v. Virginia. See* Virginia Military Institute
urban schools, 7–8, 63; race, and achievement gap, 107–14; single-sex, 6, 7–37, 121–24, 129–40, 150, 163, 169, 189. *See also specific cities and schools*

verbal interaction. *See* classroom verbal interaction
victimization, girls', 6, 15, 59, 61, 81, 109, 182, 243
video games, 104–5
violence, 3–4, 13, 94, 104, 109, 132, 189, 199
Virginia Military Institute, 1, 140, 143, 145, 151–67, 168; adversative approach, 153–58; amicus briefs in case of, 160–61; Carol Gilligan on, 58, 158, 160; hazing system, 153–54; history, 152–53; litigation, 1–3, 58, 62–63, 116–17, 121, 123, 141, 143–44, 147–49, 150–67, 172, 176–89, 237; move to coeducation, 165–67; Supreme Court opinion, 161–66; Title IX and, 173, 175, 176–87
Virginia Women's Institute for Leadership (VWIL), 155–59, 164
visual-spatial ability, 103, 105, 239
vocational education, 68–69, 70; Title IX and, 168–69, 174, 185–86
voice, 92–95
Vorchheimer, Susan, 121–24

*Vorchheimer v. School District of Philadelphia,* 121–24, 165, 268n32
voting rights, 43, 44, 45, 46, 56, 62

Wales, 208, 210
Walker School, Marietta, Georgia, 225–26
Washington, D.C., 107, 130, 133, 140, 234
Washington Irving High School, New York, 14, 70
Western High School, Baltimore, 8, 12, 32–35, 36, 37, 240; academic achievement, 33–35; alumnae, 33; description, 32–35; history, 32, 33
white students, 12, 61, 93, 110–12
Wilder, Douglas, 154
Willard, Emma, 66, 72
Wilson, Pete, 228
Winfrey, Oprah, 10, 11
Wollstonecraft, Mary, *Vindication of the Rights of Woman,* 47–48
womanhood, positive sense of, 20
women's colleges, 49–50, 66; research, 192–98
women's movement. *See* feminism
Women's Rights Convention, Seneca Falls (1848), 43
Women's Rights Project (WRP), 50–51, 145, 147, 161, 165
Wright, Benjamin, 234–35

Young Women's Leadership Foundation, 18, 21–22, 25
Young Women's Leadership School, New York, 1, 2, 8, 10–25, 35, 36, 37, 240; academic achievement, 20–25; description, 18–24; OCR complaint, 15–18; opposition to, 12–18, 24–25; planning, 11–15
Yudof, Mark, 183

CPSIA information can be obtained
at www.ICGtesting.com
Printed in the USA
BVOW06s0506160118
505322BV00002B/47/P